A BIBLIOGRAPHY OF
SIR THOMAS BROWNE

Oxford University Press, Ely House, London W.1

GLASGOW NEW YORK TORONTO MELBOURNE WELLINGTON
CAPE TOWN SALISBURY IBADAN NAIROBI LUSAKA ADDIS ABABA
BOMBAY CALCUTTA MADRAS KARACHI LAHORE DACCA
KUALA LUMPUR HONG KONG TOKYO

A BIBLIOGRAPHY OF
SIR THOMAS BROWNE
Kt. M.D.

by

GEOFFREY KEYNES
Kt. M.D.

SECOND EDITION
REVISED AND
AUGMENTED

DOMI MINA NUS TIO ILLV MEA

CLARENDON PRESS · OXFORD
1968

TO HORATIO, LORD TOWNSHEND
Raynham Hall, Norfolk

The worst newes (comes now) to this towne & my perticular, Sr. Tho:
Browne is dead, & as hee lived in an eaven temper without deep con-
cerne with how the world went, & was therein very happy so hee dyed
like a wise old philosopher. Hee fell ill on Saturday, like a feavor. All
the phisitians in towne came to him, Hee understood the busines himself, & sayd hee had a payne cross his stomack that nothing could
remove, that hee must dye, & would take nothing neither phisick nor
cordiall, but with all quietnes patience & christian meeknes dyed
yesterday, & is now pronouncd a great & happy man in his life &
death. All scholars allow him to have the most curious Learning of all
sorts & that his fellow is not left.

Norwich
October 20th 1682   THOMAS TOWNSHEND

Dedicated
to the memory of
SIR WILLIAM OSLER
Bt., M.D.

PREFACE

THE BIBLIOGRAPHY of Sir Thomas Browne was first published in 1924 by the Cambridge University Press in an edition of 500 copies. During the 43 years that have elapsed I have twice edited Browne's complete writings for Messrs. Faber and Faber and have witnessed a remarkable increase in the amount of interest taken in his philosophy, his art and the facts of his life. The original editions of his books have become much more difficult to obtain and have consequently increased greatly in value. All these tendencies have suggested that a revised edition of the Bibliography might be appreciated, the original having been long out of print. My friend and former collaborator, Cosmo Gordon, died in May 1965, so that I have not had the advantage of his help in reading the proofs, but we had both kept our interest in Browne and this new edition embodies much additional information accumulated as the years passed. I have therefore welcomed the enterprise shown by the Delegates of the Clarendon Press in taking over the publication from Cambridge.

The plan of the book remains substantially as it was before, but I have contrived not to change the numbering of the entries concerning all the more important books, that is, the original editions of Browne's works. Additions to the series have been given letters appended to the former numbers, leaving these undisturbed. The two sections on 'Imitators of *Religio Medici*' and 'Forerunners and Imitators of *Vulgar Errors*' have been retained and enlarged, but space has been saved by omitting the last two sections on 'Works of Dr. Edward Browne' and 'Simon Wilkin, Robert Southey and Sir Thomas Browne'. The nineteenth- and twentieth-century entries under 'Biography and Criticism' have been given the abbreviated form already adopted in the third edition of my *Bibliography of Dr. John Donne* (1958), thus again allowing space for the enlargement of the more strictly bibliographical material.

Several copies of most of the books have been recorded, but it must be clearly understood that the lists give no indication of their relative rarity. Wing's *Short Title Catalogue* of books from 1641 to 1700 being readily available, there seemed to be no point in further elaborating lists of library holdings. References to Wing entries have been given in the headings to each book. Some private collections formerly listed have mostly been eliminated. All the special Browne collections except my own are now lodged in public institutions. These are Wilkin's collection, formerly in the Castle Museum, now in the Central Library, Norwich, Sir William Osler's, now in the Osler Library, McGill University, Montreal, and Professor T. K. Monro's, now in the Hunterian Library, Glasgow University. My collection may ultimately find its place in the Fellows' Library at Winchester College, and has therefore been included. Apart from these the main accumulations are in the British Museum, the Bodleian Library, Cambridge University Library, the New York Academy of Medicine, Princeton University Library, the Yale Medical Library and the Houghton Library at

Harvard University. All these have been fully recorded. Holdings of other libraries have been occasionally mentioned, but this must not be taken to imply that no other relevant volumes are on their shelves.

The Cambridge University Press, having preserved the blocks of the reproductions of title-pages, have kindly transferred these to Oxford for re-use in the present edition. A few new ones have been added. The wood engraving by my late sister-in-law, Gwen Raverat, has also been used again.

I owe to Mr. T. S. Blakeney the account of Sir Thomas Browne's last hours printed facing the dedication to the memory of Sir William Osler—Mr. Blakeney found the letter in the muniment room at Raynham Hall and I am grateful to Lord Townshend for permission to print it here.

I am indebted to the late Dr W. W. Francis, cousin of Sir William Osler and first librarian of the Osler Library, for a careful survey of the former edition of this book and consequently for a number of corrections of detail. His fund of accurate and recondite bibliographical knowledge is famous. His wit and whimsical personality have added greatly to the enjoyment of my visits to Montreal during his lifetime, and I am sad that this new edition of Browne's bibliography will not come under his searching eye. I am sure to have been guilty of errors and omissions which few but he would have noticed. For these I tender to readers my apologies in advance of their detection.

Brinkley, 1967   GEOFFREY KEYNES

CONTENTS

LIST OF ILLUSTRATIONS

ABBREVIATIONS

WILKIN: *The Works of Sir Thomas Browne*. Ed. Simon Wilkin.
     London and Norwich, 1836
AUB: Amsterdam, Universiteits-Bibliothek
AUL: Aberdeen University Library
BLO: Bodleian Library, Oxford
BM: British Museum
BN: Bibliothèque Nationale, Paris
CH: H. E. Huntington Library, San Marino, California
CLC: William L. Clark Library, Los Angeles, California
CLN: Central Library, Norwich (Wilkin Collection)
DWL: Dr Williams's Library, London
ECO: Exeter College, Oxford
EUL: Edinburgh University Library
FLWC: Fellows' Library, Winchester College
GL: Guildhall Library, London
GULM: Glasgow University Library (Monro Collection)
IUL: Indiana University Library
K: Library of Geoffrey Keynes
KCCK: King's College, Cambridge, Keynes Collection

LC: Library of Congress, Washington, D.C.
LUB: Leyden, Universiteits-Bibliothek
MH: Harvard University Library, Cambridge, Mass.
MMO: Osler Library, McGill University, Montreal
MSL: Medical Society of London
NLS: National Library of Scotland
NMLB: National Library of Medicine, Bethesda, Md.
NYAM: New York Academy of Medicine
PCC: Pembroke College, Cambridge
PLC: Public Libraries, Cardiff
PUL: Princeton University Library
RCP: Royal College of Physicians of London
RCS: Royal College of Surgeons of England
RLH: Royal Library, the Hague
RSM: Royal Society of Medicine
TCC: Trinity College, Cambridge
TCD: Trinity College, Dublin
ULC: University Library, Cambridge
ULD: University Library, Durham
ULL: University of London Library
WCL: Winchester Cathedral Library
WCO: Worcester College, Oxford
WF: Folger Library, Washington, D.C.
YML: Yale Medical Library
YUL: Yale University Library

I

Religio Medici

BIBLIOGRAPHICAL PREFACE

S IR THOMAS BROWNE's *Religio Medici*, his first and most celebrated work, was probably composed about the year 1634 when he was aged 29. Credit was formerly given to a statement in Midgley's *Halifax, and its Gibbet- Law*, 1708 (see no. 307), that Browne wrote the book while living and practising medicine at Upper Shibden Hall near Halifax. Critical examination of the evidence for this by Professor F. L. Huntley[1] has reduced the statement to being no more than an improbable legend. Greater credence must now be given to Anthony Wood's assertion[2] that Browne practised for some time in Oxfordshire. Thus some unnamed place near Oxford, where he was to take his degree of M.D. in 1637, was more probably where he wrote his book. In his preface Browne confessed that he wrote *Religio Medici* for his 'private exercise and satisfaction', but that, 'being communicated unto one, it became common unto many'. The 'one' for whom it was primarily written has been conjecturally identified as John Power of Halifax, a close friend of Browne's young manhood, though it is not known how they came to be associated. The evidence for this identification is strong, though no original draft in the author's hand has survived. When the work became 'common unto many', this must have happened through multiplication of manuscript copies—a fact which has greatly complicated the establishment of a final and satisfactory text. Further difficulties have been due to revision of the manuscript by the author, who is now thought to have certainly made three, and possibly four, versions. The evidence is derived from eight manuscript copies and from the first three printed versions. All these manuscripts are different, and the brief descriptions which follow are arbitrarily designated by letters, since there is no conclusive evidence of their respective dates. None can have been copied from any existing printed edition and presumably all are to be dated before 1642, when the book was first printed.

L   *British Museum, Lansdowne MS. 489.* 30 × 20 cm. At the top of the first leaf is written: 'Mr Browne (συν θεῶ 1639)'. The text is closely written on ten pages, ff. 132*b*–137*a*. It is fragmentary, ending with the words 'can supply all these', that is, in the middle of section 18 of the printed text. It is divided into 15 sections. There are no marginal notes. The text is related to that of P, though they are not identical. Both seem to represent an early form.

P   *Pembroke College, Oxford.* 19·5 × 15 cm. Given to the College by the Rev. T. Shrigley in 1783. Headed 'Religio Medici' in a late eighteenth-century hand. Neatly written on both sides of 39 leaves (78 pp.). It is divided into 54 sections. There are no marginal notes. The text contains a number of passages and words not found anywhere else. It was edited in 1958 as an independent text by J.-J. Denonain of the University of Algiers, who claimed that it represents the earliest form (see no. 58*g*).

[1] *Sir Thomas Browne* (1962), pp. 92–7.   [2] *Athenæ Oxonienses* (ed. 2, 1721), II, 713.

J *St. John's College, Cambridge.* 20 × 13 cm. On the fly-leaf in an eighteenth-century hand is the inscription: *Ex dono | Venerabilis viri Bambridge Dean | hujus collegii olim Alumni.* Bound in contemporary calf, gilt. Written in a clear hand on 231 numbered pages with a few pages of unrelated MSS at each end. Not divided into sections. With marginal notes, some of which are not found elsewhere, though not all are likely to be by the author. The text was first fully collated by J.-J. Denonain (see no. 58*e*).

N *Norwich Record Office, Wilkin Collection, no. II.* 20 × 15 cm. No provenance is recorded. Originally without a title, but 'Religio Medici' was written later at the top of the first page. In the same hand is a long Latin note attributing the work to a Scot named Dr. Reid, or Read, who died in 1641. Charles Williams of Norwich claimed that this MS is in Browne's hand, but this is not so. Not divided into sections. No marginal notes. The text is related to J, but has many omissions and mistakes.

R *Rawlinson MS. D. 162, Bodleian Library, Oxford.* 19·5 × 15·5 cm. Closely written on 87 pages of 44 leaves. Not divided into sections. No marginal notes. The text has many omissions and mistakes. A note in Dr. Rawlinson's hand states: 'This copy of the Religio Medici by Sir Thomas Browne, Kt., is very different from all printed.'

O *Osler Library, McGill University, Montreal.* 29 × 19 cm. The MS had been in a Lancashire library for more than 250 years bound in a volume of historical pieces bearing dates from 1613 to 1631. Rebound in morocco, gilt, by Maltby of Oxford. It was sold at Sotheby's 14 December 1906, lot 273. Written on 63 leaves. Not divided into sections. No marginal notes. There are occasional blank spaces for words not deciphered.

H *Dr. de Havilland Hall.* 18·5 × 13 cm. Contains a book-plate with initials W.B. William Hall, Dr. Hall's father, told Dr. Greenhill that he found the MS 'among some old things that came from Mimms House, Herts, originally occupied by a family of Brown'. It had belonged to William Hall's grandfather who died in 1792. It was sold at Sotheby's 3 May 1928, lot 893 (Tregaskis £200). Since 1957 in Lehigh University Library, Honeyman Collection. Written on 203 leaves. Not divided into sections. With some marginal notes. Bound in contemporary calf.

W *Norwich Record Office, Wilkin Collection, no. I.* 15 × 10 cm. No provenance recorded. Closely written in a very small hand on 83 pages, the verse lines being in a taller Italian hand. Headed 'Religio Medici' in the same hand. Not divided into sections, but has some marginal notes. It is a very corrupt text. Bound in contemporary limp calf. A pencil note inside the cover in a seventeenth-century hand reads: 'The goulden griffin in Drury Lane...Warren'. On the fly-leaf is the inscription: 'J. Bohun Smyth 12 Dec. 1785'.

Religio Medici, according to Browne's statement in the first authorized edition, was composed 'with no intention for the press', but eventually the original manuscript, or one of the numerous copies, reached the hands of a discerning publisher named Andrew Crooke, who forthwith had it set up in type without the author's knowledge, and even without his name. It was published in 1642, and the venture was an immediate success, for a second edition, also unauthorized, was issued by Crooke in the same year. Some doubt has existed as to which of these was the earlier. In the former edition of this *Bibliography* I reversed the accepted order on the strength of the fresh appearance of the engraved title-page in unsophisticated copies of the book. This I later agreed was wrong, evidence based on textual differences being accepted as of greater weight, and the original order is now restored.

Meanwhile Browne was not inactive and at once prepared for the press 'a full and intended copy of that piece which was most imperfectly and surreptitiously published before'. As was pointed out by Wilkin (ii, iv), Dr. Johnson in his *Life of Browne* seems to have suspected the author 'of having contrived the anonymous publication of the work in order to try its success with the public', but our knowledge of Browne's character is sufficient disproof of his having been guilty of any such sharp practice. Nevertheless, it is quite possible that, without having intended publication, he may not have been altogether displeased at the printing of his work. Andrew Crooke at any rate seems to have been forgiven, for he was allowed to continue as publisher of the amended and first authorized edition of 1643 and to use again as title-page the plate already engraved by Marshall for the unauthorized editions. The source of the design is not known, but it presumably arose from Marshall's fancy. Clearly it met with Browne's approval, for it was used in all the separate editions, except one, published during his lifetime.

The first authorized edition of 1643 usually contains some preliminary leaves, the purpose of which has not hitherto been fully explained. The book is found in the three following forms:

(*a*) Without any preliminary leaves inserted before signature A.

(*b*) With two leaves beginning 'To such as have' inserted after the engraved title-page, the first carrying the signature A and catchword 'par'd'; the *Errata*, 14 lines, are on the second (conjugate) leaf.

(*c*) With six leaves inserted after the engraved title-page, the first, beginning 'A Letter sent', carrying the signature A2. The first four leaves have letters which passed between Browne and Sir Kenelm Digby. The next two leaves, 'To such as have' and *Errata*, have been reset with a few small changes (catchword 'pared'), and with no signature on the first of these, since it is now A6.

The engraved title-page in each of these forms is an insertion and the stub can usually be seen. It follows that A1 and A8 of the inserted leaves, being always absent, were blanks and were removed by the binder. Sometimes the inserted leaves are bound at the end of the book.

The sequence of events leading to these variations seem to have been as follows. A copy of one of the unauthorized editions had been sent by the Earl of Dorset to Sir Kenelm Digby, whose interest was instantly aroused to such a degree that he wrote his notes on the book within a few hours of reading it.

Browne somehow heard that Digby's *Observations* were to be printed, and wrote to him on 3 March protesting that the book he had read was a corrupt text not intended for publication, and telling him that 'within a few weekes I shall God willing, deliver unto the Presse the true and intended Originall', which Digby might see if he wished. Digby replied on 20 March that, immediately upon receipt of Browne's letter, he had forbidden Crooke to proceed with the printing, but that he thought there must be some mistake, since his *Observations* were 'Notes hastily set downe' and sent off to Lord Dorset within 24 hours of receiving the book. He promised that nothing should be printed without due consideration of Browne's intended text. Meanwhile the publisher, knowing of Browne's uneasiness, but not having seen Digby's disclaimer, had his own statement, 'To such as have' signed *A.B.*, set up and printed on a leaf conjugate with a leaf of *errata*, these leaves being forthwith inserted in a few copies of *Religio Medici*. Soon afterwards he saw the correspondence between Browne and Digby, which he then printed, together with a new setting of 'To such as have' and the *errata*. With this added section of six leaves the book reached its final form. Digby's undertaking was not in the end carried out, his printed *Observations* being based on the text of 1642.

Two editions were printed in 1645 with no alterations of importance. These were first shown to be distinct editions in 1924, having previously been supposed to be two issues of one edition with changes made while the book was in the press. After an interval of eleven years an edition called the fourth, but actually the sixth, appeared in 1656. This was the first edition to contain a typographical title-page, though the same plate as was used in the first edition of 1642 was still doing duty as a frontispiece. It was now so much worn and had been so many times worked over that the print is a mere caricature of Marshall's original engraving. To this edition were added the annotations by Thomas Keck of the Temple, who prefixed to his notes an interesting preface.

From this point onwards the bibliography of the *Religio Medici* is complicated by its frequent appearance in volumes containing the *Pseudodoxia Epidemica* and other works, and it is not necessary to draw attention here to each individual edition. Four more separate editions were published during the seventeenth century, that of 1669, called the sixth, being the only one issued without the usual engraved frontispiece. In this edition Digby's *Observations* were for the first time incorporated as part of the book, though the third edition of Digby had been bound in at the end of all copies of the 'fifth edition' of *Religio Medici* (1659). The 'eighth edition' of 1682 has commonly been used as the standard text of the work in recent reprints, having been published as 'corrected and amended' shortly before its author's death; but it is now realized that no edition printed after 1643 was in fact superintended by the author. Lowndes in the *Bibliographer's Manual* (1834) recorded 'an edition 1663 fol. with portrait'. This had already been mentioned in Henry Bromley's *Catalogue of Engraved British Portraits* (1793), but there is no other evidence that any such edition really exists.

Four separate editions were published during the eighteenth century, three being the result of a 'war' between the publishers Torbuck and Curll in 1736. Torbuck's edition, priced at 2*s*. 6*d*. (no. 15), seems to have been first in the field. Curll then announced his rival edition (no. 14) in *The London Evening Post*, Numb. 1334 (3–5 June 1736), as the first number of a series of publications comprising Browne's major works:

Advertisement

This Day is publish't, No. I (Price but 1*s*. 6*d*.) The Tenth Edition of Sir Thomas Browne's Religio Medici; or, The Christian Religion, as profess'd by a Physician; freed from Priest-Craft, and the Jargon of Schools. With a faithful Account of the Author's Life, Writings, and Family. Adorn'd with his Picture and Monument, finely engraved by Mr. Vandergucht and Mr. Sturt.

Printed for E. Curll, at Pope's-head in Rose Street, Covent Garden. N.B. This Edition is beautifully and correctly printed; illustrated with the Author's own Notes; not loaded with silly Annotations, heavy-headed Observations, or French Frippery. Therefore beware of a pyratical Edition impos'd on the Publicke at 2*s*. 6*d*. full of gross Errors in every Page, and the pretended Account of the Author false and greatly defective.

Torbuck retaliated by inserting in his *Religion of a Lady* (1736) (see p. 246) the following paragraph, quoted by Wilkin, II, 158; advertising his edition:

The publick are hereby cautioned against a surreptitious pamphlet just published, which contains but part of this book, being no more than seven sheets, on a gouty letter, and imposed on the world at 1*s*. 6*d*. stitched. The above new and genuine edition, with notes, annotations, and observations by Sir Kenelm Digby and other learned men, make above twelve sheets, each of which contains double the quantity of the surreptitious one, and is sold, neatly bound in a pocket size, and adorned with an emblematical frontispiece, for 2*s*. 6*d*. or sewed in blue covers for 2*s*.

Curll's advertisement accounts for the fact that some copies of his edition, though by no means all, contain prints of Browne's portrait and of his monument in St. Peter Mancroft, Norwich. These were evidently 'overs' from his edition of Browne's *Posthumous Works* (1712) (see no. 156) and so could be inserted as embellishments without further expense. Torbuck's edition was certainly the better bargain, but neither edition seems to have been very successful. Curll's is now very uncommon, and the sheets of Torbuck's were re-issued in 1738 with a reprinted title-page (no. 16). Curll published *Hydriotaphia and The Garden of Cyrus* in a uniform style (see no. 99), but the series then collapsed and the *Vulgar Errors* was not published. The only other eighteenth-century edition of *Religio Medici* is that published by Ruddiman in Edinburgh in 1754 (no. 17). This is today very seldom to be seen.

During the nineteenth and the present centuries *Religio Medici* has been many times reprinted, beginning with the very attractive edition prepared by Thomas Chapman, an Oxford undergraduate, in 1831. An edition at once scholarly and, typographically, the most satisfactory that has ever appeared, was published by William Pickering in 1845 under the editorship of Henry Gardiner, of Exeter

College, Oxford. The most authoritative text until recent times was that edited by W. A. Greenhill for Macmillan's Golden Treasury series[1]; this was first published in 1881, revised in 1885, and since then many times reprinted. Greenhill's notes are particularly valuable. The most recent recensions of the text have been made by foreign scholars—J.-J. Denonain of the University of Algiers and Dottoressa Vittoria Sanna of the University of Cagliari. The text prepared by the last named was used as the basis of that printed in my revised edition of Browne's *Works* (1964).

Religio Medici contains three examples of Browne's few attempts at versification. These are pleasant enough in their context, but do not place his name among those of the poets. Nevertheless, the third has some renown. It is what he called 'the dormitive I take to bedward', beginning:

> The night is come like to the day,
> Depart not thou great God away.

Several lines of this, with adaptations, were set to music later in the century and included in Purcell and Playford's *Harmonia Sacra: or, Divine Hymns and Dialogues. The Second Book* (London, f° 1693), pp. 23–4.

Religio Medici has not only been Browne's most popular work in English-speaking countries, but has also carried his fame to all parts of the continent of Europe through the medium of numerous translations which appeared during the seventeenth and eighteenth centuries. These have been grouped together at the end of the present section (nos. 59–72*d*). It was first translated into Latin by John Merryweather of Magdalene College, Cambridge, for whom it was twice published by Hackius at Leyden in 1644. Merryweather confessed in a letter[2] to Browne from Cambridge, 1 October 1649, that he had made the translation without telling him of it. He had afterwards visited Norwich and hoped to be able to give a copy of the translation to Browne, but unfortunately found him absent. Later he had heard rumours that Browne had died and was further discouraged. In 1644 he had tried three printers in Leyden—Hayl, de Vogel and Christian—but all refused to undertake the book. It was finally accepted by Hackius. Merryweather's only other published work, mentioned by Johnson in his *Life of Browne*, was *Directions for the Latin Tongue* (London, 1681) (A² B–D⁸). The title-page of this very rare book, which has considerable interest as an educational work, is reproduced here from a copy in my collection. Merryweather's translation was immediately reprinted at Paris in a pirated edition (no. 60), and again by Hackius at Leyden. Reprints followed at Leyden in 1650, at Strasbourg in 1652, 1665 and 1677, and at Leipzig in 1692. The last four of these contain copious annotations by Levin Nicolas von Moltke. The Paris edition of 1644 was reprinted at Zurich in 1743.

Religio Medici was next (1665) translated into Dutch by Abraham van Berckel, a philologist of Leyden and Delft. He wrote a long Latin letter[3] to Browne in

---

[1] Though bowdlerized in several places.   [2] Printed by Wilkin, I, 366–8.

[3] Printed in Browne's *Works*, ed. Keynes, 1964, IV, 331–5, with an English version by Cosmo Gordon.

DIRECTIONS

FOR THE

Latine Tongue.

BY
The Tranſlator of *Religio Medici*.

LONDON,
Printed for *Benj. Tooke*, at the *Ship*
in St. *Pauls* Church-Yard, 1681.

March 1665/6 expressing admiration for his works (see no. 68). Van Berckel's version was further translated into French by Nicolas Lefebvre and published without indication of place or printer in 1668. A fresh translation into Dutch by William Séwel, an English Quaker born at Amsterdam, was published with *Alle de Werken* in 1688.

A German translation by Christian Peganius, i.e. Christian Knorr, Baron of Rosenroth, translator of *Pseudodoxia Epidemica* in 1688 (see no. 86), is said[1] to have been published at Leipzig in 1680, but no copy is now known. The only German edition recorded here was made by Georg Venzky and published at Prenzlau in 1746.

Browne himself told John Aubrey in a letter[2] written in March 1672/3 that *Religio Medici* had also been translated into Italian, but here his memory had deceived him. No contemporary Italian version is known, the first one (by Piccolo) not being published until 1931.

Sir William Osler believed that a Polish version had been done, but a prolonged search made on his behalf by the booksellers failed to find it, and there is still no evidence of its existence.

The publication of *Religio Medici* called forth a large amount of criticism both in England and upon the continent, the religious aspect of the author's philosophy arousing the chief interest. Digby's *Observations*, written in 1642 within a few hours of receiving the book, were published in 1643. Guy Patin was already commenting upon it in a letter written in 1645. The attack by Alexander Ross, entitled *Medicus Medicatus*, was published in 1645. For these and many other works containing longer or shorter notices of Browne's book, reference may be made to the section on Biography and Criticism.

Finally, in an appendix to the present work are noticed the numerous books and essays bearing similar titles, of which *Religio Medici* was the forerunner and in many instances the inspiration.

[1] R. Watt, *Bibliotheca Britannica*, Edinburgh, 1824. This authority mentions several other imaginary editions.
[2] Keynes, 1964, IV, 376.

Title-pages of RELIGIO MEDICI 1642 and 1643

1 RELIGIO MEDICI [Wing B 5167] 8° 1642

Engraved title-page by William Marshall inserted before A1. A figure falling head-long from a rock into the sea is caught by a left hand issuing from clouds above. From the mouth of the figure come the words *à coelo falus*. Below the figure is engraved *Religio Medici*, and at the bottom of the plate *Printed for Andrew Crooke*. 1642. *Will: Marſhall. ſcu:* Plate-mark 108 × 60 mm.

Collation: Π¹ A–M⁸, 97 leaves.

Contents: Π1 *a* engraved title-page, verso blank; A1 *a*–M7 *b* (pp. 1–190) text; M8 blank.

Note: The first unauthorized edition.¹ There is no typographical title-page, the engraved title-page being inserted before A1. Type-page, excluding head-lines and catchwords, 114 × 64 mm.; 25 lines to a page. The pagination is correct. The book is divided into two parts, the second beginning on p. 135. Not divided into sections. A facsimile reprint, edited by Dr. W. A. Greenhill, was issued in 1883 (see no. 37).

Copies: BLO, BM, CLN(2), FLWC, GUL, K; CH, CLC, MH, MMO, NYAM, PUL, YUL.

2 RELIGIO MEDICI [Wing B 5166] 8° 1642

Engraved title-page by William Marshall, as in the preceding edition, inserted before A1.

Collation: Π¹ A–K⁸, 81 leaves.

Contents: Π1 *a* engraved title-page, verso blank; A1 *a*–K8 *a* (pp. 1–159) text; K8 *b* blank.

Note: The second unauthorized edition. As before there is no typographical title-page. Type-page, excluding headlines and catchwords, 119 × 72 mm.; 26 lines to a page. Page 68 is misprinted 86 in some copies; the pagination is otherwise correct. The Second Part begins on p. 110. Not divided into sections. The text of this edition has some minor changes from that of the first edition, and these later readings are generally preferable. There is no reason, however, to suppose that the author had any hand in a revision of the text.

Copies: BLO(2), BM, CLN(2, one lacking title-page), GUL, K, TCD, ULC, ULL(2); CH, LC, MH, MMO, PUL, YUL.

3 RELIGIO MEDICI [Wing B 5169] 8° 1643

Engraved title-page by William Marshall from the same plate as before. At the bottom of the engraved surface 17 mm., including the inscription, have been erased and on the space gained is inscribed: *A true and full coppy of that which was moſt imperfectly and Surreptitiously printed before vnder the name of:* Religio Medici. *Printed for Andrew Crooke:* 1643. The words *Religio Medici* below the figure have been removed and *coelo* in *à coelo falus* has been altered to *cælo*. Plate-mark 108 × 60 mm.

Collation: (*a*) Π¹ A–M⁸, 97 leaves; (*b*) Π¹ A² A–M⁸, 99 leaves; (*c*) Π¹ A⁸ A–M⁸, 105 leaves.

¹ Recorded in the first edition of this *Bibliography*, 1924, as the second edition, but this opinion was publicly reversed in 1952 (see *Times Lit. Sup.* 18 April).

Contents: (*a*) Π1*a* engraved title-page, verso blank; A1*a*–A2*b* *To the Reader*; A3*a*–M7*a* (pp. 1–183 [should be 185]) text; M7*b*–M8*b* blank.

    (*b*) Π1 engraved title-page; A1*a*–A1*b* *To such as have, or shall peruse the Observations upon a former corrupt Copy of this Booke*, signed *yours A.B.*; A2*a* *Errata*, 14 lines; A2*b* blank; A1–M8 as before.

    (*c*) Π1 engraved title-page; A1 blank, cancelled; A2*a*–A3*a* *A Letter sent* signed *Your Servant T.B.*; A3*b* blank; A4*a*–A5*b* *Worthy Sir*, a letter from Sir Kenelm Digby to Browne signed *Winchester House the 20 of March 1642, Your most humble Servant, Kenelme Digby*; A6*a*–A6*b* *To such as have*, &c. (reset); A7*a* *Errata* (reset); A7*b* blank; A8 blank, cancelled; A1–M8 as before.

Note: This, the first authorized, edition has no typographical title-page. Type-page, excluding headlines and catchwords, 122 × 70 mm.; 26 lines to a page. In the pagination pp. 171–2 are repeated, so that the actual number of pages is 185. The Second Part begins on p. 132. Both parts are divided into sections: Part I, 1–35, 35, 36–46, 46, 47–58 (total 60). Part II, 1–9, 11–15, 15 (total 15). This edition contains many changes from the text of 1642, though it repeats some of the errors, and adds others of its own, 34 of these being corrected in the list of *Errata*. Not all of these were corrected in subsequent editions. The three forms in which the book is found are described above under *Collation* and *Contents*; an explanation of these variations is given in the Bibliographical Preface. Section 56 in Part I was first added in this edition; it appears in none of the manuscripts. A few typographical variants in different copies are noted by L. C. Martin (*Religio Medici*, &c., Oxford, 1964, p. xv), who also reprints the *Errata* (p. 80). The first or second edition of Digby's *Observations* (see no. 218) is not infrequently bound up with this edition of *Religio Medici*.

Copies: BLO (2,*c*), BM (*a*, lacking title-page), CLN (4, 2*a*, 2*c*), CPL (*b*), GUL (2, *a*, *b*), K (2, *a*, *c*) ULC (*b*); CH, CLC (*b*), CN, FLWC (*b*), MH (*c*), MMO (*b*), YML (2, *b*, *c*), YUL (*c*).

4 RELIGIO MEDICI [Wing B 5170]   8° 1645

Engraved title-page as in the last edition with the date altered to 1645.

Collation: A⁶ A–L⁸ M²; 96 leaves.

Contents: A1*a* engraved title; A1*b* blank; A2*a* [misprinted A3]–A3*a* *A Letter sent*, &c.; A3*b* blank; A4*a*–A5*a* *Worthie Sir*, &c.; A5*b* blank; A6 *To such as have*, &c.; A1*a*–A2*b* *To the Reader*; A3*a*–M1*b* (pp. 1–174) text; M2 blank.

Note: No typographical title-page. Type-page, excluding headlines and catchwords, 125 × 71 mm.; 27 lines to a page. The engraved plate is the same as before, though it is a little more worn. The pagination is correct except that pp. 62, 135, 140 are misprinted 26, 335, 142. According to Dr. Greenhill this edition is 'a careless reprint of [1643], with only about one-fourth of the *errata* corrected'. The sections are misnumbered as before; in addition sections 31 and 45 are misprinted 13 and 54. Some copies are bound so that A6 follows the engraved title.

Copies: BLO(2), BM, CLN, GUL, K, PLC, TCC, TCD, ULL (imperfect); CLC, MH, MMO, NYAM, NP, WF, YUL.

5 RELIGIO MEDICI [Wing B 5171] 8° 1645

Engraved title-page as in the last edition.

Collation: A^8 A–L^8; 96 leaves.

Contents: A1 blank; A2*a* engraved title; A2*b* blank; A3*a*–A4*a* A Letter *fent*, &c.; A4*b* blank; A5*a*–A6*a* *Worthy Sir*, &c.; A6*b* blank; A7 To *fuch* as have, &c.; A8*a*–A1*b* *To the Reader*; A2*a*–L8*b* (pp. 1–174) text.

Note: No typographical title-page. Type-page, excluding headlines and catchwords, 125 × 70 mm.; 27 lines to a page. Earlier authorities supposed this to be the same edition as the preceding 'but with various corrections made in some of the sheets while they were being printed off'. The make-up of the book is, however, different throughout and a comparison of the text shows that the whole was set up afresh. The book is therefore to be regarded as a separate edition. The orthography tends to be more modern in this edition, e.g. *Worthy Sir* for *Worthie Sir* on A5*a*. The numbering of the sections is as before except that the final section is now numbered 16. Pages 57, 62, 140, 141 are numbered 75, 60, 142, 143 respectively. The plate is much more worn.

Copies: BLO (imperfect), BM, GUL, K(3), PLC; MH, MMO(2),[1] PUL, YML, YUL.

6 RELIGIO MEDICI [Wing B 5172] 8° 1656

Title, within single lines: Religio Medici. [*rule*] The fourth Edition, Corre&ted and amended. [*rule*] With Annotations Never before publi*fh*ed, upon all the ob*f*cure pa*ff*ages therein [*ornament between rules*] London, Printed by E. Cotes for Andrew Crook at the Green-Dragon in Pauls Churchyard, 1656.

Collation: A^8 A–T^8; 160 leaves.

Contents: A1*a* blank; A1*b* frontispiece; A2*a* title; A3*a*–A4*a* A Letter *fent*, &c.; A4*b* blank; A5*a*–A6*a* *Worthy Sir*, &c.; A6*b* blank; A7*a*–*b* To *fuch* as have, &c.; A8*a*–A1*b* *To the Reader*; A2*a*–L8*b* (pp. 1–174) text of *Religio Medici*; M1*a* sub-title within rule *Annotations upon Religio Medici* [rule] *Nec fatis eft vulgaffe fidem*—Pet. Arbit. *fragment.* [*ornament between rules*] *London,* &c.... 1656.; M1*b* blank; M2*a*–M4*b* The *Annotator To the Reader,* dated 24 *Martii,* 1654; M5*a*–T6*a* (pp. [183]–297) text of *Annotations;* T6*b* Errata; T7*a*–T8*b* The*fe Books following are fold by Andrew Crook at the Green Dragon in St. Pauls Church-yard.*

Frontispiece: The same plate, much worn and worked over, as was used for the engraved title of the last edition, with the date usually altered from 1645 to 1656; copies are found with the date unaltered.

Note: A reprint of the last edition, but the first to be furnished with a typographical title-page. Type-page, excluding headlines and catchwords, 125 × 67 mm.; 27 lines to a page. The pagination is correct except that pp. 185–90 are numbered 285–90. The sections are for the first time numbered correctly in both parts: 1–60 and 1–15. The author of the annotations was Thomas Keck of the Temple, whose annotated copy of

[1] One with inscription: *Robt. Bendish ex dono Authoris.* The recipient is mentioned several times in Browne's letters to his sons. References in Edward Browne's letters to 'my aunt Bendish' suggest a family relationship, probably with his mother.

Religio Medici.

The fourth Edition,
Corrected and amended.

WITH

ANNOTATIONS

Never before published, upon all
the obscure passages therein.

LONDON,
Printed by E. *Cotes* for *Andrew Crook* at the
Green-Dragon in *Pauls*·Church-yard, 1656.

the edition of 1643 is now in the Bodleian Library. The book is sometimes bound up with Digby's *Observations*, second edition 1644, or third edition 1659, but neither forms part of the book.

Copies: BLO, BM, CLN, EUL, FLWC, GUL, K(2, 1645, 1656), RCS, ULL; CLC, MH, MMO, PUL, WCL, WF, YUL.

7 RELIGIO MEDICI, &c. f° 1659

Sub-title: Religio Medici: Whereunto is added A Difcourfe of the Sepulchrall Urnes, lately found in Norfolk. Together vvith The Garden of Cyrus., or the Quincunciall Lozenge, or Net-work Plantations of the Ancients, Artificially, Naturally, Miftically Confidered. With Sundry Obfervations. [*rule*] By Thomas Brown Doctour of Phyfick [*ornament between rules*] Printed for the Good of the Commonwealth.

Collation: A–H⁴; 32 leaves.

Contents: A1 sub-title; A2 *To the Reader*; A3*a*–D3*a* (pp. 1–29) *Religio Medici*; D3*b* blank; D4*a*–E1*b* *The Epiftles Dedicatory*; E2*a*–F4*a* (pp. 35–47) *Hydriotaphia*; F4*b*–H4*b* (pp. 48–64) *The Garden of Cyrus*.

Illustrations: (i, ii) On a leaf inserted before A3 or D4 the two engravings of urns and a net-work as in the editions of *Hydriotaphia*, &c. (1658) (nos. 93 and 94). At the top of the net-work plate the words *This Networke for page:* 48. have been added.
(iii) On p. 51 (G2*a*) engraved plate of Roman legion as in nos. 93 and 94.

Note: Appended to the 1658 edition of *Pseudodoxia* (no. 75), a general title-page dated 1659 being added (no. 77). The *Religio Medici*, &c., are printed in double columns of small type and this edition may suitably be nicknamed 'the newspaper edition'; it has a very mean appearance. Pp. 3–6 are omitted in the pagination, so that the correct number of pages is 60 instead of 64. Pp. 59, 63 are both numbered 65. H2 has signature G2. All the preliminary matter of the previous editions except *To the Reader* is omitted from the *Religio Medici*. Some of the author's marginal notes are printed.

8 RELIGIO MEDICI [Wing B 5174] 8° 1659

Title, within border of ornaments: Religio Medici. [*rule*] The fifth Edition, Corrected and amended. [*rule*] With Annotations Never before publifhed, upon all the obfcure paffages therein. [*rule*] Also, Observations By Sir Kenelm Digby, now newly added [*rule*] London, Printed by Tho. Milbourn for Andrew Crook, at the Green Dragon in Pauls-Church-yard, 1659.

Collation: A⁸, A–T⁸, A–E⁸; 192 leaves.

Contents: A1*a* blank; A1*b* frontispiece; A2*a* title; A2*b* *Errata*; A3*a*–A4*b* *A Letter fent*, &c.; A5*a*–A6*b* *Worthy Sir*, &c.; A7*a*–*b* *To fuch as have*, &c.; A8*a*–A1*b* *To the Reader*; A2*a*–L8*b* (pp. 1–174) text of *Religio Medici*; M1*a* sub-title within border of ornaments *Annotations upon Religio Medici...London, Printed by Tho. Mylbourn for Andrew Crook,...* 1659.; M1*b* blank; M2*a*–M4*b* *The Annotator to the Reader*; M5*a*–T6*a* (pp. [183]–297) text of *Annotations*; T6*b*–T8*b* *The Names of fuch Books as are Printed for, and to be fold*

RELIGIO MEDICI.

The sixth Edition,
Corrected and Amended.

WITH

ANNOTATIONS
Never before published,
Upon all the obscure passages therein.

ALSO

OBSERVATIONS
By Sir KENELM DIGBY,
Now newly added.

LONDON:
Printed by *Ja.* C*otterel,* for *Andrew Crook,*
M DC LXIX.

by, Andrew Crook at the Green Dragon in St. Pauls Church-yard.; A1*a*–E8*b* Digby's *Observations*, third edition, 1659 (see no. 243).

Frontispiece: The same design as before, but newly engraved, and inscribed below *A true and full coppy of y^t which was moſt imperfeƈtly and Surreptitiouſly printed before under the name of* Religio Medici: *the 5. Edition Printed for Andrew Crooke: 1660.* Plate-mark 114 × 64 mm. Sometimes the print dated 1656 was used.

Note: A reprint of the edition of 1656. Greenhill states that only the prefatory matter has been reprinted in this edition, but in fact the whole book has been reset. Type-page, excluding headlines and catchwords, 125 × 71 mm.; 27 lines to a page. The second of the four *errata* printed on the verso of the title-page is imaginary. Page 85 is numbered 63, and pp. 185–90 are numbered 285–90, but the pagination is otherwise correct.

Copies: BLO, BM(2), CLN, EUL, K(2, 1656, 1660), MSL; MH(3), MMO, NYAM, PUL, YML, YUL.

9 RELIGIO MEDICI [Wing B 5175] 8° 1669

Title, within border of ornaments: Religio Medici. [*rule*] The ſixth Edition, Correƈted and Amended. [*rule*] With Annotations Never before publiſhed, Upon all the obſcure paſſages therein. [*rule*] Also Obſervations By Sir Kenelm Digby, Now newly added. [*rule*] London: Printed by Ja. Cotterel, for Andrew Crook, M DC LXIX.

Collation: A–Z⁸, Aa–Bb⁸; 200 leaves.

Contents: A1 blank; A2*a* title; A2*b* blank; A3*a*–A4*b* *A Letter ſent*, &c.; A5*a*–A6*b* *Worthy Sir*, &c.; A7 *To ſuch as have*, &c.; A8*a*–B1*b* *To the Reader*; B2*a*–N1*b* (pp. 1–176) text of *Religio Medici*; N2*a* sub-title *Annotations upon Religio Medici…London: Printed by Ja. Cotterel for Andrew Crook, 1668.*; N3*a*–N5*b* *The Annotator to the Reader*; N6*a*–V6*a* (pp. 185–297) text of *Annotations*; V6*b* blank; V7*a* sub-title to *Observations by Sir Kenelm Digby Knight. The fourth Edition…London…MDCLXIX*; V7*b* blank; V8*a*–Bb5*a* (pp. 300–75) text of *Observations*; Bb5*b*–Bb7*a* *The Postscript*; Bb7*b* *Books sold by Andrew Crook 1669*; Bb8 blank.

Note: This is a reprint of the edition of 1659. Pp. 57, 314, 327 are numbered 56, 312, 237; the pagination is otherwise correct. Digby's *Observations* are now for the first time printed as part of the book. This edition has no frontispiece. It is an uncommon book and had not been seen by Wilkin in 1836. It is recorded in Arber's *Term Catalogues*, I, 15, as 'Price, bound, 2*s*. 6*d*.'.

Copies: BLO, BM(2), CLN(2), GUL, K, PLC, ULL; CLC, MH, MMO, YML, YUL.

10 RELIGIO MEDICI 4° 1672

Sub-title: Religio Medici [*rule*] The ſeventh Edition, Correƈted and Amended. [*rule*] With Annotations Upon all the obſcure paſſages therein. [*rule*] Alſo Obſervations by Sir Kenelm Digby. [*rule*] London, Printed for Andrew Crook, 1672.

Collation: A–T4; 76 leaves.

RELIGIO
MEDICI.

The seventh Edition, Corrected
and Amended.

WITH

ANNOTATIONS

Upon all the obscure passages

therein.

ALSO

OBSERVATIONS

BY
Sir *KENELM DIGBY*.

LONDON,
Printed for *Andrew Crook,* 1672.

Contents: A1 sub-title; A2*a A Letter fent,* &c.; A2*b*–A3*a Worthy Sir*; A3*b To fuch as have,* &c.; A4 *To the Reader*; B1*a*–K1*a* (pp. 1–65) text of *Religio Medici*; K1*b* blank; K2*a* sub-title within rule to *Annotations upon Religio Medici...London,...*1672; K3*a*–K4*a The Annotator to the Reader*; K4*b*–Q2*a* (pp. 72–115) text of *Annotations*; Q2*b* blank; Q3–T4 Digby's *Observations*, fifth edition, 1672.

Note: Appended to the sixth edition of *Pseudodoxia Epidemica*, 1672 (see no. 79). This is a reprint of the edition of 1669, but with some variations. Page 9 is numbered 6; the pagination is otherwise correct.

11 RELIGIO MEDICI [Wing B 5177]   8° 1678

Title, within double lines: Religio Medici. [*rule*] The Seventh Edition, Corrected and Amended. [*rule*] With Annotations Never before Publifhed, Upon all the obfcure paffages therein. [*rule*] Also Obfervations By Sir Kenelm Digby, Now newly added. [*rule*] London, Printed for R. Scot, T. Baffet, J. Wright, R. Chifwell, 1678.

Collation: A–Z⁸ Aa⁸, Bb⁸; 232 leaves.

Contents: A1 frontispiece; A2 title; A3*a*–A4*b A Letter fent,* &c.; A5*a*–A6*b Worthy Sir,* &c.; A7*a*–A8*b To the Reader*; B1*a*–N3*a* (pp. 1–181) text of *Religio Medici*; N3*b* blank; N4*a* sub-title to *Annotations upon Religio Medici...London...*1677; N4*b* blank; N5*a*–N7*b The Annotator to the Reader*; N8*a*–V8*a* (pp. 181[185]–293) text of *Annotations*; V8*b* blank; X1*a* sub-title to *Observations...By Sir Kenelm Digby, Knight. The fifth Edition...London...*1678; X1*b* blank; X2*a*–Bb7*a* (pp. 297–371) text of *Observations*; Bb7*b*–8*b The Postscript*.

Frontispiece: Printed from the same plate as in the edition of 1659, with the inscription altered to read...*the 7 Edition Printed at London:* 1678.

Note: This is a reprint of the edition of 1669, but omitting the address *To such as have,* &c. The pagination of *Religio Medici* is correct, but the pages of *Annotations* are numbered 181 (misprinted 185) to 293 instead of 191–303, and the numbering of Digby's *Observations* is thrown out to the same extent.

Copies: BLO, BM, CLN, GUL, K, TCD, ULC, WCL; MH(2), MMO, NYAM, PUL, YML.

12 RELIGIO MEDICI [Wing B 5178]   8° 1682

Title within double lines: Religio Medici [*rule*] The Eighth Edition,...[&c. as in no. 11] London, Printed for R. Scot, T. Baffet, J. Wright, R. Chifwell, 1682.

Collation: As in no. 11.

Contents: As in no. 11; the dates on the sub-titles are altered to 1682. Digby's *Observations* is called the sixth edition.

Frontispiece: The usual design, but newly engraved. The inscription now reads: *A true and full coppy...the* 8 *Edition Printed at London.* 1682. Plate-mark 107×61 mm.

Note: This is an almost exact reprint of the last edition with the alterations noted above.

The type has all been reset, though the errors in pagination are reproduced; B3 is in addition misprinted B2. This was the last edition published during the author's life.

Copies: BLO, BM, CLN, GULM, K, PLC, RSM, ULC, ULL; MH, MMO, PUL, YML, YUL.

13 RELIGIO MEDICI   f° 1685

Sub-title: Religio Medici. [*rule*] The Eighth Edition, Corrected and Amended. [*rule*] With Annotations Upon all the obfcure paffages therein. [*rule*] Also Observations by Sir Kenelm Digby. [*double rule*] London, Printed for Robert Scott, Thomas Baffet, Richard Chifwell, and the Executor of John Wright. 1685.

Collation: Uu–Zz4, Aaa–Iii4, Kkk6; 58 leaves.

Contents: Uu1 sub-title; Uu2 *A Letter fent*, &c.; Uu3*a*–Uu4*a Worthy Sir*; Xx1 *To fuch as have*, &c.; Xx2*a*–Xx3*a To the Reader*; Xx3*b* blank; Xx4*a*–Ddd2*a* (pp. 1–45) text of *Religio Medici*; Ddd2*b* blank; Ddd3 sub-title to *Annotations upon Religio Medici*... *London*...1686; Ddd4*a*–Eee1*a* (pp. 49–51) *The Annotator to the Reader*; Eee1*b*–Hhh4*a* (pp. 52–81) text of *Annotations*; Hhh4*b* blank; Iii1 sub-title to Digby's *Observations*, sixth edition, 1686; Iii2*a*–Kkk6*b* (pp. 85–102) text of *Observations*.

Note: Part of the *Works* (1686) (see no. 201), reprinted from the edition of 1672 (no. 10). In my collection is a copy excerpted from the *Works* by a contemporary reader, who had it bound in calf with the title-page ruled in red. The first owner's name, dated 1687, has been obliterated. The second owner was Bishop Tillotson (1630–94).

14 RELIGIO MEDICI   8° 1736

Title: Sir Thomas Browne's Religio Medici: or, the Chriftian Religion, as Profeffed by a Phyfician; Freed from Prieft-Craft and the Jargon of Schools. [*rule*] *A Coelo Salus.* [*rule*] The Tenth Edition. [*rule*] London: Printed for E. Curll, at Pope's Head, in Rofe-Street, Covent Garden. 1736. Price 1*s*. 6*d*.

Collation: A4 B–G8 H4; 56 leaves.

Contents: A1 title; A2*a*–A3*b Some Account of the Author*; A4*a*–*b The Contents*; B1*a*–H4*a* (pp. 1–103) text; H4*b* advertisement of Pope's *Correspondence*.

Illustrations: See *Note* below.

Note: A summary account of the author's life follows the title-page, but all other prefatory matter is omitted, together with the *Annotations* and Digby's *Observations*. The Latin quotations and phrases in the text have been translated. At the end of the biographical notice the writer attributes to Browne some philosophical works, which were not by him, but by Jean de Bruyn, professor at Utrecht (see Wilkin, 1, 12). This edition is uncommon; Wilkin had never seen a copy. As already related in the Bibliographical Preface, it was advertised by Curll in the *London Evening Post*, 3–5 June 1736, with abusive remarks about a rival edition published by Torbuck at about the same time. The advertisement also stated that the book contained engravings of Browne's portrait and monument. Some copies do contain these, but the plates belong properly to the *Posthumous Works* published by Curll in 1712 (no. 156) and are not described again here.

Copies: BLO, BM, GUL, K; MMO, PUL.

Sir *Thomas Browne's*
RELIGIO MEDICI:

OR, THE

CHRISTIAN RELIGION,

AS

Profeſſed by a PHYSICIAN;

Freed from PRIEST-CRAFT

AND THE

JARGON of SCHOOLS.

A COELO SALUS.

THE TENTH EDITION.

LONDON:

Printed for E. CURLL, at *Pope's* Head, in *Rose-Street, Covent Garden.* 1736.

Price 1 *s.* 6 *d.*

15 RELIGIO MEDICI 12° 1736

Title: Religio Medici. [*rule*] By Sir Tho. Browne, Knt. M.D. [*rule*] A New Edition, Corrected and Amended. [*rule*] With Notes and Annotations Never before publifhed, Upon all the obfcure Paffages therein. To which is added The Life of the Author. [*rule*] Alfo Sir Kenelm Digby's Obfervations. [*double rule*] London: Printed for J. Torbuck, in Clare-Court, near Drury-Lane; and C. Corbett againft St. Dunftan's Church in Fleet-ftreet, M, DCC, XXXVI.

Collation: A¹² a⁶ B–M¹²; 150 leaves.

Contents: A1 frontifpiece; A2 title; A3 *a*–A4 *b* (pp. v–viii) *A Letter fent*, &c.; A5 *a*–A6 *b* (pp. ix–xii) *Worthy Sir*, &c.; A7 *a*–A9 *b* (pp. xiii–xviii) *To the Reader*; A10 *a*–a2 *a* (pp. xix–xxvii) *The Annotator to the Reader*; a2 *b*–a6 *b* (pp. xxviii–xxxvi) *The Life of Sir Thomas Browne*; B1 *a*–K3 *b* (pp. 1–198) text of *Religio Medici* with the *Annotations* at the foot of the page; K4 *a* sub-title to Digby's *Observations*; K4 *b* blank; K5 *a*–M7 *a* (pp. 201–53) text of *Observations*; M7 *b* *Books lately Publifh'd*; M8 *a*–M10 *b* *The Contents*; M11 *a*–M12 *b* *Books lately Publifh'd*.

Frontifpiece: The usual design, but newly engraved and now reversed. Some ships are added in the background. There is no inscription below. Plate-mark 143 × 85 mm.

Note: This is a reprint of the edition of 1682. Keck's *Annotations* are distributed at the bottom of the pages, and the author's marginal notes, with additions, are printed as footnotes. The *Life* is abridged from the account in the *Posthumous Works* (1712) (no. 156). Some copies have an additional imprint, *Sold by J. Joliffe, in St. James's-Street.*, pasted on at the bottom of the title.

This edition was criticized in abusive terms by Curll in an advertisement of his own edition and Torbuck replied in similar terms in a notice printed in his *Religion of a Lady* (1736) (see Bibliographical Preface above). The sheets of Torbuck's edition were reissued with a new title-page in 1738 (see next entry).

Copies: BM, CLN, FLWC, GUL, K, ULL; MH, MMO, NYAM, PUL.

16 RELIGIO MEDICI 12° 1738

Title: Religio Medici: or the Religion of a Phyfician. By Sir Tho. Browne, Knt. M.D. The Eleventh Edition Corrected and Amended. With Notes and Annotations, never before publifhed, upon all the obfcure Paffages therein. To which is added, The Life of the Author, and Sir Kenelm Digby's Obferva tions. [*rule*]

1. The Author (tho' a Phyfician) profeffes Chriftianity, without Hatred to any other Religion.
2. A particular Defcription of the Religion he profeffes.
3. His Reafons for not profeffing the *Romifh* Religion.
4. Of the Church of *England* and indifferent Things, for which no body ought to be blamed for diffenting.
5. In what Manner we ought to difpute and refolve on doubtful Matters.
6. The Author accufed of three different Herefies.
7. Of Myfteries and Faith.
8. Of God, and his Attributes; Eternity and Predeftination.

9. Of the Trinity, Divine Wiſdom, and Creation of the World.
10. Of the Nature of God, Divine Providence, and Fortune.
11. Of Atheiſm, and the Devil's Subtilty to ſeduce Mankind to it.
12. Whether the Deluge was Univerſal? How wild Beaſts came into *America*?
13. Of the Holy Scriptures, Alcoran, and the too great Number of Books.
14. If Jews and Chriſtians ſhall not make one Flock. All are not Martyrs that die for Religion.
15. Of Miracles, Reliques, Oracles, Ghoſts, Magicians, Natural Magick, good and evil Genius.
16. Of the Soul, and its Place of Reſidence at the End of the World.
17. Of Men-Eaters, Apparitions, Phantoms, &c.
18. Of Death, the Author not afraid, but aſham'd of it.
19. Of old Age; no Reaſon to be given why one Man lives longer than another.
20. Of Suicide, the End of the World, Reſurrection, Heaven, Hell, and Purgatory.
21. That there is no material Fire in Hell; and that we ought not to be afraid to hear Hell ſpoke of.
22. Of God's Goodneſs, and if there is any Salvation without Chriſt.
23. Of the Heathen Philoſophers; the Church of God ſhould not be confined to *Europe* alone.
24. Of the Number of Elect, Degrees of Glory among the Saints, and Salvation by Faith.
25. Of Good-Will to the Poor, Beggars may know a charitable Perſon by his Countenance.
26. Of Marriage, Beauty, Muſick, Converſation, Sleep, Dreams, &c.

[*rule*] With many other curious Subjects, for which the Reader is referr'd to the Table of Contents. [*rule*] London: Printed for J. Torbuck, in Clare-Court, near Drury-Lane. 1738.

Collation, contents, frontispiece: The sheets of no. 15 with a cancel title.

Note: This edition is very uncommon. The numbers preceding the summary of the contents given in two columns on the new title-page have no corresponding figures in the text. An advertisement leaflet was issued by Torbuck announcing three books: *Religio Medici, The Church of England's complaints,* and *A Collection of Travels, and Memoirs of Wales.* The title-page of each is printed with the heading: *Just Published,* and with an engraved frontispiece facing it. *Religio Medici* has added after the date 1738: [*Price 2s. 6d. neatly bound*]. An example of this leaflet is in my collection.

Copies: BM, CLN, ECO, GUL, K, ULC; MMO.

17 RELIGIO MEDICI 8° 1754

Title: Religio Medici. By Sir Tho. Browne, Knt. M.D. With the Life of the Author. To which is added, Sir Kenelm Digby's obſervations. Alſo critical notes upon All the obſcure Paſſages therein, never before publiſhed. The Tenth Edition carefully corrected. Edinburgh: Printed by W. Ruddiman jun. and Company: and ſold by the Bookſellers in Town. M.DCC.LIV.

Collation: [a]–c⁴ A–Z⁴ Aa–Zz⁴ Aaa⁴ Bbb⁴; 204 leaves.

RELIGIO MEDICI.

BY
Sir THO. BROWNE, Knt. M. D.

With the LIFE of the AUTHOR.

To which is added,
Sir *KENELM DIGBY's*
OBSERVATIONS.

ALSO
CRITICAL NOTES
UPON
All the OBSCURE PASSAGES therein,
never before publifhed.

The TENTH EDITION carefull correſted.

EDINBURGH:
Printed by W. RUDDIMAN *jun.* and COMPANY:
and fold by the Bookfellers in Town
M.DCC.LIV.

Contents: [a]1 title; [a]2*a*–[a]3*b* *A letter From the Author To Sir Kenelm Digby*; [a]4*a*–b1*b* *Sir Kenelm Digby's anſwer*; b2*a*–b4*a* *To the Reader*; b4*b*–c4*b* (pp. xvi–xxiv) *The life of Sir Tho. Browne, Knt.*; A1*a*–Ee1*b* (pp. 1–218) text of *Religio Medici*; Ee2*a* sub-title of Digby's *Observations*; Ee2*b* blank; Ee3*a*–Pp3*b* (pp. 221–202 [should be 302]) text of *Observations*; Pp4*a*–Qq1*a* (pp. 203–5) *The Poſtſcript*; Qq1*b* blank; Qq2*a*–Bbb3*b* (pp. 207–82 [382]) *Critical Notes upon Religio Medici*; Bbb4 blank.

Note: This edition is very uncommon and was unknown to Wilkin. According to Gardiner it was carefully edited, but has many unauthorized alterations in the text, which appears to have been taken mainly from the edition of 1678 or 1682. The notes are partly abridged from Keck's and are partly new. The numbers on pp. 300–82 are misprinted 200–82.

Copies: BM, EUL, GUL, K; MMO, Bibliothèque de la Ville, Versailles (Louis XV's copy, in red morocco with his arms).

18 RELIGIO MEDICI ED. CHAPMAN 12° 1831

Religio Medici. By Sir Thomas Browne, Kt. M.D. Oxford, Published by J. Vincent. MDCCCXXXI. 17 cm. in sixes. pp. xviii, 150.

Note: The short preface is signed T. C., i.e. Thomas Chapman, then an undergraduate of Exeter College, Oxford, who died in 1834 at the age of twenty-two. His annotations consist of a selection from Keck's with a few of his own added. Greenhill states that the text is probably from the edition of 1672 or 1685 with a few alterations. The book is found in three different bindings, smooth dark blue cloth, or hard-grain red or brown cloth, each with a paper label on the spine: BROWNE'S | RELIGIO | MEDICI. Usually a double leaf of *Books published by J. Vincent, Oxford*, is inserted before the fly-leaf.

Copies: BLO, BM, CLN, GUL, K; MMO.

19 RELIGIO MEDICI, &c. ED. YOUNG 8° 1831

Miscellaneous Works of Sir Thomas Browne. With some account of the author and his writings. Cambridge [U.S.A.]: Hilliard and Brown, booksellers to the university. MDCCCXXXI. pp. xxxii, 304. [Vol. III of the Library of the Old English Prose Writers, ed. Rev. Alexander Young, D.D., of Boston.]

Contents: *Religio Medici*, *Hydriotaphia*, *Letter to a Friend*, selections from *Pseudodoxia Epidemica*.

Note: The editor states in his Preface that the notes are for the most part selected from Keck's *Annotations*, but he does not specify the edition from which the text is taken.

Copies: GUL; MMO, PUL.

20 RELIGIO MEDICI ED. WILKIN 8° 1836

In Sir Thomas Browne's Works...Ed. Simon Wilkin...London William
Pickering...1836 (see no. 203).

Note: Vol. II, pp. i–xxxii and 1–158, gives a reprint of the *Religio Medici*, called by the
editor the fifteenth edition, together with a bibliographical preface and postscript, the
usual prefatory matter, and Digby's *Observations*. The copious annotations are partly
from Keck's and are partly original. The text is taken mainly from the edition of 1643,
but with numerous alterations from MSS and other printed texts.

21 RELIGIO MEDICI: HYDRIOTAPHIA ED. ST. JOHN 8° 1838

Religio Medici: to which is added, Hydriotaphia, or Urn-burial, a Discourse on
Sepulchral Urns: by Sir Thomas Browne, M.D. of Norwich. With a Preliminary Discourse and Notes, by J. A. St. John, Esq. London: Joseph Rickerby,
Sherbourn Lane, King William street, City. 1838. 17 cm. pp. 12, LII, viii, 266,
[2]. [The Masterpieces of English Prose Literature, Vol. VI.]

Note: Contains Digby's *Observations*, and numerous footnotes, mostly added by the
editor. Republished with cancel title-page by Henry Washbourne in 1841, and again,
with the addition of *Christian Morals*, in 1845 and 1848 (see no. 25).

22 RELIGIO MEDICI: HYDRIOTAPHIA ED. ST. JOHN 8° 1841

Religio Medici: to which is added, Hydriotaphia...[&c., as in no. 21] London:
Henry Washbourne, Salisbury Square, Fleet Street. 1841.

Note: The same sheets as no. 21 with cancel title.

23 RELIGIO MEDICI, CHRISTIAN MORALS ED. PEACE 8° 1844

Religio Medici. Its sequel Christian Morals. By Sir Thomas Browne, Kt. M.D.
With resemblant passages from Cowper's Task, and a verbal index. London:
Longman, Brown, Green, and Longmans, Paternoster Row. MDCCCXLIV.
20 cm. pp. xxiii, [7], 275, [1].

Note: The preface is signed *John Peace. City Library, Bristol, New Year's Day,* 1844. No
annotations except the author's marginalia. The text is that of 1643 with a few
alterations. Passages from Cowper, 15 pp. (246–61). Reprinted in America in the same
year (see next entry).

24 RELIGIO MEDICI, CHRISTIAN MORALS ED. PEACE 8° 1844

Religio Medici. Its sequel Christian Morals...Philadelphia: Lea and Blanchard.
1844. pp. [ii], xxii, 23–226.

Note: A reprint of the preceding entry.

25 RELIGIO MEDICI, &c. ED. ST. JOHN 8° 1845

Religio Medici: With Observations thereon by Sir Kenelm Digby. To which is
added, Hydriotaphia, or Urn-Burial, A Discourse on Sepulchral Urns; and also
Christian Morals: by Sir Thomas Browne, M.D. of Norwich. A New Edition,

With a Preliminary Discourse and Notes. London: Henry Washbourne, New Bridge Street, Blackfriars. MDCCCXLV. 17 cm. pp. 3–12, LII, viii, 266, 3–63, [1].

Note: This is a combination of two books, (1) *Religio Medici* and *Hydriotaphia*, ed. J. A. St. John, Rickerby (1838) (see no. 21), and (2) *Christian Morals* (Washbourne, 1845). The first two leaves of each book have been removed and a general title-page added. Issued again by Washbourne with a new title-page in 1848.

26 RELIGIO MEDICI, &c. ED. GARDINER   8° 1845

Religio Medici together with A Letter to a Friend on the Death of his Intimate Friend and Christian Morals By Sir Thomas Browne Kt. M.D. Edited by Henry Gardiner M.A. of Exeter Coll. Oxford [*Pickering's device*] London William Pickering 1845 17 cm. pp. xvi, 388.

Note: Contains a preface by the editor and notes, which are taken partly from Keck's *Annotations* and are partly original. There is also a marginal analysis of the different sections, a glossary, and a brief list of editions. The present edition is called the eighteenth. The editor 'has carefully collated the text with three of the MSS and with the most trustworthy of the Editions; and has availed himself of the corrections and annotations of former Editors'. He also gives in an appendix illustrative passages from other authors and from Sir Thomas Browne's MSS.

27 RELIGIO MEDICI, &c. ED. ST. JOHN   8° 1848

Religio Medici:...[&c. as in no.25] London: Henry Washbourne,...MDCCCXLVIII.

Note: The same sheets as in no. 25, with a new title-page.

28 RELIGIO MEDICI ED. WILKIN   8° 1852

In Sir Thomas Browne's Works...Ed. Simon Wilkin...London: H. G. Bohn...1852 (see no. 205).

Note: Vol. II, pp. 291–487. A reprint of no. 20.

29 RELIGIO MEDICI, &c. ED. FIELDS   8° 1862

Religio Medici A Letter to a Friend Christian Morals Urn Burial and Other Papers by Sir Thomas Browne, Kt. M.D. Boston Ticknor and Fields 1862 18 cm. pp. [ii], xviii, 440, [2].

Portrait: Steel engraving after White's portrait, 1686 (no. 201); unsigned.

Note: Edited by James T. Fields. The text and a selection of notes were based on those of Gardiner's edition (no. 26). Contains a biographical sketch of the author. The *Other Papers* mentioned on the title-page consist of extracts from the *Garden of Cyrus*, *Pseudodoxia Epidemica*, letters, and common-place books together with the fragment *On Dreams* and the spurious fragment *On Mummies*. Twenty-five copies were printed on large paper (22·5 cm.). A 'second edition' was issued in the same year. Imprint of Welch, Bigelow, and Co., Cambridge [Mass.], on back of title; initials in red. There were five subsequent editions; see nos. 33 and 35.

A violent attack on this edition was published in *The Philobiblon* (New York, 1868), II, 30. The reviewer seeks to convict the editor of plagiarism and incompetence.

RELIGIO MEDICI

together with

A LETTER TO A FRIEND

ON THE DEATH OF HIS INTIMATE FRIEND

and

CHRISTIAN MORALS

By

SIR THOMAS BROWNE Kт. M.D.

EDITED BY HENRY GARDINER M.A.
of Exeter Coll. Oxford

LONDON
WILLIAM PICKERING
1845

30 RELIGIO MEDICI, &c. ED. FIELDS 8° 1862

Religio Medici...[&c. as in no. 29] [Second issue] Boston Ticknor and Fields 1862.

Note: A reprint of no. 29, marked *second edition* on the back of the title-page. Portrait as before. Also with date 1863. Actually the *second issue*, since the first was printed from electrotypes; there is no alteration.

31 RELIGIO MEDICI, &c. ED. WILLIS BUND 8° 1869

Religio Medici, Hydriotaphia, and the Letter to a Friend. By Sir Thomas Browne, Knt. with an introduction and notes by J. W. Willis Bund, M.A., LL.B., Gonville and Caius College, Cambridge, of Lincoln's Inn, Barrister-at-Law. [woodcut portrait of Sir T. B.] London: Sampson Low, Son, and Marston, Crown Buildings, 188 Fleet Street. 1869. 15 cm. pp. [ii], xii, 196.

Note: It is stated in the preface that the text is taken from the edition of 1682; but Greenhill points out that if this is correct Mr. Bund's copy must be very different from the one in his possession. Reprinted in 1873, 1874, 1877, 1882, 1890 and 1903. An American edition (see next entry) appeared in 1869. Charles Williams was informed by the publishers of this edition that no reprint was issued in 1874. A copy with this date is, however, in the Glasgow University Library, Monro Collection. The woodcut on the title-page had already appeared in Friswell: *Varia* (1866) (see p. 216).

32 RELIGIO MEDICI, &c. ED. WILLIS BUND 8° 1869

Religio Medici...[&c. as in no. 31] New York: Scribner, Welford, and Co. 1869. 15 cm. pp. [ii], xii, 196.

Note: The same sheets as no. 31, with a different title-page.

33 RELIGIO MEDICI, &c. ED. FIELDS 8° 1872

Religio Medici...[&c. as in no. 29] [Fifth edition] Boston James R. Osgood and Company Late Ticknor & Fields, and Fields, Osgood, & Co. 1872 18 cm. pp. [ii], xviii, 440, [2].

Note: A reprint of no. 29, marked *Fifth edition* on the back of the title-page. Portrait as before. The imprint of Welch, Bigelow, and Company, Cambridge [Mass.], is on the back of the title-page. The initials are in red. There are copies of the third (1863) and fourth (1868) in the Osler Library, McGill University, Montreal.

34 RELIGIO MEDICI ED. SMITH 8° 1874

English School Classics Religio Medici by Sir Thomas Browne, Knt. Edited With Introduction and Notes by W. P. Smith, M.A. assistant-master at Winchester College Rivingtons London, Oxford, and Cambridge 1874. 16 cm. pp. 124.

Note: Reissued with a new title-page by Longmans and Co. in 1893.

35 RELIGIO MEDICI, &c. ED. FIELDS 8° 1878

Religio Medici A Letter to a Friend Christian Morals Urn-burial and other papers by Sir Thomas Browne, Kt. M.D. Boston Robert Brothers 1878 16 cm. pp. [ii], xviii, 440, [4].

Portrait: As in no. 29.

Note: A reprint of no. 29 with a new title-page and on smaller paper. This is therefore the sixth issue of Fields's edition. On the back of the title-page is the imprint of John Wilson and Son, Cambridge [Mass]. The book seems to have been printed from the same type as before, though the initials are now in black instead of in red.

36 RELIGIO MEDICI, &c. ED. GREENHILL 8° 1881

Sir Thomas Browne's Religio Medici Letter to a Friend &c. and Christian Morals Edited by W. A. Greenhill, M.D. Oxon. [portrait of Sir T. B. engraved on steel] London Macmillan and Co. 1881 16 cm. pp. [iv], lvi, 392. [Golden Treasury Series.]

Contents: Editor's Preface; Appendix I. Chronological table of dates connected with Sir T. B. II. Discovery of the Remains of Sir T. B. III. Brief notes of former Editors of the *Religio Medici*. IV. List of Editions. V. Collations of some old editions of the *Religio Medici* (pp. vii–lvi). Notes Critical and Explanatory (pp. 233–321). Index, general and glossarial (pp. 323–92). The three works printed are preceded by typographic facsimiles of the title-pages of the editions of 1682, 1690 and 1716 respectively.

Note: Reprinted in 1885 with additions and corrections, and in 1889, 1892, 1898, 1901, 1904, 1906, 1910, 1915, 1920, 1923, without alteration. The vignette on the title-page was engraved by C. H. Jeens after the portrait at the Royal College of Physicians.

37 RELIGIO MEDICI ED. GREENHILL 8° 1883

Religio Medici by Sir Thomas Browne Physician being A Facsimile of the First Edition published in 1642 with an introduction by W. A. Greenhill, M.D., Oxon. London Elliot Stock 62 Paternoster Row E.C. 1883 19·5 cm. pp. xxxi, [3], 190.

Note: A facsimile of the first unauthorized edition, 1642 (no. 1), with preface and bibliography by the editor. Also issued on large paper, 21 × 17·5 cm. Bound in boards, veneered with oak, and stamped with an arabesque design.

38 RELIGIO MEDICI ED. MORLEY 12° 1886

Cassell's National Library. Religio Medici. By Sir Thomas Brown, M.D. with the 'Observations' of Sir Kenelm Digby. Cassell & Company, Limited: London, Paris, New York & Melbourne. 1886. 14 cm. pp. 192.

Note: The introduction (4 pp.) is by Prof. Henry Morley. Also issued with a cancel title-page in the same year with the imprint *Leipzig, Gressner & Schramm*, and with the imprint *New York, The Cassell Publishing Co.* Reprinted in the New Series of *Cassell's National Library* in 1892, and again in 1905 with a portrait reproduced in half-tone from the engraving of 1672.

39 RELIGIO MEDICI, &c. ED. SYMONDS 8° 1886

Sir Thomas Browne's Religio Medici Urn Burial, Christian Morals, and other essays. Edited, with an Introduction by John Addington Symonds. London: Walter Scott, 24 Warwick Lane, Paternoster Row. 1886. 17 cm. pp. xxxi, 262. [The Camelot Classics.]

Note: Contains the fragment *On Dreams* and *A Letter to a Friend* in addition to the works mentioned on the title-page. The editor's introduction was reprinted in *Modern English Essays*, ed. Ernest Rhys (London, 1922), III, 89–114.

In my collection is the editor's copy, inscribed on the fly leaf: *J A Symonds August 1 1886 4 p.m.* He has corrected a number of grotesque misprints in the introductory essay, and it can only be inferred that he never saw a proof before the book went to press.

The ordinary issue is in blue cloth with a paper label on the spine. Some copies were bound in scarlet morocco, gilt, gilt edges.

40 RELIGIO MEDICI, &c. ED. LLOYD ROBERTS 8° 1892

Religio Medici and other essays By Sir Thomas Browne Edited, with an Introduction by D. Lloyd Roberts, M.D., F.R.C.P. London David Stott, 370 Oxford Street, W. 1892 11 cm. pp. xlviii, 428, [4]. [The Stott Library.]

Contents: Biographical introduction, *Religio Medici, Christian Morals, Letter to a Friend, Hydriotaphia.*

Portrait: Photomezzotype of the engraving by White, with facsimile of autograph.

Note: 100 copies were printed on large paper (16 cm.) for private circulation. In my collection is the copy given by the editor to Sir Andrew Clark, Bart., M.D., F.R.S., to whom the book was dedicated. A revised edition was published in 1898 (no. 44). This, the original, text was reprinted in 1905 (no. 49).

41 RELIGIO MEDICI, &c. ED. G. B. M. 8° 1894

Religio Medici: Urn Burial and Christian Morals, by Sir Thomas Browne, Knight, Physician of Norwich. With an illustrated memoir. London Printed for Andrew Crooke in the year 1643: and Republished by G. Moreton, 42, Burgate Street, Canterbury. 1894. (Price Nine Shillings) 22 cm. pp. viii, 210.

Contents: Contains the *Letter to a Friend* in addition to the works mentioned on the title-page.

Portrait, etc.: (i) Frontispiece. Photogravure by Dawsons after the Bodleian portrait. (ii) Facing p. vi. Photogravure of Sir T. B.'s tomb in the Church of St Peter Mancroft, Norwich. (iii) P. iv. Reduced facsimile of the engraved title-page of *Religio Medici* (1659).

Note: The memoir (6 pp.) is signed G. B. M., perhaps the publisher.

42 RELIGIO MEDICI, HYDRIOTAPHIA
ED. GREENHILL & HOLME   8° 1896

Sir Thomas Browne's Religio Medici and Urn-burial MDCCCXCVI: Published by
J. M. Dent and Co. Aldine House. London, E.C. 15 cm. pp. vii, [i], 196.
[The Temple Classics.]

Note: With engraved portrait after R. White, 1686, and glossary (13 pp.). Reprinted in
1897, 1899, 1901 and 1906. The general editor, Israel Gollancz, acknowledges
Macmillan's permission for using Greenhill's text, marginalia and glossary being
added by Miss Ursula Holme.

43 RELIGIO MEDICI ED. BELL   4° 1898

Religio Medici by Sir Thomas Browne London George Bell and Sons
MDCCCXCVIII 23 cm. pp. xii, 187, [1].

Portrait: Photogravure by Walker and Boutall of Van der Gucht's engraving (see
no. 156).

Note: Edited by Edward Bell, F.S.A. Wilkin's text, but no notes are given other than
the author's marginalia. Digby's *Observations* are added in an appendix. Printed by
Charles Whittingham & Co. on hand-made paper. Edition limited to 500 copies.
The remaining copies were re-issued in New York in 1903 (see no. 47).

44 RELIGIO MEDICI, &c. ED. LLOYD ROBERTS   8° 1898

Religio Medici. . .[&c. as in no. 40] Revised Edition London Smith Elder and
Co. 15 Waterloo Place 1898 17 cm. pp. xxxix, [i], 305, [1].

Contents: As in no. 40, with the addition of the fragment *On Dreams*.

Portrait: As in no. 40.

Note: A reprint of the text of no. 40 revised by the editor. It was re-issued with a cancel
title-page by Sherratt and Hughes, Manchester, in 1902.

45 RELIGIO MEDICI ED. BRISCOE   12° 1902

Religio Medici by Sir Thomas Browne, Kt. London Gay and Bird 1902 12 cm.
pp. xvi, 140. [The Bibelots.]

Portrait: Photogravure by Walter L. Colls after the engraving by R. White (see no. 201).

Note: Edited, with an introduction, by J. Potter Briscoe, F.R.S.L. Sixty copies on
Japanese vellum. The text is stated to be based on that of 1682.

46 RELIGIO MEDICI, &c. ED. HOLMES   f° 1902

Religio Medici, Urn burial, Christian Morals, and other essays. By Sir Thomas
Browne. *Colophon:* edited by C. J. Holmes; decorated by C. S. Ricketts
under whose supervision the book has been printed at the Ballantyne press.

Sold by Hacon & Ricketts, The Vale Press, 17 Craven Street, Strand, London, John Lane, New York, London MCMII. 29 cm. pp. cxcviii, [ii].

Note: Contains the *Letter to a Friend* and the fragment *On Dreams* in addition to the works mentioned above. 310 copies printed, 10 on vellum.

47 RELIGIO MEDICI ED. BELL   4° 1903

Religio Medici By Sir Thomas Browne New York Scott-Thaw Co. MDCCCCIII.

Note: A re-issue of the remaining copies of no. 43 with a cancel title-page.

48 RELIGIO MEDICI ED. SAYLE   8° 1904

In The Works of Sir Thomas Browne Edited by Charles Sayle London Grant Richards 1904 (see no. 206).

Note: vol. 1, pp. x–lv and 1–112. The text follows that of the edition of 1682. Keck's *Annotations* are prefixed, together with *A Letter Sent*, &c., and *To the Reader*.

49 RELIGIO MEDICI, &c.   8° [1905]

Religio Medici Christian Morals Hydriotaphia, &c. Sir Thomas Browne London: Gibbings & Company 13·5 cm. pp. xxiv, 428. [The Museum Edition.]

Contents: As on the title-page, with the addition of the *Letter to a Friend*.

Illustrations: An imaginary portrait of Sir T. B. in black and white by Frank Brangwyn, R.A., as frontispiece; Sir T. B.'s tomb and a reproduction of the engraved title-page of the 1659 edition of the *Religio Medici* in the text.

Note: The text is a reprint from the type of the issue edited by Dr. Lloyd Roberts in 1892 (see no. 40), but there is a shorter, unsigned biographical introduction.

50 RELIGIO MEDICI, &c.   8° 1906

Religio Medici and other essays by Sir Thomas Browne. London. E. Grant Richards 1906. 16 cm. pp. 192.

Portrait: Photogravure from Van Hove's engraving (see no. 79).

Contents: Religio Medici, Hydriotaphia, Brampton Urns, On Dreams.

51 RELIGIO MEDICI, &c. ED. HERFORD   8° [1906]

The Religio Medici & other writings of Sir Thomas Browne. London; published by J. M. Dent & Co. and in New York by E. P. Dutton & Co. 17 cm. pp. xvi, 296. [Everyman's Library.]

Contents: Religio Medici, Hydriotaphia, Brampton Urns, Letter to a Friend, Garden of Cyrus, Christian Morals, Glossary.

Note: Introduction by Professor C. H. Herford, based upon an essay written for Browne's Tercentenary and published in the *Manchester Guardian*. Reprinted in 1920, 1951 (see no. 58 *e*) and 1962 (see no. 58 *m*).

52 RELIGIO MEDICI, &c. ED. SONNENSCHEIN 12° [1906]

Works Religio Medici, Hydriotaphia The Garden of Cyrus Christian Morals of Sir Thomas Browne with a glossary by William Swan Sonnenschein London George Routledge & Sons, limited New York: E. P. Dutton & Co. 15 cm. pp. vi, [2], 264. [The New Universal Library.]

Note: The text is based on those of Wilkin and Greenhill, with some footnotes by the editor. It is called on the half-title *Sir Thomas Browne's Works I...*, but no more appeared. A 'more elaborate edition of Browne's works' in Messrs Routledge's English Library is announced in the preface, but did not appear.

53 RELIGIO MEDICI, HYDRIOTAPHIA ED. WALLER 8° [1906]

Religio Medici and Urn burial by Sir Thomas Browne. Methuen & Co. 36 Essex Street W.C. London. 19 cm. pp. xxii, [2], 120. [Methuen's Standard Library.]

Note: Biographical introduction by A. R. Waller. The text is that of 1682. Contains the original prefatory matter and Digby's *Observations*.

54 RELIGIO MEDICI, HYDRIOTAPHIA ED. BAYNE 8° [1906]

Religio Medici and other essays by Sir Thomas Browne with an introduction by Charles Whibley Blackie and Son Ld London. 15 cm. pp. xv, [i], 236. [The Red Letter Library.]

Portrait: Half-tone reproduction of the engraving by G. P. Harding (see no. 174).

Contents: Religio Medici and *Hydriotaphia* only.

Note: Contains the letters between Digby and Sir T. B. and *To the Reader*. The text was revised and notes prepared by Thomas Bayne. Re-issued without change in 1926.

55 RELIGIO MEDICI 8° 1909

Browne's Religio Medici And Digby's Observations At the Clarendon Press MCMIX 19 cm. pp. [xii], 183 [185], [3], 44. [Tudor & Stuart Library.]

Frontispiece: Half-tone reproduction of the engraved title of 1643.

Note: 'The text of *Religio* follows that of the first authentic edition of 1643, page for page and line for line. To preserve identity of reference the errors of pagination (pp. 171 and 172 are duplicated) and section numbering have been left undisturbed. The text has been corrected from the *Errata* page of the original; a few obvious misprints, not there noticed, have also been removed.' This type facsimile was composed from Sir William Osler's copy of the original, which happened to be an example of form (*b*) described under no. 3, but at that time unrecognized. It therefore lacks the leaves A2–5 with the letters written by Digby and Browne.

56 RELIGIO MEDICI, &c. 8° [1911]

Religio Medici and other essays by Sir Thomas Browne London: Published by Chapman & Hall, Ltd 19 cm. pp. [viii], 231, [1]. [The Books of the Verulam Club.]

Contents: Religio Medici, Hydriotaphia, Letter to a Friend, On Dreams.

Frontispiece: Photogravure reproduction of the frontispiece to Wilkin, 1836 (see no. 203).

Note: Printed at the Ballantyne Press on Aldwych hand-made paper.

57 RELIGIO MEDICI ed. murison 8° 1922

Sir Thomas Browne Religio Medici Edited by W. Murison, M.A....Cambridge At the University Press 1922 [Pitt Press Series] 17 cm. pp. xxvi, 270, [2].

Note: The text is printed from the edition of 1682 with some corrections. The notes are very copious. Reprinted without change in 1931 and 1939.

58 RELIGIO MEDICI 4° 1923

Religio Medici By Sir Thomas Browne, Physician, of Norwich Printed & sold at the Golden Cockerel Press, Waltham Saint Lawrence, Berkshire. *Colophon:* Here ends Religio Medici: cxv. copies, of which cv. are for sale, printed at the Golden Cockerel Press: Finished May 1. MCMXXIII. 26·5 cm. pp. 82, [10].

Note: Printed on Arnold's unbleached hand-made paper. Initial letters in red. Printer's device at the end in gold. Contains the author's preface *To the Reader*, but the other preliminary matter is omitted. The author's marginal notes are printed at the end.

58a RELIGIO MEDICI ed. keynes 8° 1928

In The Works of Sir Thomas Browne Edited by Geoffrey Keynes London Faber and Gwyer Limited...1928 (see no. 207a).

Note: Vol. 1, pp. ix–x, 1–98. The text is based on that edited by Greenhill, 1881 (see no. 36).

58b RELIGIO MEDICI ed. keynes f° 1939

Religio Medici By Sir Thomas Browne, Kt., M.D. Edited with a New Introduction by Geoffrey Keynes M.D., F.R.C.S. Eugene: University of Oregon Printed for the Members of The Limited Editions Club by John Henry Nash 1939 28·5 cm. pp. xix, [i], 113, [3].

Portrait, etc.: (i) Frontispiece. Photogravure reproduction of the portrait drawn by Loggan, somewhat enlarged, with a facsimile of Browne's signature below. (ii) Engraved title. The title-page of 1642 re-engraved in photogravure by Dolph Henry Murnik and enlarged to 135 × 75 mm.

Note: The text is that prepared by the same editor for the *Works,* 1929 (see no. 207a). According to the colophon on p. [114] 1500 numbered copies were printed and signed by the printer, John Henry Nash, who composed the whole of the type with his own hands in a special cutting of Benton's Cloister fount. The book and its method of production were described in *The Monthly Letter of the Limited Editions Club* (March 1939) no. 118. It was issued in quarter canvas with marbled paper sides enclosed in a slip-case; there is a paper label on the spine.

58*c* RELIGIO MEDICI &c. ED. KEYNES   12° [1940]

Sir Thomas Browne Religio Medici and Christian Morals Edited with an Introduction by Geoffrey Keynes Thomas Nelson and Sons Ltd. London [&c.]
15·5 cm. pp. xi, [i], 13–192. [Nelson Classics.]

Note: The text is that of the *Works*, ed. Keynes (1928–31). The introduction is based on
that written for no. 58*b*.

58*d* RELIGIO MEDICI INTROD. BY EDMAN   *c.* 1943

In Boethius, Anicius Manlius Severinus The Consolation of Philosophy; The
Imitation of Christ Thomas a Kempis; Religio Medici sir T. Browne with an
introduction by I. Edman New York Modern Library [*c.* 1943] 19 cm.,
pp. xxii, 406.

58*e* RELIGIO MEDICI &c. INTROD. BY HUNTLEY   8° 1951

Religio Medici and Other Writings By Sir Thomas Browne With a new intro-
duction by Frank L. Huntley New York: E. P. Dutton and Company Inc.
London: J. M. Dent and Sons, Limited 1951 17·6 cm. pp. xxii, 326.
[Everyman's Library, Philosophy and Theology 92A.]

Contents: Religio Medici, Pseudodoxia Epidemica, Book II, Chapter 3, *A Letter to a Friend,
Hydriotaphia, Urne-Buriall, The Garden of Cyrus, Christian Morals,* glossary.

Note: The text is that of the Everyman edition of 1906 (no. 51), with the addition of a
chapter from *Vulgar Errors* and omission of *Brampton Urns.*

58*f* RELIGIO MEDICI ED. DENONAIN   8° 1953

Sir Thomas Browne Religio Medici Edited from the manuscript copies and the
early editions by Jean-Jacques Denonain Professor of English Literature at the
University of Algiers Cambridge At The University Press 1953 22 cm.,
pp. xliii, [i], 120.

Note: This revised text is provided with an *apparatus criticus* on a scale never before
attempted. The editor has relied on the MS versions, particularly P (Pembroke
College, Oxford), which he claims to be the earliest and not used by any previous
editor. It is stated to provide a number of passages, phrases and words found nowhere
else, and here published for the first time.

58*g* RELIGIO MEDICI &c.   *c.* 1955

Religio Medici; Hydriotaphia; Urne-buriall; Christian Morals; On Dreams.
Chicago, Gateway [*c.* 1955] 18 cm., pp. x, 241, [1].

58*h* RELIGIO MEDICI ED. DENONAIN   8° 1955

Sir Thomas Browne Religio Medici A new edition with biographical and
critical introduction by Jean-Jacques Denonain...Cambridge At The University Press 1955 20 cm., pp. xxi, [i], 102, [4].

Note: The text is based on that of no. 58*f*, omitting the *apparatus criticus*. It is claimed to be an authoritative text, though it includes passages rejected by Browne himself without any indication of his having done so.

58*i* RELIGIO MEDICI, &c. 1956

Note: A paper-back edition is said to have been published in the United States in 1956 with an introduction by Kirk, but I have been unable to obtain a copy or any further details.

58*k* RELIGIO MEDICI ED. DENONAIN 8° [1958]

Une version primitive de Religio Medici par Sir Thomas Browne Texte inédit de la copie manuscrite au Collège de Pembroke, Oxford. Publié par Jean-Jacques Denonain Professeur de Langue et Littérature Anglaises à la Faculté des Lettres d'Alger Ouvrage publié avec le concours du Centre National de la Recherche Scientifique Presses Universitaires de France [1958] [Publications de la Faculté des Lettres d'Alger xxxvi] 25 cm., pp. 107, [1].

Frontispiece: Reproduction of p. 1 of the MS.

Note: The text is derived from P, the MS in Pembroke College, Oxford, used for the edition of 1953 (no. 58*f*). The editor claims that this is the earliest and most revealing text of the book that has survived. Critical notes are printed at the end.

58*l* RELIGIO MEDICI ED. SANNA 4° 1958

Thomas Browne Religio Medici Edizione critica con introduzione e note a cura di Vittoria Sanna Università di Cagliari Anno 1958 [Annali delle Facoltà di Lettere-Filosofia e Magistero dell'Università di Cagliari, Vol. xxvi—Parte I (II) 1958] 24·5 cm. Parte I, pp. xcii, 175, [5]; Parte II, pp. lix, [ii], 261, [3].

Note: This, the latest, full recension of the text by Dottoressa Vittoria Sanna is furnished with an extensive *apparatus criticus*. Part II contains a translation of the text into Italian with a commentary.

58*m* RELIGIO MEDICI &c. INTROD. BY SUTHERLAND 8° 1962

Sir Thomas Browne The Religio Medici and Other Writings Introduction by Halliday Sutherland, M.D., F.R.S.L. London J M Dent & Sons Ltd New York E P Dutton & Co Inc [1962] 18 cm., pp. x, [iv], 296. [Everyman's Library, no. 92]

Contents: As in no. 51, with a brief new introduction. Re-issued in 1966, ed. M. R. Ridley.

58*n* RELIGIO MEDICI ED. WINNY 8° 1963

Sir Thomas Browne Religio Medici Edited and annotated by James Winny Cambridge At The University Press 1963 18·5 cm., pp. xxxiv, [ii], 154, [2].

Note: This modernized text is based on that of Denonain (no. 58*f*) with a few changes which are listed. There are 45 pages of 'Commentary and Notes' and a Glossary.

58*o* RELIGIO MEDICI ED. KEYNES   8° 1964

> *In* The Works of Sir Thomas Browne edited by Geoffrey Keynes London
> Faber & Faber Limited [1964] (see no. 207*c*)
>
> *Note:* Vol. 1, pp. 1–93. In this revised edition of *The Works* the text of *Religio Medici* is
> adapted from the recension edited by Vittoria Sanna (1958) (see no. 58*l*). The engraved
> title-page is reproduced, but enlarged (without the editor's authorization) to twice its
> actual size.

58*p* RELIGIO MEDICI &c. ED. MARTIN   8° 1964

> Sir Thomas Browne Religio Medici and Other Works Edited by L. C. Martin
> Oxford At the Clarendon Press 1964 21·5 cm., pp. xxvii, [i], 383, [1].
>
> *Contents: Religio Medici, Hydriotaphia* with *The Garden of Cyrus, A Letter to a Friend,
> Christian Morals.*
>
> *Portrait, etc.:* Half-tone reproductions of (i) Sir Thomas and Dame Dorothy Browne
> (National Portrait Gallery). (ii) Title-page of *Religio Medici*, 1643. (iii) *Norfolk Urns.*
> (iv) Quincunx. (v) A page of Sloane MS. 1862.
>
> *Note:* The text of *Religio Medici* is that of 1643 with some deviations recorded in footnotes
> and additional passages from MSS. Appendixes give a summary of Browne's library,
> and a MS version of *A Letter to a Friend.* At the end are Textual Notes, Commentary,
> and Index of Authors cited. The last four works have type facsimiles of title-pages.

58*q* RELIGIO MEDICI ED. HUNTLEY   8° 1966

> Sir Thomas Browne Religio Medici Edited by F. L. Huntley The University
> of Michigan New York Appleton–Century–Crofts Division of Meredith
> Publishing Company [1966] 17·5 cm., pp. xiii, [iii], 109, [1].
>
> *Note:* With Introduction, Principal Dates in the life of Browne, and Glossary.

59 RELIGIO MEDICI: LATIN   12° 1644

> *Engraved title:* A copy of Marshall's design, but reversed, the figure falling to the
> left instead of to the right. The title *Religio, Medici* [sic] is engraved between the
> figure and the water, and at the bottom: *Lugd. Batavorum, Apud Francifcum
> Hackium. A°. 1644.*
>
> *Collation:* A–K¹² L⁴; 124 leaves.
>
> *Contents:* A1*a* engraved title, verso blank; A2*a Lectori S.* signed *Iohann Merryweather;*
> A2*b*–A4*b Author Lectori S.* signed *Thomas Browne;* A5*a–b In Religionem Medici Latini-
> tate donatam* and *In Eandem,* 39 Latin lines signed *Reginaldus Bokenham,* followed by *In
> Religionem Medici Anglice scriptam à D. D. Browne, & Latinitate donatam à D. Ion.
> Merryweather, amico summo,* 12 Latin lines subscribed *Hæc amicitiæ ergo T.B.D.A.;*
> A6*a*–L2*b* (pp. 11–242 [244]) text; L3*a*–L4*a Anacephalæosis;* L4*b Errata.*
>
> *Note:* Neither this edition nor the two following had been seen by Wilkin in 1836,
> though he obtained copies later. The translation is by John Merryweather of

Magdalene College, Cambridge, except for the French lines in part 2, section 4, which remain as before. There are catchwords throughout. The pagination of pp. 241–4 is misprinted 239–42. Sections 6 and 7 of part 1 of the original are included in section 6 of the translation, so that this has a total of 59 sections instead of 60. Sections 14, 29 and 41 are misnumbered 41, 30 and 35 without affecting the total. In part 2 the sections are correctly numbered 1–15. Reginald Bokenham or Bukenham, author of the Latin lines on A5, had graduated at Caius College, Cambridge, in 1637–8, and became a Fellow in 1646. He had studied medicine at Leyden in 1641 and is believed to have practised in Yarmouth, so that he is likely to have been acquainted with Browne at a later date.

Copies: BM, CLN, ECO, FLWC, GUL, K, ULC; MMO.

60 RELIGIO MEDICI: LATIN 12° 1644

Engraved Title: A roughly engraved copy of that in no. 59, omitting the comma after *Religio,* with inscription below: *Juxta Exemp Lug Batavor 1644*

Collation: ā⁴ A⁸ B–K¹² L⁴; 124 leaves.

Contents: A1*a* engraved title, verso blank; āi*a*–āiv*b* (with signatures āiii, āiiii, āv, and one leaf unsigned) *Lectori;* Aii*a*–Lii*b* (pp. 11–244) text; Liii*a*–Liiii*a Anacephalæosis;* Liiii*b* blank.

Note: The engraved title is printed on the first leaf of the second quire, the first quire with signature ā being inserted between A1 and A2. All the prefatory matter of the previous edition is omitted, and a new preface defending the author from the charge of heresy substituted. There are catchwords at the ends of quires only. The French lines on p. 197 are omitted and the space left blank. Leaves K12 and L1 are both numbered 239–40, and p. 244 is numbered 174. Signatures Av, Fiiii, Iiiii are printed Lv, Diiii, Biiii. Sections 14 and 29 of part 1 are misnumbered 41 and 30 as before; section 41 is now correctly numbered. It was of this edition that Merryweather wrote to Browne: 'When I came at Paris, the next year after [? 1643], I found it printed again, in which edition both the epistles were left out, and a preface by some papist put in their place, in which making use of, and wresting some passages in your book, he endeavoured to show that nothing but custom and education kept you from their church' (Wilkin, 1, 367).

In my collection is a contemporary manuscript copy of this edition, presumably written in France, since the binding is certainly French. The engraved title-page has been copied and enlarged in water-colours. Part 1 has been given head-lines *Pars prima de fide,* and part 11 *Pars altera de charit*[*ate*]. Each section also has a heading indicating its subject, these being set out in a list of contents derived from the *Anacephalæosis.* There is no indication of ownership.

Copies: BM(2), CLN, GUL, K; MMO.

61 RELIGIO MEDICI: LATIN 12° 1644

Engraved title: As in no. 59.

Collation: A–K¹²; 120 leaves.

Contents: A1*a* engraved title (*Religio, Medici*), verso blank; A2*a* (p. 3) *Lectori S.;* A2*b*–A3*b* (pp. 4–6) *Author Lectori S.*; A4*a–b* (pp. 7–8) Latin lines by Bokenham and Merry-weather; A5*a*–K10*a* (pp. 9–235) text; K10*b*–K12*a Anacephalæosis*; K12*b* blank.

Note: A reprint of no. 59. There are catchwords throughout. Page 197 is misprinted 179. Sections 29 and 54 in part 1 are misnumbered 30 and 45. Of this edition Merryweather wrote to Browne: 'Since my return home, I see Hackius, the Leyden printer, hath made a new impression, which furnished me afresh with some copies, and whereof that which I left with Mr Preston is one, as is easily observable by the difference of the pages, and the omission of the errata, which were noted in the first, though the title-page be the same in both' (Wilkin, I, 367). A copy of the book offered by the late Raphael King in December 1946 was inscribed on the fly-leaf: *William Berwick ejus liber ex dono authoris summi amici 1656*. The name of this friend is not otherwise known.

Copies: FLWC, GUL, K, MSL; MMO.

62 RELIGIO MEDICI: LATIN 12° 1650

Engraved title: As in no. 61, with the date altered to 1650.

Collation: A–K¹²; 120 leaves.

Contents: As in no. 61.

Note: This edition closely resembles Hackius's second edition of 1644 (no. 61), but it has been entirely reset. Some alterations have been made and the orthography has been modernized, e.g. p. 4, l. 1 cupidum for cvpidum; p. 160, l. 1 *pœnæ, summam* for *pœnæ, summā*. There are catchwords throughout. Misprints as in no. 61, with the addition of signature D5 for A5 and C4 for K4.

Copies: BLO, CLN, GUL, K, ULC(2); MH, MMO.

63 RELIGIO MEDICI: LATIN ED. VON MOLTKE 8° 1652

Engraved title: The usual design newly engraved without the title below the falling figure but inscribed below in a cartouche in three variant forms: (i) RELIGIO MEDICI | *additis annotationibus.* | M.DC.LII. (ii) RELIGIO MEDICI | *additis annotationibus.* | *Argentorati.* | *Sumptibus Friderici Spoor.* | M.DC.LII. (iii) RELIGIO MEDICI | *cum Annotationibus.* | ARGENTORATI | *Sumptibus* FRIDERICI SPOOR. | CIƆ IƆCLII. Plate-mark 146 × 78 mm.

Collation:):(⁸A–Z⁸ Aa–Gg⁸; 248 leaves.

Contents:):(1 engraved title;):(2*a*–):(5*b Præfatio auctoris annotat.* signed L. N. M. E. M.;):(6*a Lectori S.* signed *Iohann. Merryweather*;):(6*b*–):(7*a Author Lectori S.*;):(7*b*–):(8*b Præfatio Præfixa Edit. Parifienf.*; A1*a*–Ee4*b* (pp. 1–440) text of *Religio Medici* with *Annotata* after each section; Ee5*a*–Ee6*a Anacephalæofis*; Ee6*b*–Gg8*b Index Rerum quæ in Annotatis continentur*; Gg8*b Errata*.

Note: The sequence of the variant engraved title-pages recorded above is indicated by the fact that the whole cartouche has been altered in the third form to make room for the longer imprint. The rest of the book is unchanged. Signatures C4 and Aa4 are misprinted G4 and A4. The initials at the end of the *Præfatio* stand for *Levinus Nicolas Moltkenius Eques Misniensis*, that is, Levin Nicolas von Moltke of Mecklenburg-Schwerin.

Copies: BLO, BM, GUL, K (variants i, ii, iii), MSL, ULC; MH(3), MMO, PUL.

64 RELIGIO MEDICI: LATIN ED. VON MOLTKE 8° 1652 [1665]

Engraved title: As in no. 63 with the inscription altered to read (i) RELIGIO MEDICI | *cum Annotationibus* | ARGENTORAI | *Sumpt. IO. FRIDERICO SPOOR.* | CIƆIƆCLII, *or* (ii) with a cancel title, the date being altered to CIƆIƆCLXV.

Collation, contents: As in no. 63, except that the *errata* have been omitted.

Note: A reprint of no. 63 with the *errata* corrected. It seems probable that this edition was printed in 1665, but when the alteration of *Sumptibus Friderici Spoor* to *Sumptibus Io. Friderici Spoor* was made the necessary change of date was forgotten. When the mistake was discovered the leaf was cancelled and reprinted with the date changed to 1665, but meanwhile a few copies with the uncorrected date had been sold. A copy in my collection dated 1652 has the original owner's name on the title-page dated 1665. Both my copies with the date 1665 have cancel titles.

Copies: BLO, BM, CLN, FLWC, GUL, K(3, 1 i, 2 ii); MH, MMO.

65 RELIGIO MEDICI: LATIN ED. VON MOLTKE 8° 1677

Engraved title: The same plate as in no. 64, with the inscription altered to read: RELIGIO MEDICI | *cum Annotationibus.* | ARGENTORATI | *Sumpt IO FRIDERICI SPOOR* | *& REINH. WÆCHTLER.* | ANNO MDCLXXVII.

Collation, contents: As in no. 64.

Note: A reprint of no. 64. The Osler Library copy has MS notes transcribed from 'Hollman's' copy—probably that of the Göttingen philosopher, 1696–1787.

Copies: BLO, CLN, GUL, K, RCS, WCO; RLH, MH, MMO, NYAM.

66 RELIGIO MEDICI: LATIN 8° 1692

Title, in red and black: Thomae Brovvnes Medici Angli, ac Patroni Syncretisſmi univerſalis, imò crasſioris, (Hominem in quâvis Religione ſalvari poſſe) Libellus de Religione Medici Ab ipſô primum Anglicô idiomate conſcriptus, poſt à conterraneo Iohan. Merryvveather in latinum verſus nunc verò Annotationibus Eruditiſſimis, ac Satis Lutheranis illuſtratus à Politico Juvene, frequentibus migrationibus ac Principum Servitiis claro L. N. M. E. M. [*rule*] Francofurti & Lipsiæ, apud Fridericum Groschuffium, Bibl. M DC XCII.

Collation: Π²)(⁶ A–Z⁸ Aa–Gg⁸; 248 leaves.

Contents: Π1 frontispiece; Π2 title;)(1 a–)(3 a [sign.)(2,)(3] *Præfatio Auctoris annotat*;)(3 b *Lectori S.*;)(4 a–)(5 a [sign.)(5 for)(4] *Author Lectori S.*;)(5 b–)(6 b *Præfatio Præfixa Edit. Pariſienſ.*; A1–Gg8 as in no. 65.

Frontispiece: The same plate as in no. 64, rather more worn and with the inscription altered to read: RELIGIO MEDICI | THOMÆ BROWNES | ANNO MDC LXXXXII.

Note: The same sheets as in no. 65, with the exception of the preliminary matter, which has been reset.

Copies: GUL, K; MMO, NYAM, PUL.

RELIGIO
MEDICI.

Juxta Exemplar

Lugdunenſe.

ELEUTHEROPOLI.

MDCCXLIII.

67 RELIGIO MEDICI: LATIN 8° 1743

Title: Religio Medici. Juxta Exemplar Lugdunenſe. [*device of Phoenix in circle with ornaments*] Eleutheropoli. M D CC XLIII.

Collation: A–N⁸; 104 leaves. 16 cm.

Contents: A1 title; A2*a*–A4*b* (pp. III–VIII) *Lectori*; A5 *a*–N7*a* (pp. 1–197) text; N7*b*–N8*b* *Anacephalæoſis*.

Note: The preface is that of the Latin edition, Paris, 1644 (no. 60). There are no notes other than the author's marginalia. Pagination correct except that p. 147 is numbered 146. This edition was printed at Zurich.

Copies: BLO, BM (imperf.), GUL, K; MMO.

68 RELIGIO MEDICI: DUTCH 12° 1665

Title: Religio Medici. Dat is: Noodwendige beſchryvinge van Mr· Thomas Browne, Vermaert Medicijn-Meeſter tot Norwich, Aengaende ſijn Geſindtheyt, datſe over-een-komt met de geſuyverde Gods-dienſt van Engelandt. In de Nederlantſche Tale overgeſet, en met eenige Aenmerckingen verſien. [*ornament*] Gedruckt tot Laege-duynen. In 't Jaer 1665.

Collation: *⁸ A–P¹² Q²; 190 leaves.

Contents: *1*a* engraved title; *1*b* blank; *2*a* title; *2*b*–*7*a* *Voor-reden, Aen den Verſtandigen ende goetgunſtigen Leſer*; *7*a*–*8*b* *Den Inhoudt van yeder Afdeelinge*; A1*a*–Q2*b* (pp. 1–364) text.

Engraved title: A copy of the usual design, reversed, with inscription below *Gedruckt in t' Jaer* 1665. Plate-mark 115 × 68 mm.

Note: The translator, Dr. Abraham van Berckel (*c.* 1630–88), was a philologist and Rector of the Latin School at Delft. He also had close relations with the University of Leyden and addressed a Latin letter from there to Browne on 27 March 1665/6 (Sloane MS. 4062, ff. 162–3) telling him that he had made the translation with the help of Janus Rampius, Moderator of the University. He had intended sending two copies of the translation, but was prevented by the state of war between Holland and England (see *Works*, ed. Keynes, 1964, IV, 331–9). In the Preface van Berckel mentioned that he had first met with the *Religio Medici* in the house of a member of his family in Voorburg and was then advised by a friend to read it. Wilkin (II, xii–xiii) understood this passage to mean that van Berckel had met the author himself at Voorburg, but this was an error. Dr. Edward Browne in a letter to his father of October 1668 (Wilkin, I, 156) mistakenly attributed the translation to Johann Gründahl, translator of *Pseudodoxia Epidemica* (1668)—'the same man who translated your *Religio Medici* hath translated your *Vulgar Errors* into Low Dutch'. The footnotes, which are partly based on Keck's *Annotations*, 1656 (see no. 6), provide evidence of the help given by Rampius, that on p. 238 being signed *I.R.* In the Le Roy Crummer collection at the University of Indiana is a copy inscribed: *Jos Hill ex dono Dris Birkle ejusd interpretis*. Joseph Hill (1625–1707) was a nonconformist divine of Magdalene College, Cambridge, but his name was removed for nonconformity and he became pastor of the Scottish Church at Middelburg, Holland, 1667–73.

Copies: BLO, BM, GUL, K; IUL (presentation copy from the translator), MMO, NYAM.

RELIGIO MEDICI.

Dat is:

Noodwendige beſchryvinge

VAN

Mr. THOMAS BROWNE,

Vermaert Medicijn-Meeſter tot
NORWICH,

Aengaende ſijn Geſindtheyt,
datſe over-een-komt met de geſuyverde Gods-dienſt van ENGELANDT.

*In de Nederlantſche Tale overgeſet, en met
eenige Aenmerckingen verſien.*

Gedruckt tot Laege-duynen.
In 't Jaer 1 6 6 5.

69 RELIGIO MEDICI: DUTCH 12° 1683

Title: Religio Medici. Dat is: Nootwendige befchrijvinge van Mr. Thomas
Browne, Vermaert Medicijn-Meefter tot Norwich. Aengaende fijn Gesintheyt,
datfe over-een-komt met de gefuyverde Gods-dienft van Engeland. In de
Nederlandfche Tale overgefet, en in defe tweede Druck met vele Aanmerck-
ingen over des felfs donckere plaatfen vermeerdert, en doorgaens verbetert.
Beneffens De Aanmerkingen van de Heer Kenelm Digby, Ridder. [*ornament*]
Gedruckt tot Laegeduynen, in 't Jaer 1683.

Collation: *¹² A–Y¹²; 276 leaves.

Contents: *1 engraved title; *2 title; *3*a*–*6*a Voorreden Van den Autheur tot den Lezer*;
*6*b*–*10*b Voor-reden Aen den Verftandigen ende goetgunftigen Lefer*; *11*a*–*12*b Den*
Inhoud; A1*a*–T9*b* (pp. 1–450) text of *Religio Medici*; T10*a* sub-title to *Eenige Aenmerck-*
ingen; T10*b* blank; T11*a*–Y1*a* (pp. 453–505) text of *Eenige Aenmerckingen*; Y1*b*–Y2*a*
Een Na-fchrift; Y2*b Dum vitant stulti vitia, in contraria currunt. Hor. Sat.* 2 (verses in
Dutch); Y3*a*–Y11*b Regifter*; Y12*a Druk-fauten*; Y12*b Hedendaegfche Godsdienftigheyt*
(verses in Dutch).

Plates: Engraved title, re-engraved with inscription *Gedruckt in t' Iaer* 1683, plate-mark
113 × 66 mm., and sometimes seven engraved plates, without titles, to face pp. 20, 80,
166, 172, 202, 408, 420.

Note: A reprint of no. 68 with greatly extended footnotes derived mainly from Keck's
Annotations, 1656, and with the addition of a Dutch translation of Digby's *Observations*.
In his Preface the translator merely states that the notes have been increased without
acknowledging the source, no doubt because they are anonymous in the English
edition.

Copies: BLO, CLN, GUL, K; MMO (with engraved plates).

70 RELIGIO MEDICI: DUTCH 4° 1688

Sub-title: Religio Medici of de Godsdienft Eens Geneefmeefters. Befchreeven
door Thomas Brown, Ridder en Doƈtor in de Medicyne tót Norwich. Met
wydloopige Aantekeningen, Op alle de duyftere plaatfen. Mitsgaders De
Aanmerkingen Van den Heer Digby.

Collation: **⁴ ***⁴ ****² A*–P*⁴ Q*¹⁻²; 72 leaves.

Contents: **1 sub-title; **2*a*–**4*a Een Brief, Het Antwoord van den Ridder Digby*; **4*b*
Bericht signed A-B; ***1*a De Overzette Aan den Leezer* signed Wm *Séwel*; ***1*b*–
3*b De Aantekenaar Aan den Lezer*; ****4*a*–*1*b De Autheur Aan den Leezer*;
****1*b*–****2*b Inhoud Der Afdeelingen*; A*1*a*–Q*2*b* (pp. 1–124) text.

Note: Part of *Alle de Werken*, t'Amsterdam, 1688, 4° (see no. 202). Not known to any
editors. The *Religio Medici* is indexed at the end of the volume with the other works.
The footnotes are translated from Keck's *Annotations*, 1656. The translator was
William Séwel of Amsterdam (see no. 202, *Note*).

71 RELIGIO MEDICI: FRENCH 12° 1668

Title: La Religion du Medecin, C'eſt à dire: Deſcription neceſſaire par Thomas Brown, Medecin renommé à Norwich; touchant ſon Opinion accordante avec le pur ſervice Divin d'Angleterre. [*ornament*] Imprimée l'An 1668.

Collation: *¹² A–P¹²; 192 leaves.

Contents: *1 engraved title; *2 title; *3*a*–*9*b Avis au leĉteur*; *10*a*–*12*b Le Contenu de chaque Diviſion*; A1*a*–P12*b* (pp. 1–360) text.

Engraved title: A copy of the plate in the Dutch edition of 1665 (no. 68). Below the figure is inscribed, *Religion du Medecin*, and at the bottom, *Imprimee l'an 1668*.

Note: Translated from the Dutch edition of 1665 (no. 68). There is no indication of the printer, publisher, or place of publishing. It is stated by M. du Petit-Thouars in *Biographie Universelle* to have been translated by Nicolas Lefebvre and printed at La Haye, but there is no evidence for this. Greenhill says that 'it appears from pp. 99 and 169 to have been printed in Holland', but the occurrence of notes on these pages containing references to Holland and Leyden is merely due to the fact that they were translated from van Berckel's Dutch version without alteration. The late Professor Olivier Leroy recorded in his *Bibliography of Browne* (1931), p. 33, that he had seen in a Paris bookseller's catalogue an entry of a copy purporting to have on the title-page the words: *Traduit par Nicolas Le Febvre, La Haye, 1668*, but in the absence of any confirmation this can only be supposed to have been the bookseller's addition based on the statement in *Biographie Universelle*. Leroy considered the French version to have no literary merit, being an adaptation of the original rather than a translation—though this is not surprising seeing that it was not translated directly from the English. Le Febvre was a chemist and apothecary who came to England in 1660 to help King Charles II in his laboratory, and remained here until his death in 1674.

Copies: ALE, BM, GUL, K; RLH, MH(2), MMO, NYAM, PUL.

71*a* RELIGIO MEDICI: FRENCH 8° 1947

Thomas Browne Religio Medici Précédé d'une Lettre à l'éditeur de Daniel Halévy, d'une Préface de Louis Cazamian Traduit de l'anglais par Charles Chassé 1947 Éditions Stock Denonain et Boutelleau 6, rue Casimir Delavigne Paris 19 cm., pp. xxviii, 194, [2].

Note: No. 6 in the series *A la Promenade*, in an edition of 2,750 numbered copies. The translator gives no clue as to which text he used.

72 RELIGIO MEDICI: GERMAN 8° 1746

Title: Des berûmten Thomas Browns Religion eines Arztes, aus dem Original von neuem ûberſezt, und nebſt dem Kern aller vorigen Vorreden und Anmerkungen, wie auch nebſt einigen abermaligen Zuſätzen, einem Regiſter und einer neuen Vorrede, welche die Geſhichte des Verfaſſers und dieſes Buchs erzâlet, herausgegeben von Georg Venzky. [*rule*] Prenzlau und Leipzig, verlegts Chriſtian Ragoczy, 1746.

LA RELIGION
DU
MEDECIN,

C'eſt à dire : ·

Deſcription neceſſaire
PAR
THOMAS BROWN,

Medecin renommé à Norwich ;

touchant ſon Opinion accordante avec le pur ſervice Divin
d'Angleterre.

Imprimée l'An 1668.

Collation:)(–)()()(⁸ A–Y⁸ Z⁴; 204 leaves, of which 2 are cancelled.

Contents:)(1 title;)(2*a*–)(7*b* dedication *Denen vortreflichen Mitgliedern der Halberſtädſchen Geſelſchaft zur Beförderung der Freundſchaftlichen Liebe und der Wiſſenſchaften*, signed *Georg Venzky*; [)(8 cancelled, ? blank];)()(1*a*–)()()(7*b Vorrede des Ueberſetzers*; [)()()(8 cancelled, ? blank].

A1 sub-title; A2*a*–B3*a* (pp. 3–21) *Die Vorreden*; B3*b* blank; B4*a*–B8*a* (pp. 23–31) *Der Inhalt*; B8*b* blank; C1 sub-title; C2*a*–N6*a* (pp. 35–203) text of *Religion eines Arztes*; N6*b* blank; N7 sub-title to *Die Anmerkungen*; N8 sub-title to *Die erſten Anmerkungen von Kenelm Digby*; O1*a*–Q5*a* (pp. 209–49) text; Q5*b* blank; Q6 sub-title to *Die zweiten Anmerkungen eines ungenanten Engländers*; Q7*a*–T6*a* (pp. 253–99) text; T6*b* blank; T7 *Die dritte Art der Anmerkungen des Hern von Molk*; T8*a*–U7*b* (pp. 303–18) text; U8 sub-title to *Die vierte Art der Anmerkungen von Georg Venzky*; X1*a*–Y4*b* (pp. 321–44) text; Y5*a*–Z4*b Das Register.*

Frontiſpiece: Copy of the usual design, reversed, inscribed below, *Die Religion eines Arztes aus dem Engliſchen uberſetzt. Prenzlau Verlegts Chriſtian Ragoczy. Aō 1746. Brühl ſc. Lips.*

Note: Not seen by Wilkin or Greenhill.

Copies: GUL; MMO.

72*a* RELIGIO MEDICI & HYDRIOTAPHIA: ITALIAN   8° 1931

Tommaso Browne—Religio Medici e Hydriotaphia—Introduzione e traduzione di R. Piccoli [Firenze—MCMXXXI—IX] 20 cm., pp. xxvi, 252, [10].

72*b* RELIGIO MEDICI: ITALIAN   4° 1958

In Thomas Browne Religio Medici Edizione critica con introduzione e note a cura Vittoria Sanna Università di Cagliari Anno 1958 (see no. 58*l*)

Note: Part II of this edition contains a translation into Italian by the editor.

72*c* RELIGIO MEDICI & A LETTER TO A FRIEND: SWEDISH   8° 1948

Religio Medici samt Ett brev till en vän i anledning av hans nära väns död Översatt och försedd med en levnadsteckning över författaren av Ernst Abramson Lund C. W. K. Gleerups Förlag [1948] 20·5 cm., pp. 225, [3].

Frontiſpiece: Portrait of Browne from the painting in the National Portrait Gallery.

Note: Issued in stiff printed wrappers, untrimmed. With notes and a list of names at the end. The text of *A Letter to a Friend* is divided into 48 sections numbered in the margins.

72*d* RELIGIO MEDICI: JAPANESE   8° 1963

In The World's Essays on Life, vol. v, pp. 167–304: Religio Medici, translated by Daiji Hori [not seen].

II

Pseudodoxia Epidemica

BIBLIOGRAPHICAL PREFACE

SIR THOMAS BROWNE's most considerable work, entitled *Pseudodoxia Epidemica*, and commonly referred to as 'Browne's Vulgar Errors', was first published in 1646, when its author was in his forty-second year. The size and varied character of this compilation are enough in themselves to show that it had been the work of many years. Browne had settled in Norwich in 1637 and it seems unlikely that even nine years would have been enough for the large amount of thought, reading, observation and experiment, which the work must have entailed. He observed in his preface that it was 'composed by snatches of time, as medical vacations, and the fruitless importunity of uroscopy would permit us'. Such a work, moreover, was 'not to be performed upon one legg; and should smell of oyle, if duly and deservedly handled'. It is probable, therefore, that he had indulged the habit of making copious notes and extracts in commonplace books from a comparatively early age, so that the foundations of the *Vulgar Errors* may have been laid while its author was on his travels and during the time when he was practising in Oxfordshire. Some of his commonplace books have survived (though not most of those on which the *Vulgar Errors* was based) and bear witness to his industry and methodical habits. It was suggested by Wilkin (II, 161) that the idea of the book was first put into Browne's mind by Bacon's dictum that to a 'calendar of doubts or problems, I advise be annexed another calendar, as much or more material, which is a calendar of popular errors: I mean chiefly in natural history such as pass in speech and conceit, and are nevertheless detected and convicted of untruth'.[1] However this may be, Browne was doubtless following the bent of his own mind. Except in matters of religious faith, he was unwilling to accept anything without carefully examining it in the light of such facts as he could gather. He has thus expressed himself regarding his own attitude: 'In philosophy, where truth seems double-faced, there is no man more paradoxical than myself, but in divinity, I love to keep the road.'[2] The original manuscript of the *Pseudodoxia* is not known to exist, but notes on some of the matters treated of are to be found in the common-place books. A long passage[3] from one of these was added by Wilkin to book v, chapter 22, in his edition of the *Works*.

In 1646 Sir Thomas Browne was already famous, five editions of his *Religio Medici* having been sold to the public in the years 1642–5. The publisher of *Pseudodoxia Epidemica*, therefore, must have felt confident in printing a large edition of the volume, and even at the present time the first edition is not at all a scarce book. The second edition of 1650, however, besides being better printed and produced, is considerably less common than its predecessor. The first edition was published by Edward Dod, the second by Dod and Nath. Ekins in partnership. Later this partnership was dissolved and thereafter the two

---

[1] Bacon, *Advancement of Learning*, ed. Montagu (London, 1840), p. 158.
[2] *Religio Medici*, part I, sect. vi.   [3] BM Sloane MS. 1827.

publishers issued rival editions of the book. Thus the third edition came from Ekins in folio in 1658, but Dod at once brought out an edition in quarto to which *Hydriotaphia* and *The Garden of Cyrus* were added. Ekins was goaded by this to add to the sheets of the unsold part of his edition reprints of *Hydriotaphia*, *The Garden of Cyrus*, and *Religio Medici*, a general title-page dated 1659 being prefixed. The fifth edition was issued by Dod in quarto, containing an execrable portrait, in 1669. To this Ekins replied by the publication of the sixth edition, with a much better portrait engraved by Van Hove, in 1672. Of the two rival publishers Browne seems to have preferred the upstart, Ekins, for, although Dod's imprint had been the first to appear in his book, he so far favoured Ekins in 1672 as to provide him with final corrections and additions, a notice being inserted to the effect that readers were to be disabused thereby of expectation of any future enlargements, the work now being 'compleat and perfect'. This edition was evidently intended to be what is now termed by publishers a 'definitive edition'. It was well printed and produced and was accorded the dignity, at that time unusual, of having some copies printed on great paper, and in this form it is undeniably a very handsome volume—though marred by containing a large number of typographical errors. This was the last edition produced during the author's lifetime, and the *Pseudodoxia* has only appeared in English since that date in the collected editions of the *Works* published in 1686, 1836, 1852, 1904, 1928–31 and 1964.

The *Vulgar Errors* was first noticed by a foreign scholar in Denmark. In the Royal Library at Copenhagen is a Danish translation by Gabriel Acheleey Knudsen dated 1652,[1] though it was never printed. The work was also translated into Dutch by Johann Gründahl and was published at Amsterdam in 1668, the same version being reprinted in *Alle de Werken* of 1688. A German version by Christian Knorr was published at Frankfort in 1680. During the eighteenth century the *Pseudodoxia*, though neglected in England, still found favour on the continent. It was translated into French by the Abbé Souchay, and was published at both Paris and Amsterdam in 1733, though the Paris edition sold but slowly and was re-issued several times with new title-pages. The book was further translated from the French into Italian and was published at Venice in 1737. These translations are now all scarce books and difficult to obtain.

In the nineteenth century a French lexicographer borrowed extensively from Browne with due acknowledgements. The *Dictionnaire des Sciences occultes* (Paris, 1848, 2 vols.), 4°, by J. Collin de Plancy, contains 24 articles 'more or less copied out of *Pseudodoxia*: cf. the entries, *aimant, alcyon, amphisbène, animaux, arc-en-ciel, autruche, castor, cerf, chandelle, Cléopâtre, coiffe, crapaudine, dauphin, éléphant, Epicure, fumée, grossesse, hiéroglyphes, lamproies, langue primitive, lièvre, lithomancie, Milon, peau*'.[2]

A short list of Browne's fore-runners and successors in the task of refuting vulgar errors was printed by Wilkin at the end of his Preface. This list was given

[1] Press-mark Gl. Kgl. Saml. No. 218–9, fol. Noted by Dr. H. Gordon Ward.
[2] O. Leroy, *A French Bibliography of Browne* (London, 1931), pp. 43–4.

with more detail and considerable additions in an appendix to the former edition of this *Bibliography*; it has been further extended in the present edition. In the section of Biography and Criticism will also be found notices of such praise or blame of the *Pseudodoxia* as was printed soon after its first appearance. The most notable of these are to be found in *Arcana Microcosmi* (1651) of Alexander Ross, and *Endoxa* (1656), of John Robinson, whose 'still gale' seems to have passed almost unnoticed at the time. Wilkin incorporated in his notes those written by Dr. Christopher Wren, father of Sir Christopher, in his copy of the first edition of *Pseudodoxia*. He noted also a manuscript volume of *Observations on Ps.Ep.*[1] from the pen of Sir Hamon L'Estrange of Hunstanton in Norfolk. This was sent to Browne with a letter printed by Wilkin (1, 369).

[1] BM Sloane MS. 1839.

Pseudodoxia Epidemica:

OR,

ENQUIRIES

INTO

Very many received

TENENTS,

And commonly presumed

TRUTHS.

By Thomas Brovvne Dr. of Physick.

Iul. Scalig.

Ex Libris colligere qua prodiderunt Authores longe est periculosissimum; Rerum ipsarum cognitio vera è rebus ipsis est.

LONDON,
Printed by *T. H.* for *Edward Dod*, and are to be sold in *Ivie Lane.* 1646.

73 PSEUDODOXIA [Wing B 5159] fº 1646

Title within double lines: Pſeudodoxia Epidemica: or, Enquiries into Very many received Tenents, And commonly preſumed Truths. [*rule*] By Thomas Brovvne Dr. of Physick. [*rule*] IUL. SCALIG. *Ex Libris colligere quæ prodiderunt Authores longe eſt periculoſiſsimum; Rerum ipſarum cognitio vera è rebus ipſis eſt.* [*rule*]

    (*a*) London, Printed by Tho. Harper for Edvvard Dod. 1646.

    (*b*) London, Printed by T. H. for Edward Dod, and are to be ſold in Ivie Lane. 1646.

Collation: a⁶ b⁴ A–Z⁴ Aa–Zz⁴ Aaa⁴ Bbb⁶; 204 leaves.

Contents: a1 *a* blank; a1 *b* *Imprimatur*, signed *Iohn Downame, March the* 14ᵗʰ· 1645; a2 title; a3 *a*–a6 *b* *To the Reader*; b1 *a*–b4 *b* *A table of the contents*; A1 *a*–Bbb5 *b* (pp. 1–386) text (*errata*, 13 lines, at bottom of Bbb5 *b*); Bbb6 blank.

Note: Page numbers 251 and 317 are misprinted 151 and 217; the pagination is otherwise correct. Of the alternative imprints it seems that the shorter and less usual one[1] is likely to be the earlier. The rest of the title-page was printed from the same setting of type in each, so that the change was probably made while the book was in the press. There is no other alteration. The paper in otherwise identical copies of the ordinary issue varies both in weight and watermark.

    Some years ago Mr. John Carter noticed in a bookseller's catalogue a copy said to carry the date 1649. The collation provided by the American dealer who bought it was close enough to that given above to show that this was a freak copy of the book usually dated 1646. Mr. Carter did not see the book and no other copy has since come to light, so that the evidence is insufficient to justify its being listed as another issue.

    A copy of this edition offered by Messrs. Maggs in 1934 (cat. 594) had the signature nine times repeated, the first dated 1646, of George Daniel of Beswick (1615–57), with a poem of 22 lines on the licence leaf, beginning:

> If to delight, & profit, be of praise;
> Admire this Author; who hath many waies
> Oblig'd the world, in either; would you see
> Error unvail'd, by a strict scrutinie?

Copies: (*a*) WCO, (*b*) BLO,[2] BM, CLN, GUL, K, PLC, RCS, ULC, ULL; MH, MMO, NYAM, PUL, YUL.

74 PSEUDODOXIA [Wing B 5160] fº 1650

Title, within double lines: Pſeudodoxia Epidemica: or, Enquiries into Very many Received Tenents, And commonly Preſumed Truths. [*rule*] By Thomas Browne Dr of Phyſick. [*rule*] The Second Edition, Corrected and much Enlarged by the Author. Together With ſome Marginall Obſervations, and a Table Alphabeticall at the end. [*rule*] JUL. SCALIG. *Ex Libris colligere quæ prodiderunt Authores longè eſt periculoſiſsimum; Rerum ipſarum cognitio vera, è rebus*

---

[1] First reported in 1944 by the late Dr. C. H. Wilkinson, Worcester College, Oxford. A similar copy belongs to Miss Patience Burn, Newnham College, Cambridge.

[2] With marginal annotations by Dr. Christopher Wren, Dean of Windsor.

ipſis eſt. [*rule*] London, Printed by A. Miller, for Edw. Dod and Nath. Ekins, at the Gunne in Ivie Lane. 1650.

Collation: A–Z⁴ Aa–Xx⁴ Yy²; 178 leaves.

Contents: A1 title; A2*a*–B1*a To the reader*; B1*b An Advertiſement concerning the Marginall Annotations,* signed N. N., *Cal. Nov.* 1649; B2*a*–B4*a A table of the Contents*; B4*b* Downame's *Imprimatur*; C1*a*–Xx1*a* (pp. 1–329) text; Xx1*b*–Yy2*a An Alphabeticall Table* (errata, 10 lines, at bottom of Yy2*a*); Yy2*b* blank.

Note: Page numbers 271, 266 have been transposed; the pagination is otherwise correct. Wilkin considered that this edition was 'the handsomest as to typography' that had appeared (up to 1835), and his opinion can be repeated with truth today. The publisher's claim that it was 'corrected and much enlarged by the author' was fully justified. New chapters and paragraphs were freely inserted and some excisions were made. Many technical terms and quotations in the original languages were dropped, rhetorical questions were altered to positive statements, and small improvements were made throughout. Of the marginal annotations some were by the author, but others, printed in smaller type, were by an admirer of the work, who was also responsible for the *Alphabetical Table.* This is made plain in the *Advertisement* signed N. N. on B1*b*. Wilkin (II, 166) suggested that this admirer may have been the Rev. Mr. Whitefoot of Norwich, who was a close friend of the author and used the same initials in a manuscript discourse preserved in the British Museum (Add. MS. 6269). A copy of this edition sold at Hodgson's 11 June 1926, lot 380, had an inscription on the fly-leaf: *Frances Le Gros: this booke given mee by the worthy authour my honor'd freinde when I was one of his family and most happy in beeinge so 1650.* Browne later (1658) dedicated his *Hydriotaphia* to his friend, Thomas Le Gros of Crostwick. The volume also carried the bookplate of Sir William Trumbull (1639–1716), who travelled in 1663–4 with Browne's son, Edward (Wilkin, I, lxxvii).

Copies: BLO, GUL, K, PLC, ULC, ULL; MH, MMO, NYAM, PUL, YUL.

75 PSEUDODOXIA [Wing B 5161]   f° 1658

Title, within double lines: Pſeudodoxia Epidemica: or, Enquiries into Very many Received Tenents, And commonly preſumed Truths. [*rule*] By Thomas Brown D*r* of Phyſick. [*rule*] The Third Edition, Corrected and Enlarged by the Author. Together With ſome Marginall Obſervations, and a Table Alphabeticall at the end. [*the usual quotation between rules*] London, Printed by R. W. for Nath. Ekins, at the Gun in Pauls Church-Yard, 1658.

Collation: A⁶ C–Z⁴ Aa–Xx⁴; 174 leaves.

Contents: A1 title; A2*a*–A4*a To the reader*; A4*b*–A6*b A Table of the Contents*; C1*a*–Uu3*b* (pp. 1–326) text; Uu4*a*–Xx4*b An Alphabetical Table.*

Note: This edition is not commonly found in its original form. More usually the sheets have been furnished with a general title-page dated 1659 and with other works added (see no. 77). The text contains further alterations and additions by the author as noted by Wilkin. The pagination is correct. The printer was probably Robert White (1639–67).

Copies: GUL, K, PLC, ULC; MH, MMO, PUL.

76 PSEUDODOXIA, &c. [Wing B 5762]   4° 1658

Title: Pſeudodoxia Epidemica: or, Enquiries into Very many Received Tenents,
And commonly Preſumed Truths. [*rule*] By Thomas Brown Dr. of Phyſick.
[*rule*] The Fourth Edition. With Marginal Obſervations, and a Table Alphabetical. [*rule*] Whereunto are now added two Diſcourſes The one of Urn-
burial, or Sepulchrall Urns, lately found in Norfolk. The other of the Garden
of Cyrus, or Network Plantations of the Antients. [*rule*] Both Newly written
by the ſame Author. [*rule*] *Ex Libris colligere quæ prodiderunt Authores longe eſt
periculoſiſſimum Rerum ipſarum cognitio vera è rebus ipſis eſt.* Jul. Scalig. [*rule*]
London, Printed for Edward Dod, and are to be ſould by Andrew Crook at
the Green Dragon in Pauls Church-yard. 1658.

Collation: a⁴ b⁴ B–X⁴ Aa–Xx⁴ Yy² Zz² Aaa² Bbb–Nnn⁴ Ooo² Ppp⁴ Qqq⁴; 5¶⁴ 5*²
5A–5I⁴ 5K²; 280 leaves.

Contents: a1 title; a2*a*–a4*b To the reader*; b1*a*–b3*b A Table of the Contents*; b4 *Marginall
Illuſtrations omitted, or to be added to the Diſcourses of Urn-Burial, and of the Garden of Cyrus*,
followed by *Errata in the Enquiries*; B1*a*–Ooo2*b* (pp. 1–468) text of *Pſeudodoxia*;
Ppp1*a*–Qqq4*a An Alphabetical Table*; Qqq4*b* blank; 5¶1*a* longitudinal label
Dr Brown's Enquiries & Garden of Cyrus; 5¶1*b* blank; 5¶2–5K2 *Hydriotaphia* and
Garden of Cyrus (see no. 94).

Illustrations: Three engraved plates in *Hydriotaphia* and *Garden of Cyrus* (see no. 94).

Note: Signatures Y, Z do not appear. The pagination is erratic; pp. 119–34 and 357–68
are omitted altogether in the numbering, numbers 166 and 167 have been transposed,
and numbers 196, 302 are misprinted 199, 202. The correct number of pages is,
therefore, 440 instead of 468. The sub-titles of the tracts appended, as is noted under
no. 94, bear the imprint of a different publisher from the one whose name is on the
general title. The leaf 5¶1, with the longitudinal label, was probably intended to be
torn out by the bookseller and used as an advertisement in his shop; it is in consequence
often missing. The text of this edition does not differ materially from that of the last.
A few alterations have been made, but they are such as are likely to have been made by
the printer.
    In the Fellows' Library, Winchester College, is a transcript of selections from this
edition written in a small early hand on 48 leaves.

Copies: BLO, BM, CLN(2), CPL, GUL, K, NCL, ULC, ULL; MH(3), MMO, NMLB,[1]
NYAM, PUL.

77 PSEUDODOXIA, &c. [Wing B 5163]   f° 1659

Title within double lines: Pſeudodoxia Epidemica:... Whereunto is Added Religio
Medici: and A Diſcourſe of the Sepulchral Urnes lately found in Norfolk.
Together with The Garden of Cyrus. Or the Quincuncial Lozenge, or Net
work Plantations of the Ancients, Artificially, Naturally, Myſtically Conſidered.
With Sundry Obſervations. [*rule*] By Thomas Brown Doctour of Phyſick [*rule*]
The Laſt Edition, Corrected and Enlarged by the Authour. Together VVith

---

[1] With the signature of William Wordsworth.

some Marginal Obfervations, and a Table Alphabetical at the End. [*the usual quotation between rules*] London, Printed for Nath. Ekins, at the Gun in Pauls Church-yard. 1659.

Collation: Π¹ A⁶ C–Z⁴ Aa–Xx⁴ A–H⁴; 207 leaves.

Contents: Π1 general title, inserted; A1–Xx4 *Pseudodoxia Epidemica* (see no. 75); A1–H4 *Religio Medici*, *Hydriotaphia*, and *Garden of Cyrus* (see no. 7).

Note: Of this issue Wilkin says: 'No sooner had Dod brought out this edition [4°, 1658] so enriched, than Ekins, his former partner, printed, in double column, not only the Tracts appended by Dod, but also *Religio Medici*:—and thus, in 1659, produced, as altogether new, his unsold copies of the 3rd edition, with these enrichments.' The press-work of the added leaves is very inferior to that of the rest of the book.

Copies: BLO, BM, CLN, GUL, K; MMO, PUL.

78 PSEUDODOXIA, &c. [Wing B 5164] 4° 1669

Title: Pseudodoxia Epidemica:...The Fifth Edition...Whereunto are now added Two Difcourfes...[&c. as in no. 76] London, Printed for the Affigns of Edward Dod, 1669.

Collation: A⁴b⁴B–Z⁴ Aa–Zz⁴ Aaa–Ggg⁴ Hhh² Iii⁴ Kkk⁴, A–E⁴ [χ]² F–K⁴; 268 leaves.

Contents: A1 blank; A2 title; A3 *a*–A4 *b* *To the Reader*; b1 *a*–b3 *b* *A Table of the Contents*; b4 *Marginal Illuftrations omitted, or to be added to the Difcourfes of Urn-Burial, and of the Garden of Cyrus*; B1 *a*–Hhh1 *b* (pp. 1–414 [418]) text; Hhh2 blank; Iii1 *a*–Kkk4 *b* *An Alphabetical Table*; A1–K4 *Hydriotaphia* and *The Garden of Cyrus* (see no. 96).

Illustrations: (i) Frontispiece. Engraved portrait of Sir Thomas Browne, half-length, standing in front of a wall of rock beyond which on the right a landscape is seen. In the centre below is the coat of arms of Browne, and on either side the words: *Effigies viri doctiſsimi Tho: Browne | Med: Doctoris.* Unsigned. The plate-mark measures 21·7 × 15 cm. (ii)–(iv) Three engraved plates in *Hydriotaphia* and *Garden of Cyrus* (see no. 96).

Note: The pagination is erratic; numbers 193–202 are omitted while numbers 309–22 occur twice over. The correct number of pages is therefore 418 instead of 414. The other misprints are too numerous to be worth recording. The frontispiece is an engraving of very poor quality. The portrait from which it was done is not known, nor by whom it was engraved; it was suggested to Wilkin (II, 167) that it may have been executed by John Dunstall (1644–75), but this is very improbable. The authors of *Engraving in England in the Sixteenth and Seventeenth Centuries*[1] attribute it on stylistic grounds to Thomas Cross (fl. 1644–82). The resemblance to Browne is slight and Miss M. L. Tildesley pointed out that the plate had almost certainly done duty already as a portrait of someone else, the head only being re-engraved (*Sir T. Browne: His Skull, Portrait, and Ancestry*, 1923, p. 7). The plate-mark is almost the same size as the page, so that it has very often been cut into below by the binder; sometimes this has been avoided by folding up the lower part of the engraving. This edition is recorded in Arber's *Term Catalogues*, I, 11, as 'Price, bound, 6s.'. The text is similar to that of the last edition.

Copies: CLN, EUL, GUL, K, PLC, RCP, RCS, ULC; MH, MMO, NYAM, PUL.

[1] M. Corbett and M. Norton (Cambridge, 1964), p. 280.

Frontispiece to PSEUDODOXIA EPIDEMICA 1669

the 'palimpsest' plate

79 PSEUDODOXIA, &c. [Wing B 5165]   4° 1672

Title: Pſeudodoxia Epidemica: or, Enquiries Into very many Received Tenents And commonly preſumed Truths, Together with the Religio Medici. [*rule*] By Thomas Brown Knight, M.D. [*rule*] The Sixth and Laſt Edition, Correóted and Enlarged by the Author, with many Explanations, Additions and Alterations throughout. Together With many more Marginal Obſervations, and a Table Alphabetical at the end. [*the usual quotation between rules*] London, Printed by J. R. for Nath. Ekins, 1672.

Collation: Π² *⁴ **⁴ ***² B–Z⁴ Aa–Zz⁴ Aaa–Lll⁴ Mmm², A–T⁴; 314 leaves.

Contents: Π1 frontispiece; Π2 general title as above; *1 sub-title to *Pseudodoxia* as above, with the omission of the words *Together...Medici*; *2*a*–**2*b* To the Reader; **3*a* The Poſtſcript; **3*b* blank; **4*a*–***2*b* A Table of the Contents; B1*a*–Kkk4*b* (pp. 1–440) text of *Pseudodoxia*; Lll1*a*–Mmm2*a* An Alphabetical Table; Mmm2*b* blank; A1–T4 *Religio Medici* (see no. 10).

Frontispiece: On Π1*b* is an engraved portrait of Sir T. B. in an oval, signed below: *F. H. Van Hove ſculp.* Underneath is the coat of arms of Browne and the words: *Effigies viri Doctiſsimi Tho: Browne | Equ: Aur: et Med: Doótoris.* The plate-mark measures 19 × 13·3 cm. Probably copied from the Buccleuch miniature.[1]

Note: This edition is on better paper than the earlier quartos, but the text is full of mistakes. The compositor was not only careless, but also impertinent. On p. 243 (Book iv, chapter 11) where the author, referring to strange stories, mentioned one 'so strange, that we might herein accuse the printer, did not the account of Ælian accord unto it', the compositor has altered 'accuse the printer' to 'excuse the PRINTER'. The marginal notes are frequently misplaced. Nevertheless, the pagination is correct. This was the last edition published during the lifetime of the author, who has added in a Postscript on **3*a*:

Readers,

    To enform you of the Advantages of the preſent Impreſſion, and diſabuſe your expeótations of any future Enlargements; theſe are to advertiſe thee, that this Edition comes forth with very many Explanations, Additions, and Alterations throughout, beſides that of one entire Chapter: But that now this Work is compleat and perfeót, expeót no further Additions.

The additional chapter here referred to is Book v, chapter 21: 'Of the picture of Haman hanged'; it is printed here for the first time. Wilkin states (ii, 167) that 'of this edition there were *large papers*'. One such copy in the collection of Sir William Osler measures 25·5 × 19 cm., and another in my collection measures 26·5 × 20 cm. The ordinary issue measures 22 × 16 cm. This edition is recorded in Arber's *Term Catalogues*, i, 143, as 'Price, bound, 10*s*.'. This text was used for the translation into French (see no. 87).

The sub-title to *Pseudodoxia* (*1) has very frequently been removed by the binder, who may have thought that it duplicated the general title.

Copies: BLO, BM, CLN(2), FLWC, GUL, K(3),[2] PLC, TCD, ULC, ULL; RLH, MH(3) MMO(l.p.), NYAM(2),[3] PUL.

[1] M. L. Tildesley, *Sir Thomas Browne: His Skull, Portraits, and Ancestry*, 1923, p. 32.

[2] One on small paper complete with the sub-title, one on large paper complete, one on small paper lacking the sub-title with the signature of John Ray on the general title and with additions to the index in his hand.   [3] One on large paper lacking the general title-page.

80 PSEUDODOXIA F° 1686

Sub-title, within double lines: Pſeudodoxia Epidemica: or, Enquiries Into very many Received Tenents And commonly preſumed Truths. [*rule*] By Sir Thomas Brown Knight M.D. [*rule*] The Seventh and Laſt Edition,...[etc. as in no. 79] London, Printed for Richard Chiſwell, and Thomas Sawbridge. M DC LXXXVI.

Collation: A⁴ a⁴ B–Z⁴ Aa–Tt⁴; 172 leaves.

Contents: A1 sub-title; A2 *a*–a1 *a To the Reader*; a1 *b The Poſtſcript*; a2 *a*–a4 *b A Table of the Contents*; B1 *a*–Sf2 *b* (pp. 1–316) text; Sf3 *a*–Tt4 *a An Alphabetical Table*; Tt4 *b* blank.

Note: In *The Works of Sir Thomas Brown* (f°, 1686) (see no. 201). No editor is named and it may be presumed that no serious editing was done. The *Postscript* announcing that no further changes were to be expected was reprinted as in 1672 (no. 79), and the text is substantially a reprint of that edition, even the compositor's impertinent emendation in Book IV, chapter 11, being faithfully reproduced (p. 171). Wilkin stated that the collected *Works* were edited by Archbishop Tenison, but gave no authority for saying so. Tenison had edited the *Miscellany Tracts*, 1683, and may be supposed to have supervised the printing of the *Works*. The pagination in sections R–T is faulty, pp. 123–41 being misprinted 121, 122, 123, 124, 127, 128, 129, 128, 131, 130, 131, 134, 133, 136, 137, 138, 139, 138, 139.

81 PSEUDODOXIA ED. WILKIN 8° 1836

In Sir Thomas Browne's Works...Ed. Simon Wilkin...London William Pickering...1836 (see no. 203).

Note: Vol. II, p. 159–vol. III, p. 374, with a preface by the editor, additions from MSS, and numerous additional footnotes; some of the latter are copied from annotations written in the hand of Dr. Christopher Wren, Dean of Windsor, in a copy of the first edition now in the Bodleian Library. The rest of the footnotes are by Edward Brayley, the editor, and others. The additions made to the text by the author in the second, third, and sixth editions are also here noted. The text here printed is that of the *Works* (1686). Some corrections have been made and there is free alteration of chapter headings.

82 PSEUDODOXIA ED. WILKIN 8° 1852

In The Works of Sir Thomas Browne...Ed. Simon Wilkin...London: H. G. Bohn...MDCCCLII. (see no. 205).

Note: Vol. I, p. 1–vol. II, p. 289. A reprint of no. 81.

83 PSEUDODOXIA ED. SAYLE 8° 1904–1907

In The Works of Sir Thomas Browne Ed. Charles Sayle...London Grant Richards [Edinburgh John Grant] 1904 [1907].

Note: Vol. I, p. 113–vol. III, p. 85. The text is a literal reprint of that of the sixth edition, 1672.

83*a* PSEUDODOXIA ED. KEYNES 8° 1928

In The Works of Sir Thomas Browne Edited by Geoffrey Keynes London
Faber & Gwyer Limited...1928 (see no. 207*a*)

Note: Vol. II, Books I–III, pp. xii, 317, [1]. Vol. III, Books IV–VII, pp. [viii], 368. The
text is based on that of 1672 with careful revision (see no. 79). At the end of vol. II
there are additions from the first and other editions, textual notes, and an index to the
whole work. It is illustrated by two drawings of Sir Thomas Browne's skull.

83*b* PSEUDODOXIA ED. KEYNES 8° 1964

In The Works of Sir Thomas Browne...Edited by Geoffrey Keynes London
Faber & Faber Limited [1964] (see no. 207*c*)

Note: Vol. II, pp. x, 574, [2]. The text is revised from the edition of 1928, omitting the
textual notes. The illustrations are the same as before.

84 PSEUDODOXIA: DUTCH 8° 1668

Title: Pſeudo-doxia Epidemica, Dat is: Beſchryvinge van verſcheyde Algemene
Dwalingen des Volks: Ofte Onderzoekingen van vele gevoelens, welke onder
de gemene Man in zwang gaan, en doorgaans voor enkele waarheden worden
aangenomen. Voor dezen etlijke maalen in't Engels gedrukt, naagezien en
vermeerdert, door den Autheur Thomas Brown: En nu getrouwelijk Vertaalt,
door Johannes Grindal. [*device of tortoise*]. t'Amsterdam, [*rule*] By Gerrit van
Goedesbergh, Boeckverkoper op't Water, recht tegen over de Nieuwe Brugh,
1668

Collation: *⁸ A–B⁸ A–Z⁸ Aa–Yy⁸; 384 leaves.

Contents: *1 title; *2*a*–7*a Aan den Leʒer*; *7*b*–8*b d'Overʒetter Aan den Leʒer*, signed
I.G; A1*a*–B1*b Blatwijʒer der voornaamſte ʒaken*; B2*a*–B6*b Tafel, Der voornaamſte
Hooftſtukken*; B7–8 blank; A1*a*–Yy8*a* (pp. 1–719) text; Yy8*b* blank.

Note: This, the earliest printed translation of the *Vulgar Errors*, is an uncommon book
and was not seen by Wilkin. The translator, Johann Grindal, or Gründahl, does not
find a place in the usual biographical dictionaries. There are various irregularities in
the printing. Pages 49, 71, 237, are misnumbered 46, 33, 236; signatures I5, O4, V3,
Ll6 are misprinted I3, N4, V4, Ll2. The sixth leaf in each section is not signed except
in signature B (p. 27). The signatures are omitted on K5, N5, Q5, Hh3, Hh5.
Signature O3 is omitted in my copy, but not in two others examined by the late
Dr. W. W. Francis.

Copies: BLO, FLWC, K; MMO, NYAM.

85 PSEUDODOXIA: DUTCH 4° 1688

Heading: Pseudo-doxia Epidemica, of een Onderſoek der Gemeene Dwalingen
des Volks. [*No sub-title.*]

Collation: *3² **² A–Z⁴ Aa–Zz⁴ Aaa–Hhh⁴; 220 leaves.

Pseudo-doxia Epidemica,

Dat is:

BESCHRYVINGE

van verscheyde Algemene

DWALINGEN

des Volks : *Ofte*

Onderzoekingen van vele gevoelens, welke
onder de gemene Man in zwang gaan, en doorgaans voor enkele waarheden wor-
den aangenomen.

Voor dezen etlijke maalen in 't Engels gedrukt,
naagezien en vermeerdert, door den Autheur

THOMAS BROWN:

En nu getrouwelijk Vertaalt, door

JOHANNES GRINDAL.

t'A M S T E R D A M,

By *Gerrit van Goedesbergh*, Boeckverkoper op 't Water, recht tegen over de Nieuwe Brugh, 1668

Contents: *3 1*a*–**2*b Aan den Lezer*; A1*a*–Eee4*b* (pp. 1–408) text; Fff1*a*–Hhh4*b Blad-wyzer.*

Note: In *Alle de Werken*, t'Amsterdam, 1688, for which see no. 202.

86 PSEUDODOXIA: GERMAN 4° 1680

Title: Des vortrefflichen Engellånders Thomæ Brown, der Artzney Dͬ Pſeudo-doxia Epidemica, Das iſt: Unterſuchung derer Irrthůmer | ſo bey dem gemeinen Mann | und ſonſt hin und wieder im Schwange gehen. In Sieben Bůchern alſo und dergeſtalt abgefaſſet | daſs darinn anfangs von den Irrthů-mern ins Gemein | mit Beyfůgung unterſchiedlicher Curiöſer Tractåtlein | als eines Handbuchs der wieder zu recht gebrachten Naturkunſt | darinn der Grund der gantzen Chymiſchen Wiſſenſchaft enthalten; Item eines Werkes wider die gemeinen Irrthůmer von der Bewegung natůrlicher Dinge; Ingleichen Herrn D. Henrici Mori von unkórperlichen Dingen in der Welt | wider Carteſium; Und dann ferner in denen ůbrigen Sechs Bůchern von den Irrthůmern | die Mineralien | Gewåchſe | Thiere | Menſchen | Bilder und Gemåhlde Welt- und Geſchicht-Beſchreibungen betreffend | gehandelt wird. Alles mit ſonderbarem Fleiſs | aus dem Engliſchen und Lateiniſchen | mit Beyfůgung der Lateiniſchen Kunſtwórter | in die reine Hochteutſche Sprach ůberſetzet | mit ungemeinen Anmerkungen erlåutert | und unterſchiedlichen Kupferfiguren verſehen durch Chriſtian Peganium, in Teutſch Rautner genannt. Mit Churfůrſtl. Såchs. Privilegio. [*rule*] Franckfurt und Leipzig | in Chriſtoff Riegels Verlag. Anno M DC LXXX.

Collation:):(⁴ A–Z⁴ Aa–Zz⁴ Aaa–Zzz⁴ Aaaa–Zzzz⁴ Aaaaa–Zzzzz⁴ Aaaaaa–Kkkkkk⁴; 504 leaves.

Contents:):(1 title;):(2*a*–4*b An den Leſer,* signed *Thomas Brown*; Ai*a*–Jiii*a* (pp. 1–69) *Das Erſte Buch. Von den Irrthůmern ins gemein*; Jiii*b*–Bbiv*b* (pp. 70–200) *Der besondern Abhandlung Erſter Theil*; Cci*a*–Kkkii*b* (pp. 201–444) *Ein ander vortrefflicher Tractat wider die gemeinen Irrthůmer*; Kkkiii*a*–Hhhhhhi*b* (pp. 445–978) *Der abſonderlichen Abhandlung von gemeinen Irrthůmern Andertes[-Siebende] Buch*; Hhhhhhii*a*–Kkkkkkiii*b Regiſter der vornehmſten und merkwůrdigſten Sachen*; *Bericht an den Buchbinder* at bottom of Kkkkkkiii*b*; Kkkkkkiv blank.

Illustrations: Sixteen full-page engraved plates giving 71 illustrative diagrams. The plates are printed on the inner sides of eight gatherings of two leaves each. The *Bericht an den Buchbinder* directs that these leaves are to be bound immediately after the *Titul-Bogen* or at the end of the book.

Note: The existence of this translation was known to Wilkin, though he had never seen a copy. He stated (II, xiii) correctly that the translator was Christian Knorr, Baron of Rosenroth (calling himself Christian Peganius), probably having derived the informa-tion from the *Catalogus Bibliothecæ Theologicæ* of Reimmann (1731) (see no. 319). Knorr was a German theologian and orientalist, who did not restrict himself to translating Browne's *Vulgar Errors*. He interpolated two long tracts of his own between Books I and II, in which he discussed problems in natural philosophy with reference to other writers such as Hobbes and Descartes. He also inserted *Anmerckungen* of his own

ESSAI
SUR LES
ERREURS
POPULAIRES,
OU
EXAMEN DE PLUSIEURS
opinions reçues comme vrayes, qui font
fauffes ou douteufes.

Traduit de l'Anglois de Thomas Brown,
Chevalier & Docteur en Médecine.

Ex libris colligere quæ prodiderunt auctores longe eft
periculofiffimum : rer m ipfarum cognitio vera
è rebus ipfis eft. Jul Scalig.

TOME PREMIER.

A PARIS,

Chez
{
PIERRE WITTE, rue S Jacques, proche de
S. Yves, à l'Ange Gardien

DIDOT, Quay des Auguftins, près du
pont S. Michel, à la Bible d'or.
}

M. D. CC. XXXIII.

Avec Approbation & Privilege du Roi.

among Browne's chapters, so that the book became immensely longer than the original. His energies seem, however, to have become exhausted before he reached the end. Book VII lacks the conclusion of chapter XV and the four last chapters. The sentence of chapter XV where he stopped was concerning the continuous growth of the crocodile and finished with the words: *ſondern werde immer groſſer und groſſer ohn ENDE*, thus providing a suitable finale.

Book I appears to have twelve chapters instead of eleven because VII has been omitted in the numbering.

The engraved plates do not illustrate the *Vulgar Errors*. The numbers of the 71 figures will be found scattered through Knorr's interpolated tracts, thus indicating where the explanations are to be found. There are no page references on the plates.

Copies: BLO, BM, K; MMO, NYAM, YML.

87 PSEUDODOXIA: FRENCH 8° 1733

Title: Eſſai ſur les Erreurs Populaires, ou examen de pluſieurs opinions reçues comme vrayes, qui ſont fauſſes ou douteuſes. Traduit de l'anglois de Thomas Brown, Chevalier & Docteur en Médicine. [*the usual Latin quotation*] Tome premier [Suite de tome premier, second] [*ornament*] A Paris, Chez Pierre Witte, rue S Jacques, proche de S. Yves, à l'Ange Gardien. Didot, Quay des Auguſtins, près du pont S. Michel, à la Bible d'or. [*short rule*] M.D.CC.XXXIII. Avec Approbation & Privilege du Roi.

Collation: Tome I, Suite du tome I, ã⁸ ẽ⁴ ĩ⁴ A⁸ B⁴–Z⁸ Aa⁴–Mm⁸ Nn⁴+ã² Oo⁸ Pp⁴–Yy⁸ Zz²; 290 leaves. Tome II, ã⁴ A⁸ B⁴–Z⁸ Aa⁴–Dd⁸ Ee⁴ Ff² Gg² Hh⁸; 184 leaves.

Contents: Tome I, ã1 title; ã2*a*–ã3*a* *A Monſeigneur le Duc de Richelieu, et de Fronſac*, signed ✱✱✱; ã3*b*–ã7*a* *Preface de l'auteur*; ã7*b*–ĩ1*b* *Preface du traducteur*, with *Errata du premier tome* at bottom of ĩ1*b*; ĩ2*a*–ĩ3*b* *Table des Chapitres*; ĩ4 blank; A1*a*–Nn3*b* (pp. 1–430) text of Livres I–III. Suite de tome premier, ã1 title; ã2*a*–*b* *Table des Chapitres L.IV*; Nn4*a*–Zz1*b* (pp. 431–546) text of Livre IV; (Zz2 blank, usually cancelled).

Tome II, ã1 title; ã2*a*–ã3*b* *Tables Des Chapitres*; ã4*a*–*b* *Approbation*, signed *Moreau de Mautour*, and *Privilege du Roi*, signed *Faurson*, with declarations signed *Witte* and *G. Martin, December*, 1732; A1*a*–Gg1*b* (pp. 1–342) text of Livres V–VII; Hh1*a*–Hh8*b* *Table des matières*.

Note: The translator was the Abbé Jean-Baptiste Souchay, Canon of Rodez. Leroy noted that this only became known when the dispersal of Souchay's library was announced in Moréri's *Dictionnaire* (1759) (*A French Bibliography of Sir Thomas Browne*, London, 1931, p. 35). Another edition of the same translation was published at Amsterdam in the same year (see next entry) and others followed. Leroy pointed out that Souchay's version was not accurate nor even complete. He omitted passages such as that in Book VII, chapter XVI, 'Of the Woman that conceived in a Bath', and he even took fright at abstruse metaphors.

The collation of the first French edition is peculiar since the fourth book, belonging to the first volume, was detached from it and bound in front of the second volume, apparently in order to equalize the sizes of the volumes. For this purpose the last leaf of signature Nn was separated and in front of this were inserted two conjugate leaves carrying an extra title-page for *Suite de Tome premier* and a *Table des Chapitres* of Book IV.

This translation was reviewed in *Mercure de France* (Paris, 1733), pp. 2443–51, and in *Le Journal des Scavans* (Paris, 1733), pp. 316–26 and 433–42.

Copies: GUL, K; BN, MMO, NYAM.

88 PSEUDODOXIA: FRENCH   12° 1733

Title in red and black: Effai fur les Erreurs Populaires,...[&c. as in no. 87] Tome Premier [Second] [*engraved device with motto*: *Vis unita major*] A Amfterdam, aux depens de la compagnie. M.DCC.XXXIII.

Collation: Tome I, *⁸+a² **⁴ ***² A–R¹² S⁴; 224 leaves. Tome II, †⁴ A–T¹² V² X⁴; 238 leaves.

Contents: Tome I, *1 title; a1*a*–a2*b* *Avertiffement Sur cette nouvelle Edition*; *2*a*–*3*a* *A Monfeigneur le Duc de Richelieu, et de Fronfac*; *3*b*–*6*b* *Preface de l'auteur*; *7*a*–**4*a* *Preface du traducteur*; **4*b*–***2*a* *Table des chapitres*; ***2*b* *Approbation*, signed *Moreau de Mautour*, and *errata*; A1*a*–S4*a* (pp. 1–415) text of Livres I–III; S4*b* blank. Tome II, †1 title; †2*a*–†4*b* *Table des chapitres*; A1*a*–T6*b* (pp. 1–444) text of Livres IV–VII; T7*a*–V2*b* *Table des matieres*; X1*a*–X4*b* *Catalogue des livres...pour l'Année 1733*.

Notes: This is a reprint of the Paris edition of the same year. The two leaves of *Avertiffement* inserted after the title-page in vol. I draw attention to the large number of errors in the Paris edition and supply corrections.

Copies: BM, GUL, K; MMO.

89 PSEUDODOXIA: FRENCH   12° 1733

Title: Effai fur les Erreurs Populaires,...[&c. as in no. 87] Traduit de l'Anglois de Thomas Brown, Chevalier & Docteur en Médicine. [*the usual Latin quotation*] Tome premier [second]. [*ornament*] A la Haye, Chez Jean Swarte, Libraire. [*rule*] M. D. CC. XXXIII.

Collation: Tome I, a¹² b⁴ A⁸ B⁴–Mm⁸ Nn⁴; 232 leaves. Tome II, a⁴ A⁸ B⁴–Oo⁸ Pp⁴ Qq¹² Rr⁴; 250 leaves.

Contents: Tome I, a1 title; a2*a*–a3*b* dedication; a4*a*–a10*b* *Preface du traducteur*; a11*a*–b2*b* *Preface de l'auteur*; b3*a*–b4*b* *Table*; A1*a*–Nn3*b* (pp. 1–430) text of Livres I–III; Nn4 blank.

Tome II, a1 title; a2*a*–a4*b* *Table*; A1*a*–Qq1*b* (pp. 1–458) text of Livres V–VII; Qq2*a*–Rr2*b* (pp. 459–84, 4 pp. unnumbered) *Table des matieres*; Rr3*a*–Rr4*b* *Approbation* and *Privilege du Roy*.

Note: A reprint of the Amsterdam edition of the same year. The Hague edition is very uncommon and only one copy has come to my notice. This was in the collection of Professor J.–J. Denonain, who told me of it in 1947. The sheets of this edition were afterwards used in the Paris issues of 1738 (see next entry).

Copy: J.–J. Denonain.

89a PSEUDODOXIA: FRENCH 12° 1738

Title: Effai fur les Erreurs Populaires,...[&c. as in no. 87] Traduit de l'Anglois de Thom. Brown, Chevalier & Docteur en Médicine Nouvelle Edition revûe & corrigée. [*the usual Latin quotation*] Tome premier [second]. [*ornament*] A Paris, Chez Briaffon, rue Saint Jacques, à la Science & à l'Ange Gardien. [*double rule, thick and thin*] MDCC XXXVIII. Avec Approbation & Privilege du Roy.

Collation, contents: As in no. 89, with a half-title and reprinted title substituted for the title of 1733. These volumes therefore contain 233 and 251 leaves respectively.

Note: The sheets of no. 89 are found doing duty for this and other issues of the book, which does not seem to have sold off very successfully.

Copies: CLN, K.

89b PSEUDODOXIA: FRENCH 12° 1738

Title: Effai fur les Erreurs Populaires...[&c. as in no. 89a] A Paris, Chez Briaffon, rue S. Jacques, à la Science, & à l'Ange Gardien. [*double rule, thick and thin*] M. DCC. XXXVIII. Avec Approbation & Privilege du Roi.

Collation, contents: As in no. 89a.

Note: A variant issue of no. 89a with resetting of the half-title and title.

Copy: K.

89c PSEUDODOXIA: FRENCH 12° 1738

Title: Effai fur les Erreurs Populaires...[&c. as in no. 89a] A Paris, chez Barrois, aîné, Libraire, quai des Auguftins, du Côté du pont Saint-Michel. MDCCXXXVIII.

Collation, contents: As in no. 89a.

Note: This variant imprint is only in vol. 1 of the copy recorded.

Copy: University of Michigan, Ann Arbor.

89d PSEUDODOXIA: FRENCH 12° 1741

Title: Essai sur les Erreurs Populaires...[&c. as in no. 89a] A Paris, Chez Briasson, rue Saint Jacques, à la Science. [*short rule*] M. D. CC. XLI. Avec Approbation & Privilege du Roy.

Collation, contents: Not collated, but presumably as in no. 89a.

Copy: BN.

90 PSEUDODOXIA: FRENCH 12° 1753

Title: Essai sur les Erreurs Populaires...[&c. as in no. 89a] A Paris, Chez Briasson, rue S. Jacques, à la Science & à l'Ange Gardien. [*double rule*] M.DCC.LIII. Avec Approbation & Privilege du Roi.

SAGGIO

SOPRA GLI

ERRORI

POPOLARESCHI

O V V E R O

ESAME DI MOLTE OPINIONI

Ricevute come vere, che sono false
o dubbiose.

Opera scritta in Inglese

DA TOMMASO BROVVN

Cavaliere e Dottore in Medicina;

Tradotta in Francese da un Anonimo, e
trasportata in Italiano

DA SELVAGGIO CANTURANI.

*Ex libris colligere quæ prodiderunt Auctores,
longe est periculosissimum : rerum
ipsarum cognitio e rebus ipsis
est.* Jul. Scalig.

TOMO PRIMO.

IN VENEZIA, MDCCXXXVII.

PER SEBASTIANO COLETI.

Con licenza de' Superiori , e Privilegio.

Collation, contents: As in no. 89*a*.

Note: This appears to be the last attempt to sell the sheets of the edition printed in 1733. The title-page of 1738 remains in vol. I of the copy in the Wilkin Collection.

Copies: GUL, CLN.

91 PSEUDODOXIA: ITALIAN 12° 1737

Title: Saggio ſopra gli errori popolareſchi ovvero eſame di molte opinioni Ricevute come vere, che ſono falſe o dubbioſe. Opera ſcritta in Ingleſe da Tommaſo Brovvn Cavaliere e Dottore in Medicina; Tradotta in Franceſe da un Anonimo, e traſportata in Italiano da Selvaggio Canturani. [*the usual Latin quotation*] Tomo primo [ſecondo]. [*double short rule*] In Venezia, MDCCXXXVII. Per Sebaſtiano Coleti. Con licenza de' Superiori, e Privilegio.

Collation: Tomo I, *¹⁰ A–R¹² S⁴; 218 leaves. Tomo. II, *⁴ A–S¹²; 220 leaves.

Contents: Tomo I, *1 title; *2*a*–*4*a* (pp. iii–vii) *Prefazione dell'autore*; *4*b*–*8*b* (pp. viii–xvi) *Prefazione Del Traduttore Franceſe*; *9*a*–*10*b* (pp. xvii–xx) *Tavola De' Capitoli*; A1*a*–R11*b* (pp. 1–406) text of Libri I–III; R12*a*–S4*b* (pp. 407–16) *Tavola Delle Materie del tomo primo*.

Tomo II, *1 title; *2*a*–*4*a* (pp. iii–vii) *Tavola de' Capitoli*; *4*b* (p. viii) licence dated 29. *Marzo* 1736; A1*a*–S10*a* (pp. 1–427) text of Libri IV–VII; S10*b*–S12*b* (pp. 428–32) *Tavola Delle Materie contenute nel ſecondo Volume*.

Note: As noted on the title-page, this is a translation from the French and therefore has the same defects. In vol. I, pp. xx, 159, 287 and signatures H3, Q3 are printed xxiv, 139, 289, H5, Qd. In vol. II H3 is printed H5; M6 and S5 are unsigned.

Copies: BM, GUL, K; MMO.

92 PSEUDODOXIA: ITALIAN 12° 1743

Title: Saggio ſopra gli errori popolareſchi...[&c. as in no. 91] In Venezia, MDCCXLIII. Per Gio: Maria Lazzaroni. Con Licenza de' Superiori, e Privilegio.

Collation, contents: As in no. 91.

Note: This is a reprint of no. 91. The first preface is set in a larger face without increasing the number of pages. The rest of the book is a line-for-line reprint. The misprints of the former edition have been corrected, but some new ones have been introduced. In vol. I signatures S1, S2 are printed S5, S6; pp. 167, 369 are numbered 197, 366. In vol. II pp. 246, 274 are numbered 146, 174. In this volume the licence on *4*b* has been altered to conform with the change of publisher, and it is now dated *8. Giugno* 1742.

Copies: GUL, K.

92*a* PSEUDODOXIA: ITALIAN 8° 1754

Title: Saggio ſopra gli errori popolareſchi ovvero eſame di molte opinioni Ricevute come vere, che sono falſe o dubbioſe. Del Signor Tommaſo Brown Cavaliere, e Dottore in Medicina; Tradotta dall'Ingleſe. [*the usual quotation*]

Tomo primo [secondo]. [*ornament*] In Venezia, Per Giuſeppe Rosa. [*short rule*] MDCCLIV. Con licenza de' ſuperiori, e privilegio.

Collation: Tomo I, A–Y⁸; 176 leaves. Tomo II, *4 A–X⁸; 172 leaves.

Contents: Vol. I A1 title; A2*a*–A3*b Prefazione dell'autore* (pp. 3–6); A4*a*–A7*b* (pp. 7–14) *Prefazione del tradutore franceſe* A8*a*–Y3*a* (pp. 15–341) text of Libri I–III; Y3*b*–Y4*b* (pp. 342–4) *Tavola de' Capitoli*; Y5*a*–Y7*b* (pp. 345–50) *Tavola Delle Materie*; Y8 blank. Tomo II, *1 title; *2*a*–*4*a* (pp. iii–viii) *Tavola de' Capitoli*; *4*b* (p. viii) licence dated *4. Aprile 1754*; A1*a*–X6*b* (pp. 1–432) text of Libri IV–VII; X7*a*–X8*a* (pp. 433–5) *Tavola Delle Materie*; X8*b* blank.

Note: This is the third printing of the Italian version.

Copy: CLN, K.

III

Hydriotaphia and *Garden of Cyrus*

BIBLIOGRAPHICAL PREFACE

S IR THOMAS BROWNE'S *Hydriotaphia* and *Garden of Cyrus* were first printed together by their author in 1658 and until the nineteenth century they were never dissociated. The two works are therefore described here together. There is internal evidence showing that *Hydriotaphia* was composed in 1656; *The Garden of Cyrus* was probably composed in the early part of 1658.

The composition of *Hydriotaphia* was suggested to Browne by the discovery of a group of cinerary urns in a field at Walsingham near Norwich. He supposed these to be of late Roman date, though the portrayal of four of the urns in the engraved frontispiece shows that they were in fact of Saxon origin and so of much later date. This does not, however, invalidate Browne's idea of their message. He wove around them a tissue of solemn reflections in his most luxurious style, and the essay is accounted by some to be the supreme example of his art. It is dedicated to Thomas le Gros, the head of an ancient family then living at Crostwick Hall, four miles north of Norwich. *The Garden of Cyrus*, also in Browne's most fanciful style, is dedicated to Nicholas Bacon, grandson of Sir Nicholas Bacon created premier baronet by James I in 1611; he lived at Gillingham, twelve miles south-east of Norwich.

Neither work is known to exist in manuscript, though Wilkin found several passages from both in the British Museum[1] and these he incorporated in his notes. Browne afterwards wrote a brief sequel to *Hydriotaphia*, entitled *Brampton Urns*, but this is an archaeological essay rather than a literary composition. It was not printed until 1712 in Browne's *Posthumous Works*. The first edition of *Hydriotaphia* in octavo is an attractive book of no great rarity. When complete it contains a bookseller's advertisement leaf bearing the title printed longitudinally and some copies have a leaf, or pasted-on slip, of *errata*. Sometimes these *errata* have been corrected in the text by contemporary hands or the *Marginall Illustrations* have been added from the quartos, and it has been suggested that this was done by the author himself. Usually this cannot be substantiated, but careful examination of a number of copies by Mr. John Carter and Dr. Jeremiah Finch has revealed twelve containing corrections now generally accepted as having been made by the author, the number of alterations varying from three to seventy-seven. Some repeat the corrections made in the printed *errata*, others are additional and independent. A few of these books were given to his friends by the author, who seems to have been more free with gift copies of this than of any other of his works.

These important copies have been listed by Mr. Carter as follows with the number of corrections they contain:[2]

(1) Avery Library, Columbia University, New York, 77.

---

[1] Sloane MSS. 1847, 1848, 1882.
[2] See also *Hydriotaphia*, ed. Carter (1932) (no. 126*d*); J. S. Finch, *The Library* (1938), XIX, 347, and *Times Lit. Sup.* 16 March 1940; J. Carter, *Times Lit. Sup.* 22 August 1935, 27 February 1943, 30 August 1953, and *The Library* (1947), II, 191.

(2) Osler Library, McGill University, Montreal, 47.
(3) Alabama University Library, 45.
(4) Trinity College, Cambridge, 44.
(5) John Carter, London, 43.
(6) Durham University Library,[1] 42.
(7) British Museum, 40.
(8) Princeton University Library, 39.
(9) Moschcovitz copy.[2] Now in the collection of Mr Robert Pirie.
(10) J. K. Lilly Library, University of Indiana, 17.
(11) Yale University Library, 16.
(12) Cornell University Library, 3.

Corrections in other hands, but believed to have been derived from the author, are found in three copies:

(1) In (9) above, written in a second hand.
(2) Norwich Central Library, Wilkin Collection.
(3) Adelaide University Library.

The final recension of the text of *Hydriotaphia* and *The Garden of Cyrus* based on these various discoveries will be found in Mr. Carter's edition of 1958 (no. 126*f*) and in my text in the *Collected Works*, 1964 (no. 126*i*).

The two works were reprinted in quarto in the same year as they were first published, being issued with the fourth edition of *Pseudodoxia Epidemica*. They also appeared in the folio edition of 1659, in the quarto of 1669, and in all collected editions issued after that date. The second separate edition was published by Curll in 1736, and this is without exception the scarcest edition of these works. Curll had intended it to be the second instalment of a series of publications containing Browne's writings. He had advertised it in the *London Evening Post*, no. 1334, 3–5 June 1736, as part of a notice of his edition of *Religio Medici* (see p. 7):

No. II. *is in the Press, containing,*
Hydriotaphia, (Urn-Burial). Being a Discourse of the manner of Interment used by the Ancients. All Sir Thomas Browne's Works will be printed with convenient Expedition, and adorn'd with near 30 Copper-plates. Price of each Number 1*s*. 6*d*.

Curll inserted another longer notice in no. 1370, 26–28 August 1736:

This Day is publish'd
(Revised by Dr. Desaguliers, with a curious Plate given by Sir Hans Sloane) Number II. of the Works of Sir Thomas Browne of Norwich, Price 1*s*. 6*d*.
This Number contains two Tracts, viz.
I. Hydriotaphia, or Urn-Burial; including the different Manner of Funeral Interments in Use throughout the World, with an Account of the Sepulchral Urns found in Norfolk 1658 and 1662. Also Remarks upon the Tumuli of the Romans, Saxons, Danes; and of

---

[1] Inscribed by Browne *For my worthy and honord friend Mr John Robins*. With *errata* slip in its second form. Robins is mentioned several times in Browne's letters to his son.
[2] Inscribed on the fly-leaf: *D. Short—ex dono authoris*. Sold at Sotheby's 9 November 1964, lot 84 (Dawson £480). Probably the one given to Dr Peregrine Short (*Letters*, 1964, p. 74).

the artificial Hills, Mounts, or Burrows, in many Parts of England, In a Letter to Sir William Dugdale. II. The Garden of Cyrus, or the Quincuncial Lozenge or Network Plantations of the Ancients; artificially, naturally, and mystically consider'd. Reciting the Methods of Gardening and Agriculture in Use among the Ancients; with Observations on Vegetation, and the Generation of Plants, Insects and Animals.

Printed only for E. Curll, at Pope's-head in Rose-street Covent-Garden.

N.B. No. III. is in the Press, which begins with *Enquiries into Vulgar Errors*; corrected and improv'd by Dr. Desaguliers. The whole Works of this learned Author will be compleated in 12 Numbers, at 1*s*. 6*d*. each; by the Appointment of the Family his Manuscripts are communicated only to Mr. Curll, who has just published No. I, being a beautiful and correct Edition of Religio Medici, adorn'd with Sir Thomas Browne's Picture and Monument finely engraven. Price 1*s*. 6*d*. Beware of *Pyratical Counterfeits*, who dare not proceed any farther.

A similar notice appeared in no. 1374, 4–7 September 1736. It will be noted that there was now no mention of 'near 30 Copper-plates'. Curll had perhaps been discouraged by lack of success with his edition of *Religio Medici*. He was, however, now offering editorial revision by Dr. Desaguliers, that is, John Theophilus Desaguliers (1683–1744), son of a Huguenot refugee, born at La Rochelle in 1683 and brought to England by his father in 1685. He became a graduate of Christ Church, Oxford, a lecturer in experimental philosophy, and author of various works on physics and astronomy. He would have been a suitable commentator on Browne's treatises, but the book when published bore no signs of his attentions. Even the copper-plate of urns was only 'inscribed to', not 'given by', Sir Hans Sloane. Curll's edition as actually published appeared curiously truncated, the last two chapters of *The Garden of Cyrus* being entirely omitted without explanation (see no. 99). The present scarcity of the book suggests that it was again a commercial failure. This is further indicated by the fact that, though the second and third announcements added a promise of a third instalment beginning with *Enquiries into Vulgar Errors*, this larger venture was abandoned.

Hydriotaphia was not reprinted apart from *The Garden of Cyrus* until 1822 (no. 100), and Professor F. L. Huntley (*Sir Thomas Browne*, 1962) found evidence in the themes to show that their conjunction was fully intended by the author. *The Garden of Cyrus* was not reprinted alone until the Golden Cockerel Press edition of 1923 (no. 126).

The first account of *Hydriotaphia* with extracts was printed by Christopher Arnold in *Inclutæ Bibliothecæ Norimbergensis Memorabilia* (1674) (no. 275). Arnold even included an engraved copy of the plate of urns.

HYDRIOTAPHIA,

URNE-BURIALL,

OR,

A Difcourfe of the Sepulchrall
Urnes lately found in

NORFOLK.

Together with

The Garden of *CYRUS,*

OR THE

Quincunciall, Lozenge, or
Net-work Plantations of the An-
cients, Artificially, Naturally,
Myftically Confidered.

With Sundry Obfervations.

By *Thomas Browne* D. of Phyfick.

Printed for *Hen. Brome* at the Signe of the
Gun in *Ivy-lane*. 1658.

93 HYDRIOTAPHIA & GARDEN OF CYRUS [Wing B 5154] 8° 1658

Title, within single lines: Hydriotaphia, Urne-buriall, or, A Difcourfe of the Sepulchrall Urnes lately found in Norfolk. Together with The Garden of Cyrus, or the Quincunciall, Lozenge, or Net-work Plantations of the Ancients, Artificially, Naturally, Myftically Confidered. With Sundry Obfervations. [*rule*] By Thomas Browne D. of Phyfick. [*rule*] London, Printed for Hen. Brome at the Signe of the Gun in Ivy-lane. 1658.

Collation: A–O⁸; 112 leaves.

Contents: A1 title; A2*a*–A4*b To my Worthy and Honoured Friend Thomas Le Gros of Croftwick Efquire*; A5*a*–A7*a To my Worthy and Honored Friend Nicholas Bacon of Gillingham Efquire*; A7*b*–A8*a* blank; A8*b* engraved plate of urns; B1*a*–G2*b* (pp. 1–84) text of *Hydriotaphia*; G3*a* blank; G3*b* engraved plate of quincunx; G4*a* sub-title of *The Garden of Cyrus*; G4*b* blank; G5*a*–O5*b* (pp. 89–202) text of *The Garden of Cyrus*; O6*a*–*b The Stationer to the Reader*; O7*a Books Printed for Hen. Broome*; O7*b* blank; O8*a* longitudinal label *Dr Brown's Garden of Cyrus*; O8*b* blank. A leaf of *errata*, 18 or 24 lines, is found in some copies inserted after O6 or pasted to one of the blank pages at the end.

Illustrations: (i) A8*b*, engraved plate of four urns, lettered below *En fum quod digitis Quinque Levatur onus Propert.* Plate-mark, 160 × 98 mm.

(ii) G3*b*, p. [86], engraved plate of quincunx, lettered below *Quid Quincunce fpeciofius, qui, in quamcunꝗ partem fpectaueris, rectus est: Quintilian:* Plate-mark, 98 × 60 mm.

(iii) I1*b*, p. 114, engraved plate with a diagram showing the quincuncial formation of the Roman legion. Plate-mark, 38 × 74 mm.

Note: P. 202 is misprinted 102; the pagination is otherwise correct. Both works have marginal notes by the author. The leaf O6 with *The Stationer to the Reader* gives a formal denial that the book called *Nature's Cabinet Unlock'd* (1657) was by Sir Thomas Browne, by whom it purported to have been written (see no. 189).

Only a minority of copies contain the *errata*. When present these are usually in the form of a slip pasted onto Oo*b*; exceptionally, as in one of my copies, they are on an inserted leaf. The *errata* consist of 18 lines, except in one instance where they occupy 24 lines. This copy (Durham University) was first described by Mr. John Carter in 1947 (*The Library*, 5th S. II, 191–3); no other example has been reported since that time. In at least one copy[1] of the book the printing of the engraved plates has been missed. There is no reason to suppose this to have been a 'trial copy', or proof, the omission being probably accidental. Presentation and author-corrected copies have been recorded above.

Copies: BLO(3), BM(2),[2] CLN, GUL(2), K(2),[3] NLS, TCC,[4] TCD, ULD; IUL,[5] MH(3), MMO(2),[6] NYAM, PUL,[7] YML, YUL.

[1] Offered by Halliday of Leicester, November 1929. Sold at Sotheby's 17 February 1930, lot 90. Now in the Fulton collection, Sterling Library, Yale University (YML).

[2] Both with *errata* slip, one author-corrected (C.116.bb.22).

[3] One with *errata* leaf. [4] Author-corrected. [5] Author-corrected.

[6] One author-corrected, the other with *errata* slip. [7] Author-corrected.

94 HYDRIOTAPHIA & GARDEN OF CYRUS [Wing B 5154]   4° 1658

Sub-title: Hydriotaphia Urne-buriall, or, a Difcourfe of the Sepulchrall Urnes lately found in Norfolk Together with The Garden of Cyrus, or the Quin- cunciall Lozenge, or Net-work Plantations of the Ancients, Artificially, Naturally, Myftically Confidered; With Sundry Obfervations. [*rule*] By Thomas Browne D. of Phyfick. [*rule*] London, Printed for Hen. Brome at the Signe of the Gun in Ivy-lane. 1658.

Collation: 5¶⁴ 5*² 5A–5I⁴ 5K²; 40 leaves.

Contents: 5¶1*a* longitudinal label *Dr Brown's Enquiries & Garden of Cyrus*; 5¶1*b* blank; 5¶2 sub-title; 5¶3*a*–5*1*b* *The Epiftles Dedicatory*; 5*2*a* blank; 5*2*b* engraved plate of urns; 5A1*a*–5D3*b* (pp. 1–30) text of *Hydriotaphia*; 5D4*a* blank; 5D4*b* engraved plate of quincunx; 5E1 sub-title to *Garden of Cyrus*; 5E2*a*–5K1*a* (pp. 35–73) text of *Garden of Cyrus*; 5K1*b* *The Stationer to the Reader*; 5K2*a* *Books Printed for Hen. Brome*; 5K2*b* blank.

Illustrations: Three engraved plates on 5*2*b*, 5D4*b* and 5F2*a* (p. 43) as in no. 93.

Note: Appended to the fourth edition of *Pseudodoxia Epidemica*, 4°, 1658 (see no. 76), which bears the imprint of Edward Dod, although the sub-titles to the tracts appended have the name of Hen. Brome, the publisher of the edition in 8°; the list of *Books Printed for Hen. Brome* is the same in both editions. In this edition the *errata* have been corrected and the spelling to some extent modernized. On a leaf following the Table of Contents of the *Pseudodoxia* is given a list of 'Marginall Illustrations omitted, or to be added to the Discourse of Urn-Burial, and of the Garden of Cyrus'.

95 HYDRIOTAPHIA & GARDEN OF CYRUS   f° 1659

Sub-title: Religio Medici: Whereunto is added A Difcourfe of the Sepulchrall Urnes, lately found in Norfolk. Together vvith The Garden of Cyrus...[&c. see no. 7].

Collation, contents, illustrations: See no. 7.

Note: Printed together with *Religio Medici* without a separate sub-title and appended to *Pseudodoxia Epidemica* (f°, 1658) with a general title-page dated 1659 (no. 77).

96 HYDRIOTAPHIA & GARDEN OF CYRUS   4° 1669

Sub-title: Hydriotaphia, Urn-Buriall;...Together with The Garden of Cyrus;... [&c. as in no. 94] London, Printed for Henry Brome, at the Star in Little- Britain, 1669.

Collation: A–E⁴ [χ]² F–K⁴; 42 leaves.

Contents: A1 sub-title; A2*a*–A4*b* *The Epiftles Dedicatory*; B1*a*–E3*a* (pp. 1–29) text of *Hydriotaphia*; E3*b* blank; E4 sub-title to *Garden of Cyrus*; [χ] 1*a* blank; [χ]1*b* engraved plate of urns; [χ]2*a* engraved plate of quincunx; [χ]2*b* blank; F1*a*–K3*b* (pp. 33–70) text of *Garden of Cyrus*; K4 blank.

Illustrations: Three engraved plates on [χ]1*b*, [χ]2*a*, and G1*a* (p. 41) as in no. 93.

Note: Appended to the fifth edition of *Pseudodoxia Epidemica* (4°, 1669) (see no. 78). The sub-title still bears the imprint of Henry Brome, although the volume was published by Edward Dod as before. The plates are very much worn, but have not been worked over. They are sometimes differently placed, the quincunx facing p. 33. *The Stationer to the Reader* is omitted from this edition. *Marginal Illustrations* as in the quarto of 1658. The sub-title to this edition is occasionally dated 1668.

97 HYDRIOTAPHIA & GARDEN OF CYRUS   f° 1686

Sub-title: Hydriotaphia, Urn-burial, or, A Discourse of the Sepulchral Urns lately found in Norfolk. [*rule*] Together with the Garden of Cyrus, or the Quincuncial, Lozenge, or Net-work Plantations of the Ancients, Artificially, Naturally, Mystically Considered. With Sundry Observations. [*rule*] By Thomas Browne Dr. of Physick. [*ornaments between rules*] London, Printed for Charles Brome, MDCLXXXVI.

Collation: Lll–Qqq⁴ Rrr⁶; 30 leaves.

Contents: Lll1 sub-title; Lll2*a*–Lll4*a* *The Epistles Dedicatory*; Lll4*b* engraved plate of urns; Mmm1*a*–Ooo3*a* (pp. 1–21) text of *Hydriotaphia*; Ooo3*b* engraved plate of quincunx; Ooo4 as sub-title to *Garden of Cyrus*; Ppp1*a*–Rrr6*b* (pp. 25–52) text of *Garden of Cyrus*; Rrr6*b* (p. 52) *The Stationer to the Reader*.

Illustrations: Two engraved plates on Lll4*b* and Ooo3*b*, as in previous editions, and type diagrams on Ppp4*a* and in the margin of Rrr5*a*.

Note: In *The Works of Sir T. B.* (f°, 1686) (see no. 201). The engraved plates are extremely badly worn. The *Marginal Illustrations* noted in the quartos are omitted from this volume.

98 HYDRIOTAPHIA & GARDEN OF CYRUS: DUTCH   4° 1688

Sub-titles: Hydriotaphia, Of kruyk-begraavenis: Zynde Een korte Reden-voeringe van de dood-bussen Of kruyken, Onlangs gevonden in Norfolk, Door Thomas Brown. M.D.

De Lust-hof Van Cyrus, Of de vyf-regelige ruyt, Of nets-wyze boom-plantinge Der Aalouden, Konstiglyk, Natuurlyk en Geheymkundiglyk aangemerkt Door Thomas Brown. M.D.

Collation: Q*3–4 R*–Z*⁴ Aa*–Cc*⁴ Dd*1; 43 leaves (see no. 202).

Contents: Q* sub-title to *Hydriotaphia*; Q*4*a*–R*2*a* (pp. 127–31) *Toe-eygen-brief Aan…* *Thomas le Gros*; R*2*b*–X*1*b* (pp. 132–62) text of *Hydriotaphia*; X*2 sub-title to *Lust-hof Van Cyrus*; X*3*a*–Y*1*b* *Opdragt Aan…Nicolaas Bacon…* Y*2*a*–Dd*1*b* (pp. 171–210) text of *Lust-hof Van Cyrus*.

Note: In *Alle de Werken, t'Amsterdam* (4°, 1688) for which see no. 202.

Illustrations: (i) Inserted before S*1, facing p. 137, an engraved copy of the plate of urns, lettered at the top: *Kruyk Begravenis*, and with the same Latin inscription below. Plate-mark 15·5 × 9·8 cm.

    (ii) Inserted before Y*2, facing p. 171, an engraved copy of the quincunx plate, with the same Latin inscription below, and in addition: *Vyf-Regelige Ruyt. Pag.* 171. Plate-mark 10 × 6 cm.

    (iii)–(iv) Type diagrams on Z*2*b* and Cc*3*a* copied from those on Ppp4*a* and in the margin of Rrr5*a* of *Works* (1686).

HYDRIOTAPHIA:

OR,

URN-BURIAL.

TWO

DISCOURSES

OF THE

SEPULCHRAL URNS

FOUND

In *NORFOLK,*

1658 AND 1667.

By Sir THOMAS BROWNE, *M. D.*

THE FOURTH EDITION.

LONDON:

Printed for E. CURLL, at *Pope's* Head, in *Rose-Street, Covent Garden.* 1736.

Price 1 s. 6 d.

99 HYDRIOTHPIA, GARDEN OF CYRUS, & BRAMPTON URNS 8° 1736

Title: Hydriotaphia: or, Urn-burial. Two difcourfes of the Sepulchral Urns found In Norfolk, 1658 and 1667. [*rule*] By Sir Thomas Browne, M.D. [*rule*] The Fourth Edition. [*rule*] London: Printed for E. Curll, at Pope's Head, in Rofe-Street, Covent Garden. 1736. Price 1*s.* 6*d.*

Collation: A–G⁸; 56 leaves.

Contents: A1 title, A2*a*–A3*b* (pp. iii–vi) *Epiftle Dedicatory*; A4*a*–D4*a* (pp. 1–49) text of *Hydriotaphia*; D4*b*–D6*a* (pp. 50–3) *Of Artificial Hills*; D6*b*–E1*b* (pp. 54–60) *Brampton Urns*; E2 sub-title to *Garden of Cyrus* with diagram of the quincunx; E3*a*–E4*b* (pp. iii–vi) *Epiftle Dedicatory*; E5*a*–G8*b* (pp. 1–40) text of *Garden of Cyrus*.

Frontispiece: Plate of four urns newly engraved with motto, and inscribed below, *To Sir Hans Sloane, this Plate is gratefully Inscribed. E. Curll.* Plate-mark, 17·5 × 11 cm.

Note: Although called the *Fourth Edition* on the title-page this is in reality the sixth edition of *Hydriotaphia* and of *The Garden of Cyrus*. The text of the latter stops at the end of chapter III; chapters IV and V, and *The Stationer to the Reader* are omitted. Of the two tracts appended to *Hydriotaphia* the first one, *Of Artificial Hills*, was originally printed as no. IX of the *Miscellany Tracts* (see no. 127), and the second, on the *Brampton Urns*, in the *Posthumous Works* (see no. 156). There are a few unauthorized alterations in the text. The marginalia are printed as footnotes.

This edition seems to be rare. It is sometimes found bound up with Curll's edition of *Religio Medici* published in the same year (see no. 14). A copy in my collection, stitched in original wrappers and untrimmed, measures 21 × 13 cm.

Copies: BM, CLN(2), GUL, K(2), TCC, ULC.

100 HYDRIOTAPHIA, &c. ED. CROSSLEY 12° 1822

Tracts, by Sir Thomas Browne, Knight, M.D. A New Edition. William Blackwood, Edinburgh; and T. Cadell, London. MDCCCXXII. 15 cm. pp. vi, [ii], 183, [1].

Contents: Hydriotaphia, A Letter to a Friend, Musæum Clausum.

Note: Edited, with a short introduction, by James Crossley. The author's marginalia to *Hydriotaphia* are printed as footnotes. Wilkin, III, 378, notes that Crossley altered the division, calling the first chapter *Introduction* and the remaining chapters *Sections* 1, 2, 3, 4, and that he has, in several instances, altered the phraseology. The *Musæum Clausum* was originally printed in the *Miscellany Tracts* (1683) (see no. 127). The book was printed by James Ballantyne and Co., Edinburgh, and issued in blue or brown boards with printed label. It is said that in a copy of the book given by Crossley to Beckford there is a statement that '75 copies were printed for private distribution' (see S. M. Ellis, *Wilkie Collins &c.* 1931, p. 215 of present work).

Copies: CLN, GUL, K(2); MMO, PUL.

101 HYDRIOTAPHIA ED. YOUNG 8° 1831

In Miscellaneous Works of Sir Thomas Browne...[Ed. Rev. Alexander Young, D.D.] Cambridge [U.S.A.]: Hilliard and Brown...MDCCCXXXI. (see no. 19).

102 HYDRIOTAPHIA & GARDEN OF CYRUS ED. WILKIN   8° 1836

In Sir Thomas Browne's Works...Ed. Simon Wilkin...London William Pickering...1836 (see no. 203).

Note: Vol. III, pp. 375–496, with *Brampton Urns*, pp. 497–505, and a preface by the editor. This is the eighth edition of *Hydriotaphia* and the seventh of *The Garden of Cyrus*. The engraved plates are reproduced as woodcuts.

103 HYDRIOTAPHIA ED. ST. JOHN   8° 1838 & 1845

In Religio Medici: to which is added, Hydriotaphia...With a Preliminary Discourse and Notes, by J. A. St. John Esq. London: Joseph Rickerby... 1838 (see no. 21), 1845 (see no. 25).

104 HYDRIOTAPHIA & GARDEN OF CYRUS   8° 1852

In The Works of Sir Thomas Browne...Ed. Simon Wilkin...London: H. G. Bohn,...MDCCCLII. (see no. 205).

Note: Vol. II, pp. 489–564, and vol. III, pp. 1–49. Reprints of no. 102.

105 HYDRIOTAPHIA ED. FIELDS   8° 1862

In Religio Medici...and Other Papers...Boston Ticknor and Fields 1862 (see no. 29).

106 HYDRIOTAPHIA ED. WILLIS BUND   8° 1869

In Religio Medici, Hydriotaphia,...with an introduction and notes by J. W. Willis Bund...London: Sampson Low,...[1869] (see no. 31).

107 HYDRIOTAPHIA ED. FIELDS   8° 1878

In Religio Medici...and other papers...Boston Robert Brothers 1878 (see no. 35).

108 HYDRIOTAPHIA ED. SYMONDS   8° 1886

In Sir Thomas Browne's Religio Medici, Urn Burial...Edited by John Addington Symonds. London: Walter Scott...1886 (see no. 39).

109 HYDRIOTAPHIA & BRAMPTON URNS   8° 1890

Miscellanies upon various subjects. By John Aubrey, F.R.S. The fifth edition. To which is added, Hydriotaphia; or, Urn Burial. By Sir Thomas Browne. [*device*] London: Reeves and Turner 196, Strand. 1890. 17 cm. pp. xvi, 301, [3], engr. frontispiece. [Library of Old Authors.]

Note: Hydriotaphia (called tenth edition), pp. 223–85, and *Brampton Urns*, pp. 286–95. There are wood-cut reproductions of the engravings of urns on pp. 224 and 287.

110 HYDRIOTAPHIA ED. LLOYD ROBERTS   12° 1892

In Religio Medici and other essays...Edited...by D. Lloyd Roberts, M.D., F.R.C.P. London David Stott...1892 (see no. 40).

111 HYDRIOTAPHIA & BRAMPTON URNS ED. EVANS   8° 1893

Hydriotaphia Urn burial; with an account of some urns found at Brampton in Norfolk, by Sir Thomas Browne: with introduction and notes by Sir John Evans, K.C.B., F.R.S., F.S.A. London printed and issued by Charles Whittingham & Co. at the Chiswick press M DCCC XCIII 19·5 cm. pp. [viii], xxvi, 109, [5].

Portrait: Photogravure by Walker and Boutall of Van der Gucht's engraving, 1712 (see no. 156).

Note: Fifty copies on Japanese vellum and 450 on hand-made paper.

112 HYDRIOTAPHIA ED. G. B. M.   8° 1894

In Religio Medici: Urn Burial...London...G. Moreton...1894 (see no. 41).

113 HYDRIOTAPHIA ED. GREENHILL & HOLME   8° 1896

In Sir Thomas Browne's Religio Medici and Urn-burial MDCCCXCVI: ... J. M. Dent and Co....London (see no. 42).

114 HYDRIOTAPHIA & GARDEN OF CYRUS ED. GREENHILL   8° 1896

Sir Thomas Browne's Hydriotaphia and the Garden of Cyrus edited by the late W. A. Greenhill, M.D. Oxon. London Macmillan & Co., Ltd. New York: Macmillan & Co. 1896. 16 cm. pp. xxxi, [i], 208. [Golden Treasury Series.]

Note: Reprinted in 1906.

115 HYDRIOTAPHIA ED. HOLMES   F° 1902

In Religio Medici, Urn Burial,...edited by C. J. Holmes...The Vale Press,... London,...MCMII (see no. 46).

116 HYDRIOTAPHIA & GARDEN OF CYRUS ED. SAYLE   8° 1904

In The Works of Sir Thomas Browne Edited by Charles Sayle London Grant Richards 1904 (see no. 206).

Note: Vol. III, pp. 87–211, with reproductions in line of the engraved plates of the urns and quincunx.

117 HYDRIOTAPHIA & BRAMPTON URNS   8° 1906

In Religio Medici and other essays...London. E. Grant Richards 1906 (see no. 50).

HYDRIOTAPHIA

Urne-Buriall

OR

*A Discourse of the
Sepulchrall Urnes
lately found in
Norfolk*

By Sir Thomas Browne
D. of Physick

The
Riverside
Press
1907

118 HYDRIOTAPHIA, BRAMPTON URNS, GARDEN OF CYRUS
   ED. HERFORD   8° [1906]

   In The Religio Medici & other writings...London...J. M. Dent & Co....
   [1906] (see no. 51).

119 HYDRIOTAPHIA & GARDEN OF CYRUS
   ED. SONNENSCHEIN   12° [1906]

   In Works...with a glossary by William Swan Sonnenschein London George
   Routledge & Sons...[1906] (see no. 52).

120 HYDRIOTAPHIA ED. WALLER   8° [1906]

   In Religio Medici and Urn burial...Methuen & Co....London [1906] (see
   no. 53).

121 HYDRIOTAPHIA ED. BAYNE   8° [1906]

   In Religio Medici and other essays...with an introduction by Charles Whibley
   Blackie and Sons Ld London [1906] (see no. 54).

122 HYDRIOTAPHIA   8° 1907

   Hydriotaphia Urne-Buriall or A Difcourfe of the Sepulchrall Urnes lately found
   in Norfolk By Sir Thomas Browne D. of Phyfick The Riverfide Prefs 1907
   25 cm. pp. [ii], x, [2], 54, [4].

   Note: Title within ornamental border. Large 8°, in sixes. 385 copies printed for
   Houghton, Mifflin and Co., Boston and New York, under the supervision of Bruce
   Rogers.

122*a* GARDEN OF CYRUS &c. ED. SIEVEKING   8° 1908

   In Sir William Temple upon the Garden of Epicurus, with other xvii^th Century
   Garden Essays: Introduction by Albert Forbes Sieveking, F.S.A. Chatto and
   Windus, Publishers London 1908 15 cm. pp. lxxii, 272 (The King's Classics).

   Note: Pp. 85–162 contain *The Garden of Cyrus* and three pieces from *Miscellany Tracts*:
   (i) Upon Several Plants mentioned in Scripture. (ii) Of Garlands. (iii) On Grafting.
   The editor's remarks on Browne are on pp. xxv–xliii.

123 HYDRIOTAPHIA   8° [1911]

   In Religio Medici and other essays...London...Chapman & Hall L^td [1911]
   (see no. 56).

124 HYDRIOTAPHIA ED. MURISON   8° 1922

   Sir Thomas Browne Hydriotaphia Edited by W. Murison, M.A. Senior English
   Master, Aberdeen Grammar School Cambridge At the University Press 1922
   [Pitt Press Series] 17cm. pp. xxii, 146.

   Note: Re-issued 1933, 1937.

125 HYDRIOTAPHIA　　　　　　　　　　　　　　　　　　　　4° 1923

Hydriotaphia. Urn-burial...By Sir Thomas Browne, Physician, of Norwich. Printed & sold at the Golden Cockerel Press Waltham Saint Lawrence, Berkshire.

　　Colophon: Here ends Hydriotaphia...cxv. copies, of which cv. are for sale, printed at the Golden Cockerel Press: Finished March XVII. MCMXXIII. 26·5 cm. pp. 48, [8].

Note: Printed on Arnold's unbleached, hand-made paper. Initial letters, &c., in red. Printer's device at the end in gold. The marginal illustrations and notes are printed at the end.

126 GARDEN OF CYRUS　　　　　　　　　　　　　　　　　　4° 1923

The Garden of Cyrus...by Sir Thomas Browne, Physician, of Norwich. Printed & sold at the Golden Cockerel Press Waltham Saint Lawrence, Berkshire.

　　Colophon: Here ends the Garden of Cyrus...cxv. copies, of which cv. are for sale, printed at the Golden Cockerel Press & finished April VI. MCMXXIII. 26·5 cm. pp. 58, [6].

Note: Printed on Arnold's unbleached, hand-made paper. Initial letters in red. Printer's device at the end in gold. The marginal illustrations and notes are printed at the end.

126*a* HYDRIOTAPHIA & GARDEN OF CYRUS　　　　　　　　8° 1927

The Noel Douglas Replicas Thomas Browne Hydriotaphia...Noel Douglas 38 Great Ormond Street London W.C. [1927] 17·5 cm., pp. [vi], 112 leaves as in no. 93, 3 leaves blank.

Note: A photographic facsimile of the first edition from the copy in the British Museum lacking the *errata*. There was a special issue of 100 copies printed on hand-made paper and numbered. The unsigned bibliographical note on the title-page is by John Sparrow.

126*b* HYDRIOTAPHIA ED. WHIBLEY　　　　　　　　　　　32° 1927

Little Books edited by Charles Whibley Sir Thomas Browne's Hydriotaphia or Urne-burial Published by Peter Davies London, 1927 12·2 cm., pp. [ii], v, [i], 98, [2].

126*c* HYDRIOTAPHIA & GARDEN OF CYRUS ED. KEYNES　　8° 1929

In The Works of Sir Thomas Browne Ed. Geoffrey Keynes Vol. 4 London: Faber & Gwyer 1929 (see no. 207*a*).

126*d* URNE BURIAL & GARDEN OF CYRUS ED. CARTER　　4° 1932

Urne Burial and The Garden of Cyrus by Sir Thomas Browne with thirty drawings by Paul Nash Edited with an introduction by John Carter Published by Cassell and Co. Ltd. La Belle Sauvage London MCMXXXII 30·5 cm., pp. xx, 146, [2], in gatherings of ten.

Note: This very beautiful edition contains the best text that had yet been printed, with new readings derived from examination of six copies of the first edition containing corrections made by the hand of the author. An edition of 215 numbered copies was printed by the Curwen Press on Barcham Green's hand-made paper in Monotype Bembo. The title-page and large headings are in Bruce Rogers' Monotype Centaur. The drawings by Nash were reproduced in collotype by Whittingham and Griggs and stencilled in colour at the Curwen Press. The binding by Nevetts Ltd. is vellum with brown morocco inlay, with designs in gold on the covers after Nash. At the end is an *apparatus criticus* and an Appendix in which the errors of previous editors are remorselessly exposed; yet there are four errors in Carter's text. The publisher reports that part of the edition (20–30 copies) was destroyed by enemy action in 1941. Copies bound according to the original design were still available in 1965 through the Folio Society of London. The original prospectus offered one copy in two volumes at 350 guineas, the second volume containing all Nash's original drawings.

126*e* URNE BURIALL CHAP. V ED. CARTER 8° 1946

The last chapter of Urne Buriall by Sir Thomas Browne [Cambridge the Rampant Lions Press 1946] 20·5 cm., 10 unnumbered leaves.

Note: An edition of 125 copies was printed on blue tinted paper, stitched in stiff paper wrappers. The cover design and title-page are by John Piper. The text is based on that of Carter's edition of 1932.

126*f* URNE BURIALL & GARDEN OF CYRUS 8° 1958

Sir Thomas Browne Urne Buriall and The Garden of Cyrus Edited by John Carter Cambridge at the University Press 1958 19·8 cm., pp. viii, 120.

Note: The text is based on that of 1932 improved by use of readings in six more copies with corrections by the author. Nevertheless, eight gross errors have escaped the editor's eye. All the marginal notes have been omitted.

126*g* HYDRIOTAPHIA, BRAMPTON URNS & GARDEN OF CYRUS 8° 1962

In Religio Medici and Other Writings... J M Dent... [1962] [Everyman's Library, no. 92] (see no. 58*m*).

126*h* URN BURIAL 1963

In Seventeenth-Century Prose and Poetry. Second Edition. Selected and edited by Alexander M. Witherspoon and Frank J. Warnke. New York and Burlingame, California Harcourt Brace & World. 1963. pp. xxvi, 1094.

Note: Previously published in 1929 and 1946. In this edition *Urn Burial* is given in full.

126*i* HYDRIOTAPHIA & GARDEN OF CYRUS ED. KEYNES 8° 1964

> *In* The Works of Sir Thomas Browne Ed. Geoffrey Keynes Vol. 1 London Faber & Faber [1964] (see no. 207*c*).

126*k* HYDRIOTAPHIA & GARDEN OF CYRUS ED. MARTIN 8° 1964

> *In* Religio Medici and Other Works ed. L. C. Martin Oxford Clarendon Press 1964 (see no. 58*p*).

126*l* HYDRIOTAPHIA & GARDEN OF CYRUS ED. HUNTLEY 8° 1966

> Sir Thomas Browne Hydriotaphia (Urn burial) and The Garden of Cyrus Edited by F. L. Huntley The University of Michigan New York Appleton–Century–Crofts Division of Meredith Publishing Company [1966] 17·5 cm., pp. xiv, [ii], 118, [2].
>
> *Note:* With Introduction, Principal Dates in the life of Browne, Glossary and Bibliography.

126*m* HYDRIOTAPHIA CHAP. V: FRENCH 1929

> Sir Thomas Browne, Chapitre v de Hydriotaphia précédé d'Opinions de S. T. Coleridge sur Sir Thomas Browne. Traduit de l'Anglais par Valéry Larbaud. *In* Commerce, Cahiers trimestriels publiés par les soins de Paul Valéry, Léon-Paul Fargue, Valéry Larbaud, Automne 1929, Cahier xxi, pp. 185–205.

126*n* HYDRIOTAPHIA: ITALIAN 1931

> *In* Tomaso Browne—Religio Medici e Hydriotaphia—Introduzione e traduzione di R. Piccoli (see no. 72*a*).

IV

Miscellany Tracts

BIBLIOGRAPHICAL PREFACE

The *Miscellany Tracts* were edited shortly after their author's death by Archbishop Tenison, to whom Browne's own transcripts were handed by his son. As the editor remarked in his Preface, he had selected them out of 'many disordered papers'; also that they were written as letters, though he could not ascertain the names of the recipients. They were in fact written as answers to enquiries addressed to Browne by various correspondents. John Evelyn noted in his copy of the book that 'most of these letters were written to Nicholas Bacon', and that the second, 'Of Garlands', was addressed to himself. Another, 'Of Artificial Hills', was in reply to Sir William Dugdale, although erroneously headed in the printed text 'My Honoured Friend Mr. E.D.'s query'. This was used by Dugdale in his *History of Imbanking and Draining* (1662) (see no. 255). Manuscript drafts of all the *Miscellany Tracts* are extant, twelve in the British Museum[1] and one in the Bodleian.[2] All of these were used by Wilkin and myself in the collation of our texts.

When Wilkin was at work on his edition, only the issue of 1684 was known to him, though he acquired a copy of the first issue, which had belonged to Evelyn, in time to mention it in the preface to vol. IV of the *Works*.

The *Tracts* have been reprinted as a whole only in the various collected editions of the *Works*, having been translated into Dutch for that of 1688. In addition the *Musæum Clausum* was printed in the small volume edited by James Crossley in 1822, and 'Of Garlands' was printed by the Gehenna Press in 1962.

[1] Sloane MSS. 1827, 1839, 1874.   [2] MS. Rawl. D58.

CERTAIN

MISCELLANY

TRACTS.

Written by
THOMAS BROWN, Kt,
and Doctour of Physick ;
late of *NORWICH*.

LONDON,
Printed for *Charles Mearn*, Bookseller
to his most Sacred Majesty,
MDCLXXXIII.

127 MISCELLANY TRACTS [Wing B 5151] 8° 1683

Title, within double lines: Certain Miſcellany Tracts. [*rule*] Written by Thomas
Brown, K^t, and Doctour of Phyſick; late of Norwich. [*rule*] London, Printed
for Charles Mearn, Bookſeller to his moſt Sacred Majeſty, MDCLXXXIII.

Collation: A⁴ B–P⁸; 116 leaves.

Contents: A1 title; A2*a*–A3*b The Publiſher to the Reader* signed *Tho. Teniſon;* A4 *The
Contents of theſe Tracts,* with *Errata,* 7 lines, at the bottom of A4*b;* B1*a*–P4*a* (pp. 1–215)
Tracts, I–XIII; P4*b* blank; P5*a*–P7*b Index;* P8 blank.

Frontispiece: Engraved portrait in an oval, unlettered or lettered on a pedestal below:
P. Vandrebanc F | S^r· Thomas Browne M.D. Plate-mark 150 × 103 mm.

List of Tracts: I. Observations upon several Plants mention'd in Scripture.
  II. Of Garlands, and Coronary or Garland-plants.
  III. Of the Fishes eaten by our Saviour with his Disciples after the Resurrection
    from the dead.
  IV. An Answer to certain Queries relating to Fishes, Birds, Insects.
  V. Of Hawks and Falconry, ancient and modern.
  VI. Of Cymbals, &c.
  VII. Of Ropalic or Gradual Verses, &c.
  VIII. Of Languages, and particularly of the Saxon-Tongue.
  IX. Of Artificial Hills, Mounts or Boroughs in many parts of England...
  X. Of Troas, what place is meant by that Name. Also of the situations of Sodom,
    Gomorrah, Zeboim, in the Dead Sea.
  XI. Of the Answers of the Oracle of Apollo at Delphos to Crœsus King of Lydia.
  XII. A Prophecy concerning the future state of several Nations; in a Letter...
  XIII. Musæum Clausum, or, Bibliotheca Abscondita...

Note: This preliminary issue of the *Miscellany Tracts* is comparatively uncommon. Some
copies have the appearance of having been bound for 'presentation', being in red
morocco or elaborately tooled bindings in the 'Mearne' style. An additional feature
suggesting this is the presence of impressions of the portrait printed 'before letters'.
At least one copy has the signature of Dr. Edward Browne on the recto of the portrait.
It is believed that Charles Mearne seldom published books alone, and probably he
reprinted the title-page in order to include the name of Henry Bonwick (no. 128).

Copies: BLO, CLN,[1] GUL, K[2], KCCK;[3] MH,[4] MMO, PML,[5] PUL, YML.

128 MISCELLANY TRACTS [Wing B 5152] 8° 1684

Titles, within double lines: Certain Miſcellany Tracts. [*rule*] Written by Thomas
Brown, K^t, and Doctour of Phyſick; late of Norwich. [*rule*] London, Printed
for Charles Mearne, and are to be ſold by Henry Bonwick, at the Red Lyon,
in St. Paul's Church-Yard, MDCLXXXIV.

[1] John Evelyn's copy with his signature, motto and annotations.
[2] In red morocco binding and proof of portrait 'before letters'.
[3] In elaborately tooled red morocco binding by a binder who worked for Pepys.
[4] In red morocco binding with proof of portrait 'before letters'.
[5] In binding similar to the KCCK copy with proof of the portrait 'before letters'.

Collation, contents, frontispiece: As in no. 127.

Note: The sheets of no. 127 with a reprint title-page.

Copies: BLO(2), BM, CLN, FLWC, GUL, K(3), RCS, ULC; MH(3), MMO, NYAM, PUL, YUL.

129 MISCELLANY TRACTS f° 1686

Sub-title: Certain Miſcellany Tracts. [*rule*] Written by Thomas Brown, Kt and Doctour of Phyſick; late of Norwich. [*ornaments between rules*] London, Printed for Charles Mearn, Bookſeller to His moſt Sacred Majeſty, MDCLXXXVI.

Collation: Sss–Zzz⁴, Aaaa-Dddd⁴ Eeee²; 42 leaves.

Contents: Sss1 title; Sss2 *The Publiſher to the Reader*; Sss3 *The Contents*; Sss4*a*–Dddd4*a* (pp. 1–73) text; Dddd4*b* blank; Eeee1*a*–Eeee2*a Index*; Eeee2*b* blank.

Note: In *The Works of Sir T. B.* (f°, 1686) (see no. 201). Pp. 69–73 are numbered 99–103.

130 MISCELLANY TRACTS: DUTCH 4° 1688

Sub-title: Mengelſtoffe, Beſtaande in Verſcheydenerleye Verhandelingen. Beſchreeven door Thomas Brown. M.D.

Collation: Dd✳2-4, Ee✳–Qq✳⁴, Rr✳1-2; 53 leaves.

Contents: Dd✳2 sub-title; Dd✳3*a*–4*b De Uytgeever Aan den Leezer*; Ee✳1 (pp. 217–18) *De Inhoud Deezer Verhandelingen*; Ee✳2*a*–Rr✳2*b* (pp. 219–316) text.

Note: In *Alle de Werken* (t' Amsterdam, 1688), for which see no. 202.

130*a* OF ARTIFICIAL HILLS 8° 1736

In Hydriotaphia: or, Urn-Burial…The Fourth Edition. London: for E. Curll, 1736 (see no. 99).

131 MUSÆUM CLAUSUM ED. CROSSLEY 12° 1822

In Tracts, by Sir Thomas Browne,…William Blackwood, Edinburgh; and T. Cadell, London. MDCCCXXII (see no. 100).

132 MISCELLANY TRACTS ED. WILKIN 8° 1836

In Sir Thomas Browne's Works…Ed. Simon Wilkin…London William Pickering…1836 (see no. 203).

Note: In vol. IV, pp. 115–250 Wilkin gives a reprint of the *Tracts*, and appends Sir T. B.'s remarks on *Iceland* and the *Miscellanies* from the *Posthumous Works*, 1712. He has collated the text of all the *Tracts* with MSS and has added all the important variations in footnotes.

133 MISCELLANY TRACTS ED. WILKIN 8° 1852

In Sir Thomas Browne's Works…Ed. Simon Wilkin…London: H. G. Bohn…1852 (see no. 205).

Frontispiece to MISCELLANY TRACTS 1683
'proof before letters'

134 MISCELLANY TRACTS ED. SAYLE 8° 1907

In The Works of Sir Thomas Browne Ed. Charles Sayle. Volume III Edinburgh John Grant 1907 (see nos. 206, 207).

Note: Pp. 213–365 give a reprint of the *Tracts* from the text of 1684.

134*a* MISCELLANY TRACTS ED. KEYNES 8° 1931

In The Works of Sir Thomas Browne Ed. Geoffrey Keynes Volume five... London Faber & Faber Limited...1931 (see no. 207*a*).

Note: Printed from the text of 1683 with variant readings and additional passages from manuscripts.

134*b* OF GARLANDS 8° 1962

Title in red and black within a wreath of oakleaves printed in green: Of Garlands and Coronary Plants Thomas Browne to John Evelyn Esq F.R.S.

Colophon: Of this keepsake 500 copies have been printed for the Smith College Museum of Art at the Gehenna Press in Northampton Massach[etts] MCMLXII

Collation: One gathering of 8 leaves without signature or pagination in printed green paper wrappers, untrimmed. 22·8 cm.

Contents: f1 blank; f2 title; f3–5 text; f6*a* colophon; f6*b*–f8*b* blank.

Note: Printed under the direction of Leonard Baskin. Some copies contain an added slip stating that the Smith College Museum of Art had permitted the overprinting of 250 copies for presentation.

134*c* MISCELLANY TRACTS ED. KEYNES 8° 1964

In The Works of Sir Thomas Browne Ed. Geoffrey Keynes Volume III... London Faber and Faber Limited [1964] (see no. 207*c*).

Note: A reprint of the text of 134*a*.

V

A Letter to a Friend

BIBLIOGRAPHICAL PREFACE

A LETTER TO A FRIEND was first printed as a folio pamphlet of six leaves by the author's son, Dr. Edward Browne. In Arber's *Term Catalogues*, II, 306, is the following entry: '1690 Hilary Term. Reprinted. The Works of the Learned Sir T. B. Knight. To which is added, A Letter to a Friend, upon the Occasion of the Death of his intimate Friend: never before published. Folio.' This suggests that *A Letter to a Friend* was printed in folio in order that it might be bound with unsold copies of the *Works* (1686) (no. 201), perhaps with a new general title-page. The name of the publisher, Charles Brome, appeared also in the imprint of the *Works*, and the style of printing conforms closely to that of the earlier volume. The *Letter* is, however, very seldom found in this position. One is in my collection in a contemporary binding, another in a modern binding is in the British Museum, and I have heard of only two others.

It was formerly supposed that *A Letter to a Friend* was written late in Browne's life, and it was therefore placed after *Christian Morals* in collected editions of the *Works*. This view has had to be revised since the publication of Professor F. L. Huntley's *Sir Thomas Browne* (1962). It had always been plain that the *Letter* was addressed to someone whose 'intimate friend' had died of phthisis. It was also clear from the wealth of personal details that Browne was not describing a fictitious character, but was making a literary composition out of a true story for the gratification of a friend. He been in attendance on the patient and wished to console the dead man's friend, who had been absent at the time of the illness. It had always seemed probable that the two characters concerned might be identified, but this was not done until Professor F. L. Huntley put forward convincing reasons for believing that the patient was Robert Loveday, a man of letters and a member of the Loveday family of Chediston, or Cheston, in Suffolk, and that his older friend was Sir John Pettus, owner of Cheston Hall. Loveday was a talented writer, who had died of phthisis at the age of thirty-five in December 1656. He had translated almost half of Gauthier de La Calprenède's *Cléopâtre* (1647), the first part being published in 1652 as *Hymen's Præludia, or Love's Masterpiece*. There were in all twelve parts of this long prose romance, but Loveday lived to translate and publish only the first five (1652–6), the rest being completed by J. Coles. After Loveday's death his brother, Anthony, published in 1659 a volume of his letters (see no. 244) containing references to 'Dr. B. of Norwich', which almost certainly means Browne. The letters are preceded by one from Sir John Pettus urging Anthony to publish them. There is even one letter (CXLVII) in the series of a different character from the others and this may well have been addressed to Dr. Thomas Browne himself.

Sir John Pettus (1613–90), though Squire of Cheston, lived at Rackheath, only four and a half miles north-east of Norwich. It is clear from Loveday's letters that he and Pettus were good friends and references in Browne's letters show that he and Pettus were also friends, if not doctor and patient. As a young man Pettus became interested in geology and minerals and he developed into being an authority on mines. He was a royalist and contributed generously to the King's cause during the Civil War, but in 1655 under Cromwell was appointed deputy-governor of the royal mines in Wales and the west country. He is likely, therefore, to have been absent from his East Anglian home at the time of Loveday's death in 1656. His preoccupation with mines and mining led to his writing a book on the subject, *Fodinæ Regales* (London, 1670).

The third part of *Hymen's Præludia*, published in 1655, provides some evidence of Loveday's relations with Sir John Pettus, and most probably with Browne. The book is dedicated to Pettus's wife, Elizabeth, and her sister, Lady Cramond. Following an 'Address to the Reader' is a letter beginning 'Honest Robin' and signed 'Thy affectionate friend Jo. Pettus'. The next leaf has a set of six lines addressed to Loveday on his book and signed 'Ma. Browne Doc. Med.'. The last two lines run:

> The Garland's thine, O give me leave to say
> I Like thy Dawn, but better LOVE thy DAY.

The pun is trite, but it is in the manner of the time, and there is no strong reason for rejecting Browne's authorship.

Except for the evidence provided by *Hymen's Præludia*, these considerations were developed in detail by Professor Huntley, all tending to show that Browne probably wrote *A Letter to a Friend* in 1657 at about the same time as *Hydriotaphia* and a year or two before *The Garden of Cyrus*. There were many reasons, personal and political, why Browne's intimate study of his patient and of the character of his friend, to whom he gave much outspoken advice on the conduct of his life, could not be published while he was alive. There is evidence, however, that he revised it as late as 1672, when he referred to Duloir's *Travels* (1654) as being published 'yet scarce twenty years ago'. He may also have added at this time the passage on the 'Morgellons', otherwise known as 'Masquelons', a curious condition seen in children in Languedoc due to infestation of hair follicles on the back by a parasite, *Demodex follicularum*. This Browne would have seen when a student at Montpellier.

The only manuscript version is among the Sloane MSS in the British Museum. This is a shorter draft with verbal differences and some additional passages. It may be assumed that the printed text was the final form intended by Browne, but it could not be printed even after his death, Sir John Pettus having survived him. The manuscript would have passed in 1682 to Browne's son and executor, Dr. Edward Browne, and it is significant that he refrained from printing it until 1690, the year Pettus died.

A fragment concerning consumptions, apparently composed for this work, though not used, was found copied in a commonplace book compiled by Browne's daughters, Mary and Elizabeth. The book has been in my collection since 1918, and the passage has been printed with the *Letter* in my editions of the *Works* (see *Note* opposite).

A Letter to a Friend was first reprinted in the volume of *Posthumous Works* in 1712, and the concluding portion was incorporated in *Christian Morals*, first published in 1716. A century later it attracted the attention of James Crossley, at whose instance it was twice reprinted, in 1821 and 1822. It has been frequently reprinted since that date, but has only once been published separately, in 1924. It has only once been translated into any foreign language—Swedish— together with *Religio Medici*.

Note: Professor Endicott of Toronto has recently endorsed my inclusion by finding a place for its insertion marked in the manuscript.

A
LETTER
TO A
FRIEND,

Upon occasion of the

DEATH

OF HIS

Intimate Friend.

By the Learned

Sir *THOMAS BROWN*, Knight,

Doctor of Physick, late of *Norwich*.

LONDON:

Printed for *Charles Brome* at the *Gun* at the West-End
of S. *Paul's* Church-yard. 1 6 9 0.

[reduced]

135 LETTER TO A FRIEND [Wing B 5158]   f° 1690

Title: A Letter to a Friend, Upon occaſion of the Death of his Intimate Friend. [*rule*] By the Learned Sir Thomas Brown, Knight, Doĉtor of Phyſick, late of Norwich. [*double rule*] London: Printed for Charles Brome at the Gun at the Weſt-End of S. Paul's Church-yard. 1690.

Collation: A–C²; 6 leaves.

Contents: A1 title; A2a–C2b (pp. 3–12) text.

Note: With marginal notes, which have often been cut into by the binder, the book usually having been bound up with other folio tracts.

Copies: BM(2),[1] BLO, CLN, K(2),[2] ULL; MH, MMO, PUL.

136 LETTER TO A FRIEND   8° 1712

In Poſthumous Works Of the Learned Sir Thomas Browne, Kt. M.D.... London: Printed for E. Curll...1712 (see no. 156).

Note: On signatures d1–g4, pp. 25–56, without sub-title. Also in the re-issues of this volume, 1722, &c.

137 LETTER TO A FRIEND ED. CROSSLEY   8° 1821

In Blackwood's Edinburgh Magazine. Vol. IX. Edinburgh. 1821. pp. 549–55. 'Sir Thomas Browne's Letter to a Friend.'

Note: Reprinted in full except for the concluding paragraphs, which were used in the *Christian Morals*. Edited by James Crossley, whose name does not appear.

138 LETTER TO A FRIEND ED. CROSSLEY   12° 1822

In Tracts, by Sir Thomas Browne,...William Blackwood, Edinburgh,... MDCCCXXII (see no. 100).

139 LETTER TO A FRIEND ED. YOUNG   8° 1831

In Miscellaneous Works of Sir Thomas Browne...[Ed. Rev. Alexander Young, D.D.] Cambridge [U.S.A.]: Hilliard and Brown...MDCCCXXXI (see no. 19).

140 LETTER TO A FRIEND   8° 1836

In Sir Thomas Browne's Works...Ed. Simon Wilkin...London William Pickering...1836 (see no. 203).

Note: Vol. IV, pp. 33–51. Wilkin gives in footnotes some additional passages from MSS, but omits the latter part (from p. 48, *Posthumous Works*) since it was included in the *Christian Morals* (1716).

[1] One in a nineteenth-century binding with the *Works* (1686).
[2] One in an untouched contemporary binding with the *Works* (1686).

141 LETTER TO A FRIEND ED. GARDINER   8° 1845

In Religio Medici together with A Letter to a Friend...Edited by Henry Gardiner, M.A....London William Pickering 1845 (see no. 26).

Note: The editor follows Wilkin in omitting the latter part.

142 LETTER TO A FRIEND ED. WILKIN   8° 1852

In The Works of Sir Thomas Browne...Ed. Simon Wilkin...London: H. G. Bohn...MDCCCLII (see no. 205).

Note: Vol. III, pp. 61–80. A reprint of no. 140.

143 LETTER TO A FRIEND ED. FIELDS   8° 1862

In Religio Medici...and Other Papers...Boston Ticknor and Fields 1862 (see no. 29).

144 LETTER TO A FRIEND ED. WILLIS BUND   8° 1869

In Religio Medici, Hydriotaphia, and the Letter to a Friend...with an introduction and notes by J. W. Willis Bund...London: Sampson Low,...[1869] (see no. 32).

145 LETTER TO A FRIEND ED. FIELDS   8° 1878

In Religio Medici A Letter to a Friend...and other papers...Boston Robert Brothers 1878 (see no. 35).

146 LETTER TO A FRIEND ED. GREENHILL   8° 1881

In Sir Thomas Browne's Religio Medici Letter to a Friend &c....Edited by W. A. Greenhill M.D....London Macmillan and Co. 1881 (see no. 36).

147 LETTER TO A FRIEND ED. SYMONDS   8° 1886

In Sir Thomas Browne's Religio Medici...and other essays. Edited...by John Addington Symonds. London: Walter Scott...1886 (see no. 39).

148 LETTER TO A FRIEND ED. LLOYD ROBERTS   12° 1892

In Religio Medici and other essays...Edited...by D. Lloyd Roberts, M.D., F.R.C.P. London David Stott...1892 (see no. 40).

149 LETTER TO A FRIEND ED. G. B. M.   8° 1894

In Religio Medici: Urn Burial...London...G. Moreton...1844 (see no. 41).

150 LETTER TO A FRIEND ED. LLOYD ROBERTS   8° 1898

In Religio Medici and other essays...Edited by D. Lloyd Roberts, M.D., F.R.C.P. London Smith Elder and Co....1898 (see no. 44).

151 LETTER TO A FRIEND ED. HOLMES f° 1902

In Religio Medici...and other essays...edited by C. J. Holmes...The Vale Press...London...MCMII (see no. 46).

152 LETTER TO A FRIEND ED. SAYLE 8° 1904

In The Works of Sir Thomas Browne Edited by Charles Sayle London Grant Richards 1904 (see nos. 206, 207).

Note: Vol. III, pp. 367–94, in full.

153 LETTER TO A FRIEND ED. HERFORD 8° [1906]

In The Religio Medici & other writings...London...J. M. Dent & Co.... [1906] (see no. 51).

154 LETTER TO A FRIEND 8° [1911]

In Religio Medici and other essays...London...Chapman & Hall L^{td} [1911] (see no. 56).

155 LETTER TO A FRIEND & CHRISTIAN MORALS 4° 1923

A Letter to a Friend upon the Occasion of the Death of an Intimate Friend, together with Christian Morals: by Sir Thomas Browne, Physician, of Norwich. Printed & sold at the Golden Cockerel Press, Waltham Saint Lawrence, Berkshire.

Colophon: Here end A Letter to a Friend & Christian Morals: cxv. copies, of which cv. are for sale, printed at the Golden Cockerel Press: finished May XIX. MCMXXIII. 26 cm. pp. 68, [8].

Note: The marginal notes are printed at the end. Printed on Arnold's unbleached hand-made paper. Initials and headings in red. Printer's device at the end in gold.

155*a* LETTER TO A FRIEND f° 1924

The Haslewood Reprints No. 1 Sir Thomas Browne's Letter to a Friend 1690 London Printed for Frederick Etchells and Hugh Macdonald at 1a Kensington Place W. 8. 1924 34 cm., pp. [iv], 12.

Note: The first separate reprint. An edition of 425 numbered copies was printed line for line in type facsimile, except that errors in the original edition have been corrected and s substituted for long-s.

155*b* LETTER TO A FRIEND ED. KEYNES 8° 1928

In The Works of Sir Thomas Browne Edited by Geoffrey Keynes London Faber and Gwyer Limited...1928 (see no. 207*a*).

Note: The fragment on consumptions from the commonplace book of Elizabeth Browne (see no. 196) was first included here.

155*c* LETTER TO A FRIEND ED. HERFORD   8° 1951

In Religio Medici and Other Writings by Sir Thomas Browne With a new
introduction by Frank L. Huntley New York...London: J. M. Dent and
Sons, Limited 1951 (see no. 58*e*)

155*d* LETTER TO A FRIEND   8° 1962

In Religio Medici and Other Writings...J M Dent...[1962] [Everyman's
Library, no. 92] (see no. 58*m*). Re-issued in 1966, ed. M. R. Ridley.

155*e* LETTER TO A FRIEND ED. KEYNES   8° 1964

In the Works of Sir Thomas Browne edited by Geoffrey Keynes London
Faber & Faber Limited [1964] (see no. 207*c*)

Note: Vol. I, pp. 101–21, placed after *Religio Medici* in accordance with the revised dating.

155*f* LETTER TO A FRIEND ED. MARTIN   8° 1964

In Sir Thomas Browne Religio Medici and Other Works Edited by L. C. Martin
Oxford At the Clarendon Press 1964 (see no. 58*p*).

Note: The shorter MS. version of the *Letter* is printed in an appendix with a reproduction
of a page of the MS. The editor has for the first time correctly placed the marginal
note, 'See *Picotus de Rheumatismo*'. This note is placed at the bottom of p. 5 of the first
edition apparently referring to 'the *Morgellions*'. Its proper place is at the middle of
the first paragraph on p. 6 referring to 'sharp and corroding Rheums'.

155*g* A LETTER TO A FRIEND: SWEDISH   1948

In Religio Medici samt Ett brev till en vän i anledning av hans nära väns död
Översatt av Ernst Abramson [1948] (see no. 72*c*).

VI

Posthumous Works

BIBLIOGRAPHICAL PREFACE

The volume of *Posthumous Works* published in 1712 seems to have been a some-what hasty gathering of miscellaneous pieces, one of which, *A Letter to a Friend*, had been printed before. The preface stated that for these 'Remains' the editor was indebted to 'Owen Brigstock Esq; Grandson by Marriage to the Author', but it seems that Brigstocke's hand had in fact been forced by the bookseller Edmund Curll. Browne's daughter, Elizabeth Lyttelton, wrote in a letter[1] to her niece, the Countess of Buchan, under the date 19 April [1713]: 'There is lately a small thing of my fathers put out. I know not well where the bookseller had it, he was printing it by a coppy, & then Mr. Brigstock gave him that writ by my fathers own hand. My brother not putting it out, it had not bin dun now by any of us: my Cozen Tenison giving the Plate for his Monument...' It seems that Edmund Curll was the editor and that Richard Rawlinson had some hand in the matter. On 21 December 1711 Thomas Hearne wrote to Rawlinson: 'I have not yet had time to step into the Museum & indeed I am not now inclin'd to meddle in Sr. Thomas Browne's Repertorium 'till I know who the person is that publishes it.'[2] Soon afterwards he wrote again: 'I look upon Sr. Thomas Browne as a better Philosopher than Antiquary. However his Repertorium will be of use. But I like it never the better because a Bookseller is the Publisher. I see no need of Glosses unless a compleat Account be intended. That will require more Learning & Skill than a Bookseller is Master of.'[3] On 16 January 1712 Hearne wrote again: 'Mr. Richard Rawlinson of St. John's College, now Bach. of Arts there, but lately Gentleman Commoner, is printing at London Sr. Thomas Browne's Repertorium, or Account of the Monumts. of the Cathedral of Norwich. He hath given it to a Bookseller, wch. I do not at all like in him, it being not a sign of his Friendship to me, who printed two things for him before, (in Leland) & I shld. have been glad to have done this, provided it be (as he hath told me) undr the Author's own Hand, & contains things that are really valuable, as I believe it may.' Some years later Hearne added a note: 'It is a very poor Book, and I am now glad that I had it not to print.'[4]

Further information concerning the volume is afforded by a passage from a letter written by Bishop Tanner to Dr. Charlet, Master of University College, Oxford, 20 October 1712: 'Curll the bookseller, has bought of Dr. Browne's executors, some papers of Sir Thomas Browne, one of which is some account of the Cathedral, which he is printing under the title of the Antiquities of Norwich. If I had perfectly liked the thing, I should not have been backward to have given a cut; but it was hurried by him into the press without advising with anybody here, or with Mr. Le Neve, who has great collections that way. However, out of

---

[1] Sold at Sotheby's 17 December 1956, lot 82 (Pickering and Chatto, £42).

[2] Hearne's *Remarks and Collections*, edited by C. E. Doble for the Oxford Historical Society (Oxford, 1889), III, 284.

[3] *Ibid.* p. 288.   [4] *Ibid.*

regard to Mr. Hase, the herald, the Dean has suffered them to reprint his catalogue of Bishops, Deans and Prebendaries, and, I think, to send a list of the Chancellours and Archdeacons.'[1] This also evidently refers to the *Repertorium*, which, with a continuation said to be by John Hase[2] and two pieces by other writers, forms the most considerable part of the volume. This was mentioned by Archbishop Tenison in his preface to *Miscellany Tracts*, 1683: 'It was written merely for private use: and the relations of the author expect such justice from those into whose hands some imperfect copies of it are fallen, that, without their consent, they forbear the publishing of it.' As Wilkin points out, however, the work does not pretend to be a history of the antiquities of the church, but is only a brief account of the monuments to be found there.

Two manuscripts of *Repertorium*, both entirely in the author's hand, are extant. They are bound together in nineteenth-century leather and were bequeathed by William Fitch, F.S.A., to the Castle Museum, Norwich (now in the Norwich Record Office). The earlier one, consisting of 22 leaves, 19 × 14 cm., has the title: 'Some account of the tombs and monuments in the cathedrall church of Norwich 1679.' The other, 36 leaves, 19 × 14 cm., is entitled: 'Repertorium or some account of the tombs & monuments in the cathedrall Church of Norwich 1680.' *Repertorium* was never reprinted until it was included by Wilkin, with additional notes, in his edition of the *Works*.

The author of the Life at the beginning of the *Posthumous Works* is not indicated, but probably it was compiled by the publisher. Appended to it are valuable 'Minutes for the life of Sir Thomas Browne' by his friend John Whitefoot, late Rector of Heigham, in Norfolk. These were mostly incorporated by Johnson in his Life of Browne.

The *Miscellanies* include, with two extracts from commonplace books, *An Account of Iceland*, compiled at the request of the Royal Society largely through correspondence with Theodore Jonas, a Lutheran minister resident in the island. Three of the letters from Jonas are printed by Wilkin, IV, 256–69. Browne's letters to Jonas are not known to have survived. The correspondence with Dugdale includes only a portion of the letters that passed between them; a number of others will be found recorded in the section of Letters.

Brampton Urns, printed in *Posthumous Works* for the first time, forms a short sequel to *Hydriotaphia*. Of this piece there are three manuscript drafts,[3] all of which were used by Wilkin in the preparation of his text in 1836. It had previously been printed by Curll with *Hydriotaphia* in 1736 (no. 99), and has been added to some of the recent editions of that work.

As recorded below, one leaf of the anonymous Life has usually been cancelled and replaced. The cancelled leaf stated that Browne came to Norwich 'by the Persuasions of Mr. Thomas Lushington, his sometime Tutor'. On the reprinted leaf Lushington's name is replaced by those of Sir Nicholas Bacon, Sir Justinian Lewyn and Sir Charles Le Gros, all distinguished residents in Norfolk. Probably

---

[1] Ballard's MS. Letters in the Bodleian Library, IV, 58.   [2] Wilkin, IV, 3 n.
[3] BM Sloane MSS. 1862 f. 26, 1869 f. 60. Bodleian Library MS. Rawl. D 191.

both statements are true. Responsibility was first attributed to Lushington by Anthony Wood in *Athenæ Oxonienses* (1691).

The *Posthumous Works* was more than once re-issued with new title-pages, but was never reprinted as a whole. Three issues, dated 1712, 1722 and 1723, are described here. Wilkin stated that other issues dated 1715 and 1721 are mentioned, but I have found no confirmation of this. The volume is said by Kippis[1] to have been printed at Norwich, but the evidence for this statement is not known. As noted below, the make-up of the volume presents a difficult problem to the present-day bibliographer no less than it must have to the contemporary binders.

[1] *Biographia Britannica* (1730).

POSTHUMOUS
WORKS

Of the Learned

Sir *Thomas Browne*, K^t. M.D.

Late of NORWICH:

Printed from his Original *Manuscripts*.

V I Z.

I. REPERTORIUM: Or, The Antiquities of the Cathedral Church of NORWICH.

II. An Account of some URNES, &c. found at *Brampton* in *Norfolk*, *Anno* 1667.

III. LETTERS between Sir WILLIAM DUGDALE and Sir THO. BROWNE.

IV. MISCELLANIES.

To which is prefix'd his LIFE.

There is also added,

Antiquitates Capellæ D. JOHANNIS Evangelistæ; *hodie Scholæ Regiæ Norwicensis.* *Authore* JOHANNE BURTON, A.M. *ejusdem Ludimagistro.*

Illustrated with *Prospects, Portraitures,* Draughts of *Tombs, Monuments,* &c.

LONDON:

Printed for *E. Curll,* at the *Dial* and *Bible;* and *R. Gosling* at the *Mitre* in *Fleetstreet.* 1712.

Price 6 *s.*

156 POSTHUMOUS WORKS   8° 1712

Title, within double lines: Poſthumous Works Of the Learned Sir Thomas Browne, Kᵗ· M.D. Late of Norwich: Printed from his Original Manuſcripts. Viz.
 I. Repertorium: Or, The Antiquities of the Cathedral Church of Norwich.
 II. An Account of ſome Urnes, &c. found at Brampton in Norfolk, Anno 1667.
 III. Letters between Sir William Dugdale and Sir Tho. Browne.
 IV. Miscellanies.
[*rule*] To which is prefix'd his Life. [*rule*] There is alſo added, Antiquitates Capellæ D. Johannis Evangeliſtæ; hodie Scholæ Regiæ Norwicenſis. Authore Johanne Burton, A.M. ejuſdem Ludimagiſtro. [*rule*] Illuſtrated with Proſpeſts, Portraitures, Draughts of Tombs, Monuments, &c. [*rule*] London: Printed for E. Curll, at the Dial and Bible; and R. Goſling at the Mitre in Fleetſtreet. 1712. Price 6s.

Collation: Π² a–e⁴ χ¹ A–K⁴ L³ A⁴ [A]–[B]⁴ a–g⁴ A–H⁴; 138 leaves. First a 2 has usually been cancelled and replaced.

Contents: Π1 title, verso blank; Π2*a Preface*; Π2*b Contents*; a1*a*–e3*a* (pp. i–xxxvii) *The Life of Sir Thomas Browne, Kt.*; e3*b*–e4*a* (pp. xxxviii–xl) *The Diploma given to Sir Thomas Browne by the College of Physicians*; χ1*a* sub-title to *Repertorium*; χ1*b Bishop Hall's Account of the Sacrilege and Prophanation of this Church, in the Time of the Civil Wars*; B1*a*–L1*b* (pp. 1–74) text of *Repertorium*; L2*a*–L3*b Index*; A1*a* sub-title to *Miscellanies*, verso blank; A2*a* [sig. A]–A4*b* (pp. 3–8) *An Account of Island*; [A]1*a*–[B]4*b* (pp. 1–16) *Concerning some Urnes found in Brampton-Field, in Norfolk, Ann. 1667*, the plate of *A Roman Urn* being printed on p. 11 [B]2*a*, verso blank; a1*a*–c3*b* (pp. 1–22) *Some Letters Which pass'd between Mr. Dugdale, and Dʳ Browne; Ann. 1658*; c4*a*–*b* (pp. 23–4) *Against Censure, Upon Reading Hudibras*; d1*a*–g4*b* (pp. 25–56) *A Letter to a Friend*; A1*a* sub-title to *Antiquitates Capellae D. Johannis Evangelistæ, hodie Scholæ Regiæ Norwicensis*, verso blank; A2*a*–E3*a* (pp. 3–37) *De Schola Regia Norwicensi*; E3*b*–4*b* (pp. 38–40) *Appendix* (inscriptions in Aylisham and Heigham churches); F1*a*–H4*b* (pp. 41–64) *A Catalogue of the Bishops* [&c.] *to the Present Year 1712. Errata In the Antiquities of Norwich*, 7 lines, at the bottom of H4*b*. In some copies a list of books sold *At Curll's Literatory*, A1*a*–4*b* (pp. [1]–8), has been inserted at the end.

Illustrations: (i) Frontispiece. Engraved portrait of Browne in an oval copied from White's plate in the *Works* (1686), signed *M. V.ᵈᵉ Gucht Scul:*; beneath are the arms of Browne in an oval surmounting a cartouche lettered *Sʳ Thomas Browne, Kᵗ | M.D.* Plate-mark 17·5 × 11 cm.
 (ii) Facing p. xviii (*c1 b*). Browne's monument in the church of St Peter Mancroft at Norwich. Signed *J. Sturt sculp.* and inscribed *To the Reverend Edw. Tenison LL.B. Arch Deacon of Carmarthen Nephew to my Lady Browne.* Plate-mark 18·4 × 11·3 cm.
 (iii) Facing p. 1 of *Repertorium* (B1*a*). Folding plate of *Norwicensis Eccl: Cath: facies Australis.* Signed *H: Hulsbergh Sculp:* and inscribed to the Bishop of Norwich. Plate-mark 23 × 29·5 cm.
 (iv) Facing p. 3 (B2*a*). Monument of Bishop John Parkhurst. Signed *H. Hulsbergh Sc:.* Plate-mark 17·5 × 9 cm.
 (v) Facing p. 4 (B2*b*). Monument of Sir James Hobart. Unsigned. Plate-mark 15 × 10 cm.

(vi) Facing p. 6 (B3 *b*). Monument of James Goldwell, Bishop of Norwich. Inscribed to John, Bishop of Ely. Unsigned. Plate-mark 17·5 × 11 cm.

(vii) Facing p. 8 (B4 *b*). Figures of *S*: *Thomas Erpingham and his Two Ladies* from a painted window, and *The Arms of Thomas Windham and his two Wives* from a manuscript. Inscribed to Sir Henry St. George Kt. Unsigned. Plate-mark 16 × 11·5 cm.

(viii) Facing p. 14 (C3 *b*). Six coats of arms. Inscribed to William Ferdinand Lord Hunsdon, with his coat of arms. Unsigned. Plate-mark 17 × 11 cm.

(ix) Facing p. 16 (C4 *b*). *A Representation of the Standing Herse used at Bishop Redman's Publick Funeral*. Inscribed to Peter Le Neve Esq. Unsigned. Plate-mark 16 × 11·5 cm.

(x) Facing p. 20 (D2 *b*). Twelve coats of arms. Unsigned. Plate-mark 15 × 10 cm.

(xi) Facing p. 22 (D3 *b*). Twelve coats of arms. Unsigned. Plate-mark 15 × 10 cm.

(xii) Facing p. 24 (D4 *b*). Folding plate of the gate next the School. Inscribed to Charles Viscount Townshend with his arms. Signed *H: Hulsbergh Sc:* Plate-mark 29·5 × 19 cm.

(xiii) Facing p. 25 (E1 *a*). Folding plate of *Norwicensis Eccl: Cath: facies Occidentalis*. Inscribed to Sir Jacob Astley Bart. Signed *H. Hulsbergh Sculp:*. Plate-mark 30 × 17·4 cm.

(xiv) Facing p. 38 (F3 *b*). Monument of Edmund Scamler. Unsigned. Plate-mark 17 × 12 cm.

(xv) Facing p. 41 (G1 *a*). *Mrs. Astley's Monument*. Inscribed to Hobart Astley Esq. Unsigned. Plate-mark 17 × 11 cm.

(xvi) Facing p. 48 (G4 *b*). Monument of Bishop John Overall. Inscribed to William, Bishop of Chester. Signed *H. Hulsbergh Sculp:*. Plate-mark 17 × 11 cm.

(xvii) Facing p. 51 (H2 *a*). Monument of Robert Pepper. Inscribed to John Moore Esq. Unsigned. Plate-mark 17 × 11 cm.

(xviii) Facing p. 53 (H3 *a*). Monument of Bishop Edward Reynolds. Unsigned. Plate-mark 17 × 11 cm.

(xix) Facing p. 62 (I3 *b*). Monument of William Inglott. Unsigned. Plate-mark 17 × 11 cm.

(xx) Facing p. 67 (K2 *a*). Monument of Osbert Parsley. Inscribed to Mr. James Cooper. Unsigned. Plate-mark 17 × 10 cm.

(xxi) Facing p. 74 (L1 *b*). Monument of Bishop Anthony Sparrow. Inscribed to Peter Parham M.D. Unsigned. Plate-mark 17 × 11 cm.

(xxii) On p. 11 ([B]2 *a*) of *Brampton Urnes*. *A Roman Urn*. Inscribed to Dr. Hans Sloane. Unsigned. Plate-mark 17·5 × 11 cm.

(xxiii) Facing sub-title of *Antiquitates Capellae*, &c. (A1 *a*). Folding plate of *Schola Regia Norwicensis*. Signed *H. Hulsbergh Sculp:*. Plate-mark 21 × 30 cm.

Note: The collation and arrangement of this book are difficult to determine. The binders were evidently puzzled and have often varied the arrangement; if they followed the catchwords, the order would not agree with the list of Contents. In the above collation and register of Contents the order has been made to follow the list, the catchwords being ignored. This is the arrangement found in the two large paper copies in my collection, these being more likely than small paper copies to have been arranged according to the publisher's intention. The *Collation* and *Contents* given above are consequently quite different from those given in the former edition of the Bibliography. The sheets of the book have the following peculiarities:

(i) The leaf first–a2 (pp. iii–iv) is usually cancelled and replaced, as explained in the Bibliographical Preface. The original form of the leaf is found in some large paper

Sr Thomas Browne, K.^t
M.D.

Frontispiece to POSTHUMOUS WORKS 1712

copies as in one of mine and in Princeton University Library, though three such copies in the British Museum have the *cancellans*.

(ii) In the second section A–L the sub-title to *Repertorium*, here listed as χ, seems likely to have been imposed as L4, which is missing, and transferred to the beginning of the section.

(iii) In the section [A]–[B], *Brampton Urnes*, the engraved plate of a Roman Urn was printed on p. 11, [B]2*a*. All the other plates in the book are insertions with visible stubs.

(iv) Signatures C2 and E2 in *Antiquitates Capellæ* are usually signed D2.

(v) Large paper copies usually have the price 6*s*. at the bottom of the title-page erased or altered by pen to 10*s*., 12*s*. or 13*s*. These copies, trimmed by the binder, measure about 22 × 13 cm.; small paper copies are about 19·3 × 12 cm.

Copies: BLO, BM(4),[1] CLN, FLWC, K(4),[2] NCL, ULC; MH, MMO, NYAM, PUL.[3]

157 POSTHUMOUS WORKS   8° 1722

Title: Poſthumous Works Of the Learned Sir Thomas Browne, K͔ M.D....
[&c. as in no. 156] London: Printed for W. Mears, at the Lamb without
Temple Bar, and J. Hooke, at the Flower-de-Luce againſt St. Dunſtan's
Church in Fleetſtreet. MDCCXXII.

Collation, contents, illustrations: As in no. 156.

Note: The sheets of no. 156 with cancel title-page. Re-issued with another title-page in 1723.

Copies: K, CLN.

158 POSTHUMOUS WORKS   8° 1723

Title: Poſthumous Works Of the Learned Sir Thomas Browne, K͔ M.D....
[&c. as in no. 156] London: Printed for W. Mears, at the Lamb without
Temple Bar, and J. Hooke, at the Flower-de-Luce againſt St. Dunſtan's
Church in Fleetſtreet. MDCCXXIII. (Price Six Shillings.)

Collation, contents, illustrations: As in no. 156.

Note: The sheets of no. 156 with cancel title-page.

Copies: BM, K.

159 POSTHUMOUS WORKS ED. WILKIN   8° 1836

In Sir Thomas Browne's Works...Ed. Simon Wilkin...London William
Pickering...1836 (see no. 203).

Note: In vol. III, pp. 497–505 (*Brampton Urns*), and vol. IV, pp. 1–32 (*Repertorium*),
pp. 251–6 (*Miscellanies*). The correspondence between Dugdale and Sir T. B. is in
vol. I, pp. 380–93.

---

[1] Three on large paper, all with a2 *cancellans*.
[2] Two on large paper, one with a2 *cancellandum*.
[3] On large paper, with a2 *cancellandum*.

160 POSTHUMOUS WORKS ED. WILKIN   8° 1852

In The Works of Sir Thomas Browne...Ed. Simon Wilkin...London: H. G. Bohn...MDCCCLII (see no. 205).

Note: Vol. III, pp. 279–305. A reprint of no. 159 with a few omissions.

161 POSTHUMOUS WORKS ED. SAYLE   8° 1907

In The Works of Sir T. B. Ed. Charles Sayle. Vol. III Edinburgh John Grant 1907 (see no. 206).

Note: Vol. III, pp. 395–438 (*Repertorium, Miscellanies, Brampton Urns*).

162 BRAMPTON URNS VARIOUS EDD.

Reprinted with *Hydriotaphia* in nos. 99, 109, 111, 117, 118, 126g.

162*a* POSTHUMOUS WORKS ED. KEYNES   8° 1929–31

In The Works of Sir Thomas Browne Ed. Geoffrey Keynes. London Faber & Gwyer Limited. 1929–31 (see no. 207*a*).

Note: Vol. IV, pp. 55–61 (*Brampton Urns*); vol. V, pp. 147–69 (*Repertorium*); pp. 311–13 (*Account of Iceland*); vol. VI, pp. 331–58 (*Letters to Dugdale*).

162*b* POSTHUMOUS WORKS ED. KEYNES   8° 1964

In The Works of Sir Thomas Browne Ed. Geoffrey Keynes Faber and Faber Limited 1964 (see no. 207*c*).

Note: Vol. I, pp. 237–8 (*Brampton Urns*); vol. III, pp. 123–43 (*Repertorium*); vol. IV, pp. 307–27 (*Letters to Dugdale*); pp. 345–6 (*Account of Iceland*).

VII
Christian Morals

BIBLIOGRAPHICAL PREFACE

CHRISTIAN MORALS was written by Sir Thomas Browne during his later years and was stated by his daughter to be his last work, but there is no record of the exact date of composition. The chief information concerning its history is contained in the following note taken from memoranda written by White Kennett, Bishop of Peterborough, in his copy of the *Works* (1686). Whitefoot's account of Browne had been lent to Kennett by Elizabeth Lyttelton, and at the end of an abstract of this he added: 'The said Mrs. Littelton reports that the MSS. papers of her father were in the hands of her late brother Dr. Edward Brown, who lent them in a box to Dr. Thomas Tenison, vicar of St. Martin's, in the reign of James II, and that she herself, at her brother's request, went to fetch home the box, and accordingly brought it back, and delivered it to her brother, who soon after complained that he missed the choicest papers, which were a continuation of his Religio Medici, drawn up in his elder years, and which his son Dr. Brown had now intended to publish. She went back to Dr. Tenison, and desired him to look for those papers, which he could not find, but she hopes they may be still recovered, either as mislaid by the Archbishop of Canterbury [Dr. Tenison], or by her brother, whose only daughter is married to Mr. Brigstock, a member of the House of Commons.'[1] Many years later another search was made in the presence of Archbishop Tenison and this time the manuscript was found. It was returned to Mrs. Lyttelton and soon afterwards its publication was arranged under the joint editorship of Mrs. Lyttelton and John Jeffery, Archdeacon of Norwich, with a dedication by Mrs. Lyttelton addressed to her kinsman, the Earl of Buchan. Jeffery stated in his preface that 'There is nothing printed in the Discourse, or in the short notes, but what is found in the Original MS. of the Author, except only where an Oversight had made the Addition or Transposition of some words necessary.' Since the publication of the book in 1716 the author's manuscript has again been lost, but passages from it are to be found in the British Museum[2] and the Bodleian Library, Oxford.[3] The concluding paragraphs of *A Letter to a Friend* were also incorporated in *Christian Morals*. Probably, therefore, Sir Thomas Browne at the end of his life compiled this work largely from materials accumulated during many preceding years.

The first edition of *Christian Morals* is an attractive and uncommon book. A copy in my collection has a special interest. It is in its contemporary binding of red morocco and has on a fly-leaf the inscription: 'Given by Mrs. Lyttelton at Windsor, May 22, 1716'; on the title-page is the signature of the Earl of Buchan, to whom the book was dedicated. The donor has made one correction in the text (see no. 163). The second edition was published at Halle in Saxony in 1723; only two copies are known at the present time.

The book was reprinted in 1756 with notes and a Life of Browne by Dr. Samuel

---

[1] *European Magazine* (1801).
[2] Sloane MSS. 1847, 1848, 1874, 1885.   [3] MS. Rawl. cix.

Johnson, who drew largely upon the biographical material supplied by White-foot's notes printed in the *Posthumous Works* (1712). Wilkin also recorded (IV, 55) on the authority of Croker a review of *Christian Morals* by Johnson in *The Literary Magazine*, but he was afterwards able to correct this (IV, xi), the supposed review being merely some passages from the Life quoted in vol. 1 of this periodical (1756) (see no. 331). Johnson's edition was re-issued with a new title-page in 1761. The work was not printed again until edited by Wilkin in 1836. It has been many times reprinted since that date, usually in company with *Religio Medici*. Separate editions were published in 1863, 1904 and 1927.

163 CHRISTIAN MORALS ED. JEFFERY 12° 1716

Title: Chriſtian Morals, by Sʳ Thomas Brown, Of Norwich, M.D. And Author of Religio Medici. [*rule*] Publiſhed from the Original and Correct Manuſcript of the Author; by John Jeffery, D.D. Arch-Deacon of Norwich. [*rule*] Cambridge: Printed at the Univerſity-Preſs, For Cornelius Crownfield Printer to the Univerſity; And are to be Sold by Mr. Knapton at the Crown in St. Paul's Church-yard; and Mr. Morphew near Stationers-Hall, London, 1716.

Collation: ∏⁶ A–E¹² F⁶; 72 leaves.

Contents: ∏1 blank; ∏2 half-title; ∏3 title; ∏4*a*–∏5*a* dedication *To the Right Honourable David Earl of Buchan,* signed *Elizabeth Littelton;* ∏5*b*–∏6*b* *The Preface,* signed *John Jeffery Arch-Deacon of Norwich;* A1*a*–F4*a* (pp. 1–127) text; F4*b*–F5*b* *Books Printed for and Sold by Cornelius Crownfield;* F6 blank.

Note: Several copies of the book are known with inscriptions signed by the author's daughter, Mrs. Lyttelton. Others have been inscribed by the editor John Jeffery or by Archdeacon Tenison, who has sometimes inserted opposite the title-page the print of Browne's monument from *Posthumous Works* (1712). In the copy given by Mrs. Lyttelton to the Earl of Buchan she has made a correction on p. 9 (part I, section ix), altering 'when prudent simplicity hath fixed there' to 'where prudent simplicity hath fixed thee'. Some copies are printed on thicker paper than others.

Copies: BLO, BM, CLN,[1] FLWC(2), GUL, K(3),[2] ULL; MH(2),[3] MMO, NYAM, PUL.

164 CHRISTIAN MORALS ED. JEFFERY 8° 1723

Title: Christian Morals, by Sʳ Thomas Brown, Of Norwich, M.D. [*rule*] Published from the Original and Correct Manuscript of the Author; by John Jeffery, D.D. Arch-Deacon of Norwich, and printed at Cambridge by the printer to the University 1716. [*rule*] Hall in Saxony, Printed by John Frider. Krottendorff Printer to the University; And are to be Sold by the same. 1723.

Collation: A–E⁸ F⁴; 44 leaves.

Contents: A1 title; A2*a*–*b* *The Preface;* A3*a*–F4*b* (pp. 5–80, 4 ll. unnumbered) text.

Note: The book is a faithful reprint of the first edition, even the title-page being closely followed. Jeffery's Preface is reprinted, but Mrs. Lyttelton's dedication is omitted. Pages 5–80 are printed in pica and paginated; the remainder is printed in small pica and thus compressed into 8 unnumbered pages, presumably in order to avoid running over on to a fresh section. This edition is very uncommon; it was first described in a note by myself in *The Library,* (1930) n.s. x, 418–20, from a copy then in the collection of H. Gordon Ward.

Copies: CLN, GUL.

[1] With inscription from Mrs. Lyttelton to C. Lyttelton.
[2] One is in red morocco on thick paper with inscription from Mrs. Lyttelton to the Earl of Buchan with his signature on the title-page and with a correction in her hand. Another has an inscription by Edward Tenison and the plate of Browne's monument inserted.
[3] One with inscription from Mrs. Lyttelton to Edward Tenison.

CHRISTIAN
MORALS,

BY

Sʳ THOMAS BROWN,
Of NORWICH, *M. D.*

And AUTHOR of
RELIGIO MEDICI.

Publiſhed from the Original and Correct Manuſcript of the Author;
by *JOHN JEFFERY*, D. D.
ARCH-DEACON of NORWICH.

CAMBRIDGE:

Printed at the UNIVERSITY-PRESS,
For *Cornelius Crownfield* Printer to the UNIVERSITY;
And are to be Sold by Mr. *Knapton* at the Crown
in St. *Paul's* Church-yard; and Mr. *Morphew* near
Stationers-Hall, *LONDON*, 1716.

165 CHRISTIAN MORALS ED. JOHNSON   8° 1756

Title: Chriſtian Morals: by Sir Thomas Browne, Of Norwich, M.D. and author of Religio Medici. The Second Edition. With a life of the author, by Samuel Johnſon; and explanatory notes. London: Printed by Richard Hett, For J. Payne, at Pope's Head, in Pater-noſter Row. MDCCLVI.

Collation: Π² a–d⁸ B–I⁸ K⁴; 102 leaves.

Contents: Π1 half-title; Π2 title; a1 *a*–d7*a* (pp. i–lxi) *The life of Sir Thomas Browne*; d7*b*–d8*b* blank; B1 sub-title to *Chriſtian Morals* copied from the first edition but without the imprint; B2 dedication; B3 *The Preface*; B4*a*–K4*b* (pp. 7–136) text.

Note: Johnson's notes are printed at the foot of the page.

Copies: BLO, BM(2), CLN, GUL, K; MH, MMO, NYAM, PUL.

166 CHRISTIAN MORALS ED. JOHNSON   8° 1761

Title: True Chriſtian Morals: by Sir Thomas Browne, M.D. author of Religio Medici, &c. with His Life written by the celebrated Author of the Rambler; and explanatory Notes. The third edition. [*engraved vignette of a lamb: plate-mark 50 × 78 mm.*] London: Printed for, and Sold by Z. Stuart, at the Lamb, in Pater-noſter row. MDCCLXI.

Collation, contents: As in no. 165.

Note: The sheets of unsold copies of no. 165, with a new half-title and title-page. Very rare. A copy, which had belonged to Archdeacon Wrangham, was afterwards in Wilkin's possession, but neither Gardiner nor Greenhill had seen the book. Wilkin, IV, xi, stated that he believed there are similar copies dated 1765, but I have not discovered any evidence to support this.

Copies: BLO, CLN, GUL, K, ULC, ULL; MMO.

167 CHRISTIAN MORALS ED. WILKIN   8° 1836

In Sir Thomas Browne's Works...Ed. Simon Wilkin...London William Pickering...1836 (see no. 203).

Note: Vol. IV, pp. 53–114. Variant readings from MSS are given in footnotes.

168 CHRISTIAN MORALS ED. PEACE   8° 1844

In Religio Medici. Its sequel Christian Morals...London: Longman... MDCCCXLIV (see no. 23).

169 CHRISTIAN MORALS ED. PEACE   8° 1844

In Religio Medici. Its sequel Christian Morals...Philadelphia: Lea and Blanchard. 1844 (see no. 24).

170 CHRISTIAN MORALS ED. GARDINER   8° 1845

In Religio Medici together with...Christian Morals...Edited by Henry Gardiner M.A....London William Pickering 1845 (see no. 26).

TRUE
CHRISTIAN MORALS:

B Y

Sir Thomas Browne, M. D.

AUTHOR OF

RELIGIO MEDICI, &c.

WITH

His LIFE written by the celebrated Author
of the RAMBLER;

A N D

EXPLANATORY NOTES.

THE THIRD EDITION.

LONDON:
Printed for, and Sold by Z. STUART, at the
LAMB, in PATER-NOSTER ROW.
MDCCLXI.

171 CHRISTIAN MORALS ED. ST. JOHN 8° 1845

In Religio Medici...To which is added...Christian Morals...London: Henry Washbourne...MDCCCXLV (see no. 25).

Note: This edition was also issued separately (copy in CLN).

172 CHRISTIAN MORALS ED. WILKIN 8° 1852

In Sir Thomas Browne's Works...Ed. Simon Wilkin...London: H. G. Bohn...1852 (see no. 205).

Note: Vol. III, pp. 81–144. A reprint of no. 167.

173 CHRISTIAN MORALS ED. FIELDS 8° 1862

In Religio Medici...and Other Papers...Boston Ticknor and Fields 1862 (see no. 29).

174 CHRISTIAN MORALS 8° 1863

Christian Morals. By Sir Thomas Browne, Kt. M.D. London: Rivingtons, Waterloo Place. 1863. 19 cm. pp. lxix [numbered lxxiii], [3], 143, [1].

Frontispiece: Steel engraving, 11 × 9 cm., by J. Brown from a drawing by G. P. Harding, F.S.A., after the portrait in the Hall of the College of Physicians.

Note: A reprint of the second edition with Johnson's Life and a facsimile of the title-page. The plate for the frontispiece was used again in *Portraits of Illustrious Persons*, 1869 (see p. 223); it had already been published separately by M. M. Holloway, Covent Garden, in 1849.

175 CHRISTIAN MORALS ED. FIELDS 8° 1878

In Religio Medici...and other papers...Boston Robert Brothers 1878 (see no. 35).

176 CHRISTIAN MORALS ED. GREENHILL 8° 1881

In Sir Thomas Browne's Religio Medici...and Christian Morals Edited by W. A. Greenhill, M.D....London Macmillan and Co. 1881 (see no. 36).

177 CHRISTIAN MORALS ED. SYMONDS 8° 1886

In Sir Thomas Browne's Religio Medici...and other essays. Edited...by John Addington Symonds. London: Walter Scott...1886 (see no. 39).

178 CHRISTIAN MORALS ED. LLOYD ROBERTS 12° 1892

In Religio Medici and other essays...with an introduction by D. Lloyd Roberts, M.D., F.R.C.P. London David Stott...1892 (see no. 40).

179 CHRISTIAN MORALS ED. G. B. M.   8° 1894

In Religio Medici...and Christian Morals...Republished by G. Moreton...
Canterbury. 1894 (see no. 41).

180 CHRISTIAN MORALS ED. HOLMES   f° 1902

In Religio Medici...Christian Morals, and other essays...edited by C. J.
Holmes...The Vale Press...London MCMII (see no. 46).

181 CHRISTIAN MORALS   4° 1904

Christian Morals by Sir Thomas Browne [*device*] Printed at the University
Press, Cambridge, & Published At the Cambridge University Press Warehouse, Ave Maria Lane, London, E.C. MCMIV 22 cm. pp. viii, 99, [1].

Note: 250 copies printed on hand-made paper, of which 200 were for sale. A reprint of
the first edition, 1716, with type facsimile of title-page.

182 CHRISTIAN MORALS ED. SAYLE   8° 1904–7

In The Works of Sir Thomas Browne Edited by Charles Sayle London
Grant Richards 1904–7 (see nos. 206, 207).

Note: Vol. III (1907), pp. 439–510. A reprint of the first edition, 1716, with a type
facsimile of the title-page.

183 CHRISTIAN MORALS ED. HERFORD   8° 1906

In The Religio Medici & other writings of Sir Thomas Browne. London...
J. M. Dent & Co....[1906] (see no. 51).

184 CHRISTIAN MORALS ED. SONNENSCHEIN   12° 1906

In Works...of Sir Thomas Browne with a glossary by William Swan Sonnenschein London George Routledge & Sons...[1906] (see no. 52).

185 CHRISTIAN MORALS   4° 1923

In A Letter to a Friend...together with Christian Morals...Printed & sold at
the Golden Cockerel Press...[1923] (see no. 155).

185 *a* CHRISTIAN MORALS ED. ROBERTS   8° 1927

Sir Thomas Browne's Christian Morals The Second Edition with the Life of the
Author by Samuel Johnson, LL.D. Edited With an Introduction and Notes
by S. C. Roberts Cambridge At the University Press 1927 17·5 cm.,
pp. xviii, [ii], 219, [1].

185*b* CHRISTIAN MORALS ED. KEYNES 8° 1928

In The Works of Sir Thomas Browne Edited by Geoffrey Keynes London: Faber & Gwyer Limited 1928 (see no. 207*a*).

Note: Vol. I, pp. 101–56, with additional passages from manuscripts.

185*c* CHRISTIAN MORALS ED. KEYNES 8° 1940

In Religio Medici and Christian Morals Edited with an Introduction by Geoffrey Keynes Thomas Nelson and Sons Ltd London &c. [1940] (see no. 207*b*).

Note: Pp. 125–92. The marginal notes are printed as footnotes.

185*d* CHRISTIAN MORALS 8° 1962

In Religio Medici and Other Writings...J M Dent...[1962] [Everyman's Library, no. 92] (see no. 58*m*).

185*e* CHRISTIAN MORALS ED. MARTIN 8° 1964

In Sir Thomas Browne Religio Medici and Other Works Ed. L. C. Martin Oxford At the Clarendon Press 1964.

Note: Pp. 199–247, with a type facsimile of the original title-page, the Dedication and Preface, textual notes and commentary.

185*f* CHRISTIAN MORALS ED. KEYNES 8° 1964

In The Works of Sir Thomas Browne Ed. Geoffrey Keynes London Faber & Faber Limited [1964] (see no. 207*c*).

Note: Vol. I, pp. 243–90, with additional passages from manuscripts.

VIII

Other Writings

[The entries contained in this section form a somewhat miscellaneous collection of pieces which do not fall naturally into any other section of this *Bibliography*. Each is self-explanatory, and no Bibliographical Preface seems to be needed. Commendatory letters have been included as in the previous edition; other letters are transferred to a separate section.]

186 CAMDENI INSIGNIA [STC 19028]   4° 1624

Camdeni Insignia. Oxoniæ. Excudebant Iohannes Lichfield, & Iacobus Short, Academiæ Typographi. 1624.

Collation: Π² ¶⁴ ¶¶⁴ ¶¶¶² A–F⁴ G²; 38 leaves.

Latin poem: On C3 *b*, 10 Latin couplets beginning:

Quid in remotis sacra Parnassi jugis
Vatum sedetis numina.

and signed *Th. Browne Generos. Lateport.*

Note: These Latin verses formed Browne's first published composition, written when he was eighteen as an undergraduate at Broadgates Hall, afterwards Pembroke College, in honour of William Camden, who had died 9 November 1623. Other contributors were another Thomas Browne, Robert Burton, John Donne, jr., and William Strode, all of Christ Church. Browne's lines were first reprinted in a letter from me, *Times Literary Supplement* 25 February 1932. They were included in my edition of the *Works* (1964), III, 146, with an English rendering by W. R. LeFanu (see no. 207*c*).

Copies: BLO, BM, K, ULC; HN.

187 LATIN ORATION 1624 *IN* BALLIOFERGUS [Wing S 759]   4° 1668

Balliofergus, or a Commentary upon the Foundation, Founders and Affaires, of Balliol Colledge...Together with Two Tables, One of Endowments, the other of Miscellanies. By Henry Savage, Master of the said Colledge. Oxford, Printed by A. & L. Lichfield, Printers to the University. 1668.

Collation: A–S⁴; 72 leaves. A folding genealogical table facing p. 6.

Latin oration: On p. 92 under the sub-title, *Natalitia Collegii Pembrochiani Oxonii*, is the Latin oration delivered by Browne on 5 August 1624. It is headed: *Thomas Browne Studiosus non Graduatus Commensalis Collegii.*

Note: Browne had matriculated as fellow-commoner at Broadgates Hall, Oxford, early in 1623. In the following year this foundation was incorporated as Pembroke College and Browne was one of those called upon to deliver orations at the ceremony of inauguration. A translation was printed by Charles Williams among the documents collected by him in 1906. The oration was included in my edition of the *Works* (1964), III, 148–9, with an English rendering by W. R. LeFanu (see no. 207*c*).

Copies: BLO, BM, K, ULC; MH, YUL.

187*a* LOVEDAY'S HYMEN'S PRÆLUDIA, Pt. III [Wing L 114]   8° 1655

Title within single lines: Hymen's Præludia: or, Love's Master-piece. Being the third Part of that ſo much admired Romance, Intituled, *Cleopatra*. Written Originally in the French, and now rendred into Engliſh By R. Loveday. [*Latin quotation from Evander and ornament between rules*] London. Printed by J. G. for R. Lowndes, at the White-Lyon in S. Paul's Church yard, near the Weſt-end, 1655.

Collation: A–Y⁸; 176 leaves.

Contents: A1 blank; A2 title; A3*a*–A4*b Epistle Dedicatory* to Lady Cramond and Lady Pettus, signed *Loveday*; A5*a*–*b To his esteemed Friend, Mr. Robert Loveday*, signed *Jo: Pettus, Chan. Row. Westm. Feb. 2. 1654*; A7*a* six lines *To my very honoured Friend, Mr. Robert Loveday, upon his matchlefs Version intituled Love's Master-piece*, signed *Ma. Browne, Doc. Med.*; A7*b* 12 lines, unsigned, to the same; A8*a* 12 lines *Upon his teaching Cleopatra English*, signed *R.W.*; A8*b* blank; B1*a*–Y6*a* (pp. 1–331) text; Y6*b* blank; [Y7–8 not seen].

Lines to Loveday: On A7*a* signed *Ma. Browne, Doc. Med.*

Note: This very uncommon book, translated from La Calprenède's *Cleopatra*, is fully described since it contains part of the evidence for identifying the individuals con- cerned in Browne's *Letter to a Friend* as Robert Loveday and Sir John Pettus (see pp. 99–100 of the present work). It seems that the lines on A7*a* signed *Ma. Browne, Med. Doc.*, must be by Dr. Thomas Browne, a friend of both the men concerned. This evidence was not detected by Professor Huntley when engaged in his original ex- amination of the problem, but he has accepted its significance since I found Browne's lines in a copy of the book acquired in 1965.

    The page number is omitted on p. 11 and p. 300 is numbered 230; the pagination is otherwise correct.

Copies: BM, K; HCL, PUL, YUL.

188 KING'S VALE-ROYAL [Wing K 488]   f° 1656

Title: The Vale-Royall of England. Or, The County Palatine of Chefter Illuftrated. Wherein is contained a Geographicall and Hiftorical Defcription of that Famous County...Adorned with Maps and Profpects...[*rule*] Per- formed by William Smith, and William Webb, Gentlemen, Publifhed By Mr. Daniel King. [*rule*] To which is annexed, An Exact Chronology of all its Rulers and Governors...Alfo, An Excellent Difcourfe of the Ifland of Man... [*rule*] London, Printed by John Streater, in Little S. Bartholomews, and are to be fold at the Black-fpread-Eagle at the Weft-End of Pauls, 1656.

Collation: A–O⁴ Aa–Zz⁴ Aaa–Ggg⁴ Hh–Kkk² Aaaa–Mmmm⁴ Nnnn²; 278 leaves.

Illustrations: Engraved title-page, nineteen engraved plates, and four engravings in the text.

Letter: On A3*a*–*b, To His endeared Friend, Mr Daniel King*, signed, *Your old Acquaintance, and true Friend, Tho: Brown.*

Note: This letter is mentioned by Wilkin, I, xcix, and is reprinted by him, I, 419. He expresses some doubt as to the identity of the writer and remarks that the style of the letter is certainly not like Sir Thomas Browne's. In my opinion, however, the letter is undoubtedly authentic, some passages in it being very characteristic, and I have included it in the *Works* (1931), VI, 417–18, and (1964), IV, 393–4. Browne referred to King in a letter to Dugdale of 6 December 1658 as having made a draught of 'a convent of Black Friers' when he was in Norwich.[1] Browne's grandfather, Richard Browne, lived in Chester and also his father until he moved to London.

Copies: BLO, BM, K, ULC; MH, YUL.

       1 *Works*, ed. Keynes (1964), IV, 311.

HYMENS PRÆLUDIA:
OR,
LOVEs MASTER-PIECE

Being the third Part of that so much admired ROMANCE,
Intituled, *CLEOPATRA.*

Written Originally in the French, and now rendred into English

By R. LOVEDAY.

EVAND.

Quid magis optaret Cleopatra parentibus orta
Conspicuis, Comiti quam placuisse Thori?

LONDON.

Printed by *J. G.* for R. LOWNDES, at the
White-Lyon in S. *Paul's* Church yard,
neer the West-end, 1655.

To my very honoured Friend,
Mr. *Robert Loveday*, upon
his matchless Version intituled
LOVE'S MASTER-PIECE.

THe rarest Plants, & Flowers somtimes improve
Their growth and beauty, by a kind remove.
Sydney's the Phosher; thou the splendent Sun,
Deserves the lawrell of our English Tongue.
The Garland's thine, O give me leave to say,
I like thy Dawn, but better LOVE thy DAY.

Ma. Browne, *Doc. Med.*

To

189 NATURE'S CABINET UNLOCK'D [spurious] [Wing B 5065]   1657

Title, within single line: Nature's Cabinet Unlock'd. Wherein is Difcovered The natural Caufes of Metals, Stones, Precious Earths, Juyces, Humors, and Spirits, The nature of Plants in general; their Affections, Parts, and Kinds in Particular. Together with A Defcription of the Individual Parts and Species of all Animate Bodies, Similar and Diffimilar, Median and Organical, Perfect and Imperfect. With a compendious Anatomy of the Body of Man, As alfo the Manner of his Formation in the Womb. [rule] All things are Artificial, for Nature is the Art of God. By *Tho. Brown* D. of Phyfick. [rule] London, Printed for Edw. Farnham in Popes-head alley near Cornhil. 1657.

Collation: π² A² C–R¹²; 184 leaves.

Contents: π1 blank; π2 title; A1 *a*–A2 *b* The Preface; C1 *a*–R10 *a* (pp. 1–331) text; R10 *b*– R11 *a* advertisement of *Natural Magic*, by John Baptist Porta; R11 *b*–R12 *b* blank.

Note: This scarce and curious work treats of physiology, but is not in any way worthy of Browne, with whose name it was falsely associated. Presumably in order to give colour to this attribution, the *Preface* concludes: 'Let us but contemplate on thofe prodigious Pieces of Nature, Whales, Dromedaries, &c. or on the leaft of Creatures, and we fhall immediately fall into Meanders, and tedious Labyrinths: in every Creature Gods handywork is exceedingly difcovered, *Reafon may go to fchool to the very Bees, Ants, and Spiders:* So faith   *Religio Medici.*'¹

A formal disclaimer of the authorship of this work was soon issued on Dr. Thomas Browne's behalf, a notice to this effect being printed by the publisher, Henry Brome, at the end of *Hydriotaphia*, 1658, 8° and 4° (see nos. 93 and 94, *The Stationer to the Reader*). A reference to this attempted imposition is also to be found in *Baconiana*, London, 1679, edited by Thomas Tenison, pp. 76–7. The true author of *Nature's Cabinet Unlock'd* is not known.

Copies: BM, CLN, GUL, K; NYAM.

190 COMMENDATORY EPISTLE [Wing B 5125]   8° 1678

Title: A compleat Treatife of Preternatural Tumours, Both General and Particular, As they appear in Humane Body From Head to Foot. To which alfo are added many Excellent and Modern Hiftorical Obfervations, conclud-ing moft Chapters in the Whole Difcourfe. [rule] Collected from the Learned Labours both of Ancient and Modern Phyficians and Chirurgions, compofed and digefted into this new Method by the Care and Induftry of John Brown, Sworn Chirurgion in Ordinary to the Kings moft Excellent Majefty. [rule]

*Poft varios cafus Artem Experientia fecit,
Exemplo monftrante viam.—*

[rule] London, Printed by S. R. for R. Clavel, at the Peacock at the Weft end of S. Pauls; and George Rofe, Bookfeller in Norwich. 1678.

¹ 'Out of this ranke Solomon chose the object of his admiration, indeed what reason may not goe to Schoole to the wisdome of Bees, Aunts, and Spiders?' (*Religio Medici*, pt. 1, sect. 15).

Collation: A–Z⁸ Aa–Cc⁸; 208 leaves.

Illustrations: Portrait, engraved by R. White, facing the title, and five plates of surgical operations and appliances facing pp. 166, 205, 245, 256, 340.

Commendatory Epistle: On A6*a*, *To the Author*, signed *Tho. Brown*.

Note: John Brown was the son of a Norwich tailor and lived in the city until the age of seventeen. In January 1659/60 he was apprenticed to a London surgeon, John Bishop, and was also a pupil of Thomas Hollyer at St. Thomas's Hospital. From 1663 to 1666 he served in the Navy and then returned to Norwich, where he practised for about ten years. In 1675 he moved to London and assumed the title of 'sworne Chirurgeon to the King'. From 1683 he served for a time on the staff of St. Thomas's Hospital, but was suspended by the governors after eight years for breach of orders, and in spite of repeated appeals was not reinstated. He died probably in 1702.

   Brown wrote a number of books on surgery and anatomy and for two of these he managed to obtain Commendatory Letters from Sir Thomas Browne, whom he had no doubt known during his years at Norwich. He was a systematic plagiary and his books contain little or nothing that is new. His pretensions were ruthlessly exposed by another surgeon, James Young, in *Medicaster Medicatus, Or a Remedy for the Itch of Scribbling* (London, 1685). Wilkin (I, 338) rightly described Sir Thomas's Commendatory Letter in the *Treatise of Preternatural Tumours* as 'a brief note of cautious recommendation'. John Brown referred to Sir Thomas Browne in *Adenochoiradologia* (1684), his book on touching for the King's evil (see no. 289), and is himself mentioned by Sir Thomas in a letter to Edward Browne 31 March [1682].[1] For a full account of John Brown see K. F. Russell, *Bulletin of the History of Medicine*, XXXIII (1959), 393–414, 503–25.

Copies: BLO, BM, GUL, K, MSL, ULC; YML.

191 COMMENDATORY EPISTLE [Wing B 5124]   4° 1678

Title, within double lines: A Compleat Difcourse of Wounds Both in General and Particular: Whereunto are Added the feverall Fractures of the Skull, with their variety of Figures. As alfo a Treatife Of Gunfhot-Wounds in General. [*rule*] Collected and Reduced into a New method By John Brown…and may be of fingular ufe to all Practitioners in the Art of Chirurgery. [*rule*]
        Satis nunquam Dicitur, quod nunquam Satis Difcitur.
[*rule*] London, Printed by E. Flefher, for William Jacob, at the Black Swan in Holborn. 1678.

Collation: A–Z⁴ Aa–Yy⁴; 180 leaves.

Illustrations: Portrait by R. White facing the title, and eight plates of surgical operations, &c., facing pp. 36, 37, 104, 124, 144, 145, 170, 171.

Commendatory Epistle: On A3*b*, *To Mr. John Brown* signed *Thomas Brown*; preceded by a recommendation signed by the King's surgeons and followed by another Commendatory Epistle signed by Thomas Hollier (surgeon to St. Thomas's Hospital).

Note: For a note on the author see last entry. The letter by Sir Thomas Browne in the

---

[1] *Works*, ed. Keynes (1964), IV, 217.

present work is of the same character as that in Brown's *Treatise of Preternatural Tumours*, published in the same year.

Copies: BLO, BM, K, ULC.

192 HOOKE'S WORKS
f° 1705

The Posthumous Works of Robert Hooke, M.D. S.R.S....Publish'd by Richard Waller, R.S. Secr. London: Printed by Sam Smith and Benj. Walford, (Printers to the Royal Society) at the Princes Arms in St. Paul's Church-yard. 1705. f°.

Account of a fossil bone: p. 313, in 'A discourse of Earthquakes'. Quotation from an 'account from the Learned Dr. Brown concerning a petrified Bone of a prodigious bigness, discover'd by the falling of some Cliffs [near Winterton in Norfolk] in 1666'.

Note: Hooke quoted this account by Browne of the fossil bones from Winterton, Norfolk, to illustrate: 'The motion of the water another cause of alteration in the Earth'; in this instance the bones were exposed by erosion of a cliff by the sea. The account was part of a communication by Browne to the Royal Society on 27 February 1667/8, when the Society received from him 'a great petrified bone, a double goose-egg, the one included in the other, and a stone bottle, which had been filled seven years before with Malaga sack, and was well stopped, but now found almost empty, and the outside covered all over with a mossy coat'.[1] An abbreviated account of the same curiosities was printed in Hooke's *Philosophical Experiments and Observations*, ed. Derham (1726), p. 31. Another account of the fossil bones in Browne's hand is in the British Museum;[2] this differs considerably from the version printed from Hooke's papers.

193 WOTTON'S ESSAY
4° 1753

An Effay on the Education of Children, in the Firft Rudiments of Learning. Together with A Narrative of what Knowledge William Wotton, a Child fix Years of Age, had attained unto, upon the Improvement of thofe Rudiments, in the Latin, Greek, and Hebrew Tongues. [*rule*] By Henry Wotton, Of Corpus Chrifti College, Cambridge, and Minifter of Wrentham in Suffolk. [*double rule*] London: Printed for T. Waller, at the Mitre and Crown, in Fleet-ftreet, MDCCLIII. [Price 1s.]

Collation: A–G⁴ H²; 30 leaves.

Contents: A1 title; A2*a*–A3*b* dedication to Charles II; A4*a*–B2*b* (pp. vii–xii) preface; B3*a*–H2*a* (pp. 1–59) text; H2*b* Modern Pamphlets, fold by T. Waller.

Testimony by Browne: pp. 58–9. Testimony as to the proficiency of William Wotton, signed *Tho. Browne* and dated *July* 20, 1672.

Note: Browne set the child to read a stanza from Spenser and passages in Latin, Greek, and Hebrew, all of which he pronounced and construed correctly. The certificate is printed in the *Works*, ed. Keynes (1964), IV, 399.

Copies: BM, K.

---

[1] Birch's *History of the Royal Society* (1756), IV, 253.
[2] Sloane MS. 1882, ff. 19–20; printed in the *Works*, ed. Keynes (1964), III, 350–1.

194 DIALOGUE BETWEEN TWO TWINS [spurious]   8° 1855

Conjectural Restoration of the lost Dialogue Between Two Twins, By Sir Thomas
    Browne, M.D.CLXXXIII. Edited by B. Dockray: Author of Egeria; or Casual
    Thoughts and Suggestions. London: W & F. G. Cash. 5, Bishopsgate Street
    Without. 1855. 21 cm., pp. xi, [i], 20, [4].

Note: This was the subject of a note in Browne's miscellaneous manuscripts suggesting
    'A dialogue between two Twins in the womb concerning the world they were to
    come into',[1] but Browne himself did not take it any further. It has been suggested
    that the 'Conjectural Restoration' was written by James Crossley (see *The Palatine
    Note-book*, 1883, p. 214 of the present work); on the other hand a copy of the *Dialogue*
    in my collection is inscribed: 'Dr. Stebbing with *grateful* respects of a "namesake"
    J. "D". Parry.' This is presumably John Docwra Parry, topographer and author of
    various compilations, none, according to the *DNB*, of much value. The pamphlet
    was afterwards bound up with another work, with a general title-page as follows:
    *Two Dialogues. I. Our Human Nature. II. Conjectural Restoration of a Lost Dialogue by
    Sir Thomas Browne. B. Dockray, Author of the first, Editor of the second. Lancaster:
    T. Edmondson, Printer...1859.* I have a copy of this inscribed to Prince Louis Lucien
    Bonaparte by 'The Author & Editor' and dated 'Lancaster Decr 12 1859'. The
    general character of the writing, though larger as befitting the occasion, is similar to
    that in the other copy. The date of Parry's death was unknown to the writer of the
    DNB article and he may well have been alive in 1859, since he graduated at Cam-
    bridge in 1824. Moreover Crossley lived in Manchester, not Lancaster. It seems
    probable, therefore, from the form of the first inscription, that Parry was the author.

195 NATURAL HISTORY OF NORFOLK   8° 1902

Notes and Letters on the Natural History of Norfolk more especially on the
    birds and fishes from the MSS. of Sir Thomas Browne, M.D. (1605–1682)
    In the Sloane Collection in the Library of the British Museum and in the
    Bodleian Library, Oxford with notes by Thomas Southwell, F.Z.S. Member
    of the British Ornithologists' Union; Vice-President of the Norfolk and
    Norwich Naturalists' Society London Jarrold & Sons, 10 & 11 Warwick
    Lane, E.C. [all rights reserved] 1902 22 cm. pp. xxvi, 102.

Facsimile: Part of a letter from Browne to Doctor Christopher Merrett.

Note: The notes were written for the benefit of Dr. Christopher Merrett. Most of the
    notes and letters printed in this volume are to be found in Wilkin, but they are
    given here in a more accessible form and more fully annotated. The *Notes on the
    Natural History of Norfolk* were freshly transcribed from the manuscripts[2] for the
    Works, ed. Keynes (1931), V, 377–412, and (1964), III, 401–31. Southwell's edition is
    found in two different bindings—quarter roan or blue cloth, with gilt title-blocks on
    the front covers and spines. The Osler copy is a variant, having no date on the title-
    page.

---

[1] See *Works*, ed. Keynes (1964), III, 278; also a passage in *Hydriotaphia*, ch. IV (*ibid.* I, 162).
[2] Sloane MS. 1830, ff. 5–31, &c.

196 ELIZABETH LYTTELTON   8° 1919

The Commonplace Book of Elizabeth Lyttelton daughter of Sir Thomas
Browne Description by Geoffrey Keynes M.D. Cambridge Printed at the
University Press 1919 22 cm. pp. 34, [2].

Note: The typographical style of this pamphlet was designed by Bruce Rogers. Fifty-
four copies were printed on hand-made paper for private circulation in printed paper
wrappers. The manuscript here described, which has been in my collection since
1918, formerly belonged to Browne's second daughter, Elizabeth Lyttelton. In it she
has recorded a fragment, 'Of consumptions', composed by Sir T. B. probably for his
Letter to a Friend, a poem by him, 'upon a tempest at sea', written in 1630, and a list
of 'The books which my daughter Elizabeth hath read unto me at nights till she read
y^m all out'. These are all printed here for the first time, with other extracts from the
MS. The pieces mentioned above were also printed in an article in the *Times Literary
Supplement*, 4 September 1919, p. 470.

197 ON DREAMS   8° 1920

On Dreams by Sir Thomas Browne, Kt. with decorations by I. de B. Lockyer
London: At the de la More Press [1920] [The Saint George Series Number II]
20 cm. pp. 14, [2].

Note: First printed by Wilkin (IV, 355–9) from Sloane MS. 1874, ff. 112, 120. Reprinted
here separately for the first time. On hand-made paper, issued in printed wrappers.

198 LECTURE ON THE SKIN   4° 1924

Notes for a Lecture on the Skin by Sir Thomas Browne, Kt., M.D. Edited by
Geoffrey Keynes, M.D., F.R.C.S. London John Murray, Albemarle Street,
W. 1924 24 cm. pp. 7, [1].

Note: First printed in *St. Bartholomew's Hospital Reports*, vol. LVII, part ii, pp. 108–13,
1924. Fifty copies with title-page as above were printed for the editor.

199 ON DREAMS   8° 1929

On Dreams by Thomas Browne, Kt. and Doctor of Physick: late of Norwich
[*vignette*] Norwich Printed and Published by Martin Kinder at the Walpole
Press, 18 Elm Hill 1929 22·3 cm. pp. 12, [4].

Note: 250 numbered copies were issued in printed boards and printed green paper
wrappers.

200 MISCELLANEOUS WRITINGS ED. KEYNES   8° 1946

The Miscellaneous Writings of Sir Thomas Browne Including Miscellany
Tracts and Repertorium Edited by Geoffrey Keynes Faber and Faber Limited
24 Russell Square [1946] 19 cm. pp. xx, 474.

Note: The stock of sheets of the *Works* (1928–31) was destroyed by enemy action in 1941
with the exception of those of a few copies of vols. V and VI. This is therefore a
reissue of vol. V with a cancel title-page and a leaf of *errata* added after p. xviii. It is
bound in brown cloth.

IX

Letters

[It seemed convenient in this revised *Bibliography* to give a separate account of the letters as they have appeared. A few were printed in scattered books and journals. The majority remained in manuscript until collected and printed by Wilkin in his edition of the *Works* (1836). More complete collections will be found in the *Works*, ed. Keynes (1931, 1964).]

200*a* LETTER TO EVELYN   1664

> *In* Sylva, Or a Difcourfe of Foreft-Trees...By J. E. Efq...To which is annexed
> Pomona...Also Kalendarium Hortenfe...London, Printed by Jo. Martyn,
> and Ja. Allestry, Printers to the Royal Society, and are to be fold at their Shop
> at the Bell in S. Paul's Church-yard. MDCLXIV.

> *Letter: Sylva*, p. 82, description of 'an extraordinary large...Lime-tree', written in a
> letter from Browne to Evelyn about 1664.

> *Note:* Evelyn had been corresponding with Browne for several years before this. All of
> their letters that survive are printed in the *Works*, ed. Keynes (1964), vol. IV. Evelyn
> sent a copy of *Sylva* to Browne and also his *Sculptura* (1662).[1] For Evelyn's visit to
> Browne at Norwich see no. 271 on p. 193.

200*b* LETTERS TO DUGDALE   1712

> *In* Posthumous Works, London, 1712 (see no. 156).

> *Note:* Seven of the letters which passed between Browne and Dugdale are printed at
> pp. 1–22.

200*c* LETTER TO HENRY POWER[?]   1735

> *In* A General Dictionary, Historical and Critical:...A New...Translation of
> that of Mr. Bayle...By J. P. Bernard, Thomas Birch and John Lockman.
> Vol. III. London, 1735.

> *Note:* Extensive annotations have been added by Thomas Birch to Bayle's article on
> Browne, pp. 609–13. Among these, pp. 612–3, is a letter from Browne 'communicated
> by Richard Middleton Massey M.D., F.R.S.'. It is dated at Bury, April the 29th. 1653.
> The article was reprinted in the *Biographia Britannica* of Andrew Kippis, II (1780),
> 633, but the date was omitted, and it has hitherto been accepted as probably addressed
> to Henry Power, *c.* 1646, since it contains advice on what a young man should read
> in preparation for a medical career. If the date given above is correct, this attribution
> becomes unlikely, Power being by then established in practice. The original document
> is not known to be extant, and the name of the recipient remains in doubt. The printing
> of 1735 was first noticed by Professor N. J. Endicott of the University of Toronto.

200*d* LETTERS TO EDWARD BROWNE   1820

> *In* The Retrospective Review, Vol. I, London, 1820.

> *Note:* Pp. 161–4. Art. x. 'A MS. Volume of Sir Thomas Browne's Letters to his Son.'
> Extracts are given, somewhat inaccurately, from four letters in Sloane MS. 1847.

[1] This copy was sold on three occasions at Sotheby's: 10 March 1901 (Pickering, £40);
4 June 1902 (Denham, £69); 16 June 1903 (£38). It is now in the Pierpont Morgan Library.

200*e* LETTERS TO DUGDALE 1827

In The Life, Diary, and Correspondence of Sir William Dugdale, Knight. Edited by William Hamper, F.S.A. London. 1827.

Note: Pp. 337–52 give the letters first printed in *Posthumous Works* (1712) (see no. 156).

200*f* COLLECTED CORRESPONDENCE 1836

In Sir Thomas Browne's Works. Edited by Simon Wilkin. Vol. 1. London. 1836 (see no. 203).

Note: Wilkin was the first editor to transcribe and publish Browne's correspondence from manuscripts and other sources, including letters to his sons, Thomas and Edward, and to Power, Evelyn, Dugdale, Ashmole, Merrett, and Aubrey, with some to miscellaneous correspondents. Sometimes both sides of the correspondence are given, notably that from Edward Browne. The collection is necessarily incomplete, but Wilkin included a number of letters written to Browne which are not printed elsewhere. Wilkin's edition was reprinted in 1852 and the letters are there placed at the end of vol. III (see no. 205).

200*g* LETTER TO DUGDALE 1872–3

In Eastern Counties Collectanea. Norwich. 1872–3.

Note: Pp. 193–5 give an undated second letter to Dugdale concerning the fish bones found at Conington Down. It was largely reprinted by Southwell in *Notes on the Natural History of Norfolk* (1902) (see no. 195), and extracts were given by T. K. Monro in the *Scottish Historical Review*, 1921. The original MS is in the Osler Collection, McGill University, Montreal. It was first described in *Historical Manuscripts Commission* (1897), xv, pt. 2, 294.

200*h* LETTER TO DUGDALE 1904

In Transactions of the Norfolk and Norwich Naturalists' Society. Vol. VII. Norwich. 1904.

Note: Pp. 360–3 give an article by Thomas Southwell, F.Z.S., 'On an unpublished letter from Dr. Thomas Browne to Mr. William Dugdale'. It is dated 17 November [1660] and is chiefly concerning fossil fish bones found at Happisburgh, with a reference in a postscript to Dugdale's *Monasticon*. The original MS is in the library of Pembroke College, Cambridge. It was first recorded and extracts printed in the *Fifth Report of the Royal Commission on Historical Manuscripts* (London, 1876), appendix, pp. 487–8. The letter is printed in the *Works*, ed. Keynes (1964), IV, 325–6.

200*i* LETTER TO DUGDALE 1921

In The Scottish Historical Review, vol. XIX. Glasgow. 1921.

Note: Pp. 49–57 give an article by Professor T. K. Monro on 'An unpublished letter of Sir Thomas Browne, M.D.'. It prints the first letter, 16 November 1659, to Dugdale concerning the fish bones found at Conington Down with facsimiles of the original MS. It was formerly in the Morrison Collection and is now in the Monro Collection, Glasgow University. The letter is printed in the *Works*, ed. Keynes (1964), IV, 319–21.

200*j* LETTER TO DUGDALE 1924

In Annals of Medical History, vol. VI. New York. 1924.

Note: Pp. 287–96. 'An Unpublished Letter of Sir Thomas Browne', by Eli Moschcowitz, printing Browne's letter to Dugdale, 11 December 1658. The original document was sold at Sotheby's 2 March 1965, lot 475. A draft of Browne's remarks on the draining of flooded lands in Holsatia by the Duke of Holstein in 1610, sent with the letter, was separated from it and sold as lot 476. Both documents are printed in the *Works*, ed. Keynes (1964), IV, 312–16.

200*k* COLLECTED LETTERS ED. KEYNES 8° 1931

In The Works of Sir Thomas Browne   Ed. Geoffrey Keynes   Volume six London 1931 (see no. 207*a*).

Note: This volume embodies the first attempt to present a complete collection of the letters written by Browne. They were freshly transcribed from the manuscripts where these existed. A number of letters written to Browne by various correspondents and printed by Wilkin are not given here, but where both sides of an exchange have survived all are given with the exception of those written to Browne by his sons. Between forty and fifty entire letters by Browne are printed for the first time and many others are supplemented. Those to Sir Hamon L'Estrange of Hunstanton Hall and to Henry Oldenburg, Secretary of the Royal Society, were not known to Wilkin.

200*l* COLLECTED LETTERS ED. KEYNES 8° 1946

The Letters of Sir Thomas Browne   Edited by Geoffrey Keynes   Faber and Faber Limited   24 Russell Square   London   19 cm. pp. xiv, 440, 1 leaf (307*a*) inserted.

Note: The stock of sheets of the *Works* (1928–31) (see no. 207*a*) was destroyed by enemy action in 1941 except for a few sheets of vols. v and vi. The sheets of vol. vi containing the letters were accordingly re-issued in 1946 with a cancel title-page, a leaf of *errata* inserted after the Preface, and an additional letter from Browne to Evelyn inserted on an extra leaf following p. 307. These copies were bound in brown cloth.

200*m* LETTER TO DR. SAMUEL BAVE 1953

In Bulletin of the History of Medicine   Vol. XXVII, no. 6, New Haven, 1953.

Note: Pp. 503–11 give an article by Murdock MacKinnon, 'An Unpublished Consultation Letter of Sir Thomas Browne'. The letter was written to Dr. Samuel Bave of Bath, 8 May 1642, about a patient, Sir Charles Le Gros. The original Latin text is printed, followed by an English version and a list of the drugs mentioned in Browne's prescriptions. The manuscript with two letters from Bave was acquired by the British Museum in 1947 (Add. MS. 46378B). Reprinted in the *Works*, ed. Keynes (1964) IV, 242–4.

200*n* COLLECTED LETTERS ED. KEYNES   8° 1964

In The Works of Sir Thomas Browne Volume IV Letters Edited by Geoffrey Keynes London Faber and Faber Limited [1964] (see no. 207*c*).

Note: This volume is a revised reprint of vol. VI of the *Works*, VI vol., 1931, with the following additions: (1) Two letters to Evelyn, one of which was added to the separate edition of the *Letters* (1946). (2) The original version of a tract on Artificial Hills written to Dugdale in 1658. (3) A letter to a member of the Coke family. (4) Latin letters to and from Dr. Samuel Bave of Bath with one from Dr. John Maplet (English versions by W. R. LeFanu). (5) A Latin letter from Dr. Abraham van Berckel of Leyden University (English version by Cosmo Gordon). This edition contains every letter written by Browne known at the present time.

X

Collected Works

BIBLIOGRAPHICAL PREFACE

The first collected edition of Sir Thomas Browne's works was printed under the supervision of Archbishop Tenison and published in a handsome folio in 1686 four years after the author's death. This contains all the principal works issued during Browne's lifetime. The whole collection was almost immediately translated into Dutch and published at Amsterdam in 1688. This translation is of some rarity; there are but three copies known in Holland, one in East Germany, three in Great Britain, and two in North America.

Probably a large edition of the volume of 1686 was published, for it is even now quite a common book. Evidently it satisfied the contemporary demand, and no other collected edition was published for 150 years. Ultimately the four-volume edition prepared by Simon Wilkin, a printer of Norwich, was issued in the years 1835–6; this included the correspondence and much other fresh material from manuscript sources, and it enjoys the reputation of being one of the best edited books in the English language. An account of Wilkin's labours and the part played therein by Robert Southey will be found in an appendix added to the former edition of this *Bibliography*.

A third collected edition edited by Charles Sayle was published in the years 1904–7, but this omitted the correspondence and most of the new material added by Wilkin. The omission was remedied by the publication in 1928–31 of the six volumes edited by myself for Messrs. Faber and Faber. This edition included everything by Browne that was known at the time except for the writings in Latin, and all the manuscript material was freshly transcribed from the original papers. Nevertheless, it sold but slowly, and a large part of the sheets still lying in a warehouse in Paternoster Row was destroyed by enemy action in 1941. The copies already in circulation did not satisfy the greatly increased demand which arose during the next twenty years and so I set about the preparation of a complete revised edition, using the latest recensions of the texts and including the Latin writings with English versions added. This was published in four volumes in 1964.

ALLE DE WERKEN

Van

THOMAS BROWN,

In ſijn Leven Ridder en Doctor in de Medicyne tót Norwich.

Verdeelt in vijf Deelen,

Behelſende

I. **PSEUDO-DOXIA EPIDEMICA,** *of een Onderſoek der Gemeene Dwalingen des Volks.*

II. **RELIGIO MEDICI,** *of de Godsdienſt eens Genees-meeſters, met wydloopige Aantekeningen voorzien, neffens de Aanmerkingen van den Heer* Kenelm Digby.

III. **HYDRIOTAPHIA,** *of Kruyk-begraavenis.*

IV. **DE LUSTHOF VAN CYRUS,** *of de Vyf-Regeligen Ruyt,*

V. **MENGELSTOFFE,** *beſtaande in verſcheydene Verhandelingen.*

Voorſien met naukeurige Regiſters.

Door een Liefhebber uyt het Engelſch Vertaalt.

t' A M S T E R D A M,

By de WEDUWE van STEVEN SWART, Boekverkoopſter ter zyden de Beurs, 1688.

201 WORKS [Wing B 5150]   Fº 1686

Title, in red and black, within double lines: The Works Of the Learned Sʳ Thomas
Brown, Kt. Doctor of Phyſick, late of Norwich. [*rule*] Containing
   I. Enquiries into Vulgar and Common Errors.
  II. Religio Medici: With Annotations and Obſervations upon it.
 III. Hydriotaphia; or, Urn-Burial: Together with The Garden of Cyrus.
 IV. Certain Miſcellany Tracts.
[*rule*] With Alphabetical Tables. [*rule*] London, Printed for Tho. Baſſet, Ric.
Chiſwell, Tho. Sawbridge, Charles Mearn, and Charles Brome. M̄DCLXXXVI.

Collation: Π² A⁴ a⁴ B–Z⁴ Aa–Zz⁴ Aaa–Iii⁴ Kkk⁶ Lll–Qqq⁴ Rrr⁶ Sſſ–Zzz⁴ Aaaa–Dddd⁴
Eeee²; 304 leaves.

Contents: Π1 frontispiece; Π2 general title; A1–Tt4 *Pseudodoxia Epidemica* (see no. 80);
Uu1–Kk6 *Religio Medici* (see no. 13); Lll1–Rrr6 *Hydriotaphia* and *Garden of Cyrus* (see
no. 97); Sſſ1–Eeee2 *Miscellany Tracts* (see no. 129).

Illustrations: (i) Frontispiece. Portrait of Browne in an oval. Signed R. *White ſculpsit.*
Below are the arms of Browne and the words: *The true Effigies of Sʳ Tho: Brown of
Norwich Kᵗ M.D.* The plate-mark measures 24·5 × 15·5 cm.
(ii)–(v) See no. 97.

Copies: BLO, BM(2),[1] CLN, FLWC, K(2),[2] NCL, NLS, TCD, ULC; BN, RLH, MH,
MMO, NYAM(2), PUL, YUL.

202 WORKS: DUTCH   4º 1688

Title: Alle de Werken Van Thomas Brown, In ſijn Leven Ridder en Doctor in
de Medicyne tót Norwich. Verdeelt in vijf Deelen, Behelſende...[*see facsimile*]
Voorſien met naukeurige Regiſters. Door een Liefhebber uyt het Engelſch
Vertaalt. [*swag ornament*] t'Amſterdan, [*rule*]
  (*a*) By Joannes en Gillis Janſſonius van Waeſberge, Boekverkoopers op't
Water, 1668.
  (*b*) By de Weduwe van Steven Swart, Boekverkoopſter ter zyden de Beurs,
1688.
  (*c*) By Johannes Wolters, Boekverkooper op't Water, in Seneca 1688.

Collation: *⁴ **² A–Z⁴ Aa–Zz⁴ Aaa–Hhh⁴ **⁴ ***⁴ ****² A*–Z*⁴ Aa*–Ss*⁴ Tt*²;
398 leaves.[3]

Contents: *1 frontispiece; *2 general title; *3*a*–**2*b* *Aan den Lezer*; A1*a*–Eee4*b*
(pp. 1–408) *Onderſoek der Gemena Dwalingen*; Fff1*a*–Hhh4*b* *Bladwyzer* (see no. 85);
**1*a*–Q*2*b* *Religio Medici* (see no. 70); Q*3*a*–Dd*1*b* *Hydriotaphia* and *Luſthof van Cyrus*
(see no. 98); Dd*2*a*–Rr*2*b* *Mengelſtoffe* (see no. 130); Rr*3*a*–Tt*1*b* *Blad-wyzer Op de
Godſdeenſt Eens Geneeſmeeſters en volgende Verhandelingen*; Tt*2 usually blank. *Drukfouten*
at bottom of Tt*1*b*, or on Tt*2*a* in one copy (AUB).

[1] One with *A Letter to a Friend* in a modern binding.
[2] One from the library of Narcissus Luttrell, the other in a contemporary binding with
A Letter to a Friend at the end.
[3] An untrimmed copy in Leyden University Library measures 25·5 × 21·3 cm.

Illustrations: (i) Frontispiece, on *1 *b*. An engraved copy, slightly reduced, of the portrait by R. White in the *Works*, 1686. The engraving is unsigned. Below the portrait are the arms of Browne and the inscription: *Thomas Brown,* | *In ſyn Leven Ridder en Doctor* | *in de Medicyne tót Norwich.* The plate-mark measures 19 × 14 cm.

(ii)–(v) See no. 98.

Note: This book was unknown to bibliographers until a copy was obtained from a bookseller at Utrecht by the late Professor T. K. Monro of Glasgow University in 1900. Sir William Osler tried for many years to find another copy, but was unsuccessful, though his friends added a copy to his library after his death. Since that time seven other copies have been located, making nine in all. The title-pages of these are identical except for variations in the imprint. As recorded above, the risk seems to have been shared among three different Amsterdam booksellers, whose names appear in the imprints. Four of the known copies carry the name of the Janssonius van Waesberges, two have that of the widow of Steven Swart, and three have that of Johannes Wolters. The translation is based on the *Works* of 1686, the constitution of this volume being closely followed; the only changes are the addition of a translator's preface before *Religio Medici* and the provision of a general index to all the works after *Pseudodoxia Epidemica* instead of the index to *Miscellany Tracts.* This preface gives the only indication that can be found of the identity of the 'Liefhebber' who translated the books. It is signed by *Wm Séwel*, a Quaker historian (1654–1720), born of English parents at Amsterdam. As pointed out by Monro, however, the text of *Pseudodoxia* appears to be that of Gründahl published in 1668 (see no. 84), so that Séwel was responsible for part of the volume only. He was also author of *A New Dictionary English and Dutch*, t'Amsterdam, By de Weduwe van Steven Swart (1691, 4°), with an engraved title by I. Luiken.

Several sections of *Pseudodoxia Epidemica*, probably taken from *Alle de Werken*, were reprinted by Jan van Gaveren in *Boekzaal der Geleerde Wereld*, July–August 1707.

Copies: AUB (2, *c*, no portraits), GUL (Monro Collection, 2, *a* and *b*), K(*b*); LUB(*a*), MMO(*a*), NYAM(*c*). There is an impression of the frontispiece in the BM Dept. of Prints and Drawings. The late Arundel Esdaile told me that there was a copy in the Göttingen University Library. Enquiries have not elicited any reply, though it is stated in *Bibliotheca Osleriana*, 4573, that this copy is in category (*a*).

203 WORKS ED. WILKIN   8° 1835–6

Sir Thomas Browne's Works including his Life and Correspondence Edited by Simon Wilkin F.L.S. Volume I [II–IV]. [*Pickering's device*] London William Pickering Josiah Fletcher Norwich 1836 [1835] 22 cm. Vol. I, pp. viii, 9–16, xvii–cx, [4],¹ 471, [1]. Vol. II, pp. viii, xxxii, 538, [2]. Vol. III, pp. viii, 505, [3] (last leaf blank). Vol. IV, pp. xvi, 546, [2].

Contents: Vol. I.   Memoirs of Sir Thomas Browne.
                              Domestic Correspondence, Journals, etc.
                              Miscellaneous Correspondence.
            Vol. II.   *Religio Medici.*
                              Pseudodoxia Epidemica, Books I–III.

¹ The second of these two leaves is a fly-title for *Memoirs of Sir T.B.* and evidently meant to be inserted before p. xvii, but, having been printed out of place, has sometimes been omitted.

SIR THOMAS BROWNE'S WORKS

INCLUDING HIS LIFE AND CORRESPONDENCE

EDITED BY SIMON WILKIN F.L.S.

VOLUME I.

LONDON

WILLIAM PICKERING

JOSIAH FLETCHER NORWICH

1836

Vol. III. *Pseudodoxia Epidemica*, Books IV–VII.
  The Garden of Cyrus.
  Hydriotaphia.
  Brampton Urns.
Vol. IV. *Repertorium.*
  Letter to a Friend.
  Christian Morals.
  Miscellany Tracts.
  Latin letters from Theodore Jonas.
  Unpublished papers.
  Dr. Thomas Browne's journey with Dr. Plot, August 1693.
  An account of the MS. collections of Sir T. and Dr. Edward Browne.
  General index.

Illustrations, etc.: Vol. I. (i) Frontispiece. Portrait of Sir T. B., 11 × 9 cm., engraved on steel by W. C. Edwards after White's plate in *Works* (1686). Below are the arms of Browne, and a facsimile of Sir T. B.'s autograph.

(ii)–(iv) Pedigrees nos. 1–3, on leaves, two of which are folding, inserted between pp. 16 and xvii.

Vol. II. Facsimile, folding, of Sir T. B.'s will, inserted between pp. viii and ix.

Vol. III. (i) Frontispiece. Lithographed plate of Sir T. B.'s monument.
  (ii) P. 376. A network.
  (iii) P. 451. Four urns. Woodcut after the original engraving.
  (iv) P. 498. A Roman urn. Ditto.

Vol. IV. (i) Frontispiece. Elevation of the north side of the Cathedral, and Plan of the Green-yard, at Norwich (engraved).

(ii) Facing p. 20. Escutcheons on the inside of the steeple over the choir at Norwich (engraved).

Note: Among the *Memoirs of Sir Thomas Browne* the editor has included an important *Supplementary Memoir* of his own. For this he made extensive researches and even circulated a manifesto (reproduced here, and see p. 229) asking for copies of parish registers. He has also prefixed to each work a biographical and bibliographical preface. Wilkin was the first editor to print most of the correspondence and extensive extracts from commonplace books and other manuscripts, including the compositions in Latin. He began his work on Browne about 1823 at the age of thirty-three, and in 1824 he attempted to obtain the services of Robert Southey as editor. This Southey declined in a letter dated 24 June. In another letter dated 29 June 1831[1] he refused also to write an account of Browne, saying he could not improve on Johnson's *Life*.

In April 1827 Wilkin issued a double leaf of Proposals, announcing his book as 'To be published by subscription, In Four Volumes, 8vo, Price £2 12s. 6d.'. In addition 'A few Copies will be worked on fine thick royal paper, price £4 4s.'. He assigned the printing to his partner in Norwich, Josiah Fletcher; the publication in London was to be undertaken by William Pickering. Fifty copies were printed on large paper (26 × 16·5 cm., untrimmed); the number of small paper copies is not known.

Part of Wilkin's manuscript material is preserved in the Norwich Central Library

---

[1] This letter was in the collection of Captain F. L. Pleadwell, Medical Corps, U.S.N., who sent me a copy in 1929. All the other Southey documents mentioned are in my collection.

To all whom it may Concern.

WANTED,

Copies of the following Registers; for which 2s. 6d. each will be paid, on application to MR. FLETCHER, UPPER HAYMARKET, within a week:—Marriage of Dr. Thomas Browne to Dorothy Mileham in 1641— Births and Burials of Children of the said Thomas and Dorothy Browne between 1641 and 1650. It not being known in what Parish of Norwich he resided during that period.

PRINTED BY JOSIAH FLETCHER, NORWICH.

together with letters from Pickering and various learned correspondents, such as Philip Bliss, John Payne Collier, Daniel Gurney, William Macmichael, Sir Harris Nicolas, and Adam Sedgwick. James Crossley of Manchester was another correspondent, who played Wilkin a trick by sending the spurious 'Fragment on Mummies', which he printed in good faith (IV, 273–6). The greater part of the book was printed in 1835, and this date is found on the title-pages of vols. II–IV, but there was delay in completing the first volume, which bears the date 1836. Much of Wilkin's manuscript material was loaned to me when I was compiling the first edition of this *Bibliography* and formed the basis of an Appendix giving an account of Wilkin[1] and his work on Sir Thomas Browne. After publication Wilkin made great efforts to obtain a review by Southey, who wrote him a number of letters first printed in my Appendix together with the first part of his review, never completed or published.

Pickering did not succeed in subscribing the whole edition, and part of it was re-issued by Bohn with title-pages dated 1846.

A copy of the *Works* with the editor's corrections is in the Central Library, Norwich. A special off-print of *Religio Medici* pulled on hand-made paper with water-mark T EDMONDS 1823 and measuring 27·5 × 21 cm. is also in the Wilkin Collection.

204 WORKS ED. WILKIN   8° 1846

The Works of Sir Thomas Browne. Including his unpublished correspondence, and a memoir. Edited by Simon Wilkin, F.L.S. Vol. 1 [&c.]. London: Henry G. Bohn, York Street, Covent Garden. 1846.

Note: The sheets of the remaining copies of the edition of 1835–6 with new title-pages.

205 WORKS ED. WILKIN   8° 1852

The Works of Sir Thomas Browne. Edited by Simon Wilkin, F.L.S. Vol. 1 [&c.] containing four books of Vulgar Errors [&c.]. London: Henry G. Bohn, York Street, Covent Garden. MDCCCLII. 18 cm. Vol. I, pp. [iv], lxxxii, 463, [1]. Vol. II, pp. iv, 563, [1]. Vol. III, pp. vii, [i], 552 [Bohn's Antiquarian Library]

Illustrations: Vol. I. Frontispiece. Portrait of Sir T. B., 10 × 8 cm., engraved by Hinchliff after the Bodleian portrait.

Vol. II, p. 490, Quincunx.

Vol. III, p. 2, Woodcut of urns; p. 52, Woodcut of Brampton Urn.

Note: A reprint of no. 203, with the Correspondence at the end of vol. III. Considerable passages are omitted, especially from the Supplementary Memoir, and there are a few corrections. The spurious fragment, *On Mummies,* is omitted.

The sheets of this edition were re-issued later by George Bell and Sons. Dr. K. Garth Huston tells me that he has a copy in which a cancel title-page in vol. I has the imprint: *George Bell and Sons, York Street, Covent Garden, 1880.* Vol. II has a cancel title-page dated 1872. Vol. III has the original title-page of 1852.

[1] See also *DNB*, LXI, 259. A corrected proof of the article by his son, Martin Hood Wilkin, is in my collection, and details of the family are written in the family Bible, which I bought at Hodgson's in October 1921 and gave to the Castle Museum, Norwich (it is now in the Ecclesiastical Museum, St. Peter Hungate).

206 WORKS ED. SAYLE 8° 1904–7

The Works of Sir Thomas Browne Edited by Charles Sayle. Volume I [II].
London Grant Richards 1904 [Volume III. Edinburgh John Grant 1907]
[The English Library] 20 cm. Vol. I, pp. lv, [i], 351, [1]. Vol. II, pp. [ii], x,
400. Vol. III, pp. [ii], ix, [i], 601, [3].

Contents: Vol. I.   *Religio Medici.*
                Pseudodoxia Epidemica, Books I–III.
           Vol. II. *Pseudodoxia Epidemica*, Books III–VI.
           Vol. III. *Pseudodoxia Epidemica*, Book VII.
                Hydriotaphia and *Garden of Cyrus.*
                Certain Miscellany Tracts.
                A Letter to a Friend.
                Posthumous Works.
                Christian Morals.
                Selection from MSS. (Notes on certain Birds found in Norfolk;
                Notes on certain Fishes and Marine Animals found in Norfolk; On
                the Ostrich; Boulimia Centenaria; Upon the dark Mist, 27th Novem-
                ber, 1674; Account of a Thunderstorm at Norwich, 1665; On
                Dreams; Observations on Grafting.)

Illustrations: Vol. I. Frontispiece. Photogravure reproduction, reduced, of Van Hove's
       portrait, 1672 (no. 79).
       Vol. II. Frontispiece. Photogravure reproduction of a photograph of Sir T. B.'s skull.
       Vol. III. (i) Facing p. 97. Four urns. Half-tone reproduction of the original
       engraving, 1658.
       (ii) Facing p. 147. Net-work.

Note: Vol. III appeared three years after vols. I and II with the imprint of a different
       publisher. Re-issued with new title-pages in 1912.
       The editor states in his Preface that his text reproduces 'as faithfully as seems
       advisable' the form in which it was presented at the time of the author's death. Hence
       Religio Medici 'follows more particularly the issue of 1682'. The *Vulgar Errors* is
       based on the edition of 1672 'with careful revision'. In the text of *Hydriotaphia* con-
       sideration has been given to corrections made by the author in the presentation copy
       now in the library of Trinity College, Cambridge. Reviewed in *The Athenæum*,
       London, 11 June 1904.

207 WORKS ED. SAYLE 8° 1912

The Works of Sir Thomas Browne Edited by Charles Sayle. Volume I [etc.].
Edinburgh John Grant 1912.

Contents, etc.: As in no. 206.

Note: A re-issue of no. 206 with new title-pages.

207a WORKS ED. KEYNES 8° 1928–31

The Works of Sir Thomas Browne Volume One [Two–Six]…Edited by
Geoffrey Keynes London: Faber & Gwyer Limited New York: William

Edwin Rudge, Publisher 1928 [–1931] 19 cm., untrimmed. Vol. I, 1928, pp. xii, 189, [3]. Vol. II, 1928, pp. xii, 317, [3]. Vol. III, 1928, pp. [viii], 368, Vol. IV, 1929, pp. xii, 130, [2]. Vol. V, 1931, pp. xx, 473, [3]. Vol. VI, 1931, pp. xii, 440.

Contents: Vol. I. *Religio Medici*
               Christian Morals
               A Letter to a Friend
     Vol. II. *Pseudodoxia Epidemica*, Books I–III
     Vol. III. *Pseudodoxia Epidemica*, Books IV–VII
     Vol. IV. *Hydriotaphia*
               Brampton Urns
               The Garden of Cyrus
     Vol. V. *Miscellany Tracts*
               Repertorium
               Miscellaneous Writings
               Fragment on Mummies (spurious)
     Vol. VI. Letters

Illustrations in collotype: Vol. I, frontispiece. Sir Thomas Browne, from a drawing attributed to David Loggan.

    Title-page of *Religio Medici*, 1642, engraved by Marshall, facing p. 2.

    Vol. II, frontispiece. The Skull of Sir Thomas Browne, *norma frontalis*, from a drawing by T. L. Poulton.

    Vol. III, frontispiece. The Skull of Sir Thomas Browne, *norma lateralis*, from a drawing by T. L. Poulton.

    Vol. IV, frontispiece. Sir Thomas Browne, from the oil painting in St. Peter Mancroft, Norwich.
                 Plate of urns, facing p. 7.
                 Quincunx (line block), p. 68.
                 Roman *Battalia* (line block), p. 81.

    Vol. V, frontispiece. Sir Thomas Browne, from the miniature in the collection of the Duke of Buccleuch.

    Vol. VI, frontispiece. Sir Thomas and Dame Dorothy Browne, from the oil painting attributed to Joan Carlile in the National Portrait Gallery.
                 Ureters and *vesica* of a carp (half-tone block), p. 73.
                 Head of an ostrich after Ray (half-tone block), p. 239.

Note: In this edition the entire text has been revised, from manuscript sources whenever possible, these being freshly transcribed. The text, especially that of the Letters, contains many additions, though the Latin writings are omitted. There is a Preface by the editor in each volume except vol. III. The ordinary edition is bound in blue buckram with a monogram TB on the title-page and front cover of each volume reproduced from an engraving by Stephen Gooden, R.A. A limited edition is described under the next entry. Part of the ordinary edition was destroyed by enemy action in 1941 except for some copies of vols. V and VI (see nos. 200 and 200*l*).

207*b* WORKS ED. KEYNES [Limited edition] 8° 1928–31

The Works of Sir Thomas Browne [&c. as in no. 207*a*] 19 cm., untrimmed. Vol. I, pp. xvi, 189, [3]. Vol. II, pp. xv, [i], 317, [3]. Vol. III, pp. viii, 368. Vol. IV, pp. [ii], xii, 130, [2]. Vol. V, pp. xxiv, 473, [3]. Vol. VI, pp. xvi, 440.

Contents, illustrations: As in no. 207*a*.

Note: Of this edition 210 numbered copies were printed on Kelmscott hand-made paper, bound in blue parchment with monogram as before. Vol. I of each set was signed by the editor on the leaf before the half-title.

207*c* WORKS ED. KEYNES 8° 1964

The Works of Sir Thomas Browne Volume I [II–IV]...Edited by Geoffrey Keynes London Faber & Faber Limited [1964] 21·6 cm., trimmed. Vol. I, pp. xii, 295, [1]. Vol. II, pp. x, 574. Vol. III, pp. xvii, [i], 482. Vol. IV, pp. xiii, [i], 415, [1].

Contents: Vol. I.   *Religio Medici*
               A Letter to a Friend
               Hydriotaphia and *Garden of Cyrus*
               Brampton Urns
               Christian Morals
      Vol. II.   *Pseudodoxia Epidemica*, Books I–VII
      Vol. III. *Certain Miscellany Tracts*
               Repertorium
               Latin Writings with translations into English
               Miscellaneous Writings
               Fragment on Mummies (spurious)
      Vol. IV. Letters

Illustrations in collotype:
    Vol. I, frontispiece. Sir Thomas Browne, from a drawing attributed to David Loggan. Title-page of *Religio Medici*, 1642 (enlarged), facing p. I. Sir Thomas Browne, from the oil painting in St. Peter Mancroft, Norwich, facing p. 129. Plate of Urns, facing p. 135. Quincunx (line block, enlarged), p. 178. Roman *Battalia* (line block), p. 189.
    Vol. II. The Skull of Sir Thomas Browne, *norma frontalis* and *lateralis*, from drawings by T. L. Poulton, frontispiece and facing p. 1.
    Vol. III, frontispiece. Sir Thomas Browne from the miniature in the collection of the Duke of Buccleuch.
    Vol. IV, frontispiece. Sir Thomas and Dame Dorothy Browne, from the oil painting attributed to Joan Carlile in the National Portrait Gallery. Ureters and *vesica* of a carp (half-tone block), p. 64. Head of an ostrich after Ray (half-tone block), p. 207.

Note: This edition is a reprint of no. 207*a* extensively revised and augmented. The text of *Religio Medici* is based on that edited by Dottoressa Vittoria Sanna in 1958 (see no. 58*l*). *Hydriotaphia* and *The Garden of Cyrus* follow John Carter's edition of 1958 (see no. 126*f*). Vol. III contains for the first time since 1836 all the Latin writings with

English versions by W. R. LeFanu. The Letters in vol. IV have several additions, including some Latin letters with English versions. The illustrations are the same as before. The binding of grey cloth with red labels and the title-pages have the monogram by Gooden.

207*d* WORKS ED. KEYNES (University of Chicago Press)   8° 1964

Note: Part of the edition of no. 207*c* was issued by the University of Chicago Press with its imprint.

XI

Selections

207*e* THE DORMITIVE f° 1693

In Harmonia Sacra: or, Divine Hymns and Dialogues [Edited by Henry Playford]...The Second Book...London: E. Jones for Henry Playford. 1693.

Poem: On pp. 23–4 is part of Browne's 'Dormitive', 'The night is come like to the day', from *Religio Medici*, part II, section 12. Ten lines have been altered and adapted, and set to music probably by Pelham Humphreys.

Note: In the third edition of *Harmonia Sacra* (1714) Browne's lines are placed after Donne's 'Wilt thou forgive that sin' at pp. 67–8. The music for Donne's lines is by Humphreys.

207*f* GOLDEN SENTENCES ED. BATES 12° 1826
[Not seen]

208 SELECTIONS ED. MONTAGU 8° 1829

Selections from the Works of Taylor, Hooker, Barrow, South, Latimer, Brown, Milton, and Bacon; by Basil Montagu, Esq. A.M. Third Edition. London William Pickering. MDCCCXXIX. 16 cm. pp. xv, [1], 422.

Selections: pp. 329–50, passages from *Religio Medici* and *Hydriotaphia*.

Note: The passages from Browne were not included in the two previous editions. Republished in 1899 by Dent under the title *Thoughts of divines and philosophers selected by Basil Montagu*. This is also the title of another and distinct work by Montagu, published by Pickering in 1832, which contains one short passage from *Religio Medici*.

209 SELECTIONS ED. ALLIBONE 8° 1876

Prose Quotations from Socrates to Macaulay...By S. Austin Allibone... Philadelphia: J. B. Lippincott & Co. 1876. 24 cm. pp. 764.

Selections: Contains 78 quotations from Browne's works (see index).

209*a* SELECTIONS ED. WHYTE 8° 1898

Sir Thomas Browne an Appreciation with some of the best passages of the Physicians Writings selected and arranged by Alexander Whyte D.D. Edinburgh. Oliphant Anderson & Ferrier 1898 18·5 cm. pp. 90, [6].

210 SELECTIONS ED. MINCHIN 8° 1905

Simples from Sir Thomas Browne's Garden Gathered by Harry Christopher Minchin Author of 'The Arcadians' and 'A Little Gallery of English Poets'... Oxford B. H. Blackwell, Broad Street MCMV 17 cm. pp. [viii], 154, [6].

Selections: From *Religio Medici*, *Christian Morals*, *Pseudodoxia*, *Hydriotaphia*, and three letters to Mrs. Lyttelton, with a preface.

Frontispiece: Engraved portrait by R. White reproduced in half-tone.

211 SELECTIONS ED. WILKIN 8° 1905

Quaint Sayings from the Works of Sir Thomas Browne. Compiled by Mrs.
Martin Hood Wilkin. London Elliot Stock, 62, Paternoster Row, E.C. 1905
14 cm. pp. xi, [i], 95, [1].

Selections: From *Religio Medici, Christian Morals, Hydriotaphia* and commonplace books.

Frontispiece: Engraved portrait by R. White reproduced in half-tone.

Note: With a biographical introduction. Published as a memorial of Martin Hood
Wilkin, son of Simon Wilkin.

212 SELECTIONS ED. JENKINS 8° [1908]

Golden Thoughts from Sir Thomas Browne edited with a preface by Herbert
Ives [Jenkins]...London: John Lane, the Bodley Head. New York: John
Lane Company [The Library of Golden Thoughts] 15 cm. pp. xvi, 71, [1].

Frontispiece: Engraved portrait by R. White reproduced in half-tone.

213 SELECTIONS ED. TOWNSEND 8° [1911]

Selections from the Writings of Sir Thomas Browne by Lewis W. Townsend
London Headley Brothers Bishopsgate [1911] [The Religion of Life Series]
17 cm. pp. 67, [1].

Selections: From *Religio Medici, Christian Morals* and *A Letter to a Friend,* with an introduction.

XII

Sale Catalogue of Browne's Library

BIBLIOGRAPHICAL PREFACE

In a passage in *Religio Medici* (part I, sect. xxiv) Browne deplored the multiplicity of books, and wished 'for the benefit of learning, to reduce it as it lay at first in a few and solid Authors; and to condemne to the fire those swarms and millions of *Rhapsodies*, begotten onely to distract and abuse the weaker judgements of Scholars, and to maintaine the Trade and Mystery of Typographers'. But the wish was a rhetorical expression and not to be taken too literally, for we know that he was himself a persistent and omnivorous reader, and that he even compiled in his *Musæum Clausum, or Bibliotheca Abscondita*, a long list of curious works no longer, or never, in existence, though he would have wished to see them. The evidence of his wide reading has survived in the references to other authors abounding in his works, in the portentous list of books read to him at nights by his daughter Elizabeth 'until she read them all out' (see no. 196), and finally in the catalogue of his library printed when the books were to be sold by auction in January 1710/11 after the death of Thomas Browne, Sir Thomas's grandson. The sale catalogue described here can only have survived by fortunate accidents, but four copies being known to be extant at the present time. Of these, the British Museum copy belonged to Sir Hans Sloane and provides evidence that he was a buyer at the sale, though neither this nor any other copy has been priced.[1] The title-page, reproduced here, shows that some of the books were added by Dr. Edward Browne, though relatively few have dates after 1682, the year of Sir Thomas's death, suggesting that the greater part of the collection was formed by Sir Thomas himself.

The catalogue lists 2,377 lots, the books being classified under the following headings: *Libri Theologici*; *Historici, Philologici*; *Medici, Philosophici*; *Mathematici*; *Livres Francois*; *Libri Italiani*; *Libros Espannolos*; *Libri Teutonicè & Belgicè*; *English Books*; *Libri Omissi*; *English Folios Omitted*. The books under each heading are further divided up according to size.

It is remarkable that, although so large a collection of books belonging to Sir Thomas Browne or to his son has been dispersed, so few can now be identified as having belonged to either of them. One volume thus identifiable is his copy of Evelyn's *Sculptura* (1662), though this is known only by the author's presentation inscription (see no. 200 a). It is clear, in fact, that Browne was not in the habit of putting his name in his books, so that the volumes which he loved and read cannot usually be distinguished from other copies. In my collection, however, is a copy of Leland's *Cygnea Cantio* (London, 1658) containing evidence that it certainly did belong to him. The fly-leaf bears the signature of Edward Browne and beneath this is the title of the book, *Lelandi Cygnea Cantio*, written in his father's hand. The volume was sold at Sotheby's on 21 December 1921 with part of the Blaenpant Library formed by Edward Browne's son-in-law, Owen Brigstocke, whose bookplate and signature dated 1734 also appear in the book.

[1] See Jeremiah S. Finch, 'Sir Hans Sloane's Printed Books', *The Library* (1941), p. 67.

Browne referred to Leland's works in a letter to Dugdale dated 6 December 1658,[1] mentioning one with the title *Itinerarium Cantii*, but the *Cygnea Cantio* was not relevant to the subject under discussion—the source of a quotation made by Browne at second hand. He may not have obtained the book until later and it was perhaps given by Edward to his son-in-law. I have in my collection one other book that may have belonged to Sir Thomas near the end of his life. It is an English translation of de Scudéry's *Celia. An Excellent New Romance* (London, f°, 1678), and is inscribed twice inside the cover by Browne's grandson: *Thomas Browne his Book 1699*, and on the fly-leaf and title-page: *Brigstocke*, indicating that it also came into the Blaenpant Library. Several other books from this library have been examined, but none contains evidence of Sir Thomas's ownership, even when it was a book known to have been in his library.[2] The sale catalogue must, therefore, remain the chief evidence of the sources from which his erudition was derived, and it is consequently of great interest and importance. A study of the catalogue with a reprint has long been in preparation by Dr. Jeremiah S. Finch, but is still awaited.

[1] *Works*, ed. Keynes (1964), IV, 311.
[2] In *The Bookman's Journal and Print Collector*, 9 July 1920, Fleming Patrick reported finding a copy of Edward Topsell's *The Reward of Religion* (London, Windet, 1601) (STC 24129) 'with the autograph of Sir Thomas Browne when a young man at college'. I have not seen this and can express no opinion as to its authenticity. There were many people of the same name, whose signatures have often been wrongly attributed to Sir Thomas.

A
CATALOGUE

Of the LIBRARIES of the Learned

Sir *Thomas Brown*,

AND

Dr. *Edward Brown*, his Son,

Late Prefident of the College of Phyficians.

Confifting of many very Valuable and Uncommon Books, in moft *Faculties* and *Languages*.

Chiefly in

PHYSICK,	}{	DIVINITY,
CHIRURGERY,	}{	PHILOLOGY,
CHYMISTRY,	}{	HISTORY,

And other Polite Parts of *Learning*.

Moft of the Claffics *Not Varior*. Old *Elzevir*'s, and other
Choice Editions, well Bound, and very Fair.

ALSO

BOOKS of SCULPTURE & PAINTING,

with Choice Manufcripts.

WHICH

Will begin to be Sold by AUCTION, at the
Black-boy Coffee-houfe in *Ave-Mary-Lane*, near
Ludgate, on MONDAY the 8th Day of *January*,
17$\frac{10}{11}$, beginning every Evening at Four of the
Clock, till the Sale is finifh'd.

By **Thomas Ballard**, Bookfeller,
at the *Rifing-Sun* in *Little-Britain*.

Where Catalogues may be had; as alfo of Mr. *King* in *Weftmin-
fter-hall*, Mr. *Stokoe* againft the Mews Gate, Mr. *Vaillant* againft
Bedford-buildings in the *Strand*, Mr. *Brown* without *Temple-bar*,
Mr. *Clements* in St. *Paul*'s Church-yard, Mr. *Strahan* in *Cornhill*,
Bookfellers, at both Univerfities, and at the Place of Sale. Pr. 6 d.

214 SALE CATALOGUE

Title: A Catalogue Of the Libraries of the Learned Sir Thomas Brown, and Dr. Edward Brown, his Son, Late President of the College of Physicians... Which Will begin to be Sold by Auction, at the Black-boy Coffee-house in Ave-Mary-Lane, near Ludgate, on Monday the 8ᵗʰ Day of January, 1710/11, beginning every Evening at Four of the Clock, till the Sale is finish'd. By Thomas Ballard, Bookseller, at the Rising-Sun in Little-Britain...[&c.; see facsimile]

Collation: Π¹ B⁴ C⁵ (C1 detached) D–H⁴ I¹. Π1 and I1 are conjugate, being wrapped round the other sheets of the book.

Contents: Π1 *a* title; Π1 *b Conditions of sale*; B1 *a*–I1 *b* (pp. 1–58 [should be 60]) *Catalogue.*

Note: The page numbers are omitted from pp. 16 and 18; pp. 19–60 are numbered 17–58. The copy of the *Catalogue* at Worcester College, Oxford, one of the books given to the College by its benefactor George Clarke (1661–1736), is unsophisticated, having never been bound. The three original stab holes are visible and the sheets are now secured by early stitching, so that the peculiar constitution described above can be clearly seen. It seems probable that the first and last leaves, Π1 and I1, were imposed with the detached leaf C1, the single resulting blank leaf being removed. There is no watermark by which this might be tested.

Copies: BM (Sir Hans Sloane's copy), WCO (given by George Clarke); MMO (given to Sir William Osler by A. Forbes Sieveking), YML (acquired by J. F. Fulton after a sale at Sotheby's of books derived from the library of the Royal Society).

XIII

Biography and Criticism

BIBLIOGRAPHICAL PREFACE

Materials for a biography of Sir Thomas Browne begin with autobiographical passages in *Religio Medici* (1642), and within a few hours of its publication Sir Kenelm Digby was penning his *Observations* on the contents, thus initiating the long series of entries included in this section as criticism. It is convenient for bibliographical purposes to combine biographical and critical materials in one section and to arrange them within the period 1633–1800 according to the date of publication. Any difficulty introduced by this method of presentment will be resolved by reference to the General Index. The form of entry has been varied according to the bibliographical or other interest of the individual items.

The uneventfulness of Browne's life has resulted in the accumulation of more critical than biographical matter. Indeed the only works of importance concerned with his life are Whitefoot's Minutes in the *Posthumous Works* (1712) (no. 310), Kippis's *Biographia Britannica* (1730), Mrs. Lyttelton's notes printed in the *European Magazine* (1801), Wood's *Athenæ Oxonienses* (1826), Wilkin's edition of the *Works* (1836) (no. 203) and the recent biographical studies by Dr. Jeremiah S. Finch (1950) and Professor Frank L. Huntley (1962), these having superseded Sir Edmund Gosse's book of 1905. Samuel Johnson's *Life of Browne* in his edition of *Christian Morals* (1756) is chiefly of interest as criticism. Isolated incidents in Browne's life are related in *A Tryal of Witches* before Sir Matthew Hale, 1682 (no. 287), in John Browne's *Adenochoiradelogia*, 1684 (no. 289), in Evelyn's *Diary* and elsewhere. Browne's letters to his family and friends are also a most important source of information about his daily life and medical practice in Norwich. These may be read in the fourth volume of his collected *Works* published in 1964, and may be supplemented by the letters to him from his sons printed in the first volume of Wilkin's edition of the *Works* (1836). A frivolous anecdote, probably fictitious, is to be found in Gideon Harvey's *Conclave of Physicians* (1683) (no. 288). A considerable number of entries are concerned with Browne's posthumous biography, beginning with the exhumation of his skull in 1840 and ending with its reinterment in 1922. The controversy concerning this relic bore fruit in the publication of a monograph by the Galton Laboratory dealing fully and authoritatively with the question not only of the skull but also of the portraiture.

The number of entries in this section is very much larger than was printed in the former edition of this *Bibliography*. Greater familiarity with the literature of the seventeenth century has led to detection of many more interesting references to Browne and his works. Since 1924 scholarly criticism has become increasingly aware of the merits and interest of Browne's writings, with a corresponding growth in the output of critical studies and theses.

Contemporary criticism of Browne's works after the publication of Digby's *Observations* was voiced most loudly by Alexander Ross in his *Medicus Medicatus* (1645) (no. 225), and *Arcana Microcosmi* (1651) (no. 232), and by John Robinson in *Endoxa* (1656) (no. 239). Browne was occasionally addressed by contemporary versifiers. The earliest of these was Dr. John Collop in his *Poesis Rediviva* (1656) (no. 237), first reprinted in 1924. A Latin poem by James Duport, Master of Magdalene College, Cambridge, was published in 1676 (no. 279). Brief references to Browne are to be found in many other books, beginning with Guy Patin's letters (1644), and Howell's *Epistolæ Ho-Elianæ* (1645). A large proportion of these occur in the writings of continental authors, who were familiar with his works, particularly *Religio Medici*, through the numerous editions of this work in Latin. These authors were concerned chiefly with Browne's philosophical and religious attitudes. Sometimes he was attacked as an atheist, and *Religio Medici* was duly placed on the *Index Expurgatorius* on 18 March 1645. On the other hand an interesting *Apologia* for Browne by Elias Fredericus Heister was published in 1736. Browne's works were admired by Lamb, Coleridge, Southey, de Quincey and Hazlitt. Among the more recent appreciations are the introductions to the numerous editions of the various works by editors such as Gardiner, Greenhill, Symonds, Whibley and Denonain, and the essays by writers such as Leslie Stephen, Walter Pater, Lytton Strachey and Basil Willey. This section does not, however, attempt to furnish a complete list of recent works containing critical material. Every literary history covering the seventeenth century must contain longer or shorter passages concerning Sir Thomas Browne, but a compilation of a list of these books has not been considered necessary.

I owe many of the references in French to the late Professor Olivier Leroy's *A French Bibliography of Browne* (London, 1931).

OBSERVATIONS
VPON
Religio Medici.

Occaſionally Written
By Sir *Kenelome Digby*, Knight

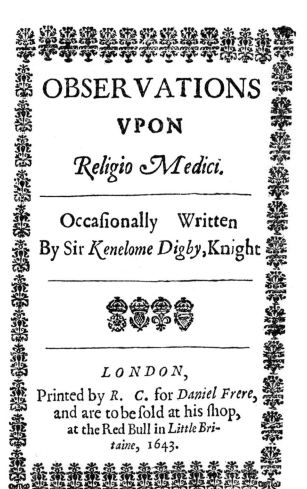

LONDON,
Printed by *R. C.* for *Daniel Frere,*
and are to be ſold at his ſhop,
at the Red Bull in *Little Bri-*
taine, 1643.

(i) 1633–1800
(*In cronological order*)

LEYDEN UNIVERSITY   1633

215 *In* Album Studiosorum Academiae Lugduno-Batavae, 1575–1875. 's Gravenhage. 1875.

Reference: p. 259, recording Browne's matriculation at Leyden as a medical student on 3 December 1633.

216 *In* Archieven van Senaaten Faculteiten der Leidsche Universiteit, no. 9: Volumen Inscriptionum sive Catalogus Studiosorum Academiae Leydensis, 1631–1645.

Reference: f. 89, recording that Browne lodged in Leyden at the house of Richardus Monck in the Sonneveltsteeg.

217 *In* Bronnen tot de Geschiedenis der Leidsche Universiteit, II, 1610–1647, ed. P. C. Molhuysen. 's Gravenhage. 1916.

Reference: p. 181, recording Browne's examination for his degree eighteen days after his matriculation: '*Acta Sen. 1633 Dec. xxi. Visus est dignus Thomas Broune, cui supremus in Medicina gradus conferatur, quem illi tribuit Adolphus Vorstius.*'

218 DIGBY'S OBSERVATIONS [Wing D 1442]   8° 1643

Title, within ornamental border: Obſervations vpon Religio Medici. [*rule*] Occaſionally Written By Sir Kenelome Digby, Knight [*ornaments between rules*] London, Printed by R. C. for Daniel Frere, and are to be ſold at his ſhop, at the Red Bull in Little Britaine, 1643.

Collation: A–H⁸; 64 leaves.

Contents: A1 blank; A2 title; A3 *a*–H7 *b* (pp. 1–122) *Obſervations*, addressed *To the Right Honourable Edward Earle of Dorſet*, and dated *December* 22–23, 1642; H7 *b*–H8 *b* (pp. 122–4) *The Poſtſcript*.

Note: Signature H3 is misprinted G3. The pagination is correct. A variant title-page is recorded under the next entry. Digby's volume is often found bound up with *Religio Medici* (1642, 1643). Digby's manuscript is in the British Museum (MS. 904, ff. 223–39).
    This work was translated by William Séwel into Dutch for the *Works* of 1688 (no. 202), and was included in Venzky's German edition of the *Religio Medici*, 1746 (no. 72). It was also translated into Latin and annotated by Morhof, but this was never published (*Polyhistor*, 4°, 1732, vol. I, p. 68).

Copies: BLO, BM, CLN, K; MH, MMO, PUL, YML.

219 DIGBY'S OBSERVATIONS [variant issue, Wing D 1441] 8° 1643

Title, within ornamental border: Observations vpon Religio Medici. [*rule*] Occasionally Written By Sir Kenelme Digby, Knight [*ornaments between rules*] London, Printed by R. C. for Lawrence Chapman and Daniel Frere, 1643.

Collation, contents: As in no. 218.

Copies: ULC; MH, YML.

220 DIGBY'S OBSERVATIONS 8° 1644

Title, within ornamental border: Observations vpon Religio Medici. [*rule*] Occasionally Written By Sir Kenelme Digby, Knight [*three ornaments between rules*] London, Printed by F.L. for Lawrence Chapman and Daniel Frere, 1644.

Collation: A–H⁸; 64 leaves.

Contents: A1 blank; A2 title; A3 *a*–H7 *b* (pp. 1–122) *Observations*; H7 *b*–H8 *b* (pp. 122–4). *The Postscript.*

Note: In most copies the ornaments between rules are replaced by *The second Edition*, &c. (see next entry). Neither the rest of the title-page nor any other part of the book has been reset, so that the change was made while the book was in the press. This volume is often found bound up with *Religio Medici* (1643, 1645 and 1656). Digby's *Observations on the 22. Stanza of the 2d. Book of Spencer's Faery Queen, London* (1644) is sometimes added.

Copies: K; MH.

221 DIGBY'S OBSERVATIONS [variant issue, Wing D 1443] 8° 1644

Title, within ornamental border: Observations...Knight (as in no. 220) [*rule*] The second Edition corrected and amended. [*rule*] London...(as in no. 220).

Collation, contents: As in no. 220.

Note: This issue has the more usual form of the title-page.

Copies: BLO, BM, CLN, K; MH, MMO, YUL.

222 BRUNE: JOK EN ERNST 1644 [1672]

Alle Volgeestige Werken van Jan de Brune de Jonge...Te Harlingen... MDCLXXII. 4°.

References: Contains three works separately paged; the second, *Jok en Ernst*, first published in 1644, has two references to *Religio Medici* on pp. 131, 139.

223 PATIN: LETTERS 1644–1657

In Lettres de Gui Patin Nouvelle Édition augmentée de lettres inédites, précédées d'une Notice Biographique, accompagnées de remarques par J.-H. Réveillé-Parise. Paris. Londres. 3 vols. 1846.

References: I, 340, 21 October 1644; I, 354, 16 April 1645, 21 October 1646; II, 351, 26 July 1650; II, 77, 21 October 1653; II, 321, 19 June 1657, all concerning *Religio Medici*.

Note: Leroy in his *Bibliography of Browne* (1931), pp. 47–9, regards these references as 'superficial, scanty and somewhat incoherent', though they were the first criticisms of Browne to be made in France. See also Osler, Sir William, *The Athenaeum* (1909).

224 HOWELL: EPISTOLÆ HO-ELIANÆ [Wing H 3071] 4° 1645

Epistolæ Ho-Elianæ. Familiar Letters Domestic and Forren; Divided into Six Sections...By J.H. Esq;: One of the Clerks of His Majesties most Honourable Privy Councell. London, Printed for Humphrey Moseley...1645. Engraved title-page. A4 *4 (*a*)² B–M4 Aa–Pp4 Aaa–Eee4 Aaaa–Ffff4 Aaaaa–Mmmmm4.

Reference: On Mmmmm2, Sect. 6, letter lx, To Tho. Young Esq., p. 91: 'But to passe from these motheaten Philosophers to a *modern* Physicion of our own, it was a most unmanly thing in him, while he displayes his *own Religion*, to wish that ther were a way to propagat the world without conjunction with women, (and *Paracelsus* undertakes to shew him the way) wherby he seem's to repine (though I understand he was Wiv'd a little after) at the honourable degree of *marriage*, which I hold to be the prime Link of human society.' In the second edition, 1650, the letter is dated 28 April 1645. The reference is to *Religio Medici*, part II, section 9.

225 ROSS: MEDICUS MEDICATUS [Wing R 1961] 8° 1645

Title, within double lines: Medicus Medicatus: or the phyſicians religion cured, by a lenitive or gentle potion: With ſome Animadverſions upon Sir Kenelme Digbie's Obſervations on Religio Medici. [*rule*] By Alexander Roſs. [*rule*] London, Printed by James Young, and are to be ſold by Charles Green, at the Signe of the Gun in Ivie-lane. Anno Dom. 1645.

Collation: A–H8; 64 leaves.

Contents: A1 blank; A2 title; A3*a*–A4*b* dedication to *Mr Edward Benlowes, Eſquire,* signed *A. R.*; A5*a*–A6*b The Contents*; A7*a The Contents of the ſecond part*; A7*b*–A8*a The Contents of the Animadverſions*; A8*b Imprimatur*, signed *John Downame*; B1*a*–F8*b* (pp. 1–80) *Medicus Medicatus*; G1 sub-title, within double lines: *Animadverſions...* [*device between rules*] *London, Printed for James Young*; G2*a*–H8*b* (pp. 83–112) *Animadverſions*.

Note: The device on the sub-title of *Animadversions* is the smaller one used originally by Robert Young, 1625–43 (McKerrow's *Printers' and Publishers' Devices*, 1913, no. 404). This work is often to be found bound up with the early editions of *Religio Medici*.

Copies: BLO, BM, CLN, EUL, K; MH, MMO, NYAM, PUL, YML.

226 BUCK: HISTORY OF RICHARD III [Wing B 5306] f° 1646

The History of the Life and Reigne of Richard The Third. Composed in five Bookes by Geo: Buck Esquire. London, Printed by W. Wilson, and are to be sold by W.L.H.M. and D.P. 1646. A² B–V4 *4.

Reference: On A2b in the Dedication to Philip Earl of Pembroke and Montgomery is the passage: 'I am with his opinion, in his excellent Religio Medici, who holds it an offence to Charity, and as bloody a thought one way, as Nero's in another.'

Note: The 'offence to charity' is by miscalling whole professions or nations by opprobrious epithets—*Religio Medici*, part II, section 4.

227 DANIEL: POEMS   1646–8

The Poems of George Daniel Esq. of Beswick, Yorkshire (1616–1657) from The Original MSS. in the British Museum: hitherto unprinted. Edited by the Rev. Alexander B. Grosart LL.D., F.S.A. In four volumes. Printed for Private Circulation Only. 1878 (100 subscribers).

References: Vol. I, p. 191. 'To the Reader of Doctor Browne's booke Entituled Pseudodoxia Epidemica', a poem of 22 lines, dated Decemb. 11th. 1648. Vol. I, pp. 205–8. 'Upon an excellent Treatise Written by T:B: M:D: called Religio Medici', a poem of 76 lines dated August 1 1646. See also p. 55.

Note: In the Introduction the editor states that Daniel seemed to be personally acquainted with Browne. In line 40 are the words, 'I know him by his Booke', but there is no indication of any closer friendship.

228 VOX NORWICI [Wing V 722]   4° 1646

Title, within ornamental border: Vox Norwici: or, The Cry of Norwich, Vindicating their Minifters...from the foule and falfe afperfions and flanders, which are unchriftianly throwne upon them in a lying and fcurrilous Libell, lately come forth, intituled *Vox Populi*, or the Peoples cry againft the Clergy, or rather the voice of a Scifmaticke projecting the difcouragement, and driving away of our faithfull Teachers, but we hope his lies fhall not fo effect it.
Ier. 48. 30 [quotation between rules]
London, Printed for William Franckling, and are to be fold by Richard Tomlins, at the Signe of the Sun in Pie-Corner. MDCXLVI.

Collation: A–B⁴; 8 leaves.

Contents: A1 title; A2*a To the Impartiall Reader*; A2*b Vox Norwici. A true Coppy of the Act of Common Councell*; A3*a*–B4*a The Cry of Norwich, Vindicating their Minifters*; B4*b* blank.

Reference: B4*a*. Among the names of the fifteen signatories appears that of *Thomas Browne*.

Note: This pamphlet was called forth by the publication of Louis Du Moulin's *Vox Populi, expressed in xxxv. motions* (London, 1641), concerning the reforming of the Church. Although Browne's name appears among the fifteen signatories there is no evidence that he had any hand in the composition of *The Cry of Norwich*. Attention was first drawn to Browne's association with *Vox Norwici* by Arundell Esdaile in a letter to the *Times Literary Supplement* 25 December 1919. *Vox Populi* was also attacked in *An Hue-and-Cry after Vox Populi. Or, An Answer to Vox Diaboli, or a Libellous Pamphlet falsely styled Vox Populi, reviling the Magistracy and Ministry of Norfolk.*

Printed for Edward Martin, Bookseller in Norwich, at the signe of the upper Halfe Moone in the Market-place. 1646. A–E⁴. Professor F. L. Huntley has noted that three leaves of *Vox Norwici* are to be seen used as end-papers in the BM copy of *Logica analytica*, London, 1650, by Thomas Lushington, Browne's tutor and friend.

Copy: BM. (*An Hue-and-Cry*, ULC.)

229 POWER: A LETTER 1647

A Letter from Dr. Henry Power to Dr. (*later* Sir) Thomas Browne [10 February 1647] [100 copies reprinted from *The Works*...1931, for The Roxburghe Club of San Francisco by Thomas Cowles, John T. Johnck, and Lawton R. Kennedy January, 1933] 15 cm., pp. [4].

230 SAUMAISE, CLAUDE DE 1648

In De Briefwisseling van Constantijn Huygens, ed. Worp. 's Gravenhage. 1911–17.

Reference: vol. IV, p. 456. Saumaise writes to Huygens in 1648 asking his help in finding Browne's *Pseudodoxia Epidemica*. He had heard that Browne lived at the Hague.

231 CHARLETON: HELMONT'S TERNARY OF PARADOXES
[Wing H 1401] 4° 1650

A ternary of paradoxes. Written originally by Joh. Bapt. Van Helmont, and Translated...by Walter Charleton, Doctor in Physick. London, Printed by James Flesher for William Lee, dwelling in Fleetstreet, at the sign of the Turks-head. 1650. A–Z⁴ Aa–Bb⁴. (An engraved title was added to the second impression, 1650.)

Reference: On B3*a* in *The Epistle Dedicatory* addressed by Charleton to Viscount Brouncker. Writing in favour of Latin as a source of English terms and as 'the most symphonicall and concordant Language of the Rationall Soule', he refers to 'the skill and sweate of those two Heroicall Wits, the Lord St. Albans, and the now flourishing Dr. Browne'.

232 ROSS: ARCANA MICROCOSMI [Wing R 1946] 12° 1651

Title, within double lines: Arcana Microcofmi: or, The hid Secrets of Mans Body difclofed; Firft, In an Anatomical Duel between Ariftotle & Galen, About the Parts thereof. Secondly, By a Difcovery of the ftrange and marvellous Difeafes, Symptomes, and Accidents of Mans Body. With A Refutation of Doctor Browns Vulgar Errors, And the Ancient Opinions vindicated. [*rule*] By Alexander Ross. [*rule*] London, Printed by Thomas Newcomb, and are to be fold by George Latham at the Bifhops Head in St. Pauls Church-yard 1651.

Collation: A⁸⁺² B–M¹² N²; 144 leaves.

Contents: A1 blank; A2 title; two leaves inserted, the first with signature A2, *The Epistle Dedicatory* to *Edward Watson Esquire, Son to the Lord Rockingame*; A3*a*–A8*b* Contents; B1*a*–N2*b* (pp. 1–292) *Arcana Microcosmi*.

Arcana Microcosmi :
OR,
The hid Secrets of M A N S
Body disclosed ;

F I R S T,
In an Anatomical Duel between
A R I S T O T L E
&
G A L E N,
About the Parts thereof.

S E C O N D L Y,
By a Discovery of the strange and
marvellous Diseases, Symptomes,
and Accidents of Mans Body.

W I T H
A Refutation of Doctor *Browns*
VULGAR ERRORS,
And the Ancient Opinions vindicated.

By A L E X A N D E R R O S S.

LONDON,
Printed by *Th. mas Newcomb*, and are to be sold by
George Latham at the Bishops Head in
St. *Pauls* Church-yard 1651.

12-2

Note: By the author of *Medicus Medicatus*, 1645 (see no. 225). On pp. 143–292 is a criticism of *Pseudodoxia Epidemica*, headed: 'The fecond Book, Of the ftrange Difeafes and Accidents of Mans Body; Wherein divers of Dr *Browns* vulgar errors and Affertions are refuted, and the ancient Tenents maintained.' This edition of the work seems to be extremely rare and was not known to Wilkin, who was, however, familiar with the second edition published in 1652 (see next entry). A3, the first leaf after the two leaves inserted, has signature *A*. The collation was wrongly given in the former edition of this *Bibliography*, the BM copy being then the only one known to me. The correct constitution of the book can be plainly seen in my copy acquired since 1924.

Copies: BLO, BM, K; YML.

233 ROSS: ARCANA MICROCOSMI [Wing R 1947]   8° 1652

Title, in red and black, within double lines: Arcana Microcofmi: or, The hid Secret of Man's Body difcovered; In an Anatomical Duel between Ariftotle and Galen concerning the Parts thereof: As alfo, By a Difcovery of the ftrange and marveilous Difeafes, Symptomes & Accidents of Man's Body. With A Refutation of Doctor Brown's Vulgar Errors, The Lord Bacon's Natural Hiftory, And Doctor Harvy's Book De Generatione, Comenius, and Others; Whereto is annexed a Letter from Doctor Pr. to the Author, and his Anfwer thereto, touching Doctor Harvy's Book de Generatione. [*rule*] By A. R. [*rule*] London, Printed by Tho. Newcombe, and are to bee fold by John Clark, entring into Mercers-Chappel at the lower end of Cheapfide, 1652.

Collation: A–S⁸ T⁴; 148 leaves.

Contents: A1 title; A2 dedication to *Edward Watfon, Efq.*, A3 *a*–A8 *a The Contents*; A8 *b* blank; B1 *a*–O8 *a* (pp. 1–207) *Arcana Microcofmi*; O8 *b* blank; P1 sub-title to *An appendix*; P2 dedication to *Andrew Henley, Efq.*; P3 *a*–S8 *a* (pp. 209–67) *An appendix*; S8 *b* blank; T1 *a*–T4 *a* Latin letter from *I. P.* and Ross's answer; T4 *b* blank.

Note: Second edition of no. 232. *Dr. Pr.* and *I.P.* are short for *Dr James Primrose* (see p. 288).
The criticism of *Pseudodoxia Epidemica* is on pp. 92–207, with heading as before.

Copies: BLO, BM, CLN, EUL, K, ULC; MH, MMO, PUL, YML.

234 BULWER: ANTHROPOMETAMORPHOSIS [Wing B 5461]   1653

Anthropometamorphosis: Man Transform'd: or, The Artificiall Changling Historically presented...By John Bulwer...London Printed by William Hunt Anno. Dom. 1653. A⁴*–*****⁴ ******¹ B–Z⁴ Aa–Zz⁴ Aaa–Zzz⁴ Aaaa–Gggg⁴. With engraved frontispiece and explanation facing, and engraved portrait by W. Faithorne.

References: On ****3 *a*, 'A List of Divines, Poets, Historians, Philosophers, Anatomists, Physicians and others...empanell'd for the Triall of the Artificiall Changling...' This contains the name 'Dr. Brown'. Also references, marginal and textual, as follows:
P. 128, *Pseud. Epid.* Book VI, ch. 10, on the shapes of noses.
P. 276, *ibid.* Book VII, ch. 14, on the wish of Philoxenes.

P. 378, *ibid*. Book IV, ch. 10, on the carnality of Jewish women.

P. 448, *ibid*. Book V, ch. 5, on the creation of Adam and Eve.

P. 467, *ibid*. Book VI, ch. 10, on the blackness of negroes.

Note: Reissued with a new title-page in 1654.

Copies: BM, ULC(2); BN, CH, MH, MMO, YML.

235 HOLLAND: GRAND PREROGATIVE [Wing H 2417]   8° 1653

The Grand Prerogative of Humane Nature...By G[uy] H[olland] Gent. Now first published according to the perfect Copie, and the Authours mind... London; Printed by Roger Daniel, and to be sold by Anthony Williamson... An. 1653. *⁎*⁎4 B–I8 K4

Reference: Pp. 6–7, Quoting Browne's views on 'the entity of the form' in *Religio Medici*, pt. 1, sect. 21.

Copies: BLO, BM, TCC, ULC.

236 WHITLOCK: ZΩOTOMIA [Wing W 2030]   8° 1654

Zωotomia, or, Observations on the Present Manners of the English. By Richard Whitlock M.D. Late Fellow of All Souls Colledge in Oxford. London, Printed by Tho. Roycroft, and are to be sold by Humphrey Moseley, at the Princes Armes in St. Pauls Church-yard, 1654. A8 a8 B–Z8 Aa–Oo8 Pp4, with A8, Moseley's catalogue. Engraved frontispiece.

Reference: On p. 232 to writers [like Ross] who must write to eat. 'Write they must against Things or Men that they can neither Master nor Conquer, Sparing neither Bacons, Harveys, Digbys, Brownes, or any the like of *Improvement* COLLEDGE (as I may terme them)'.

237 COLLOP: POESIS REDIVIVA [Wing C 5395]   8° 1656

Title: Poeſis Rediviva: or, Poeſie Reviv'd. By John Collop M.D. [*rule*]

         Odi prophanum vulgus & arceo.

[*rule*] London, Printed for Humphrey Moſeley, and are to be ſold at his Shop at the Princes Armes in S. Pauls Church-yard. 1656.

Collation: A–H8 χ1; 65 leaves.

Contents: A1 title; A2 *a*–A4 *b Epistle Dedicatory* to the Marquis of Dorchester; A5 *a*–H3 *b* (pp. 1–110) text; H4 *a*–H7 *a Contents*; H7 *b*–H8 *b* blank; χ1 (inserted) *errata*.

Poem: P. 60, twenty-two lines as follows:

On Doctor Brown.

His Religio Medici and vulgar errors

Religio Medici though th' wor[l]d Atheism call,

The wou[r]ld shows none, and the Physitian all.

More zeal and charity *Brown* in twelve sheets shows,

Then twelve past ages writ, or th' present knows;

What *Paracelsus* brag'd of doth disclose,

He 'twixt the Pope and *Luther* might compose.
Though gut-inspired zelots bark at him,
He hath more knowledge then their Sanedrim.
Or the *Scotch* pedant a worm in every book,
To maim the words and make the sence mistook.
Dul lumps of earth not yet concoćted mud,
In natures count scarce Cyphers understood.
Let these lick up the indigested phlegm
Which Cruder stomach'd *Sciolists* belch'd 'fore them:
Dog-like to vomits run and lick each sore,
Think learning to repeat what's said before.
While these can prize truths weapons by the rust,
Crawl with the aged serpent in the dust.
Shine out dispelling th' ages darker night,
Knowledge makes only Children of the light.
Folli's unmask'd, and errors bald pate show'n,
Brown others errors, others write their own.

Note: The author of this poem was certainly the John Collop of Flitwick who was admitted at Pembroke College, Cambridge, in 1641, as an Exhibitioner from Charterhouse (Venn, *Alumni Cantabrigienses*, I, 375). On the leaf of *errata* at the end of the book, the author remarks: 'Ingenuity is so much a stranger to the Presse, that it hath forgot what it is to be ingenious, and tainted with ignorance infects the most ingenious pieces. For the Presses faults the Author desires a pardon, who scorns to intreat it for his own...' The Pembroke copy (given to the college library by William Quarles) has no *errata* leaf, but includes a 20-page list of books printed for Humphrey Moseley. Some Latin verses (*Author de Libro*) are also written on the blank page facing the title and most of the *errata* are corrected in the same handwriting.

Copies: BLO, BM, K, PCC, ULC; LC, MH, NYAM, PUL, YUL.

238 COLLOP: MEDICI CATHOLICON [Wing C 5394]   8° 1656

Medici Catholicon, or A Catholick Medicine for the Diseases of Charitie...By J.C. M.D. London, Printed for Humphrey Moseley, and are to be sold at his Shop at the Princes Armes in S. Pauls Church-yard. 1656.

Collation: A–K⁸ χ¹ (errata).

Reference: On A8*a*, '...If you were acquainted with [so] much felicity as to be intituled to the knowledge of Dr. Browne's *Religio Medici*, you might bee induced to beleeve a Physitian still may prove an evangelist.'

Note: By the author of *Poesis Rediviva*. In 1924 this book was placed among the imitations of *Religio Medici*, but the present position seems to be more suitable, although the theme has certain similarities.

Copies: BLO, BM, PCC, ULC.

239 ROBINSON: ENDOXA [Latin] [Wing R 1702]   8° 1656

Title: Endoxa feu Quæftionum quarundam mifcellanearum Examen probabile, ut et Lapis ad Altare five Exploratio Locorum paucorum difficiliorum S.

Scripturæ, Unà cum Pfeudodoxiæ Epidemicæ Ventilatione Tranquilla, [*rule*] Per Johannem Robinfonum, M.D. [*device of triple head between rules*] fint variæ quamvis facies mentefque alienæ, Unus fit Cordis nexus amore boni. [*rule*] Londini, Typis T. N. impenfis Sa. Thomfon, ad infigne equi albi in Cœmiterio Paulino, 1656.

Collation: A⁴ B–L⁸, with two leaves inserted; 86 leaves.

Contents: A1 title; leaf, without signature, inserted, with commendatory letter signed *Tho. Allen*; A2*a Ad Abftrufam methodum Clavis adaptata*; A2*b*–A4*a Lectori candido S.*; A4*b Contenta*; B1–E8*a* (pp. 1–63) *Endoxa*; E8*b* blank; F1 sub-title to *Lapis ad Altare*; F2 *Chriftiano Judiciofo Salutem*; F3*a*–H3*b* (pp. 69–102) text; H4*a Locorum Syllabus*; H4*b* blank; H5 sub-title to *Pfeudodoxiæ Epidemicæ D. Thomæ Brunii Medicinæ Doctoris, Perfpicacitate & Induftriâ Nemini Secundi, Ventilatio Tranquilla, Spirante aurâ placidâ*; H6 *Praefatio*; H7*a*–L5*a* (pp. 109–55) text; L5*b* blank; L6*a*–L8*b* (pp. 157–62) *Contenta*. Additional leaf, *errata*.

Note: John Robinson was a doctor practising in Norwich. Little is known of him beyond the opinions expressed in his published works. According to Wilkin (II, 169 n.) the first part of *Endoxa* had been published in English as: *Miscellaneous Propositions and Quaeres, by J.R. Dr. in Physick in Norwich. London, Printed for R. Royston, at the Angel in Ivie Lane. 1649.* No copy of this book is recorded in Wing's *Short Title Catalogue.* It is here translated into Latin with the addition of *Lapis ad Altare* and *Ventilatio Tranquilla.* The title of this attack on *Vulgar Errors* was derived from *Religio Medici*, part I, section 32: 'whosoever feels not the warm gale and gentle ventilation of this Spirit...' There was, as Wilkin remarked, 'little in this *gale* to ruffle a far more excitable antagonist than Sir Thomas, and it seems to have died away unnoticed'. The whole work was issued in English two years later (see no. 241).

Copies: BLO, BM, TCD; BN.

240 EVELYN: LETTER   1658

In The London Magazine, vol. x. London. 1824.

Letter: Pp. 589–92, Evelyn's letter to Browne giving an account of a portion of his unpublished work on Gardens, dated 28 January [1657/8].

Note: First reprinted by Wilkin, I, 374, with others from Browne to Evelyn.

241 ROBINSON: ENDOXA [English] [Wing R 1700]   8° 1658

Title, within single lines: Endoxa, or, Some probable Inquiries into Truth ,both Divine and Humane: Together with A Stone to the Altar: or, Short Difquifitions on a few difficult places of Scripture; as alfo, A Calm Ventilation of Pfeudo-doxia Epidemica. By John Robinfon, Dr. of Phyfick. Tranflated and augmented by the Author, [*engraved vignette of a heart containing a head with five faces*]

> Though divers Heads, Faces averfe you fee;
> Yet for Truth's fake, they all in Heart agree.

[*rule*] London, Printed by J. Streater, for Francis Tyton, 1658.

ENDOXA,
OR,
Some probable *Inquiries*
INTO
TRUTH,
BOTH
Divine and *Humane* :
Together with
A STONE to the ALTAR:
OR,
Short Disquisitions on a few difficult places of
SCRIPTURE;
AS ALSO,
A CALM VENTILATION
OF
PSEUDO-DOXIA EPIDEMICA.

By *John Robinson*, Dr. of Physick.
Translated and augmented by the Author,

Though divers Heads, Faces averse you see ;
Yet for Truth's sake, they all in Heart agree.

London, Printed by *J. Streater*, for *Francis Tyton*, 1658.

Collation: A⁴ B–K⁸ L⁴; 80 leaves.

Contents: A1 title; A2 *a The Contents of the Endoxa*; A2 *b A Key to the Work*; A3 *a*–A4 *b The Preface, To the candid Reader*; B1 *a*–E5 *a* (pp. 1–57) *Endoxa, or, Some profitable Inquiries into Truth*; E5 *b* blank; E6 sub-title to *A Stone to the Altar*; E7 *a–b The Index*; E8 *a–b To the Understanding Christian*; F1 *a*–H4 *b* (pp. 65–104) *A Stone to the Altar*; H5 subtitle to *A Calm Ventilation*; H6 *a*–H7 *b The Contents*; H8 *a–b Preface*; I1 *a*–L4 *a* (pp. 113–51) *A Calm Ventilation*; L4 *b* blank. An *errata* slip is sometimes pasted onto the verso of the title-page.

Sub-title on H5 *a:* A Calm Ventilation, of Pſeudodoxia Epidemica; or, Doſtrine of Vulgar Errours, Set forth by the hand of the moſt ſedulous Thomas Brown, Dr. in Phyſick, By the ſtill Gale of John Robinson, His Fellow-Citizen and Collegian.
            Pro captu Leſtoris, habent ſua fata libelli.
[*rule*] London, Printed by J. Streater, for Francis Titon, at the three Daggers in Fleet-ſtreet, 1658.

Note: In his preface to *A Calm Ventilation* Robinson refers to Browne as 'my honoured Friend and Author; who, in his maturer years, is willing to reſtifie, what himself, and others, in their younger days, were falsely seasoned withall'.

Copies: BLO, BM, K; MH(2).

242 SCHUPP: SALOMO   12° 1658

Salomo, Oder Regenten-Spiegel Vorgestellet...Von Antenore [J. B. Schupp], Einem Liebhaber der H. Schrift. [no place] 1658 𝔄–𝔛¹² 𝔐¹⁰ A–E¹²

Reference: On D5 *a* in ch. x (misnumbered ix) is a reference to *Religio Medici*.

243 DIGBY: OBSERVATIONS [Wing D 1444]   8° 1659

Title, within single line: Observations upon Religio Medici [*rule*] Occasionally Written by Sʳ Kenelm Digby Knight. [*printer's ornamental block between rules*] London, Printed by A.M. for L.C. and are to be sold by Andrew Crook at the Green-Dragon in Sᵗ Pauls Church-yard, 1659. A–E⁸.

Note: This edition of Digby's *Observations*, although it has a separate collation, is mentioned on the title-page of *Religio Medici* (1659) (no. 8) and is not found separately. The *Observations* were first printed as an integral part of the book in 1669 (no. 9).

244 LOVEDAY: LETTERS [Wing L 3225]   8° 1659

Loveday's Letters Domestick and Forrein. By R. Loveday Gent. London, Printed by J.G. for Nath. Brook, at the Angel in Corn-hill, 1659. A–T⁸. Engraved frontispiece.

References: It seems clear that references by Loveday to his medical adviser in Norwich are meant to indicate that he was under Browne for the phthisis from which he was suffering. Sometimes the reference is to 'Dr. B. of Norwich'. The letter numbers and pages are as follows: xxii, p. 40; xxxix, p. 77; lvi, p. 106; lxxx, p. 153; ci, p. 186; civ, pp. 192–3; cxii, p. 206. It seems likely that Letter cxlvii, pp. 271–3, was addressed to Browne himself.

A

Calm Ventilation,

OF

Pseudodoxia Epidemica;

O R,

Doctrine of Vulgar Errours,

Set forth by the hand of the most sedulous

THOMAS BROWN,

Dr. in Physick,

By the still G A L E

O F

JOHN ROBINSON,

His Fellow-Citizen and Collegian.

Pro captu Lectoris, habent sua fata libelli.

LONDON,

Printed by *J. Streater*, for *Francis Titon*, at the three
Daggers in *Fleet-street*, 1658.

Note: Loveday died at the age of thirty-five in December 1656. Professor F. L. Huntley has demonstrated that Loveday was almost certainly the young man whose death gave rise to the composition of *A Letter to a Friend,* 1690, his intimate friend being Sir John Pettus. For references see under Huntley. Six further editions were published up to 1684.

Copies: BLO, BM, PC; MH.

245 PHILIPOTT: VILLARE CANTIANUM [Wing P 1989]   1659

Villare Cantianum: or Kent Surveyed and Illustrated...By Thomas Philipott Esq; formerly of Clare Hall in Cambridge...London, Printed by William Godbid...M.DC.LIX. a⁴ A²B–Z⁴ Aa–Zz⁴ Aaa–Eee⁴ [Fff]².

Reference: On pp. 249–51 is a passage beginning: 'At this Parish of Newington, not long since were digged up many *Roman* Urns...' Much of this is clearly based on Browne's *Urne-Buriall,* ch. III, though none of it is quoted word for word.

Note: In one of his commonplace books, in a passage on plagiarisms, Browne added a note: 'Mr Philips in his *Villare Cantianum* transcribes half a side of my hydriotaphia, or urn buriall, without mention of the author.' (See *Works,* ed. Keynes, 1964, III, 289.)

Copies: BLO, BM, ULC; CH.

246 MICRAELIUS: DE PRAEADAMITIS   4° [*c.* 1660]

Monstrosae de praeadamitis opinionis abominanda foeditas. Demonstrata a John. Micraelio, Pomerano. Stetini Impensis et Typis Johan-Valentini Rhetii. [*c.* 1660])(⁴)( )(⁴ B–O⁴.

Note: This work is stated by J. S. Green, jr., to contain references to *Religio Medici,* but I have been unable to verify this.

247 HALL: WORKS [Wing H 416]   4° 1660

The Shaking of the Olive-Tree. The Remaining Works Of that Incomparable Prelate Joseph Hall, D.D. Late Lord Bishop of Norwich...London, Printed by J. Cadwel for J. Crooke, at the Ship in S. Paul's Church-Yard. 1660 a–b⁴ A–Z⁴ Aa–Zz⁴ Aaa–Ddd⁴.

Reference: a₃ b–a₄a. Preface: 'After his prevailing infirmities had wasted all the strengths of nature, and the Arts of his learned and excellent Physician D. Brown of Norwich (to whom under God, we and the whole Church are ingaged for many Years preserving his life as a blessing to us)...'

248 RAY: CAMBRIDGE CATALOGUE [Wing R 383]   8° 1660

Catalogus plantarum circa Cantabrigiam nascentium. Cantabrigiae: Excudebat Joann. Field. Impensis Gulielmi Nealand Bibliopolae. Ann. Dom. 1660. *⁸ **⁸ A–S⁸.

Reference: Pp. 171–2. Quoting Browne's *Garden of Cyrus* concerning the germination of plants.

249 SHARROCK: HISTORY OF VEGETABLES [Wing S 3010]   8° 1660

The History of the Propagation & Improvement of Vegetables By the con-
currence of Art and Nature. By Robert Sharrock, Fellow of New College,
Oxford: Printed by A. Lichfield, Printer to the University, for Tho. Robinson.
1660. A–K⁸ L⁴. Engraved plate with leaf of explanation at p. 70.

Reference: Pp. 142–3 [numbered 140–1] 'As to leaves, the Learned Doctor Brown hath
made the Quincunx famous, which may with as great aptness be applyed, and, I
think, more universally, to the scituation of Buds, or Germens.' This is followed by
examples of three kinds of quincunx.

250 BOYLE: ESSAYS [Wing B 3929]   4° 1661

Certain Physiological Essays. By the Honourable Robert Boyle. London,
Printed for Henry Herringman at the Anchor in the Lower walk in the New-
Exchange, 1661. A² B–O⁴ P¹⁰ [P3 cancelled, 7 leaves inserted] Q–Z⁴ Aa–Ii⁴
Kk².

Reference: Pp. 98–9. In the second of 'Two Essays Concerning the unsuccessfulness of
Experiments'. Describing experiments with oil and other fluids, Boyle wrote: 'And
so having been inform'd that the learned Dr. Brown somewhere delivers, that *Aqua
fortis* will quickly coagulate common Oyle, we pour'd some of those Liquors together, and let them stand for a considerable space of time in an open Vessel, without
finding in the Oyle the change by him promis'd.' Later by changing the liquors the
experiment succeeded. Boyle was 'concern'd for the reputation of a person that so
well deserves a good one'. Wilkin (I, lxxxix) noted that in *Biogr. Britan.* the experiment was wrongly attributed to Edward Browne. Sir Thomas Browne's MS notes on
coagulation refer to experiments with aqua fortis and milk, but not with oil (see
Works, ed. Keynes, 1964, III, 452).

251 BROME: SONGS (Wing B 4852]   8° 1661

Songs and other Poems. By Alex. Brome, Gent....London, Printed for Henry
Brome, at the Gun in Ivy-Lane. 1661. Π² A–U⁸.

Reference: p. 173, in *Epistle: The Answer*

      Thou next would'st have me turn Divine,
      And Doctor too, indeed 'tis fine,
      Physick and preaching ill agree,
      There is but one *Religio Medici*.

252 GLANVILL: VANITY OF DOGMATIZING [Wing G 834]   8° 1661

The Vanity of Dogmatizing: By Jos. Glanvill, M.A. London, Printed by E.C.
for Henry Eversden at the Grey-Hound in St. Pauls Church-Yard. 1661. A–S⁸.

Reference: P. 204. In a description of magnetized needles Browne's observations are
mentioned. See *Pseud. Epid.* Book II, ch. 2, 'Concerning the Loadstone'.

253 BAYFIELD: DE TUMORIBUS [Wing B 1469] 1662

Tractatus de tumoribus Præter naturam. Or, A Treatise of preternatural Tumors: divided into four Sections, and adorned with many choice and rare Observations. By Robert Bayfield, Physician...London Printed for Richard Tomlins, at the Sun and Bible near Pye-Corner, 1662. A–K¹² L⁶, errata on L6*a*. With engraved portrait of the author, aet. 27, by Faithorne.

Reference: Each of the four sections has a separate dedication. On C11*a*, p. 69, is the dedication: *Famosissimo Philosopho Thomæ Brown, Medicinæ Doctori, Robertus Bayfield hanc suam secundam Sectionem De Tumoribus a Bile ortis, humillime dedicat.*

Note: The other dedications are to Edward, Bishop of Norwich, Robert Gawsell, J.P., and James Le Franc, pastor of the French Church in Norwich. Robert Bayfield, of whom little is known, was a young medical practitioner in Norwich. Presumably he was acquainted with Browne.

Copies: BLO, BM, EUL, MSL, ULC(2); YML.

254 CHAPELAIN: LETTERS 1662

In Lettres de Jean Chapelain de l'Academie Française publiées par Th. Tamizey de Larroque. Paris. 2 vols. 4°. 1880–3.

Reference: Vol. II, p. 201, col. 1, in a letter to M. Huet à Caen, Feb. 1662, mentioning Browne's views on *The Three Impostors* (*Religio Medici*, part 1, section 20).

255 DUGDALE: IMBANKING AND DRAYNING [Wing D 2481] f° 1662

The History of Imbanking and Drayning of Divers Fenns and Marshes. By William Dugdale Esquire, Norroy King of Arms. London, Printed by Alice Warren, in the Year of our Lord MDCLXII. A–Z⁴ Aa–Zz⁴ Aaa–Hhh⁴ Iii¹ A² B³ [5 extra leaves substituted for Iii2 blank]. 11 engraved maps.

Reference: P. 175. 'Touching which kind of *Urne Buriall* see farther in that excellent discourse of the learned Dr *Tho. Brown* of Norwich, printed at London in An. 1658, from whom I acknowledge to have received much direction for my better guidance in this present work.'

Note: For the full extent of Dugdale's debt to Browne see *Miscellany Tracts* and their correspondence, *Works*, ed. Keynes, 1964, IV, 301–27.

256 DUGDALE: LETTER 1662

In The European Magazine and London Review, vol. XXXIV. London. 1798.

Letter: P. 152, 'Original Letter from [Sir William] Dugdale to Browne, 5 Apr. 1662'.

Note: There is no indication of the source of the original document. The letter was printed by Wilkin, I, 392, and, more correctly, in *Works*, ed. Keynes, 1964, IV, 326–7.

257 FULLER: WORTHIES [Wing F 2440]   f° 1662

> The History of the Worthies of England. Endeavoured by Thomas Fuller, D.D.
> London, Printed by J.G.W.L. and W.G. MDCLXII. A–Z⁴ Aa–Zz⁴ Aaa⁴ Bbb²
> Aa–Nn⁴ Oo² P–T⁴ Vv–Zz⁴ Aaa–Yyy⁴ Aaa–Zzz⁴ Aaaa–Ffff⁴ Aaaaa–Hhhhh⁴
> Iiiii². Engraved frontispiece.

> *Reference:* On Eeeee3. The Principality of Wales, p. 29. Discussing the tradition that
> Merlin had an Incubus as father, Fuller commented: 'But a Learned Pen demon-
> strateth the impossibility of such Conjunctions. And let us not load Satan with
> groundless sins, whom I believe the Father of Lyes, but (in a literal sense) no Father
> of Bastards', with a marginal reference to 'Dr Brown in his vulgar Errors, Book 7,
> Ch. 16'. (See Browne's *Works*, ed. Keynes, 1964, II, 528.)

258 SPIZELIUS: SCRUTINIUM ATHEISMI   4° 1663

> Theophili Spizelii Ecclesiastæ Augustani, Scrutinium Atheismi Historicoætio-
> logicum. Augustæ Vindelicorum, Formis Io. Prætorii. M. DC. LXIII. *A*⁴
> A–H⁸ I⁴.

> *Reference:* Pp. 111–13. Quotation from *Religio Medici*, part 1, section 18, with comments.

259 BYSSHE: VISITATION OF NORFOLK   1664

> The Visitation of Norfolk A.D. 1664 by Sir Edward Bysshe, Knt. Vol. 1 A–L
> Ed. A. W. Hughes Clarke and A. Campling. London. 1933.

> *Reference:* p. 37. 'Browne of Norwich', from Richard Browne of Cheshire to Sir Thomas
> Browne and his family.

260 LAWRENCE: MERCURIUS CENTRALIS [Wing L 686–7]   12° 1664

> *Title within double lines:* Mercurius Centralis: or, A Discourse of Subterraneal
> Cockle, Muscle, and Oyster-shels, Found in the digging of a Well at Sir
> William Doylie's in Norfolk, many foot under ground, and at considerable
> distance from the Sea. [*rule*] Sent in a Letter to Thomas Brown, M.D. By
> Tho. Lawrence, A.M. [*rule*] London: Printed by J.G. for R. Royston [J.
> Collins], and are to be sold at the Angel in Ivielane. 1664.

> *Collation:* A–D¹² E⁶; 54 leaves.

> *Contents:* A1*a* blank; A1*b Imprimatur* dated *June 13. 1664*; A2 title; A3*a*–A6*b To the*
> *Reader* signed *T.L.*; A7*a*–E6*b* (pp. 1–94) *Mercurius Centralis.* Woodcut on p. 84.

> *Note:* A3 has signature A4. In some copies the name *J. Collins* has been substituted in the
> imprint for *R. Royston.* The rest of the title-page has not been reset and the volume is
> otherwise unchanged. The book was reissued by Collins with a new title-page in 1668
> (see no. 267). Sir William D'Oyley lived at Shotesham, six miles south of Norwich.

> *Copies:* BLO, BM, CLN, K (2, Royston, Collins), ULC (Collins); MH.

261 PETIT, PIERRE 1664

In Œuvres Completes de Christian Huygens. 's Gravenhage. 1890.

Reference: vol. IV, p. 378. Petit writes to Huygens concerning the unpublished translation of *Pseudodoxia Epidemica* by Isaac Gruterus, suggesting that it would have found readers among the learned had Gruterus shown more energy in having it published. Five letters from Gruterus to Browne are in BLO (MS. Rawl. D 391) and eight in BM (MS. Sloane 4062).

262 PETTY, SIR WILLIAM 1664

In The Diary of Samuel Pepys. Edited by Henry B. Wheatley, F.S.A. London. 1924. 8°.

Reference: Vol. IV, p. 22, under the date 26–27 January 1663/4: 'Up and to the office, and at noon to the Coffee-house, where I sat with Sir G. Ascue and Sir William Petty, who in discourse is, methinks, one of the most rational men that ever I heard speak with a tongue, having all his notions the most distinct and clear, and, among other things (saying, that in all his life these three books were the most esteemed and generally cried up for wit in the world—Religio Medici, Osborne's Advice to a Son, and Hudibras)—did say that in these—in the two first principally—the wit lies, and confirming some pretty sayings, which are generally like paradoxes, by some argument smartly and pleasantly urged...'

263 POWER: EXPERIMENTAL PHILOSOPHY [Wing P 3099] 4° 1664

Experimental philosophy In Three Books. By Henry Power, Dr. of Physick. London, Printed by T. Roycroft, for John Martin, and James Allestry, at the Bell in S. Pauls Church-yard. 1664. a–c⁴ B–Z⁴ Aa–Bb⁴, *errata* 1 leaf. 1 engraved plate.

References: (1) On B3 *a*, quoting *Religio Medici*, part 1, section 15, 'Who admires not Regio-Montanus his Fly beyond his Eagle', i.e. Johann Muller of Konigsberg (1436–76), who constructed an iron fly and a wooden eagle.

(2) P. 8, quoting *Pseud. Epid.* concerning the scales on butterflies' wings and 'how vastly they were mistaken, that held this mealy dust to be an exudation of atoms out of their wings'.

(3) P. 37, drawing attention to Browne's mistake in believing the eyes of a snail to be 'amongst the Vulgar errours of the multitude' (*Pseud. Epid.* Book III, ch. 20). This refers to the first edition, 1646; later Browne corrected this opinion, perhaps following Power's criticism. (See *Works*, ed. Keynes, 1964, II, 224.)

(4) P. 42, confirming Browne's observation that the liver of the lamprey is coloured green. See *Pseud. Epid.* Book III, ch. 19 (*Works*, ed. Keynes, 1964, II, 223).

(5) P. 58, agreeing with Browne's Doctrine of Effluxions. See *Pseud. Epid.* Book II, ch. 2 (*Works*, ed. Keynes, 1964, II, 90).

Note: For Browne's relations with Power see their correspondence (*Works*, ed. Keynes, 1964, IV, 255–70).

Copies: BLO, BM, K, ULC; MMO, YML, YUL.

264 THE NEWES: ACCOUNT OF A THUNDERSTORM 4° 1665

The Newes. Published for Satisfaction and Information of the People. With Privilege. [London] Thursday July 20. 1665.

Reference: P. 608, 'I had almost forgot to tell you, that upon *Wednesday was sennight* likewise there break a most terrible clap of *Thunder* just over *Norwich* that shaked the whole City, and a *Ball* of *Fire* fell upon *Dr Browne's* house, and did him some little damage, brake some of the *Glass-windows* in his *Court-yard*, and other houses near, and so ran (in the sight of divers people) down the walk in the Market-place, but (God be praised) did not hurt any person.'

Note: A description of the incident by Browne himself is in Sloane MS. 1866, ff. 2–3 (see *Works*, ed. Keynes, 1964, III, 239–40). The storm took place on 28 June 1665, and considerable damage was done to his house, which was probably at the southern end of the Gentleman's Walk, Haymarket. The newspaper reference was first recorded by P. J. Dobell in his catalogue of *Books of the Time of the Restoration*, July 1920, p. 36.

Copy: K.

265 MERRETT: PINAX [Wing M 1839] 8° 1666

Pinax Rerum Naturalium Britannicarum, continens Vegetabilia, Animalia, et Fossilia, In hac Insula reperta inchoatus. Londini, Typis T. Roycroft, Impensis Cave Pulleyn. 1666. *⁸ A–P⁸.

Reference: P. 2, to 'the sweet-smelling flag found by Dr. Brown neer Lyn'.

Note: Christopher Merrett (1614–95) was a Fellow of the College of Physicians and Librarian, 1654–81. His *Pinax* was re-issued twice in 1667 with the reference to Browne on p. 2 as before. From 1668 he corresponded with Browne, who supplied him with extensive notes on the natural history of Norfolk for an enlarged edition of *Pinax*, but this was never published. For the letters see *Works*, ed. Keynes, 1964, IV, 343–62.

Copies: BLO, BM, K; MH, MMO.

266 ROYAL SOCIETY 4° 1667

Philosophical Transactions. Vol. II. For Anno 1667. In the Savoy. Printed by T.N. for John Martyn at the Bell, a little without Temple-Bar, Printer to the Royal Society.

Reference: In Number 29, 11 November 1667, pp. 546–8: 'Anatomical Observations on a Humane Body, dead of odd Diseases; as they were communicated by Dr. Nathaniel Fairfax.' The article gives an account of a young woman of Rumborough in Suffolk, who had been under the care of Browne and others. She suffered from 'a frightful jolking in her Breast', when she shook herself. She gradually became 'stopt up', and died after about five years' illness. Postmortem she was found to have a large collection of purulent fluid in her thorax. 'Dr. Brown saith, he hath met with the like in an *Italian* author. His opinion was to salivate her.' The description suggests an infected hydatid cyst.

267 LAWRENCE: DISCOURSE [Wing L 685]   12° 1668

Title, within single lines: A Difcourfe of Subterraneal Treasure. Occafioned by
fome late Difcoveries thereof in the County of Norfolk, And fent in a Letter
To Thomas Brown, M.D. [*rules*] London, Printed for J. Collins, at the Kings
Head in Weftminfter-Hall, 1668. A–D¹² E⁶.

Note: A re-issue of the sheets of no. 260 with a reprint title-page.

Copies: BLO, CLN, ULC.

268 WILD: ITER BOREALE [Wing W 2136]   8° 1668

Iter Boreale, With large Additions of several other Poems. The Author R. Wild,
D.D. Printed for the Booksellers in London, MDCLXVIII. A–H⁸.

Reference: P. 68, in 'The Grateful Nonconformist: or, Return of Thanks to Sir J.B.
Knight who sent the Author Ten Crowns 1665'.

>   Ten Crowns at once! Sir you'l suspected be
> For no good Protestant, you are so free.
> So much at once! sure you ne'r gave before,
> Or else, I doubt, mean to do so no more.
> This is enough to make a man protest
> *Religio Medici* to be the best.

Note: Robert Wild (1609–79), incumbent of Aynhoe, first published *Iter Boreale* on
General Monk in 1660.

269 REISERUS   8° 1669

Antonii Reiseri Augustani, De Origine, Progressu et Incremento Antitheismi,
Seu Atheismi, Epistolaris Dissertatio, Ad Clariss. Virum Theophilum
Spizelium, Augustanum. Augustæ Vindelicorum, Impensis Gottlieb Goebelii,
Bibliopolæ ibid, M.DC.LXIX. A–Y⁸.

Reference: P. 286 to *Religio Medici* and the annotations by Moltkenius.

270 RAY: CATALOGUS PLANTARUM [Wing R 381]   8° 1670

Catalogus Plantarum Angliæ. Opera Joannis Raii M.A. Londini Typis E.C. &
A.C. Impensis J. Martyn, Regalis Societatis Typographi, ad Insigne Campanæ
in Cœmeterio D. Pauli. MDCLXX. Π⁴ A–Z⁸ Aa⁴.

Reference: P. 7, recording Browne's discovery of 'The sweet-smelling Flag or Calamus'
in the Yare near Norwich. Also pp. 125–6, the *Fungus phalloides*, 'This was brought
to Doctor Browne at Norwich'; p. 313, mentioning the 'Shrub-Stonecrop', shown
to him by Browne, thus suggesting that Ray had visited Browne at Norwich.

271 EVELYN, JOHN   1671

In The Diary of John Evelyn. Edited by E. S. de Beer. Oxford. 6 vols. 1955.

Reference: Vol. III, pp. 592–5, under the date 17 October 1671, an account of Evelyn's
visit to Norwich in order to see Sir Thomas Browne and his collections.

272 GREW: ANATOMY OF VEGETABLES [Wing G 1946]   8° 1672

The Anatomy of Vegetables Begun. With a General Account of Vegetation Founded thereon. By Nehemiah Grew, M.D. and Fellow of the Royal Society. London, Printed for Spencer Hickman, Printer to the R. Society, at the Rose in S. Pauls Church-Yard, 1672. A^8 a^8 B–O^8. 3 engraved plates.

References: Pp. 132, 143, to the Learned Dr. Browne's observations on the petals of flowers (in *The Garden of Cyrus*).

273 RAY: OBSERVATIONS IN THE LOW-COUNTRIES [Wing R 399]   8° 1673

Observations Made in a Journey through part of the Low-Countries, Germany, Italy, and France. By John Ray, Fellow of the Royal Society. London: Printed for John Martyn, Printer to the Royal Society, at the Bell in St. Paul's Church-yard, 1673. A–Z^8 Aa–Ii^8 Kk^2 Aaa–Ggg^8 Hhh^6. 4 engraved plates.

Reference: P. 237. 'Among other things we took notice of [in the Duke's Palace at Modena] a humane head petrified; a hens egg having on one side the signature of the Sun, which I rather noted, because some years before Sir *Thomas Brown* of *Norwich* sent me the picture of one having the perfect signature of a Duck swimming upon it, which he assured me was natural.'

274 STEVENSON: POEMS [Wing S 5508]   8° 1673

Poems: or, A Miscellany of Sonnets, Satyrs, Drollery, Panegyricks, Elegies, &c....By the Author, M. Stevenson...London, Printed for R. Reynolds at the Sun and Bible, and John Lutton at the Blew Anchor in the Poultrey, Booksellers. 1673. A–I^8.

Reference: P. 30, to the knighting of 'the so famous Brown', in a poem 'Upon His Majesties Progress into Norfolk, Sept. 28. 1671.'

Note: Matthew Stevenson, fl. 1654–85, was a minor poet of whom not much is known. The sheets of the *Poems* were twice re-issued with new title-pages as *Norfolk Drollery* (London, 1673) and *The Wits, or Poems and Songs on Various Occasions* (London, 1685).

275 LEIBNITZ & ARNOLD: MEMORABILIA   4° 1674

Inclutæ Bibliothecæ Norimbergensis Memorabilia, quae Joh. Jacobus Leibnitzius solemniter recensuit. Accedit Christopheri Arnoldi, V.C. Hydriotaphia, hoc est, Urnis sepulchralibus, in agro Anglorum Nortfolciensi repertis, Epistola gratulatoria. Norimbergæ, Apud Wolffgangum Mauritium Endterum, & Johannis Andreæ Endteri Heredes. MDCLXXIV. A–G^4 H^2. 8 engraved plates.

Reference: Pp. 45–51. *Epistola gratulatoria* from Arnold to Leibnitz, including an account of *Hydriotaphia* with an engraved copy of the plate of urns facing p. 46.

Copies: K(2).

276 PLACCIUS: DE SCRIPTIS ANONYMIS 4° 1674

De Scriptis & Scriptoribus Anonymis atque Pseudonymis Syntagma Vincentii Placcii, J. U. L. Hamburgensis. Hamburgi, Sumptibus Christiani Guthii, Anno M.DC.LXXIV.)(⁴)( )(⁴ A–Z⁴ Aa–Mm⁴ A–H⁴.

Reference: Pp. 26–8. A discussion of *Religio Medici*.

277 RAY: COLLECTION OF WORDS [Wing R 388] 8° 1674

A Collection of English Words Not Generally used. By John Ray, Fellow of the Royal Society. London, Printed by H. Bruges for Tho. Burrell, at the Golden Ball under St. Dunstan's Church in Fleetstreet, 1674. A–K⁸ L⁴.

Reference: On A7–8 in *To the Reader*, acknowledging 'Pictures of Birds which I have received from the Learned and deservedly Famous Sr. Thomas Brown of Norwich', with brief descriptions of five birds omitted from his Catalogue of English Birds.

278 PATRICK: PARAPHRASE 8° 1675

A Paraphrase upon the Books of Ecclesiastes and the Song of Solomon. By Symon Patrick D.D. Dean of Peterborough. London, Printed for Rich. Royston, Bookseller to the King's most Sacred Majesty. MDCLXXV. A⁴ B–Z⁸ Aa–Ss⁸ Tt⁴. Engraved frontispiece.

Reference: On Qq3 *b*, p. 178 of *The Song of Solomon Paraphrased*, ch. VII, v. 7: 'Our learned Countryman, Sir Tho. Brown, (in his Miscellan. Tracts, p. 78) hath ingeniously observed, that they speak emphatically when they say they will go up to take hold of the Boughs of this Tree [the palm, or date, tree].'

279 DUPORT: MUSÆ SUBSECIVÆ [Wing D 2652] 8° 1676

Title: Muſæ Subſecivæ ſeu Poetica Stromata. Autore J. D. Cantabrigienſi. Cantabrigiæ, Ex Officina Joann. Hayes, celeberrimæ Academiæ Typographi. 1676. a⁴ B–Z⁸ Aa–Pp⁸.

Poem: Pp. 210–11. Sixteen elegiac lines *Ad Cl. Virum, D. Thomam Brownum, Equitem, & Doctorem Medicum, De ſua Religione Medici, & Pſeudodoxia Epidemica.*

Note: By James Duport, D.D., 1606–79. Master of Magdalene College, Cambridge. Duport was Vice-Master of Trinity College when Edward Browne entered under him in October, 1657 (Wilkin, I, lxxv, note). Reprinted by Wilkin, I, 4.

280 RAY: ORNITHOLOGIA [Wing W 2879] f° 1676

Francisci Willughbii Ornithologiæ Libri Tres: Totum opus recognovit, digressit, supplevit Joannes Raius. Sumptus in Chalcographos fecit Illustriss. D. Emma Willughby, Vidua. Londini; Impensis Joannis Martyn, Regiæ Societatis Typographi, ad insigne Campanæ in Cœmeterio D. Pauli. MDCLXXVI. Π² a⁴ A–Z⁴ Aa–Qq⁴. 77 engraved plates, 2 folding tables.

References: On a2 *b*–3 *a* acknowledging drawings of birds received from Sir Thomas Browne and used for the illustrations. Some of these, such as the stone curlew (p. 228), are mentioned in the text. See also the English edition of 1678.

281 PLOT: OXFORDSHIRE [Wing P 2585]   f° 1677

The Natural History of Oxfordshire. By R. P. LL.D. Printed at the Theatre in Oxford, and are to be had there: And in London at Mr. S. Millers, at the Star near the West-end of St. Pauls Church-yard. 1677. Π² b⁴ B–Z⁴ Aa–Yy⁴ Zz² Aaa–Bbb². Engraved map and 16 plates.

References: P. 142, mentioning Browne's description of the *Toad-stone* in *Pseudodoxia Epidemica* (Book III, chap. 13). P. 329, citing *Hydriotaphia*, ch. 3, on burials of noble families.

282 WAGNER: EXAMEN ATHEISMI   4° 1677

Examen Elencticum Atheismi Speculativi, Institutum A Tobia Wagnero, SS.Th. Tubingæ, Typis Johann. Henrici Reisi, Anno M DC LXXVII.):(²A–M⁴ N².

References: Pp. 11, 15 to *Religio Medici*.

283 WEBSTER: WITCHCRAFT [Wing W 1230]   f° 1677

The Displaying of supposed Witchcraft...By John Webster, Practitioner in Physick. London, Printed by J.M. and are to be sold by the Booksellers in London. 1677. Π⁴ a⁴ B–Z⁴ Aa–Xx⁴ Yy².

Reference: P. 283, discussing the nature of satyrs and pigmies, Browne is quoted on the devil appearing in the shape of a goat (*Pseud. Epidem.* Book V, ch. 22, xix), and on pigmies (*Ibid.* Book IV, ch. 11).

284 [GRANT]: LETTER   1680

Strange and Wonderful News from Norwich: the like not in all England beside. In a letter from Norwich to a friend in London. 1680. (One sheet, f°.)

Reference: ...We lately elected Members here to serve next Parliament, and sure nobody will blame us for chusing those who serv'd us well in the last; for you must note we hate Abhorrers. And tho' we like *Religio Medici* very well, presented them with an address against Popery.

Note: Taken from a bookseller's catalogue, where the *Letter* is attributed to 'Colonel Grant'.

285 TYSON: PHOCÆNA [Wing T 3599]   4° 1680

Phocæna, or the Anatomy of a porpess, dissected at Gresham Colledge: with a preliminary Discourse concerning Anatomy, and a Natural History of Animals. *The World was made to be inhabited by Beasts, but studied and contemplated by Man: 'tis the Debt of our Reason we owe unto God, and the Homage we pay him for not being Beasts.*   Religio Medici
London, Printed for Benj. Tooke at the Ship in St. Paul's Church-yard; 1680. A² B–G⁴ H². 2 engraved plates.

Quotation: on the title-page from *Religio Medici*, part 1, section 13.

Note: The dedication to the President of the Royal Society is signed by Dr. Edward Tyson (1650–1708).

286 GREW: MUSEUM REGALIS SOCIETATIS [Wing G 1952] f° 1681

Museum Regalis Societatis or A Catalogue & Description Of the Natural and Artificial Rarities Belonging to the Royal Society And preserved at Gresham Colledge. Made by Nehemiah Grew M.D. Fellow of the Royal Society and of the Colledge of Physicians...London, Printed by W. Rawlins for the Author, 1681. A⁶ B–Z⁴ Aa–Zz⁴ Aaa–Ddd⁴ A–E⁴ F². 31 engraved plates.

References: Sir Thomas Browne's contributions to the museum are recorded as the leg bone of an elephant (p. 32), and a swan's egg with another within it (p. 78, illustrated on pl. 6). There are references to *Pseudodoxia Epidemica* on pp. 42 and 49, and to *Religio Medici* on p. 254.

286a SWAMMERDAM: EPHEMERI VITA [Wing S 6233] 4° 1681

Ephemeri Vita: or the Natural History and Anatomy of the Ephemeron, A Fly that Lives but Five Hours. Written Originally in Low-Dutch by Jo. Swammerdam, M.D. of Amsterdam. London. Printed for Henry Faithorne, and John Kersey, at the Rose in St. Paul's Church-yard, 1681. A–G⁴ H². 3 engraved plates.

Quotation: On A2a–b, in *To the Reader* signed by Edward Tyson, is a quotation from *Religio Medici*, part 1, section 13: 'The Wisdom of God receives small honour from those vulgar heads, that rudely stare about, and with a gross Rusticity admire His Works; Those highly Magnifie him, whose judicious inquiry into his Acts, and deliberate research into his Creatures, return the Duty of a devout and learned Admiration.'

287 TRYAL OF WITCHES [Wing T 2240] 8° 1682

Title, within double lines: A Tryal of Witches, at the aſſizes held at Bury St. Edmonds for the County of Suffolk; on the Tenth day of March, 1664. Before Sir Matthew Hale Kᵗ· then Lord Chief Baron of His Majeſties Court of Exchequer. [*rule*] Taken by a Perſon then Attending the Court [*rule*] London, Printed for William Shrewsbery at the Bible in Duck-Lane. 1682.

Collation: A² B–D⁸ E⁶; 32 leaves.

Contents: A1 title; A2 *To the Reader*; B1a–E6a (pp. 1–59) text; E6b blank.

Note: An account of a trial before Sir Matthew Hale of Rose Cullender and Amy Duny for witchcraft; the accused were found guilty and condemned to death. On pp. 41–2 is given the evidence of *Dr Brown of Norwich*, who 'was clearly of Opinion, that the persons were Bewitched'. The passage is reprinted by Wilkin, 1, lxxxiii, note, who gives also a passage relating to the same incident from Aikin's *General Biography* (p. 210), and discusses Sir T. B.'s attitude towards withcraft. See also Malcolm Letts in *Notes and Queries*, March 1912.

A TRYAL

OF

WITCHES,

AT THE

ASSIZES

HELD AT

Bury St. Edmonds for the County
of *SUFFOLK*; on the
Tenth day of *March*, 1664.

BEFORE

Sir Matthew Hale Kt.

THEN

*Lord Chief Baron of His Majesties
Court of EXCHEQUER.*

Taken by a Person then Attending the Court

LONDON,
Printed for *William Shrewsbery* at the
Bible in *Duck-Lane.* 1682.

This pamphlet is usually found appended to another work by Sir Matthew Hale entitled: *A Short Treatiſe Touching Sheriffs Accompts...To which is added, A Tryal of Witches...London, Printed, and are to be ſold by Will. Shrowsbery, at the Bible in Duke-Lane.* 1683. A4 B–H8. The sheets of the whole volume were reissued in 1716, and were added to Hale's *Pleas of the Crown* (1707).

The *Tryal of Witches* has been several times reprinted: London, P. Deck, 1771, 12°; London, Longman and Co., 1835, with an Appendix on witchcraft; London, J. Russell Smith, 1838; also in *Witchcraft farther Display'd*, London, E. Curll, 1712, 8°; Hale's *Pleas of the Crown*, London, 1716, 8°; Hutchinson's *Historical Essay concerning Witchcraft*, London, 1718 and 1720, 8°; Cobbett and Howell's *State Trials*, VI, 687–702.

Copies: BLO, BM, GUL, K(1682, 1716, 1718, 1771, 1835, 1838); MH, MMO(1716).

288 HARVEY: CONCLAVE OF PHYSICIANS [Wing h 1059] 12° 1683

Title, within double lines: The Conclave of Phyſicians. Detecting Their Intrigues, Frauds, and Plots, Againſt Their Patients. Alſo a Peculiar Diſcourſe of the Jeſuits Bark: The Hiſtory thereof, with its True Uſe, and Abuſe. Moreover, A Narrative of an eminent Caſe in Phyſick. [*rule*] By Gideon Harvey, M.D. Phyſician in Ordinary to His Majeſty. [*rule*] London: Printed for James Partridge at the Poſt-houſe between Charing-Croſs and White-hall, MDCLXXXIII.

Collation: Π12 A–I12 K6; 126 leaves.

Contents: Π1–3 blank; Π4 title; Π5 dedication to *Sir Philip Howard K^t*; Π6a–Π11b Introduction; Π12a Errata; Π12b blank; A1a–K6b (pp. 1–228) text.

Reference: ch. IV, pp. 59–61. 'Some *Physicasters* by reputing themselves *Virtuoso's*, *Mathematicians*, *Philosophers*, and witty *Cracks*, have insinuated this *Enthymeme* to the Commonalty, that therefore they must necessarily arrive to the top of their profession; for since their porous Brain was capable to imbibe such knotty Mysteries, it's not improbable, they might much easier suck up the quintessence of the Art of Medicine. To this Category belonged that famed Doctor of *Norw.* who being Posted away from his House with a Coach and Four to a Sick Gentleman in the Countrey, an unhappy gawdy *Butterfly* thwarted the Coach, upon which a halt was made, and the Doctor with the assistance of the Coach-driver, hunted so long, untill they had him under the broad brimm'd Beaver. Here an *harangue* was to be made to his conducting Auditor upon the admirable Structure, Shape, Organs, and colours of the Butterfly, particularly upon the transparent yellow, of which colour a Cap would better have fitted him than the black Velvet one. The Butter-fly being cag'd up in a Box, and reserv'd to a further consideration, the Journey was pursu'd, at the end whereof the Doctor found the Patient just expir'd of a Syncopal-fit, and the new Widow accosting him with the information, "That her dear Husband had passed through many of them by the help of a Cordial, and so probably might this, had she not, wretched Creature as she was! expected his coming to prescribe another." But whether the Doctor, besides the Reprimend, and the want of his *Sostrum*,[1] had the Justice done him, to be sent home on foot, I know not.'

---

[1] There is no such word in English or Latin dictionaries. Presumably it refers to the doctor's fee.

Note: This book by Gideon Harvey (about 1640–1700) contains an attack upon the College of Physicians, and there can be no doubt that the passage quoted above is intended to ridicule Sir Thomas Browne. There is no reason for supposing that the anecdote, which apparently was not known to Wilkin, is anything more than a fabrication founded on Sir Thomas Browne's well-known interest is natural history. Harvey also wrote a *Religio Philosophi* (see p. 235).

A second enlarged edition of *The Conclave of Physicians* was published in 1686 (see no. 291). At the same time a defence of Browne was included in an anonymous reply to Harvey's book as a whole under the title: *A Dialogue between Philiatus and Momus* (1686) (see no. 292).

Copies: BLO, BM, K, RCS, RSM, ULC; MMO, YML.

289 BROWNE: ADENOCHOIRADELOGIA [Wing B 5122]   8° 1684

Title, within double lines: Adenochoiradelogia: or, An Anatomick-Chirurgical Treatiſe of Glandules & Strumaes, Or Kings-Evil-Swellings. Together with the Royal gift of Healing, Or Cure thereof by Contact or Impoſition of Hands, performed for above 640 Years by our Kings of England...All which are ſuccinctly deſcribed By John Browne, One of His Majeſties Chirurgeons in Ordinary, and Chirurgeon of His Majeſties Hoſpital...London: printed by Tho. Newcomb for Sam. Lowndes, over againſt Exeter-Exchange in the Strand. 1684. A⁸ a–d⁸ B–Z⁸ Aa⁴ Bb–Qq⁸. Engraved frontispiece.

Reference: In the Third Book, pp. 187–9, is an account of the part played by Sir Thomas Browne in bringing about the cure of a scrofulous child by the King's touch.

Note: The account is reprinted in full by Wilkin, I, xcix n. Browne refers several times in his correspondence to sending patients to the King (see *Works*, ed. Keynes, 1964, IV, 132, 134, 192).

Copies: BLO, BM, K, RCP; MH, MMO.

290 GUIDOTT: GIDEON'S FLEECE [Wing G 2194]   4° 1684

Gideon's Fleece: or, The Sieur de Frisk. An Heroic Poem, Written on the cursory perusal of a late Book, call'd The Conclave of Physicians. By a Friend to the Muses. London, Printed for Sam. Smith at the Princes Arms in St. Paul's Church-yard, 1684. A–E⁴.

Reference: Pp. 19–20, to Gideon Harvey's anecdote (no. 288) in ten lines of doggerel.

Note: This pamphlet attacking Harvey's book was by Thomas Guidott, a physician practising in Bath. He had taken his M.B. at Oxford in 1666, and his name was known to Browne, who referred to him in a letter to Edward Browne (*Works*, ed. Keynes, 1964, IV, 123).

291 HARVEY: CONCLAVE OF PHYSICIANS [second edition] [Wing H 1060]   12° 1686

Title, within double lines: The Conclave of Physicians. In Two Parts. Detecting Their Intrigues, Frauds, and Plots, Against Their Patients, And their destroying the Faculty of Physick...Moreover an Account of some Eminent Cases and new Principles in Physick, of greater use than any yet known [*rule*] The second Edition with many Alterations. [*rule*] By Gideon Harvey, M.D. Physician in Ordinary to His Majesty. [*rule*] London, Printed for James Partridge, Stationer to his Royal Highness George Hereditary Prince of Denmark...MDCLXXXVI.

Collation: A¹² A–F¹² (F11, 12 with signatures A2, 3) B–F¹²; 144 leaves.

Contents: A1 general title; A2 subtitle to *The First Part*; A3 *a–b* dedication to *Sir Philip Howard*; A4*a*–10*a* Introduction; A10*b*–11*b* Contents, Part One; A11*b*–12*b* Books Printed for James Partridge; A1*a*–F9*b* (pp. 1–138) *The First Part*; F10 subtitle to *The Second Part* dated 1685; F11*a*–F12*b* (pp. 1–124) *The Second Part*.

References: First Part, pp. 49–51, the anecdote of Browne and the butterfly as before. Second part, p. 69, an indirect reference to Browne: 'There is no Trust to be put in *Religio Medici* many of whom, I verily dare affirm, believe there is neither God, Heaven, Devil nor Hell.'

Copies: K, MSL, RCP, ULC; MMO, YML.

292 ANON: A DIALOGUE BETWEEN PHILIATER AND MOMUS
[Wing D 1321]   8° 1686

Title, within double lines: A Dialogue between Philiater and Momus, Concerning a late Scandalous Pamphlet called The Conclave of Physicians. [*rule*] *A Whip for the Ass, and a Rod for the Fool's Back.* [*rule*] London, Printed for Walter Kettilby at the Bishop's Head in St Paul's Church-Yard, 1686.

Collation: A–O⁸ P⁴; 108 leaves.

Contents: A1*a* blank; A1*b* Imprimatur dated *March* 22. 1685/6; A2 title; A3*a*–P3*b* (pp. 1–226) *A Dialogue*; P4*a–b* Books Printed for Walter Kettilby. *Errata* at bottom of P3*b*.

Reference: Pp. 105–9, a defence of Sir Thomas Browne against Gideon Harvey's attack in *The Conclave of Physicians* (see p. 235).

Copies: BM, K, TCC, ULC; YML.

293 RAY: SYNOPSIS METHODICA [Wing R 406]   8° 1690

Synopsis Methodica Stirpium Britannicarum, Auctore Joanne Raio, E Societate Regia. Londini: Prostant apud Sam. Smith ad Insignia Principis in Cœmetario D. Pauli. MDCXC. π⁴ (a)⁸ B–X⁸. 2 engraved plates.

Reference: Pp. 37–8, to Browne's finding Shrub-stonecrop on the Norfolk coast. P. 206, to his finding the sweet smelling flag or Calamus in the river Yare near Norwich.

294 BAXTER: WORLDS OF SPIRITS [Wing B 1214–15]   8° 1691

The Certainty of the Worlds of Spirits. Fully evinced by unquestionable Histories of Apparitions and Witchcrafts...Written for the Conviction of Sadduces &

Infidels By Richard Baxter. London, Printed for T. Parkhurst and J. Salus-
bury. 1691. A–R⁸.

Reference: P. 152, 'But as *Religio Medici* says, The Devil hath them [atheists] in too fast a
Noose, for to appear to them would be to convert them from their error.' See *Religio
Medici*, part I, section 30.

295 CARR: EPISTOLÆ MEDICINALES [Wing C 629]   8° 1691

Epistolæ Medicinales variis occasionibus conscriptæ. Authore Ricardo Carr,
M.D. Londini, Impensis Stafford Anson, ad insigne trium Columbarum in
Cœmetario D. Pauli, 1693. A–O⁸.

Reference: P. 199, to Browne with a quotation on sleep from *Religio Medici*, part II,
section 12.

Note: See also the English version: *Dr. Carr's Medicinal Epistles Upon Several Occasions.
Done into English By John Quincy. London: for W. Newton and J. Phillips* (1714), p. 168.

296 [DUNTON]: ATHENIAN GAZETTE   1691

The Athenian Gazette: or Casuistical Mercury, Resolving all the most Nice and
Curious Questions proposed by the Ingenious: from Tuesday August 18th to
Saturday October 17th, 1691. The First Volume...London, for John Dunton
at the Raven in the Poultry...1691. [30 numbers]

Reference: No. 20. *Quest.* Doctor Brown in his Religio Medici, P. 150 [ed. 1672] says: He
hopes he does not break the fifth Commandment...[quoting the passage on friendship, part II, section 5, and asking whether Browne is justified].
   Answ: Dr. Brown has throughout that Book shew'd such a great Spirit, solid
Judgment and evenness of Temper...&c. [reassuring the questioner].

297 RAY: COLLECTION OF WORDS [second edition] [Wing R 389] 12° 1691

A Collection of English Words not Generally used...The Second Edition,
augmented with many hundreds of Words, Observations, Letters, &c. By
John Ray: Fellow of the Royal Society. London: Printed for Christopher
Wilkinson, at the Black Boy over against S. Dunstan's in Fleetstreet. 1691.
A–K¹².

Reference: On A9*b* in the preface, to 'Sir Tho. Brown's eighth Tract, which is of
Languages.'

Note: The catalogue of birds and fishes, containing other references to Browne in the
first edition, is here omitted. The tract mentioned is in *Miscellany Tracts* (1683) (see
no. 127).

298 KOELMAN: LASTERINGEN   1692

Lasteringen van Jacob Koelman, In zijn zoo genaamde Wederlegging van B.
Bekkers Betooverde Wereldt. Rotterdam: I. van Ruynes. 1692.

Reference: pp. 7–8. Antony van Dale had been accused by Koelman of being the trans-lator of *Religio Medici* into Dutch. He denied this, though admitted that he had read the book and regarded it as dangerous for young persons.

299 RAY: WISDOM OF GOD [second edition] [Wing R 411]   8° 1692

The Wisdom of God Manifested in the Works of the Creation, In Two Parts...
The Second Edition, very much enlarged. London: Printed for Samuel Smith,
at the Princes Arms in St. Paul's Church-yard. 1692. A⁸ a⁸ B–O⁸ Aa–Ll⁸.

Reference: Part II, p. 102, to Browne's experiments on keeping frogs alive under water.

300 KOELMAN: WEDERLEGGING   1692

Wederlegging, van B. Bekkers Betooverde Wereldt...Amsterdam: J. Boek-
holt. 1692.

Reference: p. 143. Koelman attacks Browne and his Dutch translator, van Berckel, on
grounds of heresy. (See J. Schmidt in *Nederlandsch Archief voor Kerkgeschiedenis* (1932),
pp. 135–6, 'Een Verloren Gewaand Werk van Jacobus Koelman'.)

301 BLOUNT: ORACLES OF REASON [Wing B 3312]   12° 1693

The Oracles of Reason. In several Letters to Mr. Hobbs and other Persons of
Eminent Quality, and Learning. By Chas. Blount Esq; Mr. Gildon and Others.
London. Printed 1693. A–I¹² K⁶.

Reference: Pp. 3–8, in 'A Letter to Mr Gildon in Vindication of Dr. Burnet'. 'Nor is
Dr. Burnet the only ingenious Man either of this Age or Nation who has been, upon
Enquiry, startled at some Passages in the Mosaic History: For Dr. Brown (so justly
admired as well by Foreigners as his own Country-men, upon the Account of his
Knowledge in all Gentile sorts of Literature) does both in his *Religio Medici* and
Vulgar Errors, betray his many Doubts and Scruples as well upon this Subject as
others.' This is followed by long quotations from *Religio Medici*, part I, section 21,
and from *Pseud. Epidem.* Book I, ch. 1.

302 CONNOR: EVANGELIUM MEDICI [Wing C 5886]   8° 1697

Evangelium Medici: seu Medicina Mystica; de Suspensis Naturæ Legibus, sive
De Miraculis...A Bernardo Connor, M.D. è Regali Societate Londinensi, nec
non è Regali Medicorum Londinensium Collegio. Londini, Sumptibus
Bibliopolarum Richardi Wellington...Henrici Nelme...& Samuelis Briscoe
...MDCXCVII. A–O⁸ Aa–Ff⁴.

Reference: On A8 (pp. vii–viii) the author refers to Browne's *Religio Medici* because both
works touch on some of the same points.

Note: This work was formerly placed among the imitations of *Religio Medici*, but as
Wilkin remarked, II, xix, it is not properly an imitation, constituting an attack on
miracles, with a curious consideration of the resurrection of the body and how it is to
be accomplished. The book was reprinted in London in the same year and at
Amsterdam in 1699 and 1724.

Copies: BM, EUL, K, RCP; BN, MH, MMO.

303 CHAMBERLAYNE: LITHOBOLIA [Wing C 1862]   1698

Lithobolia: or, The Stone-Throwing Devil. Being An Exact and True Account (by way of Journal) of the various Actions of Infernal Spirits, or (Devils Incarnate) Witches, or both; and the great Disturbance and Amazement they gave to George Waltons Family, at a place call'd Great Island in the Province of New-Hantshire in New-England...By R.C. Esq; who was a Sojouner in the same Family the whole Time, and an Ocular Witness of these Diabolick Inventions...London, Printed and are to be Sold by E. Whitlook [*sic*] near Stationers-Hall, 1698. A² A–B⁴.

Reference: On second A1 *a* in seven verses of three lines each:

> To tell strange feats of Dæmons, here I am;
> Strange, but most true they are, ev'n to a Dram
> Tho' Sadduceans cry, 'tis all a Sham.
>
> Here's Stony Arguments of persuasive Dint,
> They'l not believe it, told, nor yet in Print:
> What should the Reason be? The Devil's in't.
>
> And yet they wish to be convinc'd by Sight,
> Assum'd by Apparition of a Sprite;
> But Learned Broun doth state the matter right.
>
> Satan will never Instrumental be
> Of so much Good, to' Appear to them; for he
> Hath them sure by their Fidelity.

See *Pseudodoxia Epidemica*, Book I, ch. 10 (*Works*, 1964, ii, 69).

Note: The incidents resulted from a dispute between George Walton and his neighbour, an old woman, over possession of a piece of land. The BM copy is inscribed on the title-page: *By Richard Chamberline | ex dono Authoris: 20 Oct: 1698.*

Copies: BLO, BM; MH.

304 TYSON: ORANG–OUTANG [Wing T 3598]   4° 1699

Orang-Outang, sive Homo Sylvestris. Or, the Anatomy of a Pygmie Compared with that of a Monkey, an Ape, and a Man. To which is added, A Philological Essay Concerning the Pygmies, the Cynocephali, the Satyrs, and Sphinges of the Ancients. Wherein it will appear that they are all either Apes or Monkeys, and not Men, as formerly pretended. By Edward Tyson M.D. Fellow of the Colledge of Physicians, and the Royal Society...London: Printed for Thomas Bennet at the Half-Moon in St. Paul's Church-yard; and Daniel Brown at the Black Swan and Bible without Temple-Bar and are to be had of Mr. Hunt at the Repository in Gresham-Colledge. MDC XCIX. Π⁴ A² B–P⁴ B–H⁴ I². 8 engraved plates.

References: In the Philological Essay: (1) p. 16, to Browne's chapter 'Of Pigmies' in *Pseudodoxia Epidemica*, Book IV, ch. 11, disagreeing with his assertion that Aristotle had contradicted himself in writing of pigmies; (2) p. 25, quoting from the same chapter a long passage on the testimony of the scriptures against the existence of human pigmies (see *Works*, ed. Keynes, 1964, II, 304–5). On p. 22 is a reference to Edward Browne's *Travels*.

305 PATIN, GUI. *Naudæana et Patineana. Ou singularitez remarquables, prises des conversations de Mess. Naudé et Patin.* Amsterdam. 1703. 8°. In *Patiniana*, p. 25, is a paragraph mentioning *Religio Medici*, and attributing to Browne a work, *De lue venerea*. Also published à la Haye, 1748.

306 CONRING, HERMANN. *Conringiana Epistolica. Sive animadversiones variæ eruditionis ex B. Hermanni Conringii.* Helmstadt. 1708. 12°. Reference on p. 10: *Religio Medici vehementer me delectavit. Utinam nemo Medicorum, imo Theologorum, illo Homine sit minus religiosus.*

307 MIDGLEY, SAMUEL. *Halifax, and its Gibbet-Law Placed in a true Light. With an account of the Gentry, and other Eminent Persons Born and Inhabiting within the Said Town.* London. 1708. 12°. Reference on pp. 88–9 stating that Browne lived and wrote *Religio Medici* near Halifax in Shibden-dale, i.e. at Old, or Upper, Shibden Hall. See Dale, Brian, 1896. There is no clear evidence for this statement. See Huntley, F. L., for a critical examination of its truth. Reprinted 1761, 1886.

308 HEARNE, THOMAS. *Remarks and Collections.* Vols. III–IV. Ed. C. E. Doble. Oxford, for the Oxford Historical Society. In vol. III is a series of remarks on the publication of Browne's *Posthumous Works* (1712). See p. 109 of the present work.

309 KENNETT, WHITE. In *The European Magazine and London Review*, XL (1801), 89–90. 'Sir Thomas Browne'. A letter signed C.D. stating that in a copy of Browne's *Works* (1686), formerly in the library of the Bishop of Peterborough, he had found a long inscription in Kennett's hand. This gave an account of Browne by Whitefoot, with additions by Mrs. Lyttelton concerning Browne's life, the picture of the family at Devonshire House, and the papers lent to Thomas Tenison. The latter part was reprinted by Wilkin, I, cx.

310 WHITEFOOT, JOHN. *Posthumous Works of Sir Thomas Browne.* London. 1712. 8°. Pp. i–xxxvii, 'the Life of Sir Thomas Browne' (anonymous), and 'Minutes for the Life of Sir Thomas Browne by John Whitefoot, M.A., late Rector of Heigham in Norfolk'. Also 'The Diploma given to Sir Thomas Browne by the College of Physicians, London'. See no. 156.

311 LILIENTHAL, MICHAEL. *De Machievellismo Literario, sive de perversis quorundam in Republica Literaria inclarescendi artibus dissertatio historicomoralis.* Königsberg & Leipzig. 1713. 8°. Reference: §6, p. 19, to a passage in *Pseud. Epid.* Book I, ch. 6 (*tanto quamque sententiam magis suspectam esse, quanto sit antiquior & pervulgatior, crepantes*). Index reference: *Browne, Thom. novaturiens.*

312 BAYLE, PIERRE. *Dictionnaire historique et critique.* 4 vols. Rotterdam. 1720. References: III, 2508, a long note on *Rel. Med.* part II, section 9 (first ed., 1697, II, part 2, 990); IV, 3005–6, quotation from *Rel. Med.* part I, section 8, on religious dogmas, with comments.

313 BAYLE, PIERRE. *Œuvres diverses.* La Haye, 4 vols. 1725–7. f°. I, 25, another reference to Patin and *Rel. Med.* quoting the same passage (part I, section 8).

314 REIMMANN, J. F. *Historia Universalis Atheismi et Atheorum.* Hildesia. 1725. 8. Reference pp. 446–8: a marginal note: *Thomas Browne non fuit Atheus,* with an account of *Rel. Med.* and *Pseud. Epid.*

315 JÖCHER, CHRISTIAN GOTTLIEB. *Compendiöses Gelehrten-Lexicon.* Leipzig. 1726. 8°. Article, I, 478, 'Browne, Thomas'.

316 ECCLESIASTICAL REGISTER. *A Register and Chronicle Ecclesiastical and Civil from the Manuscript Collections of the Lord Bishop of Peterborough.* London. 1728. f°. Reference, p. 345, in a list of contributors to a fund for the repair of Christ Church Cathedral, Oxon., is the name: *Dr Thomas Brown cxxx lib.* It seems probable that this refers to Thomas Browne, B.D. (1604–73), of Christ Church.

317 KIPPIS, ANDREW. *Biographia Britannica.* Second edition. London. 1730. f°. II, 627–37, 'Browne, Sir Thomas'. II, 638–41, 'Browne, Edward'.

318 MANGET, J. J. *Bibliotheca Scriptorum Medicorum.* 2 vols. Geneva. 1731. f°. References, pp. 483–6, to *Works* (1686), *Rel. Med.* and translations into Latin.

319 REIMMANN, J. F. *Bibliotheca Reimmanniana.* Hildesia. 1731. 8°. References, pp. 685–6, to *Pseud. Epid.* (1680), described as *opus aureum* with further remarks; p. 1052, to *Rel. Med.* (1692 and 1667 [1677]).

320 NICERON, J. P. *Mémoires pour servir à l'Histoire des Hommes Illustres dans la République des Lettres.* Tome XXIII. Paris. 1733. 8°. Pp. 353–60, 'Thomas Browne, le Médecin'.

321 PRÉVOST D'EXILES, A. F. *Le Pour et Contre. Ouvrage périodique.* Paris. 1733. I, 230–2, an account of the French translation of *Pseud. Epid.*

322 WATTS, ISAAC. *Reliquiæ Juveniles; Miscellaneous Thoughts in Prose and Verse.* London. 1734. 8°. Reference, p. 133, to a passage in *Rel. Med.* concerning pride.

323 HEISTER, ELIAS FREDERICUS. *Apologia pro medicis*. Amsterdam. 1736. 8°. Defending a number of medical writers from the charge of atheism. See pp. 133–9: *Apologia Brownii*, with other references and quotations from *Rel. Med. passim*. Sir William Osler noted in his catalogue: 'It is a learned work for so young a man and of special interest as dealing with the old question *Ubi tres medici duo athei.*'

324 BUDDEUS, JOAN. FRANCISCUS. *Theses theologicæ de atheismo et superstitione*. Utrecht. 1737. 8°. References, ch. I, pp. 132, 135–7, *An dentur Athei?*, giving an account of the views expressed in *Rel. Med.*

325 BAYLE, PETER. *Dictionary Historical and Critical*, Second edition. London. 1738. f°. References v, 6, to the passage in *Rel. Med.* on procreation; v, 834–5, on scepticism in the same.

326 WRIGHT, THOMAS. *The Antiquities of the Town of Halifax in Yorkshire*. Leeds. 1738. 12°. Reference, p. 152, to Browne's reputed residence at Upper Shibden Hall.

327 CHAUFEPIÉ, J. G. DE. *Nouveau dictionnaire historique et critique pour servir de supplément ou de continuation au Dictionnaire de Bayle*. Amsterdam & la Haye. 4 vols. 1740–6. f°. II, 452 n., a translation of Henry Power's letter to Browne; 449–52, biographical account from *Posthumous Works* (1712).

328 DUCLOS, ABBÉ. *Dictionnaire bibliographique, historique et critique*. Paris. 3 vols. 1740. 8°. i. 200. References to *Rel. Med.* (Latin) (1664) and (French) (1668).

329 MORHOF, DANIEL GEORGE. *Polyhistor. Ed. quarta*. Lubeck. 1747. 4°. II, Book II, ch. I, 131. References to *Rel. Med.* and *Pseud. Epid.* III, Book v, ch. I, 532. References to *Rel. Med.*, *Pseud. Epid.*, Digby's *Observations*, Ross's *Arcana Microcosmi* and some translations.

330 RICCI, F. M. In *S. Capricius. De principiis rerum*. Venice. 2 vols. 1754. 8°. (Translated into Italian by Canturani and annotated by F. M. Ricci.) Reference, I, 161. The author has been speaking of the extinction of one body before the production of another. Ricci quotes Boyle (*Origin of Forms and Qualities*), and then says: 'It is further a pleasure to introduce the learned Thomas Brown, who in his *Pseud. Epid.*, Book III, ch. 27, is of the opinion that "the forms of things lie deeper than we conceive them; seminal principles may not be dead in the divided atoms of plants; but wandering in the ocean of nature, when they hit upon proportionable materials, may unite and return to their visible selves again"' (*Works*, ed. Keynes, 1964, II, 264).

331 JOHNSON, SAMUEL. 'The Life of Sir Thomas Browne', in *Christian Morals*, London. 1756 (see no. 165). First reprinted in *Miscellaneous and Fugitive Pieces*, vol. 1, London, 1773. 8°, and later in various editions of Johnson's *Collected Works*. Two pages of the 'Life' were reprinted in *The Literary Magazine*, vol. 1, London, 1756. In *The Adventurer*, no. 1, 28 April 1753, p. 296, Johnson wrote: 'The devils, says Sir Thomas Brown, do not tell lies to one another; for truth is necessary to all societies; nor can the society of hell subsist without it.' Boswell also reported Johnson's saying on 15 April 1778: 'I remember this remark of Sir Thomas Brown's, Do the devils lie? No, for then Hell could not subsist' (Birkbeck Hill, *Boswell's Life of Johnson*, 1934, III, 293). Neither passage occurs in Browne's writings, and the source of Johnson's mistaken attribution is not known. One of the two BM copies of *Christian Morals* is inscribed: *Bought at the Sale of Dr Samuel Johnson's Books Feb^ry 16. 1788*, with the engraved ticket of Charles Burney. There are no annotations.

332 MORÉRI, LOUIS. *Le grand dictionnaire historique*. 10 vols., Paris. 1759. f°. II, 314, biographical account of Browne and list of his works.

333 CHAUDON, L. M. *Nouveau dictionnaire historique*. 4 vols., Amsterdam. 1766. 8°. I, 362, biographical account of Browne.

334 CARRÈRE, J.-F. *Bibliothèque littéraire, historique et critique de la médicine ancienne et moderne*. 2 vols., Paris. 1776. II, 180, biographical account, and analysis of *Pseud. Epid.*

335 ELOY, N. F. J. *Dictionnaire historique de la médecine ancienne et moderne*. Paris. 1778. 4°. P. 459, an appreciation of *Rel. Med.* and *Pseud. Epid.*

336 JORTIN, JOHN. *Tracts, Philosophical, Critical and Miscellaneous*. 2 vols. London. 1790. I, 373, reference to a passage in *Rel. Med.* ('methinks there be not impossibilities enough') and to Digby's remarks. This occurs in Jortin's 'Remarks on Tillotson', the Bishop having referred in his 140th sermon to Browne's wish for impossibilities on which to exercise his faith.

(ii) 1801–1966

(*In alphabetical order, names not indexed*)

ABRAMSON, E. *Times Lit. Sup.* (1948), 24 July. 'The Maid of Germany', i.e. Eva Flegen of Mörs. See *Rel. Med.*, *Works*, ed. Keynes (1964), 1, 41.

ADAMS, E. W. *Gent. Mag.* (1896), CCLXXVIII, 185–201. 'Sir Thomas Browne.'

AIKIN, JOHN. *General Biography: or Lives, Critical and Historical*. London. 10 vols. 4°. 1801. II, 325–7. 'Browne, Sir Thomas.'

ALLEN, H. *Appleton's Pop. Science Monthly* (1897), I, 80–9. 'Two Scientific Worthies' (Sir T.B. and Sir T. Stamford Raffles).

ALLEN, R. J. *N. & Q.* (1852), S.1, VI, 415. Query about a passage in *Rel. Med.* pt. 1, section 58, on resuscitation of plants. See also 518 for a reply.

ALLIBONE, S. A. *A Critical Dictionary of English Literature*. Philadelphia. 1859. I, 263–5. 'Browne, Sir Thomas, M.D.'

ANDERTON, B. (City Librarian, Newcastle upon Tyne). *Sketches from a Library Window*. Cambridge. 22 cm. 1922. Pp. 135–72. 'Sir Thomas Browne.' Published also New York, 1923. Reprinted in *Camb. Pub. Libr. Rec. and Bk-list* (1935), VII, 69–73, 110–16.

ANON. *Penny Encyclopaedia*. London. 1836. v. 475–6. 'Browne, Thomas.'

—— *Quart. Rev.* (1851), LXXXIX. 'Wilkin's edition of Sir Thomas Browne.'

—— *Brit. Quart. Rev.* (1857), XXV, 172. 'Sir Thomas Browne.'

—— *Harper's New Month. Mag.* (1882), LXV, 396–7. 'Some Worthies of Old Norwich', with woodcut portrait.

—— *The East Anglian* (1806), n.s. I, 194–5. Notes on Sir T.B.

—— *Lit. World* (Boston, 1882), XIII, 37. 'A New Edition of Sir Thomas Browne.'

—— *Brit. Med. Journ.* (1898), I, 1659–61. 'Sir Thomas Browne.' Review of *Religio Medici, and Other Essays*, ed. D. Lloyd Roberts.

—— *Practitioner* (1898), LX, 274–9. 'The Author of Rel. Med.'

—— *Yarmouth Mercury* (1893), 23 Dec. Statement on the removal of Browne's skull from St. Peter Mancroft. Quoted by W. B. Gevish in *N. & Q.* s.s. VI, 64–5.

—— [? JOHNSON LIONEL]. *Daily Chron.* (1899), 24 Apr. Unsigned article on Sir T.B. written in a parody of his style.

—— *The Sketch* (1899), 10 May. 'Why not a statue of Sir Thomas Browne?' Illustrated.

—— *Times* (1899), 11 April. Leading article on the proposed memorial to Browne at Norwich.

—— *Quart. Rev.* (1902), CXCVI, 82–106. 'Golden Age of English Prose', a review of Dowden's *Studies in Eng. Lit.*

(1900), and *Eng. Prose Sel.*, ed. Craik (1893–6). With many references to Browne.

—— *The Times* (1904), 23 Dec. 'Browne's Christian Morals.'

—— *Brit. Med. Journ.* (1905), II, 1121–5. 'The Tercentenary of Sir Thomas Browne.'

—— *East. Daily Press*, Norwich, 19–20 Oct. 1905. Articles concerning the unveiling by Lord Avebury of Henry Pegram's statue of Browne at Norwich on 19 Oct. 1905. A volume containing a large number of excerpts from the *Daily Press* concerning this event is preserved in the Central Library, Norwich. See also *Order of Service*.

—— *Norfolk News*. Norwich (1905), 21 Oct. 'The Browne Statue Unveiled.' With full account of the luncheon, Lord Avebury's Speech, &c.

—— *Times Lit. Sup.* (1905), 13 Oct. 'Sir Thomas Browne', leading article.

—— *Putnam's Monthly & Reader* (1908), IV, III. 'Idle Notes. Sir T.B.'s Mouldy Pastures.'

—— *Encyclop. Brit.* (1910), IV, 666–7. 'Sir Thomas Browne.'

—— *East. Daily Press* (1922), 4 July. 'Sir Thomas Browne.' Leading article on the reburial of the skull, attributing the original theft of the skull to an antiquary and phrenologist named Fitch.

—— *East. Daily Press,* (1922), 5 July. 'Sir Thomas Browne. Reburial of the Skull. Ceremony in St. Peter Mancroft.'

—— *Times Lit. Sup.* (1923), 28 June, 436. 'Sir Thomas Browne.' Review of Golden Cockerel Press editions of *Religio Medici, Urn Burial, Garden of Cyprus.*

—— *Brit. Med. Journ.* (1923), II. 'The Skull of Sir Thomas Browne.' A notice of the volume by M. L. Tildesley.

—— *Times Lit. Sup.* (1924), 24 Aug. Review of Keynes, *Bibliography of Sir T.B.*

—— *East. Daily Press* (1925), 4 May.

'Death of Mr D. T. Potter.' A notice of the death in St. Peter Mancroft Church, Norwich, of the verger, Douro T. Potter, a recognized authority on Browne.

—— *Times Lit. Sup.* (1928), 24 May. Leading article on *Works*, ed. Keynes, vol. I, and *Christian Morals*, ed. Roberts.

—— *Times Lit. Sup.* (1932), 21 April. Review of *Works*, ed. Keynes, vols. V, VI.

—— *Times Lit. Sup.* (1933), 19 Jan. Review of *Urne Buriall and The Garden of Cyprus*, ed. Carter. (See no. 126*d*.)

—— *Clin. Excerpts*, Winthrop Chem. Co., Inc. (1946), XX, 67–74. 'Sir Thomas Browne.'

—— *N. & Q.* (1954), CXCIX, 184. Review of *Rel. Med.* ed. Denonain.

—— *Seventeenth Century News* (1960), XVIII. Notice of Denonain's *La Personalité de Sir Thomas Browne*.

—— *Times Lit. Sup.* (1962), 14 Dec., 972. 'Great and Glorious Physician.' A review of Mrs Bennett's *Sir Thomas Browne*.

—— *Seventeenth Cent. News* (1963), Autumn, 38. Notice of *Rel. Med.* ed. Winny.

ASCOLI, G. *La Grande-Bretagne devant l'opinion française au XVIIᵉ siecle*, 2 vols. Paris. 8°. 1930. Vol. I, pp. 79–80: 'Thomas Browne et la Religio Medici.'

ASHTON, A. J. *Eng. Rev.* (1926–7), XLIII–IV, 693–707, 59–68. 'Sir T.B. *en famille*.'

AUBREY, J. *Aubrey's Brief Lives*, ed. A. Clark, vol. I, Oxford, 1898, pp. 37, 210, 211. References to his introduction to *Religio Medici*, and to Browne's friendship with Dr. Arthur Dee, son of John Dee.

BACON, F. *Library of the World's Best Literature*, ed. C. D. Warner, vol. V, New York, 1896, pp. 2473–81. 'Sir Thomas Browne.'

BALDENSPERGER, F. *Revue des Cours et Conférences*, University of Paris, 1913, 740–56. '*La tradition moderne de l'humour*.' Browne is compared with Montaigne and Burton.

BALFOUR, R. D. *Some Seventeenth Century Worthies in a Twentieth Century Mirror*. Chapel Hill, 1940. Contains 'The Wisdom of Sir T.B.'.

BARNES, W. H. *Isis* (Bruges, 1934), XX, 337–43. 'Browne's Hydriotaphia with a reference to adipocere.'

BARRETT, J. H. *American Whig Rev.* (1848), VIII, 22, 'Sir Thomas Browne.'

BATHURST, CHARLES, Hon. and Rev. *Notes on Nets; or, The Quincunx Practically Considered*. London [*c.* 1840]. References, pp. 14, 63, to *The Garden of Cyrus*.

BEAN, WM. *Trans. Assoc. Am. Physicians* (1959), LXXII, 40–55. 'The Natural History of Error, *Pseudodoxia Epidemica*.' Reprinted, slightly modified, in *Am. Med. Ass. Arch. Int. Med.* (1960), CV, 184–93.

—— *Arch. Intern. Med.* (1964), 113. 'The Doctor's Religion. A Browne Study.'

BEECHENO, F. R. *East. Daily Press*, Norwich, 21 Feb. 1912. Letter on 'The First Residence of Sir Thomas Browne in Norwich'.

BENNETT, J. *Studies in the Renaissance* (1956), III, 175–84. 'A Note on *Religio Medici* and Some of its Critics.'

—— *Sir Thomas Browne*. Cambridge University Press, 1962. 21.5 cm., pp. viii, 255, [1].

—— *Camb. Rev.* (Oct. 1964). 'Wise beyond Wisdom?', review of *Works*, ed. Keynes, 1964.

BENSLEY, E. *N. & Q.* (1903), S. 9, XI. Browne's reference to Lipsius. *N. & Q.* (1905), S. 10, IV, 214. Spurious passage on Oblivion. *N. & Q.* (1906), S. 10, V, 346, 397. Sir T.B.'s Skull.

—— *N. & Q.* (1910). S. 11, I, 290–1, 353. Sir T.B. on Olybius's Lamp.

—— *N. & Q.* (1911), S. 11, III, 131. Note on Pyrrhus's Toe; see also p. 174, further note by S.W.S. *N. & Q.* (1912), S. 11, VI, 97. Browne's quotation from Ptolemy.

—— *N. & Q.* (1922), S. 12, XI, 108, 347. 'A Spanish Quotation in Sir Thomas

Browne's "Religio Medici".' *N. & Q.* (1924), S. 13, CXLVI, 364. Browne's quotation from Ausonius.

BETT, W. R. *Medical Press* (1955), CCXXIV, 380. 'Sir Thomas Browne.' Lines on his birthday.

BEVERLEY, M. *British Medical Association Annual Meeting, June 1890.* Presidential Address, Norwich, 1890, pp. 14–18. Sir Thomas Browne, Edward Browne, in 'Some Norwich Medical Worthies'.

BEVINGTON, M. M. *N. & Q.* (1960), CCV, 73. 'Locke and Stevenson on Comparative Morality.' Including notes on the influence of Browne on R. L. Stevenson, especially in 'Pulvis et Umbra'.

BIOGRAPHIE GÉNÉRALE. *Nouvelle biographie générale.* Paris, 1855. VII, 555. 'Browne, Thomas.'

[BIRKBECK, G.] Sale catalogue of contents of Stoke Holy Cross Hall, nr. Norwich, by direction of Geoffrey Birkbeck, Esq., June 1930, lot 370, 'The historic oak overmantel' from Browne's house, bought by Henry Birkbeck when the house was demolished in 1845 (400 gns.). Now in the Castle Museum, Norwich.

BIRRELL, A. *New Statesman* (1923), XXI, 326. 'Sir Thomas Browne.'

BIRRELL, F. *Nat. & Athen.* (1924), XXV, 650. Review of Keynes, *Bibliography of Browne.*

BISCHOFF, D. *Sir Thomas Browne als Stilkünstler. Ein Beitrag zur Deutung der englischen Barockliteratur.* Heidelberg, 1943. 23 cm., pp. [iv], 88. Frontispiece after the portrait in the Nat. Port. Gall.

BIZOUARD, J. *Des rapports de l'homme avec le démon, essai historique et philosophique.* Paris, 1863, III, 160–3, references to Browne.

BLAKISTON, Capt. *Memoirs Illustrative of the History and Antiquities of Norfolk and the City of Norwich.* London. Archeological Institute. 1851. Pp. 219–22. 'Remarks on Sir Thomas Browne.'

BLAND, D. S. *N. & Q.* (1964), CCIX, 356–7. Review of *Rel. Med.* ed. Winny.

BLATCHFORD, R. *My Favourite Books. Sir Thomas Browne's Hydriotaphia.* Clarion Pamphlet, no. 32. London, 1899, pp. 12, in printed wrappers.

BLAU, J. L. *Pub. Mod. Langu. Assoc. Amer.* (1934), XLIX, 963–4. 'Browne's interest in Cabalism.'

BLOMEFIELD, FRANCIS. *An Essay towards a Topographical History of the County of Norfolk.* London, 1806. References, vol. III, p. 414, short accounts of Sir Thomas and Edward Browne; vol. IV, pp. 193–4, account of the tombs in St. Peter Mancroft, Norwich.

BOTTRALL, M. *Every Man a Phoenix. Studies in seventeenth century autobiography.* London [1958]. 21.5 cm., pp. vi, 174. Pp. 30–56. 'Browne's Religio Medici.'

BOWES, W. A., jr. *Pharos* (1960), XXIII, 21–30. 'The Knight of Norwich. Sir T.B.'

BRIDGES, R. *Collected Essays Papers &c.* Oxford, 1934, pp. 133–46. XVIII. 'Sir Thomas Browne.' In phonetic spelling. First printed in *The Speaker*, London, 14 May 1904, as a review of Browne's *Works*, ed. Sayle (1904), vol. I.

BRIGSTOCKE, G. R. *N. & Q.* (1905), S. 10, III, 267. Sir T.B.'s epitaph. See also 452–3. Note on Owen Brigstocke.

BRITTEN, J. *Times Lit. Sup.* (1919), 18 Sept. 'Sir T.B.'s Plant-names', a letter.

BROWNE, S. J. *The World of Imagery.* London, 1927. P. 25, discussing Browne's symbols.

BRUNET, J.-C. *Manuel du libraire et de l'amateur de livres.* Paris, 1860. Vol. I (5th ed.), col. 1281, various works quoted.

BRYANT, M. *Encyclop. Brit.* Cambridge, 1910. IV, 666–7. 'Browne, Sir Thomas.' Revised from the article in the ninth edition, 1876.

BUCHINGER, H. *Beiträge zur Erkenntnis des individuellen Moments in Wortschatz der Religio Medici des Sir Thomas Browne.* Inaugural-Dissertation zur Erlungung der Doktorwürde der Albertus-Universität zu Königsberg i. Pr. Borna-Leipzig, 1936. Pp. xi, 64, [2].

BULLEN, A. H. *Dict. Nat. Biogr.* VII. London, 1886 [re-issue 1908]. 64–72. 'Browne, Sir Thomas.'

BULWER, E., LORD LYTTON. In *Misc. Prose Works* (London, 1868), I, 159 ff. 'Sir Thomas Browne.'

—— *Edinb. Rev.* (1837), LXIV, 1–37. 'Sir Thomas Browne's Works.' Review of Wilkin. Reprinted in Lord Lytton's *Quarterly Essays* (London, 1875), pp. 137–75.

BURNETT, G. In *Specimens of Engl. Prose Writers*. London, 1807.

BUSH, D. *English Literature in the Seventeenth Century*. Oxford, 1962. See pp. 286–9, 349–58, and *passim*.

BUTLER, H. B. and FLETCHER, C. R. L. *Historical Portraits 1600–1700. The Lives. The Portraits chosen by Emery Walker*. Oxford, 1911. Pp. 216–18. 'Sir Thomas Browne', with reproduction of the portrait in the Royal College of Physicians.

BUTTERWORTH, S. *N. & Q.* (1907), S. 10, VIII, 173–4. Sir T.B.'s Knighthood.

BUXTON, D. W. *Concerning Sir Thomas Browne Kt., M.D. and some Ideals of Professional Life*. London. 21.5 cm. 1909. Pp. 11, [1]. Reprinted from *The Gazette of the Royal Dental Hospital of London*, Feb. 1909.

CAMBRIDGE. *Cambridge History of English Literature*. Ed. A. W. Ward and A. R. Waller. 15 vols. Cambridge, 1908–27. See index, vol. xv for references, esp. vol. VII.

CARRITT, E. F. *The Open Window* (1910), II, 93–122. 'Hydrolatry', an essay on bathing in the style of Browne.

CARTER, J. Prospectus of *Urne Buriall and The Garden of Cyrus*, ed. John Carter [1932], [8] pp., 4°, with specimen pages and separate order form. See no. 126 d.

—— *The Iniquity of Oblivion Foil'd*. London, 1933. 50 copies reprinted from *The*

Colophon (1933), describing six author-corrected copies of *Urne-Buriall*.

—— *Times Lit. Sup.* (1935), 22 Aug. 'Browne's Urne-Buriall', describing a seventh author-corrected copy.

—— *Library* (1939), S. 4, XIX, 492–3. 'Browne's Autograph Corrections.' See also 347–53.

—— *Times Lit. Sup.* (1940), 11 May. 'An Author-corrected Urne-Buriall.'

—— *Times Lit. Sup.* (1943), 27 Feb. 'Urne Buriall.' A letter recording two additional copies of *Urne Buriall* corrected by the author.

—— *Library* (1947) S. v, II, 191–3. 'Browne's *Urn Burial*', a note on a copy with corrections by the author and an *errata* list of 24 lines, with reproductions of both *errata* lists.

—— *Times Lit. Sup.* (1957), 30 Aug. 'Browne's Hydriotaphia', a letter on the copy at Durham University Library, with author-corrections and the *errata* in the second form (see p. 77).

—— *The Book Collector* (1966), XV, 279–82. 'The Iniquity of Oblivion foil'd'. An account of author-corrected copies of *Hydriotaphia*, with folding plate of p. 135 from four copies.

CAWLEY, R. R. *Publ. Mod. Langu. Assoc. of America* (1933), XLVIII, 426–70. 'Sir Thomas Browne and his Reading.'

CAWLEY, R. R. & YOST, G. *Studies in Sir Thomas Browne*. (The Timeliness of *Pseudodoxia Epidemica*; Sir T. B. and Aristotle; Sir T. B. and his Reading.) Eugene: Univ. of Oregon Books, 1965, pp. ix, 166. Revd. in *Seventeenth Century News*, Autumn, 1966.

CHALMERS, ALEXANDER. *The General Biographical Dictionary*. New edition. 8°. London, 1813. Vol. VII, pp. 141–7. 'Browne, Sir Thomas.'

CHALMERS, G. K. *Harvard Summaries of Theses*. 1934. 281–4. 'Sir T.B.'s Thought and its Relation to Contemporary Ideas.'

—— *Virgin. Quart. Rev.* (1935), XI, 547–60: 'Hieroglyphs and Sir Thomas Browne.'

—— *Mod. Philol.* (1936), XXXIII, 243 ff. 'Three Terms of Corpuscularian Philosophy.' With reference to Browne's use of *effluvium*.

—— *Osiris* (1936), II, part 3, 28–79. 'Sir Thomas Browne, True Scientist.'

—— *Philos. of Science* (1937), IV, 75–95. 'The Lodestone and the Understanding of Matter in Seventeenth Century England.' With emphasis on Gilbert and Browne.

—— '*Virgin Quart. Rev.* (1950), XXVI.' That Universal and Publick Manuscript.'

CHAPMAN, R. W. *Times Lit. Sup.* (1937), 10 April. 'Contrive or Continue.' A letter referring to a reading in *Urne-Buriall*.

CHASLES, PHILARÈTE. *Études sur l'Antiquité.* Paris, 1847. 18°. Pp. 139–92. 'Essai sur les destinées et les sources des langues teutonique et latines', with remarks on Browne (p. 172).

—— *Études sur le XVIIIe Siècle en Angleterre.* Paris. 12°. 1847. Pp. 122–36. 'Un livre bizarre de Southey', with reference to *Hydriotaphia* (p. 123).

—— *Études sur la littérature et les mœurs de l'Angleterre au XIXe siècle.* Paris. 12°. 1851. Pp. 3–29, 'Du génie de la langue anglaise', with remarks on Browne (p. 20).

CHEVRILLON, A. *Qui fuerint sæculo xvii imprimis apud Hobbesium Anglicæ Solutæ orationis progressum.* Insulæ, 1893 (thesis). References to Browne, pp. 25, 26, 86, 88, 89.

CICCIO, D. *Narrativa* (1960), V, 73–5. 'Browne fonte dei "Sepolcri".'

CLARK, A. C. *Prose Rhythm in English.* London, 1913. References to Browne.

CLINE, J. M. *Five Studies in Literature.* Ed. B. H. Bronson. *Univ. of Calif. Publications*, VIII, 1940, pp. 73–100. 'Hydriotaphia.'

COLERIDGE, S. T. *Blackwood's Mag.* (1820), VI, 197–8. 'Character of Sir Thomas Browne as a writer', a fragment, preceded by a letter signed G. J.

—— *The Literary Remains.* 2 vols. London,

1836. Vol. I, pp. 241–8. 'Notes on Sir Thomas Browne's Religio Medici, 1802.' Communicated by Mr. Wordsworth. Vol. II, pp. 398–416. 'Notes on Sir Thomas Browne's Religio Medici made during a second perusal, 1808.' Notes on...Garden of Cyrus.' 'Notes on...Vulgar Errors, 1804.' 'Letter on Sir Thomas Browne.' See also *Miscellaneous Criticism*, ed. T. M. Raysor (London, 1936), p. 254.

COLIE, R. L. *Neophilologus.* Groningen (1952), XXXVI, 162–71. 'Sir Thomas Browne's "Entertainment" in XVIIth century Holland.'

—— *Bodl. Libr. Rec.* (1960), VI, 541–51. 'Dean Wren's Marginalia and Early Science in Oxford.'

COLLIN DE PLANCY, J. *Dictionnaire des sciences occultes.* Paris. 2 vols. 4°. 1848. Reference, vol. I, col. 272, to Browne as author of *Pseud. Epidem.*, with an analysis of the work and an allusion to the trial of witches at Bury St. Edmunds. The dictionary contains 24 notices copied with acknowledgment from *Pseud. Epidem.*

CONSTABLE, K. M. *Rev. Eng. Stud.* (1929), V, 218–19. 'Sir Thomas Browne's Christian Morals' (review of no. 185*a*).

COOK, ELIZABETH. *Harvard Libr. Bull.* (1948), II, 22–31. 'The First Edition of *Religio Medici*.'

CORFIELD, B. M. *Unpub. Doct. Diss.*, Radcliffe Coll. (1957). 'Studies in Sir T.B.'s *Pseud. Epid.*'

CORIE, THOMAS. *The Correspondence of Thomas Corie (1604–1689), Town Clerk of Norwich*, with his Annotations to Edward Browne's Travels. Ed. R. H. Hill, M.A. Norfolk Record Society, 1956. References: p. 16, Corie was a friend and neighbour of Sir T. Browne; 57, his comments on *Pseudodoxia Epidemica* in marginalia on Edward Browne's *Travel's*, 1673.

COUPLAND, W. H. *Edinb. Med. Journ.* (1905), 370–89. 'Sir Thomas Browne Knt.'

COURTNEY, W. L. *Daily Telegraph* (1905), 3 Oct. 'Sir Thomas Browne, Consulting Metaphysician.'

COWLES, T. *Isis* (1933–4), XX, 348. 'Dr. Henry Power, disciple of Sir Thomas Browne.'

CROLL, M. *Stud. in Philol.* (1921), XVIII, 79–128. 'Attic Prose in the Seventeenth Century.'

—— References in 'The Baroque Style in Prose', *Studies in Engl. Philol. in Honor of Frederick Klaeber.* Minneapolis, 1929, pp. 427 ff.

CROSSLEY, JAMES. *Blackwood's Edinb. Mag.* (1820), VI, 435–7. 'Sir Thomas Browne', a letter to the Editor.

—— *Retrospect. Rev.* (1820), I, 83–94. 'Art. VII. Hydriotaphia, Urn Burial... 1686.' An account of the book, unsigned.

   Ibid., 161–4. 'Art X. A MS volume of Sir Thomas Browne's Letters to his Son', with extracts, unsigned.

[CROSSLEY, JAMES] *The Palatine Note-book*, vol. III. Manchester, 1883, pp. 221–9. 'The late Mr James Crossley', with a woodcut after Walker's portrait of Crossley. Mentions all his contributions concerning Browne in periodicals and gives an account by Samuel Crompton of Crossley's behaviour on being challenged with having himself written the 'Fragment on Mummies' (see p. 154 of the present work).

CURRIE, H. MacL. *N. & Q.* (1958), CCIII, 143. 'Notes on Sir Thomas Browne's *Christian Morals*.'

D., C. *Europ. Mag.* (1801), XL, 89–90. 'Sir Thomas Browne.' A letter on a copy of the *Works* (1686), formerly belonging to Dr. White Kennett, Bishop of Peterborough, with a manuscript account of Browne and his family by J. Whitefoot; also, in the hand of Mrs Lyttelton, an account of Browne's MSS and the Devonshire painting of the Browne family. See no. 310.

DALE, B. *The Bradford Antiquary.* Bradford, 1896, pp. 45–57. 'Shibden Dale and Sir Thomas Browne's Religio Medici.'

DANIELS, R. B. *Some Seventeenth-century Worthies in a Twentieth-century Mirror.* Chapel Hill. 1940. pp. X, 156. Contains an essay on Browne.

DE BEER, E. S. *Library* (1938), XIX, 103–6. 'The Correspondence between Sir T.B. and John Evelyn.' With special reference to the dating of the letters.

DECHAMBRE, A. *Dictionnaire encyclopédique des sciences médicales* Paris, 1869. Vol. XI, p. 171. Short article on Browne and *Religio Medici*.

DE QUINCEY, T. *Confessions of an English Opium Eater.* London, 1822, p. 106, reference to a passage on music in *Religio Medici*, part II, section 9.

—— *Style and Rhetoric and Other Papers.* Edinburgh, 1862 (*Collected Works*, vol. X). Pp. 43–5, references to Browne's style in an essay on 'Rhetoric'.

DEROQUIGNY, J. *Charles Lamb, sa vie et ses œuvres*, Lille, 1904, pp. 334–5. Lamb and Browne compared.

DEZEIMERIS, O., et RAIGE-DELORME. *Dictionnaire historique de la médécine ancienne et moderne.* Vol. I. Paris, 1828. P. 536, remarks on Browne.

DOBRÉE, B. *The Listener* (1962), LXVIII, 979. Reviews of Bennett, *Sir T.B.*, and Huntley, *Sir T.B.*, 1962.

—— *The Listener* (1964), 1 Oct. 'Several Worlds.' Review of *Works*, ed. Keynes, and *Religio Medici*, &c. ed. Martin.

D[ONNE], W. [BODHAM] *Athenæum* (1829), no. 93, 487–8. 'Shades of the Dead', no. IV. The Humanists: I. 'Sir Thomas Browne.'

DOUGLAS, D. C. *English Scholars*, London, 1939, 22 cm., pp. 381, [I]. Pp. 28–30 and other references relating Browne to other scholars of the seventeenth century.

DOWDEN, E. *Puritan and Anglican: Studies in Literature*, London, 1900, pp. 35–68. 'Sir Thomas Browne.'

DOYLE, B. R. *McGill Med. Journ.* (1963)

32. 'Sir Thomas Browne, physician and humanist.'

DRAKE, NATHAN. *Evenings in Autumn—A Series of Essays Narrative and Miscellaneous.* London. 2 vols. 8°. 1822. Vol. II, pp. 63–99, 197–221. 'On the Character and Writings of Sir Thomas Browne, with extracts from, and Observations on, his Religio Medici.'

DUMONT, J. *Analyse d'un ouvrage de Thomas Browne, médecin anglais intitulé: Religio Medici (la Religion du Médecin).* Angers, 1859. 8°. pp. 34.

DUNN, W. P. *Sir Thomas Browne. A Study in Religious Philosophy* [1926]. pp. [vi], 190, [4]. Second edition. Minneapolis. [1951], pp. viii, 182.

DUTT, W. A. *Some Literary Associations of East Anglia.* London, 1907, pp. 126–51. 'Sir Thomas Browne and Bishop Hall.'

EADE, SIR PETER. *Sir Thomas Browne.* A paper read at a meeting of the C.E.Y.M.S. Literary Class, 12 March 1894, pp. 8. Reprinted from the Society's Journal and in *Addresses and Papers* (1908), pp. 121–38.

EDWARDS, A. B. *The Photographic Historical Portrait Gallery.* London, 1864. P. 87, biographical notice. Plate XLIV, 'Sir Thomas Browne', from a miniature in the collection of the Duke of Buccleugh.

ELLIS, S. M. *Wilkie Collins, Le Fanu and Others.* London, 1931. 22.5 cm., pp. [x], 343, [1]. Pp. 223–65. 'James Crossley', with remarks on his edition of Browne's *Tracts* and his fictitious 'Fragment on Mummies'.

ELMES, J. *N. & Q.* (1858), S. 2, VI, 284–5. 'Sir T.B.'s English undefiled.' A note on his Latinisms (*Pseud. Epid.* preface).

ELTON, O. *A Sheaf of Papers.* London, 1922. 'English Prose Numbers.'

EMERSON, R. W. *The Journals and Miscellaneous Notebooks.* Ed. A. R. Ferguson. 4 vols. Harvard Univ. Press, Cambridge, Mass., 1964. References in vols. III and IV (see indexes).

ENDICOTT, N. J. *Univ. of Toronto Quart.* (1961), XXX, 180–210. 'Sir Thomas Browne as "Orphan", with Some Account of his Stepfather, Sir Thomas Dutton.'

—— *N. & Q.* (1962), CCVII, 273–4. Readers' Queries. 'Sir Thomas Browne', on the date of Browne's birth and the last paragraph of *The Garden of Cyrus.*

—— *Times Lit. Sup.* (1962), 24 Aug., p. 645. 'Sir Thomas Browne, Montpellier, and the Tract "Of Languages".' See also a letter from D. E. Rhodes concerning Mario Equicola mentioned in Endicott's article.

—— *Times Lit. Sup.* (1966), 15 Sept. 'Browne's "Letter to a Friend".' Criticizing Huntley's identification of the characters concerned.

—— *Univ. of Toronto Quart.* (1966), XXXVI, 68–86. 'Sir Thomas Browne's *Letter to a Friend.*'

EOYANG, E. *Seventeenth Century News,* Spring and Summer 1963. Notice of Joan Bennett's *Sir Thomas Browne.*

ESDAILE, ARUNDELL. *Times Lit. Sup.* (1919), 25 Dec. 'Sir Thomas Browne', a letter drawing attention to *Vox Norwici* (see no. 228).

EUREN, H. F. *Portraits of and by Norwich Notables,* 1902. Contains 'Sir Thomas Browne: Walter Pater's Appreciation', 'Scotch Appreciations', 'A Quarterly Reviewer on Browne's Style', extracted from *The Norwich Mercury,* 19 Feb. 1902, 'Norwich Notables, III'.

EWING, M. *Philol. Quart.* (1942), XXI, 425–7. 'A Note on the Browne–Sir William Dugdale Letters.' On the dating of the letters.

—— *Philol. Quart.* (1943), XXII, 111–18. 'Mrs Piozzi Peruses Browne.' An account of Mrs Piozzi's marginalia in her copy of *Pseud. Epid.* (1669), now in the library of the University of Virginia.

FELLER, ABBÉ F. X. DE. *Dictionnaire historique des hommes qui se sont fait un nom par le génie.* 10 vols. Lyon. 1821–3. Vol. II, pp. 531–2. Biographical details of Browne.

FILON, A. *Histoire de la littérature anglaise.* Paris, 1883. Pp. 237–8, a passage of ignorant criticism, refuted in Leroy's *Le Chevalier Thomas Browne* (1931).

FINCH, J. S. *Abstr. of Diss.*, Cornell Univ., Ithaca, 1936. 'Sir T.B.: A Study of his Mind, Works, and Influence.'

—— *Times Lit. Sup.* (1937), 13 Nov. 'Museum Clausum.' Suggesting that the tract was addressed to Dr. Charleton.

—— *The Library* (1939) S. 4, XIX, 347–53. 'A newly discovered Urne-Buriall' (the eighth author-corrected copy).

—— *Rev. Eng. Stud.* (1939), XV, 468–70. 'Sir Thomas Browne and the strolling players in Norwich.'

—— *Publ. Mod. Langu. Assoc. Amer.* (1940), LV, 742–7. 'Early drafts of the Garden of Cyrus.'

—— *Stud. in Philol.* (1940), XXXVII, 274–82. 'Browne and the Quincunx.'

—— *Times Lit. Sup.* (1940), 16 March. 'An Author-corrected "Urne-Buriall".'

—— *Library* (1941–2), XXII, 67–72. 'Sir Hans Sloane's Printed Books.' Contains an account of Sloane's copy of the Sale Catalogue of Browne's library.

—— *Stud. in Bibliogr.* (1949), II, 196–201. 'Sir Thomas Browne: Early Biographical Notices and the Disposition of his Library and Manuscripts.'

—— *Princeton Univ. Libr. Chron.* (1950), XI, no. 4. 'The Norfolk Persuaders of Sir Thomas Browne: A Variant Copy of the 1712 Posthumous Works.'

—— *Sir Thomas Browne A Doctor's Life of Science and Faith.* New York. H. Schuman. 1950. 25 cm., pp. X, 319. Illustr.

—— *Bull. N.Y. Acad. Med.* (1951), XXVII. 'The Humanity of Sir Thomas Browne.'

—— *Trans. & Stud. of College of Physic. of Philadelphia* (1956), XXIV, 59–69. 'The Lasting Influence of Sir Thomas Browne.'

FISCH, H. *Isis*, Bruges (1953), 44, 252–65. 'The Scientist as Priest: A Note on Robert Boyle's Natural Theology', with references to Browne as echoed by Boyle.

FITCH, ROBERT. *Memoirs Illustrative of the History and Antiquities of Norfolk and the City of Norwich.* London. Archeological Institute. 8°. 1851. Pp. 223–4. 'Notes on the Discovery of the Remains of Sir Thomas Browne in 1840.'

FRAYNE, J. P. *Sir Thomas Browne, antiquarian and virtuoso.* [New York, ?1858] 28 cm., 100 leaves. M.A. thesis for Columbia University (NYAM).

FRISWELL, J. H. *Varia: readings from rare books.* London. 1866. Pp. 251–84. 'Sir Thomas Browne', with woodcut frontispiece by J. Cooper after the Norwich portrait.

GAY, R. M. *The Explic.* (1942), 1, 11 Nov. 'Browne's Hydriotaphia.'

GEORGE, E. A. *Seventeenth Century Men of Latitude.* London. 1908. 18·5 cm. pp. xviii, [ii], 199, [5]. Pp. 151–66. 'Sir Thomas Browne', with portrait.

GORDON, C. A. *Times Lit. Sup.* (1965), 6 May. 'Works of Sir Thomas Browne.' A letter on his introduction to Browne by Charles Sayle.

GORDON, G. S. *The Lives of Authors.* London, 1950. Pp. [viii], 208. Pp. 101–10, 'Sir Thomas Browne.' Essays, reprinted from *Times Lit. Sup.*, 24 May 1928, 21 April 1932.

GOSSE, SIR EDMUND. *English Literature. An Illustrated Record.* 4 vols. London, 1903. III, 52–4. 'Sir Thomas Browne', illustrated.

—— *Sir Thomas Browne.* London, 1905. 18·5 cm., pp. vi, [i], 215, [1]. (English Men of Letters series.) Reviewed in *The Times*, 13 Oct. 1905, and *Times Lit. Sup.*, 13 Oct. 1905.

—— *Sunday Times* (1924), 17 Aug. Review of Keynes, *Bibliography of Browne.*

—— *Sunday Times* (1928), 27 May. Unfinished review of *Works*, ed. Keynes, vol. 1. Written by Sir Edmund on his death-bed. The MS is in the collection of Sir Geoffrey Keynes.

GRAESSE, J. C. C. *Trésor de livres rares et précieux*. 7 vols. 4°. Dresden, 1859. Vol. I, p. 549, references to various works by Browne.

GREEN, P. M. *Sir Thomas Browne*. Publ. for The British Council and the National Book League by Longmans, Green & Co. [1959]. 21·5 cm., pp. 39. With a portrait. (Writers and their Work, No. 108.)

GREEN, S. S. *Proc. Amer. Antiqu. Soc.* 29 April 1903. 'Did Sir Thomas Browne write "Fragment on Mummies"?' Reprinted as a pamphlet. Worcester, Mass., 1903, pp. 8.

GREENHILL, W. A. *The Bibliographer*. London (1882). I, 166–9, a letter on the bibliography of *Religio Medici*. Reprinted separately, 1882. See vol. III, 1883, for a further note by Greenhill.

—— *N. & Q.* (1882), S. 6, V. 'Sir T.B.'s *Rel. Med.*'

GREG, W. W. *English Literary Autographs*, part III—Prose Writers and Appendix. Oxford University Press. 1932. LXXXIX: 'Sir Thomas Browne.' An account of Browne with a transcript and facsimile of part of Browne's letter to Dugdale, 27 Oct. 1658 (BM MS. Harl. 4712. fo. 171*a*), and of signature to a letter, *Amico clarissimo*, with a phrase adapted from Catullus, XXXV, 7 (BM MS. Sloane 1827, f. 86*a*).

GRIGSON, G. *Country Life* (1964), 3 Sept. 'A Mighty User of Words.' Review of *Works*, ed. Keynes.

GROSS, J. *The Observer* (1964), 9 Aug. 'The great amphibium.' Review of the *Works*, ed. Keynes, and *Religio Medici*, &c. ed. Martin.

GUTHRIE, D. *The Lancet*. London. II. 1943. Pp. 462–3. 'Religio Medici. A Tercentenary Tribute.'

HALLAM, HENRY. *Introduction to the Literature of Europe in the 15th, 16th, and 17th Centuries*. Fourth edition. London. 8°. 1854. Vol. II, pp. 516, 517; vol. III, pp. 237–8, 542, references to Browne.

HALLIWELL, J. O. *Catalogue of the miscellaneous manuscripts and letters in the possession of the Royal Society*. London. 1840. Nos. 422–40: Browne, Edward. Nos. 441–4: Browne, Sir T. Also VII (I), 9: Browne, Sir T.; XV (I), 34, XVII, 8: Browne, Edward.

HALSEY, A. H. *Camb. Rev.* (1964), 10 Oct. 'Wise beyond Wisdom?' Review of *Works*, ed. Keynes.

HARPER, G. M. *Literary Appreciations*, Indianapolis, 1937. 'The Family Correspondence of Sir Thomas Browne.'

HAYWARD, J. *The Criterion* (1932), XI, 328–31. Review of *Works*, ed. Keynes, vol. VI.

HAZLITT, W. *Lectures chiefly on the Dramatic Literature of the Age of Elizabeth*. London, 1820. 8°. Lect. VII, pp. 292–306. 'Character of Sir T. Brown as a writer', with a long quotation from *Urn Burial* and from Coleridge's marginalia.

—— *Literary Remains*. 2 vols. London, 1836. II, 335–7. Essay XVIII, 'Of Persons one would wish to have seen', incl. Lamb's remarks on Browne.

HEARN, LAFCADIO. *Interpretations of English Literature*. 3 vols. London. 8°. 1916. Vol. II, pp. 60–70. 'Sir Thomas Browne.'

HEIDEMAN, M. A. *Univ. of Toronto Quart.* (1950), XIX, 235–46. 'Hydriotaphia and The Garden of Cyrus. A Paradox and a Cosmic Vision.'

HEPPLE, R. B. *N. & Q.* (1938), CLXXIV, 446. See also 387; CLXXV: R. Hussey, 16, 123; L. R. M. Strachan, 67. 'Elijah's Prophecy' (in *Rel. Med.* part 1, sect. 46).

HODGART, M. *New Statesman* (1964), 11 Sept. 'All Shall Awake.' Review of *Works*, ed. Keynes, and *Religio Medici*, &c. ed. Martin.

HÖLTGEN, K. J. *Times Lit. Supp.* (1966), 20 Oct. Letter on Endicott's letter of 15 Sept. 1966, on *A Letter to a Friend*.

HOOD, E. P. *Sunday At Home* (1884), 364–7. 'Great and Good Books. IV. Sir Thomas Browne: The Urn Burial, and Religio Medici.'

HOOPER, J. *N. & Q.* (1894) S. 8, VI, 233–4. The skull of Sir T.B. See also VIII, 325. Note on the coffin-plate. *N. & Q.* (1915), S. 11. XI, 97. Note on burials at Brampton.

HOPE, H. G. *N. & Q.* (1903), S. 11, XI, 12. Notes on Browne's marriage.

HORI, DAIJI. *Swift and other Authors.* Tokyo, 1959, pp. 3–87. 'Sir Thomas Browne.'

HORTON, D. *Harvard Med. Alum. Bull.* (1956), Oct. 'Religio Medici.'

HOUGHTON, W. E. *Journ. Hist. Ideas* (1942), III, 51–73. 'The English Virtuoso in the Seventeenth Century.'

HOWELL, A. C. *Stud. in Philol.* (1925), XXII, 61–80. 'Sir Thomas Browne and Seventeenth Century Scientific Thought.'

—— *Stud. in Philol.* (1925), XXII, 412–17. 'A Note on Sir Thomas Browne's Knowledge of Languages.'

—— *Stud. in Philol.* (1931), XXVIII, 87 ff. 'Sir Thomas Browne and the Elizabethans.'

—— *Stud. in Philol.* (1945), XLII, 564–77. 'Sir Thomas Browne as Wit and Humorist.'

HUNTLEY, F. L. *Bull. Hist. of Med.* (1951), XXV, 236–47. 'Sir Thomas Browne, M.D., William Harvey, and the Metaphor of the Circle.'

—— *Mod. Philol.* (1951), XLVIII, 157–71. 'The Occasion and Date of Sir Thomas Browne's *A Letter to a Friend*.'

—— *Rev. Engl. Stud.* (1951), II, 262–7. 'Robert Loveday: Commonwealth Man of Letters.'

—— *Journ. Hist. of Ideas* (1953), XIV, 353–64. 'Sir Thomas Browne and the Metaphor of the Circle.'

—— *Times Lit. Sup.* (1953), 8 May. 'Sir Thomas Browne's Leyden thesis', a letter asking for information.

—— *Libr. Quart.* (1955), XXV, 203–18. 'The Publication and Immediate Reception of *Religio Medici*.'

—— *Hist. Ideas Newsletter* (1956), II, 50–3.

'Sir Thomas Browne and his Oxford Tutor; or, Academic Guilt by Association.'

—— *Michigan Alumni Quart. Rev.* (1956), LIII, 23–33. 'A Garland for Sir Thomas Browne, M.D., Knight.'

—— *Stud. in Philol.* (1956), LII, 204–18. 'Sir Thomas Browne. The Relationship of *Urn Burial* and *The Garden of Cyrus*.'

—— *Mod. Philol.* (1959), LVIII, 58–62. Review of Denonain's *Une version primitive de Religio Medici*. The hypothesis that the Pembroke MS. is '*une version primitive*' is not accepted.

—— *Sir Thomas Browne. A Biographical and Critical Study.* Ann Arbor, 1962. 21 cm., pp. viii, [ii], 283.

—— *Journ. Hist. Med.* (1964), XIX, 310–12. Review of *Religio Medici*, ed. Winny.

—— *Seventeenth Century News* (1965), IX. Review of *Rel. Med.*, ed. Martin.

—— *Philosophical Dictionary.* New York, 1965. Article on Browne.

—— *Times Lit. Sup.* (1967), 9 Feb. 'Sir Thomas Browne's *Letter to a Friend*', a reply to N. J. Endicott's letter of 15 Sept. 1966.

HUTCHINSON, G. E. *The Itinerant Ivory Tower.* London, 1953. Contains 'Tuba Mirum Spargens Sonum' (an essay on Browne and recent books about him).

INDEX EXPURGATORIUS. *Index of Prohibited Books*, Vatican, Polyglot Press, 1930, p. 440. *Religio Medici* was proscribed on 18 March 1645.

IRVINE, W. F. *The Cheshire Sheaf* (1901), S. 3, III, 100, 107–8, 118–19. A query and replies by Irvine on the ancestry of Browne and the Brownes of Upton, proving that he was grandson of Richard Browne and son of Thomas Browne (m. Anne Garraway) of Upton and later of London.

ISEMAN, J. S. *A Perfect Sympathy: Charles Lamb and Sir Thomas Browne.* Cambridge, Mass. 1937, pp. 90, [6]. (Harvard Honors Theses in English, no. 10.)

JAFFÉ, M. *Cambr. Journ.* (1949), II, 752–7. 'Sir Thomas Browne at Midnight.'

JANELLE, P. *Études Anglaises* (1962), XV, 269–71. 'Note sur *Religio Medici.*'

JEAFFERSON, J. C. *A Book about Doctors.* 2 vols. London. 1860. 19 cm. Vol. I, pp. 43–58. Ch. IV, 'Sir Thomas Browne and Sir Kenelm Digby'.

JESSOPP, A. *The Norfolk Antiquarian Miscellany.* Ed. Walter Rye. Norwich, 1883. 8°. II, 279, in 'The Wooing and the Married Life of Elizabeth, Lady L'Estrange, née Isham', reference to Browne's advice against the use of 'Goddard's drops' in treating Sir Edward Walpole for stone in the bladder.

JOHNSON, F., BARNARD, G. W. G. and BRIGSTOCK, G. R. *N. & Q.* (1909), S. 10, XI, 473–4. 'Notes on Sir T.B.'s relationship to Anne Townshend.' See also XII, 36–7.

JOHNSON, LIONEL. *Acad.* (1894), no. 1144, 291. 'Dr Johnson and Sir T.B.'

—— *The Daily Chronicle*, London, 1 April 1898 p. 3. 'A Letter to Sir Thomas Browne', an article on his style and writings.

JOHNSTON, D. *Living Age* (1905), CCXLVII, 289. 'Sir Thomas Browne.' Also in *Macmillan's Magazine* (1905), XCII, 414–22.

JONES, R. F. *Publ. Mod. Langu. Assoc. Amer.* (1930), XLV, 991–1009. 'Science and English Prose Style in the Third Quarter of the Seventeenth Century.' A note on Browne's style and the Royal Society.

—— *Journ. Eng. and Germ. Philol.* (1932), XXXI, 315–31. 'Science and Language in England in the middle of the Seventeenth Century.'

JUSSERAND, J. J. *Historie littéraure du peuple anglais.* 2 vols. Paris, 1894–1904. Reference, vol. II, ch. IX, pp. 871–3.

KANE, R. J. *Rev. Eng. Stud.* (1933), IX, 266–74. 'James Crossley, Sir Thomas Browne, and the *Fragment on Mummies.*'

(The greater part of the *Fragment* was printed by Prof. R. M. Gray as Browne's in *The College Book of Prose*, Boston and New York, Houghton Mifflin Co., 1929, p. 701.)

KEITH, SIR ARTHUR. *Times Lit. Sup.* (1922), 11 May, 307. 'The Skull of Sir Thomas Browne.' A letter giving the results of an investigation of the reputed skull of Sir T.B. See also under Tildesley.

—— *Phrenological Studies of the Skull and Brain Cast of Sir Thomas Browne of Norwich.* Edinburgh. 24.7 cm. 1924, pp. [ii], 30. (Henderson Trust Lecture, no. III.)

KELLETT, C. E. *Annals of Med. Hist.* (1935), VII, 467–79. 'Sir Thomas Browne and the disease called the Morgellons.'

KETTON-CREMER, R. W. *Charles Harbord.* Privately Printed. 1949. 21 cm., pp. 26. With passages concerning Browne's younger son, Thomas.

—— *Times Lit. Sup.* (1951), 2 Nov. 'Sir Thomas Browne prescribes', extracts from a household book at Gunton Park, Norfolk.

—— *East. Daily Press* (1964), 17 Aug. 'Norfolk's Greatest Writer.' Review of *Works*, ed. Keynes and *Religio Medici*, &c. ed. Martin.

KEYNES, F. A. *Times Lit. Sup.* (1936), 11 June. 'Abyssinia in the 17th. Century', quoting part of a letter from Browne to his son Edward about a History of Aethiopia.

—— *The Parents' Review* (1954), LXV, 45–9. 'Sir Thomas Browne and his Family.'

KEYNES, SIR GEOFFREY. *St. Barthol. Hosp. Journ.* (1912), XIX, 158–61. 'Sir Thomas Browne, M.D.'

—— *Times Lit. Sup.* (1919), 4 Sept. 470. 'A Daughter of Sir T.B.' [Elizabeth Lyttelton].

—— *A Bibliography of Sir Thomas Browne, Kt., M.D.* Cambridge At the University Press Ann. Dom. MCMXXIV 25 cm., pp. xii, 255, [1]. Edition of 500 copies.

—— *The Library* (1930), n.s. X, 418–20.

'An unrecorded edition of Browne's Christian Morals.' (See no. 164.)

—— *Times Lit. Sup.* (1932), 25 Feb. 132. 'France and Sir Thomas Browne', review of Leroy's *French Bibliography of Browne*.

—— *Times Lit. Sup.* (1932), 25 Feb. 134. 'The earliest compositions of Sir Thomas Browne.' See nos. 186, 187.

—— *Times Lit. Sup.* (1938), 19 Nov. 'Browne's *Letter to a Friend*' (Antiquarian Notes).

—— *Cambridge Bibliography of English Literature.* Vol. i. Cambridge, 1940, pp. 834–5, 'Sir Thomas Browne', and *Supplement*, vol. v, 1957, pp. 341–2.

—— *The Lancet* (1943), ii. 'Religio Medici', a letter concerning Guthrie's 'Tercentenary Tribute' (see p. 217).

—— *Country Life* (1951), 23 Feb. 557–8. 'Sir Thomas Browne on trees', a letter.

—— *Times Lit. Sup.* (1952), 18 April. 'Sir Thomas Browne's Religio Medici', a letter concerning the order of the two editions of 1642.

—— *Lancet* (1963). i.1166. 'Sir T.B.: the St. Peter Mancroft Restoration Fund', a letter appealing for contributions signed with F. S. Jarvis, Vicar, and J. M. Ridley Thomas. Published also in *Brit. Med. Journ.* and *Journ. Amer. Med. Assoc.*

—— *Brit. Med. Journ.* (1965), ii, 1505–10. 'Sir Thomas Browne.' A lecture delivered to the Norfolk Branch of the B.M.A. in Norwich on 31 March 1965. 50 reprints.

KIRBY, T. F. *Winchester Scholars*, London, 1888, p. 167. See also Tildesley, M. L. (1923).

KNOTT, J. *Brit. Med. Journ.* (1905), ii, 975–61, 1046–9. 'Medicine and Witchcraft in the days of Sir Thomas Browne.'

—— *Dublin Journ. Med. Science* (1905), CXXI, 241–64. 'Sir T.B., Knight.'

KNYVETT, THOMAS. *The Knyvett Letters, 1624–1644.* Ed. B. Schofield, M.D. Norfolk Record Society, 1949. References: p. 137 to medical attendance by Browne

12 April 1644; p. 142 to help from Dr. Browne in resisting the collector of rents, Richard Browne: 'You must ingage Mr. Balliston in this, & Dr. Browne who I hear was once his master.'

KOSZUL, A. *Anthologie de la littérature anglaise.* 2 vols. Paris, 1912. Vol. i, pp. 252–3, a notice of Browne, with a translation of *Religio Medici*, part i, section 32.

KRUTCH, J. W. *Thoreau Soc. Bull.* (1949), XXIX, 3. 'Thoreau and Sir T.B.'

LAMB, C. In *The Works of Charles and Mary Lamb*, ed. E. V. Lucas. London, 1903. i, p. 203; iv, pp. 65, 207; vi, p. 289; vii, p. 699.

—— In *The Life, Letters and Writings*, ed. Percy Fitzgerald. 6 vols. London. 1924 (Enfield Edition). Vol. iii, pp. 220–30: 'Imperfect Sympathies'; pp. 231–9: 'Witches and other Night Fears', written in imitation of Browne's style. Vol. vi, pp. 144–8. 'The Religion of Actors.'

—— In *The Works.* London, 1935. References i, pp. 678, 772; ii, pp. 305, 306, 377, 392, 833, 881; iii, pp. 10, 24, 25, 27, 68; iv, pp. 46, 911, 932.

LAROUSSE, P. *Grand dictionnaire universel du XIXᵉ siècle.* Paris, 1866. Vol. ii, p. 1324, article on Browne.

LEFANU, W. R. *The Book Collector* (1964), Winter. Pp. 518–19. Review of *Works*, ed. Keynes (1964).

LEGOUIS, E. *Histoire de la littérature anglaise.* Paris, 1924, pp. 512–16. Observations on Browne.

LEROY, O. *A French Bibliography of Sir Thomas Browne.* London. 25.3 cm. 1931, pp. [x], 97, [3]. Edition of 225 copies.

—— *Le Chevalier Thomas Browne.* Paris, 1931. 24.8 cm., pp. [iv], xii, 422, with portrait drawn by P. Dagnas. Edition of 342 copies. Re-issued in 1939 with a different imprint and an additional *erratum*.

LETTS, M. *N. & Q.* (1912), S. 11, V, 221–3. 'Sir T.B. and Witchcraft.'

—— *N. & Q.* (1912), S. 11, VI, 188. Note on Browne's reference, *Pseud. Ep.* I, iv, to doubling the altar at 'Delphos'.

—— *N. & Q.* (1914), S. 11, X, 1914, 321–3, 342–4, 361–2. 'Sir Thomas Browne and his books' (notes on the *Sale Catalogue*, see no. 214).

—— *N. & Q.* (1916), S. 12, II, 446. 'Sir Thomas Browne: Counterfeit Basilisks.' A note on their manufacture.

LEWIS, K. M. *N. & Q.* (1915), S. 11, XI, 1. 'An Analogy to Sir T.B.'

LOISEAU, J. *Revue Anglo-Américaine* (1933), X, 385–98. 'Sir Thomas Browne écrivain métaphysique.'

LONG, S. H. *East. Daily Press* (1923), 25 Sept. 'Sir Thomas Browne. Four recently discovered portraits.' A notice of the volume by M. L. Tildesley.

LOWELL, J. R. *Among my Books*, Boston, 1870, pp. 152–3.

—— *Atlantic Monthly* (1890), LXVI, 63. 'In a volume of Sir Thomas Browne', poem of 14 lines.

MABBOTT, T. O. *N. & Q.* (1931), CLXI, 317, A note on *Urne Buriall*, 'What Song the Sirens Sang'. See also G. H. White, 429–30.

MACAULAY, ROSE. *Time and Tide* (1932), 7 May. 'Sir Thomas Browne.' Review of *Works*, ed. Keynes, vols. V. and VI.

McC., H. *More Books*. Boston Pub. Libr. (1939), XIV, 29. 'Browne on Vulgar Errors'.

MACKINNON, M. *Bull. Hist. Med.* (1953), XXVII, 503–11. 'An Unpublished Consultation Letter of Browne.' A letter to Dr Samuel Bave of Bath (see *Works*, ed. Keynes, 1964, IV, 240–8).

McKNIGHT, W. L. *Abstr. of Theses, Univ. of Pittsburg Bull.* (1935), XI, 312–2. 'Sir T.B. A Study in Attitudes.'

MACMICHAEL, W. *Lives of the British Physicians*. London, 1830, pp. 60–83, 'Sir Thomas Browne', with a portrait engraved on steel by W. C. Edwards after the engraving by Vandrebanc, 1683 (no. 127).

MADDISON, C. *Mod. Langu. Notes* (1960), LXXV, 468–78. 'Brave Prick Song. An Answer to Sir Thomas Browne.' On the nightingale sitting with her breast against a thorn. *Pseud. Epid.* Book III, ch. 28 (*Works*, 1964, II, 268).

MALCOLM, J. P. *Lives of Topographers and Antiquaries*. London, 1815. 3 pp. 'Sir Thomas Browne', with portrait 13 × 10.5 cm. engraved by T. Trotter after R. White (*Works*, 1686). The engraving was published separately in 1798.

MANDEVILLE, Sister Scholastica. *Unpub. Doct. Diss.* St Louis Univ. (1961). 'The Rhetorical Tradition of the Sententia: with a Study of its Influence on the prose of Sir Francis Bacon and of Sir T.B.' Abstr. in *Diss. Abstr.* (1961), XXI, 3099.

MARKLAND, J. H. *N. & Q.* (1853), S. I, VIII, 10. Note on Bishop Ken and Browne's 'Midnight Hymn'. See also *N. & Q.* (1854), X, 110, and under Montgomery (see p. 222*b*).

—— *N. & Q.* (1853), VIII, 10–11. 'Bishop Ken.' Concerning Browne's 'Midnight Hymn'. See also IX, 220, 258; X, 110–11.

MARSHALL, EDWARD. *N. & Q.* (1882), S. 6, V, 102–4, 243–4. 'Notes on the *Rel. Med.* of Sir T.B.' *N. & Q.* (1885), S. 6, XII, 95. Notes on the *Rel. Med.* Atomist.

MARSHALL, EMMA. *In the East Country with Sir Thomas Browne, Kt., Physician and Philosopher of the City of Norwich*. London, 1884 [second edn. 1886, reissued 1908]. 8°, pp. XVI, 398. A novel in which Browne is the central figure.

MARSHALL, E. and WILLIAMS, C. A. *N. & Q.* (1886), S. 7, I, 155. Notes on Browne's skull.

MARTIN, H. *N. & Q.* (1854), X, 110–11. 'Sir T.B. and Bishop Ken.'

MASTERMAN, J. H. B. In *The Age of Milton*. London, 1897, pp. 146–59.

MEATH, GERARD, O. P. *The Tablet* (1964), 3 Oct. 'Sir Thomas Browne Today.' Review of *Works*, ed. Keynes, and *Religio Medici*, &c. ed. Martin.

MENAUGH, J. J. *N. & Q.* (1938), CLXXV, 132. 'A possible source of a French Quotation in the Religio Medici' (see Ward, H. G.); see also Keynes, G., 175.

MERTON, E. S. *Isis* (1956), XLVII, 161–71. 'The Botany of Sir Thomas Browne.'

—— *Journ. Hist. Med.* (1948), III, 214–28. 'Sir Thomas Browne's Scientific Quest.'

—— *Philol. Quart.* (1949), XXVIII, 497–503. 'Browne's Interpretation of Dreams.'

—— *Science and Imagination in Sir Thomas Browne.* Columbia Univ. New York, 1949, 20.5 cm., pp. x, 156.

—— *Journ. Hist. Med.* (1950), V, 416–21. 'Browne's Embryological Theory.'

—— *Osiris* (1950), IX, 413–34. 'Sir Thomas Browne as Zoologist.'

—— *Osiris* (1952), X, 206–23. 'Sir Thomas Browne's Theories of Respiration and Combustion.'

—— *Hist. of Ideas News Letter* (1957), III, 54–7. 'Microcosm, Epitome and Seed: Some Seventeenth Century Analogies.' Illustrations largely from Browne.

—— *Hist. of Ideas News Letter* (1958), IV, 86. 'Sir Thomas Browne on Astronomy.'

MEYRICK, F. J. (Vicar of St. Peter Mancroft). *Brit. Med. Journ.* London. 1. 1922, pp. 725–6. 'Sir Thomas Browne: the story of his skull, his wig, and his coffin plate.'

MILSAND, J. A. *Rev. des Deux-Mondes* (1858), XIV, 646–85; XVI, 631–61. 'Thomas Browne le médecin philosophe de Norwich.' These articles are summarized in Leroy's *Bibliogr. of Browne* (1931), pp. 58–61.

MINTO, W. *A Manual of Engl. Prose Lit.* Edinburgh, 1872.

MOLONEY, M. F. *Journ. Engl. and Germ. Philol.* (1959). LVIII, 60–7. 'Metre and *Cursus* in Sir Thomas Browne's Prose.'

MONRO, T. K. *Scottish Hist. Rev.* (1921), XIX, 49–57. 'An Unpublished Letter of Sir Thomas Browne, M.D.' (See *Works*, ed. Keynes, 1964, IV, 319.)

—— *Notes on the Early Editions of Sir T.B.* Glasgow, 1923. 26.5 cm., pp. [iii], 19, [3]. Reprinted from *Rec. Glasgow Bibliogr. Soc.* (1922).

MONTGOMERY, JAMES. *The Christian Poet; or, Selections in Verse on Sacred Subjects.* Glasgow, 1827. Pp. 186–7. Note on Browne, with his 'Colloquy with God' from *Religio Medici*, part II, section 12. The probable indebtedness of Ken's Evening Hymn to these lines is pointed out.

MOORE, SIR NORMAN. *The History of the Study of Medicine in the British Isles.* Oxford, 1908. 22 cm., pp. viii, 202. Pp. 69–83, an account of the life and education of Dr. Edward Browne with many references to Sir Thomas.

MORAN, B. *N. & Q.* (1952), CXCVII, 380–2, 403–6. 'Browne's Reading on the Turks.'

MORE, PAUL ELMER. *Shelburne Essays.* Sixth Series. New York and London, 1909. Pp. 154–86. 'Sir Thomas Browne.' First printed in *The Nation* (New York, 1908), LXXXVI, 508.

MORERI, L. *Le Grand Dictionnaire Historique:* nouvelle edn. Paris, 1759. P. 314, article on Browne.

MORETON, G. Prospectus of *The Works of Sir Thomas Browne, M.D.*, with order form. A double leaf, 8°, dated December 1893. See no. 41.

MORGAN, E. *Cambridge Journ.* (1951), IV, 481–91. 'Strong Lines and Strong Minds: Reflections on the prose of Browne and Johnson.'

MOSCHCOWITZ, ELI. *Annals Med. Hist.* (1924), VI, 287–96. 'An Unpublished Letter of Sir Thomas Browne', printing Browne's letter to Dugdale, 11 Dec. 1658. See no. 200*j*.

—— *Ann. Med. Hist.* (1924), VI, 363–8. 'The first editions of Sir Thomas Browne.'

MOULE, T. *Portraits of Illustrious Persons in English History, drawn by G. P. Harding.* London, 1869. Pp. 31–2, biographical notice. Plate 15, portrait after the painting in the College of Physicians.

MOULTON, C. W. (Ed). *The Library of Literary Criticism of English and American Authors.* New York, 1901. Pp. 339–45, 'Sir Thomas Browne', with numerous references.

MULLIK, B. R. *Critical Studies.* Vol. IX. *Browne's Religio Medici.* 1961. S. Chand & Co. Delhi. Jullundur-Lucknow. 17.7 cm., pp. [iv], 27. Consists almost entirely of quotations from other writers.

—— *Studies in Prose Writers.* Vol. II. Browne (Second Edition) 1963. S. Chand and Co. Delhi-New Delhi-Jullundur-Lucknow-Bombay, 17.8 cm., pp. [iv], 61. First published 1957. Consists almost entirely of quotations from other writers.

MURDOCH, K. B. *Living Church* (1951), 2 Dec. 16–18. 'The Golden Age of Anglican Literature.'

MURISON, W. *Aberdeen Univ. Rev.* (1922), June. 'Sir T.B. and his Religio Medici.'

MURRAY, Prof. *Homiletic Rev.* (1899), 'Sir Thomas Browne—his place in a minister's library.'

NATHANSON, L. I. *Unpub. Doct. Diss.*, Univ. of Wisconsin. 'The Strategy of Truth. A Study of Sir T. B.'s *Rel. Med.*' Abstr. in *Diss. Abstr.* (1959), XX, 2295.

NEEDHAM, J. *The Great Amphibium. Four Lectures on the position of religion in a world dominated by science.* 19 cm., pp. 180. References to Browne, including a long quotation from *TLS*, 1928, 24 May.

—— *History of Embryology.* Cambridge 23 cm. 1934, pp. 110–12. Browne as the earlier experimenter in chemical embryology. Other references *passim.* Second edition, 1959, pp. 131–3.

NEUBEYER, M. *Isis* (1944), XXXV, 16–28. 'An Historical Survey of the Concept of Nature from a Medical Viewpoint.' See p. 20, a note on Browne's phrase 'Nature is the Art of God' (*Rel. Med.* part I, section xvi).

NEVINSON, H. W. *Books and Personalities.* London and New York, 1905. Pp. 191–5, 'A Memorial to Sir Thomas Browne' (a parody of his style).

NICHOLSON, W. A. *Trans. Norf. and Norwich Nat. Hist. Soc.* (1904), VII, 72–89. 'Sir T.B. as a Naturalist.'

NICKLIN, J. A. *Westminster Gaz.* (1909), 20 Nov. Idylls of Literature 1. 'Sir Thomas Browne at the Tavern', poem of 65 lines, with quot. from *Rel. Med.* part II, section 9: 'even that vulgar and Tavern Musicke...ears of God'.

NORFOLK & NORWICH HOSPITAL. *East. Daily Press*, Norwich, 16 April 1906. Report of the Annual Meeting of the Board of Governors of the Hospital at which the question of replacing Browne's skull in his coffin was discussed.

NORFOLK RECORDS. *The Visitation of Norwich A.D. 1664.* Vol. I. A–L. Ed. A. W. Hughes-Clarke, F.S.A., and A. Campling. Norfolk Record Society, 1934. Reference, p. 37: Browne of Norwich (arms, crest and pedigree).

—— *East Anglian Pedigrees.* Ed. A. Campling, F.S.A. Norfolk Record Society, 1940. Reference, pp. 154–5: Pedigree of Mileham of Burlingham St. Peter (Dorothy Mileham, wife of Sir T. Browne).

—— *Index of Wills Proved in the Consistory Court of Norwich.* Compiled by M. A. Farrow and T. F. Barton. Norfolk Record Society, 1958. Reference, p. 38: 1682, Sir T. Browne, original Will, Registry Book, 38.

OCKERHAUSEN, G. *Rationalismus and Mystik in der 'Religio Medici' von Sir Thomas Browne.* Diss. Marburg, 1930, pp. 56.

OLIVERO, F. *Nuova Antologia* (1925), Apr., 406–23. 'Sir Thomas Browne.'

—— *Studi Brit.* Torino, 1931, pp. 57–101. 'Sir Thomas Browne.'

OPPENHEIMER, JANE M. *Bull. Hist. Med.* (1947), XXI, 17–32. 'John Hunter, Sir Thomas Browne and the Experimental Method.'

ORDER OF SERVICE. Order of Service at Eight o'clock on the Evening of Thursday, October 19th, 1905, the day of the unveiling of a memorial Statue in the Haymarket, Norwich, of Sir Thomas Browne, M.D....Who worshipped and lies buried in this church (St. Peter Mancroft, Norwich), 20.5 cm., pp. [8].

OSBORN, E. B. *Nightcaps*, 1924, pp. 122–37. 'Three August Arguments by Sir Thomas Browne' (from *Hydriotaphia* and *Religio Medici*).

OSLER, SIR WILLIAM. *The Lancet* (1903), I, 200. 'Sir Thomas Browne's Evening Hymn', a letter concerning Ken's debt to Browne.

—— *Brit. Med. Journ.* (1905), II, 993–8. 'Religio Medici.' An Address delivered at Guy's Hospital Physical Society, 12 Oct. 1905. Reprinted in *The Library* (1906), n.s. VII, 1–31, in *An Alabama Student* (Oxford, 1908), pp. 248–77, and in *Selected Writings* (Oxford, 1951), pp. 40–61.

—— *Athenæum* (1909), no. 4247, 29 Mar., 347. 'Gui Patin's "Judgement on the Religio Medici".' A letter quoting Gui Patin's comments on *Rel. Med.* found by Osler with a collection of his letters in the Bibl. Nat. It is not altogether flattering.

OWEN, E. *Times* (1905). 24 Oct. 'The Skull of Sir Thomas Browne.'

PARKER, E. L. *Publ. Mod. Langu. Assoc. of America* (1938), LIII, 1037–53. 'The Cursus in Sir Thomas Browne.'

PARRY, T. W. *Camb. Univ. Med. Soc. Mag.* (1931), VIII, 109. 'Sir Thomas Browne' (poem).

PATER, WALTER. *Macmillan's Mag.* (1886), LIV, 5–18. 'Sir Thomas Browne.' Reprinted in *Appreciations* (1889), 127–66.

PEACHEY, G. C. *N. & Q.* (1901), S. 9, VIII, 271. Note on editions of *Pseud. Epid.*

PEACOCK, E. *Index to English speaking Students who have graduated at Leyden University*. London: Index Society, 1883, 1, 13. 'Brown, Thomas, Anglus Londinensis, 3 Dec. 1633. 259', probably referring to Browne.

PEARSON, KARL. *Times Lit. Sup.* (1923), 25 Jan. 'A missing edition of Sir Thomas Browne's Religio Medici, folio, 1663.'

PENNELL, C. *Kansas Mag.* (1965), 82–6. 'The Learned Sir Thomas Browne: Some Seventeenth Century Viewpoints.'

PETERSON, R. T. *Journ. Hist. Med.* (1963), XVIII, 200–2. Review of Bennett's *Sir T.B.* and Huntley's *Sir T.B.*

PETIT-THOUARS, M. DU. In *Biographie Universelle*. Vol. VI. Paris, 1812. Pp. 61–3. 'Browne (Thomas).'

PHELPS, G. *From Donne to Marvell*. Penguin Books, 1956. 'The Prose of Donne and Browne.'

PICCOLI, R. *Poesia e vita spirituale*. Bari, 1934. 8°, pp. viii, 235. Contains an essay on Sir T.B.

PICKFORD, J. *N. & Q.* (1902), S. 9, IX, 85. Sir T.B.'s skull (the casket presented by Dr Osler).

PINTO, V. de S. *N. & Q.* (1958), CCIII, 550–51. Review of *Urne Buriall*, ed. Carter.

POLLARD, A. W. *Library* (1924), V, 184–9. Review of Keynes, *Bibliography of Sir T.B.*

POTTER, D. T. (verger, St. Peter Mancroft). *East. Evening News*, Norwich, 4 Nov. 1921. 'The Skull of Sir Thomas Browne.'

POTTER, D. T. *East. Daily Press*, Norwich, 18 Oct. 1924. 'Sir Thomas Browne's Birthday.'

POWYS, LL. *Sat. Rev. Lit.* (1932), VIII, 765–6. 'The Quincuncial Doctor.'

PRAZ, M. *Engl. Stud.* Amsterdam (1929), XI, 161–71. 'Sir Thomas Browne.'

Reprinted in Italian in *La Cultura* (1929), VII, 591–602.

—— *Studi e Svaghi Inglesi.* Florence, 1937, pp. viii, 348. Contains an essay on Sir T.B.

PRIDEAUX, W. R. B. *N. & Q.* (1901), S. 9, VIII, 191. Note on the spelling of Browne's name.

PRITCHARD, A. *Philol. Quart.* (1961), XL, 302–7. 'Wither's *Motto* and Browne's *Religio Medici.*'

QUENNELL, P. *New Statesman* (1928), 25 Aug. Review of *Works*, ed. Keynes, vol. I.

QUIVIS. *N. & Q.* (1864), S. 3, V, 400–1. A note on Browne and witchcraft.

RAUBER, D. F. *Unpub. Doct. Diss.*, Univ. of Oregon (1958). 'Sir T.B.: A Study in the Middle Way.' Abstr. in *Diss. Abstr.* (1958), XVIII, 236.

RAVEN, C. E. *John Ray, Naturalist. His Life and Works.* Cambridge, 1942, pp. xx, 502, [2]. For references see index.

—— *English Naturalists from Neckam to Ray.* Cambridge, 1947, pp. x, 379, [1]. For references see index.

REXROTH, K. *The Nation*, N.Y. (1964), 26 Oct. 'Blesse Mee and Thee.' Review of *Works*, ed. Keynes.

RICHARDSON, SIR BENJAMIN WARD. *The Asclepiad* (1892), S. 11, IX, 269–97. 'Sir Thomas Browne and the *Religio Medici*', with autotype reproduction of the portrait in Wilkin, 1836. Reprinted in *Disciples of Aesculapius* (London, 1900), vol. II, pp. 636–55.

RIEWALD, J. G. *Eng. Stud.* (1947), XXVIII, 171–3. 'Sir T.B.'s Supposed Visit to the Continent.'

RIGHT, E. *N. & Q.* (1873), S. 4, XI, 233–4. 'Milton and Sir T.B.' A note on parallel passages.

RINDER, F. *Glasgow Herald* (1924), 28 Nov. Review of Keynes, *Bibliography of Browne*.

ROBERTSON, S. *Journ. Engl. and Germ. Philol.* (1921), XX, 371–84. 'Sir Thomas Browne and R. L. Stevenson.'

ROLLESTON, SIR HUMPHRY, Bt. *Ann. Med. Hist.* (1930), n.s. II, 1–12. 'Sir Thomas Browne, M.D.'

RYE, WALTER. *Norfolk Antiquarian Miscellany.* Norwich, 1883. 8°. Vol. II, p. 358, in 'St Peter Mancroft, Norwich. Its parish history', entry: '1656 Recd. of Dr. Browne for his child's grave, 000.10.00.'

—— *Norfolk Antiquarian Miscellany.* Second Series. Norwich, 1906, p. 83. 'What brought Sir Thomas Browne to Norwich?'

—— *Some Hist. Essays chiefly relating to Norfolk.* Pt. VI. Norwich, 1928, 449–54. 'Sir T.B.: his descent and arms, and his possible connection with the family of Dr. Dee, the mystic.' Suggesting that Browne had two uncles already living in Norwich when he came there.

S. *N. & Q.* (1875), S. 5, III, 341–3, suggesting that a MS. play, 'The Female Rebellion', may be by Browne. Discredited by J. Crossley, p. 398, Reply by S., pp. 489–91.

SAINTSBURY, G. *The Cambridge History of English Literature.* Vol. VII. Cambridge, 1911, pp. 232 ff. Ch. x. 'Antiquaries. Sir Thomas Browne.' Bibliography, pp. 460–2.

SAINTSBURY, G. *A History of English Prose Rhythm.* London. 22.5 cm. 1912, pp. xvi, 489, [3]. Ch. VI, pp. 221–3. 'The triumph of the ornate style.' Other references *passim*.

SAYERS, D. *Gaudy Night.* London, 1935. (Harriet finds a copy of *Rel. Med.* in Lord Peter Wimsey's blazer pocket, and reads from it.)

SAYLE, C. *Sir Thomas Browne.* Cambridge. 22 cm. 1915, pp. 20. Reprinted from *The Cambridge Review* (1915), XXXVII, 71–4.

SCHNENCK, J. M. *Am. Journ. Psych.* (1958), CXIV, 657–60. 'Sir T.B., *Religio Medici*, and the History of Psychiatry.'

SCHONACK, W. *Janus* (1911). Seizième

Année, 217–36. 'Sir Thomas Brown's
Religio Medici.'
—— *Sir Thomas Browne's Religio Medici. Ein
verschollenes Denkmal des englischen Deismus.*
Tübingen. 26 cm. 1911, pp. x, 553,
[3].
—— *Sokrates*, Berlin (1915), LXIX, 1–3.
'Das Urteil eines Englischen Arztes
(Sir T. Browne) der 17 Jahrhunderts
über die Philologen.'
SCHULENBURG, S., Gr. von der. *MS. Diss.*
Berlin, 1956, pp. ii, 205. 'Die Denkform
Sir T. B.'s.'
SENCOURT, R. *Outflying Philosophy. A
Literary Study of the Religious Element in
John Donne and in the Works of Sir
Thomas Browne and Henry Vaughan.*
20 cm. [*c.* 1923], pp. 356, [2]. Printed
abroad. Oxford thesis.
SHAW, A. BATTY. *Proc. Roy. Soc. Med.*
(1966), LIX, 1241. 'A Historical Exhibi-
tion from the Norfolk and Norwich
Hospital', with five casts of Sir Thomas
Browne's skull and their history.
SMITH, L. D. *Rev. Eng. Stud.* (1931), VII,
458. A note on articles by Joseph
Milsand.
—— *Abstr. of Diss.*, Ohio State Univ.
(1932), 295–302. 'The Influence of Sir
T.B. and the History of his Reputation
through the Nineteenth Century.'
SMITH, R. E. *The Lancet* (1965), I, 611.
'Charity begins at home', a letter on the
true source (John Wycliffe) of the
phrase attributed to Browne.
SMITH, R. W. I. *English-speaking Students of
Medicine at the University of Leyden.*
London, 1932, pp. xxii, 258. Contains
notes on Browne.
SOUTHEY, ROBERT. *Life and Correspondence.*
Vol. v. London, 1850. P. 332, reference
to Browne's *Works* in a letter to
Grosvenor C. Bedford, 28 Nov. 1825.
—— *Common-place Book.* Fourth Series.
London. 8°. 1851, p. 334. 'Hannah More
once read through a shelf of books at
Hampton. In her list of them she
enumerates Sir Thomas Browne's "very

learned miscellanies (and eke very
obscure)", and this is all her comment.'
SPAETH, J. W. *Classical Weekly* (1923), XVI,
135. 'Some Echoes of Cicero in English.'
SPARROW, J. *Rev. Engl. Stud.* (1957), VIII,
71–7. Rev. of *Religio Medici*, ed.
Denonain.
SPROTT, S. E. *Tom Browne's Schooldays*,
reconstructing the Winchester curri-
culum in Browne's time. A Columbia
University dissertation, 1954 (described
in *17th Cent. News*, 1955).
STEARN, W. T. *Huntia* (1965), II, 180–4.
'The five brethren of the rose: an old
botanical riddle.' With a reference to a
passage in *Hydriotaphia* on the sepals of
the dog-rose.
STEPHEN, G. A. (Norwich City Librarian).
Three Centuries of a City Library. Nor-
wich, 1917, 25.5 cm. P. 21: reference to
Browne, who presented the *Opera* of
Justus Lipsius, 8 vols. Antwerp, 1606–17,
in 1666, with a reproduction of the entry
facing p. 46. He also gave 'Opera Sua
viz. Religio Medici, Vulgar Errors, &c.'.
STEPHEN, LESLIE. *Hours in a Library,
Second Series.* London, 1876. Pp. 1–43.
'Sir Thomas Browne.'
STRACHAN, L. R. M. *N. & Q.* (1938),
CLXXIV, 67, 462–3. 'Elijah's Prophecy.'
Notes on passages in *Rel. Med.* and
Urne-Buriall.
STRACHEY, L. *Independent Rev.* (1906),
VIII. 'Sir Thomas Browne.' Reprinted
in *Books and Characters French and English.*
London, 1922, pp. 31–44.
SYMONDS, J. A. *Sat. Rev.* London (1864),
XVII, 795. 'Sir Thomas Browne.' Review
of *Christian Morals* (1863) (no. 174).
SYMONS, A. *Journ. Gypsy Lore Soc.* Liverpool
(1911–12, n.s. v, 109–13. 'Sir T. B. on
the Gipsies.'

TAINE, H. *Histoire de la littérature anglaise.*
Paris, 1863. Vol. I, Book II, pp. 360–5,
article on Browne. See also Sainte-
Beuve, C. A., *Nouveaux Lundis* (Paris,
1863–72), vol. VIII, pp. 96–8.

—— *A History of English Literature.* Translated by H. van Laun. Edinburgh. 8°. 1872 (first published in French 1863). *References:* Vol. I, pp. 207, 208, 213–15, 378, 382.

TALBOTT, J. H. *Journ. Am. Med. Assoc.* (1961), 13 May, 523. 'Religio Medici.'

'TAU, SIGMA'. *N. & Q.* (1909), S. 10, XI, 410. Query re Anne Townshend, niece of Sir T. B. See 473–4 for replies. See also XII, 36–7, for further queries.

TEMPEST, N. R. *Rev. Engl. Stud.* (1927), III, 308–18. 'Rhythm in the Prose of Sir Thomas Browne.'

—— *The Rhythm of English Prose.* Cambridge, 1930. References pp. 17, 23, 44, 48, 56, 59, 61, 65, 102, 125–7.

TEXTE, JOSEPH. *Études de Littérature Européenne.* Paris, 1898, pp. 51–93. 'La descendance de Montaigne: Sir Thomas Browne.' Also printed in *Revue de Belgique*, S. 2, 30ᵉ Année, 1898, pp. 170–85, 236–54.

THALER, A. *Shakesp. Ass. of Am. N.Y.* (1931), pp. 60–4. 'Shakespere and Sir Thomas Browne.'

—— *Stud. in Philol.* (1931), XXVIII, 87–117. 'Sir Thomas Browne and the Elizabethans.' See *English Literature 1660–1800* (1950), I, 186–7, for critique by M. E. Prior.

THOMA, H. E. *The Explic.* (1943), 1 Feb. 'Browne's Hydriotaphia.'

THOMAS, P. J. *Mod. Langu. Rev.* (1912), VII, 241–2. 'Drummond and Browne.'

THOMPSON, E. N. S. *The Seventeenth Cent. Engl. Essay.* Iowa City, 1926.

THORNTON, J. L. *Libr. World* (1952), LIV, 69–73. 'Dr Edward Browne (1642–1700) as a Bibliophile.'

TILDESLEY, M. L. *Sir Thomas Browne. His Skull, Portraits, and Artistry.* Introd. note by Sir Arthur Keith, and a report by Prof. G. Elliot Smith. 27.5 cm., pp. [iv], 76, [2]. With frontisp. 24 pl. and folding pedigree. Repro. from *Biometrika* (1923), XV. Two hundred copies printed for subscribers by the Galton Laboratory. In an appendix are all the entries concerning Browne in the Winchester College records. A volume of correspondence between Dr. Karl Pearson, Sir Arthur Keith and Dr Sydney Long of Norwich concerning the skull has been deposited (1966) in the library of the Royal College of Surgeons by Dr Long's wish [by G.K.].

TOYNBEE, M. *Norfolk Archaeology* (1957), XXXI, part IV, 377–94. 'Sir Thomas Browne and some of his friends.'

TOYNBEE, M. and ISHAM, SIR GYLES. *Burlington Mag.* (1954), XCVI, 275–7. 'Joan Carlile (1606?–1679), An Identification.' With references to her portraits of Sir Thomas and Lady Browne in the Nat. Port. Gallery.

TREVOR-ROPER, H. *Sunday Telegr.* (1964), Aug. 'Ancient and Modern.' Review of *Works*, ed. Keynes, and *Religio Medici*, &c. ed. Martin.

TUCKERMAN, H. T. *South. Lit. Messenger*, Richmond, Va. (1848), XIV, 177. 'Sir Thomas Browne.'

—— *Characteristics of Literature, illustrated by the genius of distinguished men.* Philadelphia, 1849. Pp. 2–38. 'The Philosopher, Sir Thomas Browne.'

TUELL, A. K. *The Catholic World*, New York (1931), CXXXIII, 186. 'Sir Thomas Browne again.'

TURNER, DAWSON. *Narrative of the Visit of His Majesty King Charles II to Norwich in September 1671.* Yarmouth, 1846. Pp. 9, 11, references to the knighting of Dr. Thomas Browne.

TYLER, DOROTHY. *Anglia* (1930), LIV, 179–95. 'Sir Thomas Browne's part in a Witchcraft Trial.'

—— *Michigan Alumn. Quart. Rev.* (1954), LXI, 60–5. 'Sir William Osler and Sir Thomas Browne: A Friendship across the Centuries.'

'UNEDA'. *N. & Q.* (1880), S. 6, II, 265, note on the punctuation in *Religio Medici* (1685), part II, section 13, where

Browne apparently confesses himself an atheist. 1, 393, 451, further notes by E. Marshall, Chr. Wordsworth and W. A. G.; see v (1882), pp. 102–4, 182–4, 243–4, for notes by E. Marshall and W. A. Greenhill.

VAN DE KIEFT, R. M. *Unpub. Doct. Diss.*, Univ. of Michigan (1957). 'The Nineteenth Century Reputation of Sir T.B.' Abstr. in *Diss. Abstr.* (1958), XVIII, 2151.

VAUGHAN, HENRY [?]. *Brit. Quart. Rev.* (1857), XXV, 143–76. Rev. of *Works*, ed. Wilkin.

W., R. D. *N. & Q.* S. 7, 1, 163–4. Notes on some passages in *Rel. Med.*

WAGLEY, M. F. and P. F. *Bull. Hist. Med.* (1957), XXXI, 318–26. 'Comments on Johnson's Biography of Sir T. B.'

WALKER, H. *The English Essay and Essayists.* London. 20 cm. 1915, pp. 69–81. 'Sir Thomas Browne.' Other references *passim*.

WARD, C. A. *N. & Q.* (1880) S. 6, XI, 517. Notes on the *Rel. Med.* Atomist.

WARD, H. G. *N. & Q.* (1922), S. 12, XI, 108. 'Portugese and Spanish: Alternative Use.' Note on readings in *Rel. Med.* part II, section x; see also Bensley, E., 347.
—— *A Seventeenth Century Mock Catalogue.* Edited by H. Gordon Ward. London. Kegan Paul, Trench, Trübner and Co., Ltd. 1928. 21 cm., pp. 16 (Rabelais' 'La Librairie de Sainct Victor' was a forerunner of Browne's *Musæum Clausum*.)
—— *Rev. Eng. Stud.* (1929), V, 59–60. 'Joachim du Bellay and Sir Thomas Browne', identifying the source of French lines misquoted in *Religio Medici*, part II, section 4 (see *Works*, ed. Keynes, 1964, I, 76).

WARD, H. G. AND BENSLEY, E. *N. & Q.* (1922), S. 12, XI, 108, 347. 'Notes on a Spanish quotation' by Sir T.B. in *Religio Medici*, part 2, section x (see *Works*, ed. Keynes, 1964, I, 86).

WARREN, A. *Kenyon Rev.* (1951), XIII, 674–90. 'The Style of Sir T.B.'

WATERHOUSE, G. *The Literary Relations of England and Germany in the Seventeenth Century.* Cambridge. 22 cm. 1914, pp. 91–4, 124. References to Browne by continental writers and translations of his works.

WATERS, W. G. *Norfolk in Literature*, 1923, pp. 38–47. 'Sir Thomas Browne.'

WESTFALL, T. M. *Princeton Dissertation* (unpublished). 'Sir Thomas Browne's revisions of the Pseudodoxia Epidemica, a study in the development of his mind.'

WHALLON, W. *Journ. of Eng. Lit. Hist.* (1961), XXVIII, 335–52. 'Hebraic Synonymy in Sir T.B.'

WHIBLEY, C. *Essays in Biography.* London. 19.5 cm. 1913. Pp. [viii], 311. Pp. 277–311. 'Sir Thomas Browne.'

[WHISTLER, L.] *Times Lit. Sup.* (1965), 25 March. 'Browne's Handsome Groves and Delectable Odours.' Review of *Works*, ed. Keynes, and *Religio Medici*, &c. ed. Martin.

WHITE, Mother E. S. *Unpub. Doct. Diss.*, Catholic Univ. of Am. (1963), 'A Study of Symmetrical and Asymmetrical Tendencies in the Sentence Structure of Sir T.B.'s Urne Buriall.' Abstr. in *Diss. Abstr.* (1963), XXIV, 733.

WHITE, G. H. *N. & Q.* (1931), CLXI, 429–30. A note on Sir T.B. See under Mabbott.

WHITHINGTON, R. *Internat. Journ. Ethics* (1932–3), XLIII, 413–28. 'Religio Duorum Medicorum.' This does not belong in the *Religio* series, being a commentary on Browne and Oliver Wendell Holmes.

WHYTE, A. *Sir Thomas Browne. An Appreciation with writings selected.* 1898. See no. 209*a*.

WILCOCK, J. *N. & Q.* (1908), S. 10, X, 56. Note on 'What song the Sirens sang'.

WILEY, M. L. *Journ. Hist. Ideas* (1948), IX, 302–22. 'Browne and the Genesis of

Paradox.' Reprinted in *The Subtle Knot. Creative Scepticism in Seventeenth Century England* (London, 1952), pp. 137–60.

WILKIN, S. Prospectus of *Complete Edition of Sir Thomas Browne's Works*. Single leaf, 8°, dated October 11th, 1826.

[WILKIN, S.] *Manifesto* 'To all whom it may Concern', requesting copies of Registers of Browne's marriage and of births and deaths of his children (see facsimile, p. 153), *c.* 1826. Wilkin has noted on the back of his copy four entries from the Register of St Martin's: Edward s. of Thos. Browne baptized 17 June 1642. Sarah d. of Thos. Browne baptized 11 August 1644. Edward Browne buried 18 June 1642. Sarah Browne buried 20 December 1644.

WILKINSON, C. H. *Times Lit. Sup.* (1948), 21 Aug. 'The Maid of Germany' (see under Abramson, E.).

WILLEY, B. *The Seventeenth Century Background*. London, 1934, pp. 41–56. 'Sir Thomas Browne.' For other references see index.

—— *The English Moralists*. London, 1964, ch. XII, pp. 190–6. 'A Note on Sir Thomas Browne as a Moralist.'

WILLIAMS, A. *The Common Expositor*. An Account of the Commentaries on Genesis, 1527–1633. Chapel Hill, N.C., 1948.

WILLIAMS, C. *N. & Q.* (1886), S. 7, I, 155. Note on the skull (taken from the grave by George Potter and sold to Dr. Richard Lubbock).

—— *N. & Q.* (1894), S. 8, VI, 269–70. 'The Skull of Sir Thomas Browne', in reply to queries in *N. & Q.* S. 8, VI, 64, 233.

—— *The Portraits of Sir Thomas Browne*. London and Norwich. 8°. 1895. Reprinted from *N. & Q.* (1895), S. 8, VIII, 21–3.

—— *Lancet* (1895), I, 1453–4. 'The Measurements of the Skull of Thomas Browne.'

—— [Circular] Norwich, June 1899. 'Sir T. Browne Memorial Statue.'

—— [Letter to the press] (1901), 26 Sep. 'Sir T. Browne', concerning the site of his house in Norwich.

—— *The Pedigree of Sir Thomas Browne*, drawn up by Simon Wilkin, 1836, with additions and corrections, 1902. A folding sheet, 26 × 47.5 cm. [Norwich, 1903.] Reprinted from *Norfolk Archaeology* (1902–4), XV, 109–13.

—— *The Bibliography of the 'Religio Medici'*. Norwich, 1905, 25 cm., pp. 15, [1]. An annotated hand-list. Second edition, 1907, pp. 20, [2].

—— *Souvenir of Sir Thomas Browne, With Twelve Illustrations, and Notes*. London and Norwich, 1905. 31 cm., pp. [30].

—— *N. & Q.* (1906), S. 10 v, 169. Query re the Boswille family; and see 232, reply by W.C.B.

—— *The Will of Thomas Browne, Mercer, Cheapside, London, father of Sir T.B. of Norwich, together with the Oration delivered by him at the Inauguration of Pembroke College, Oxford, 1624; also the Will of Sir T.B., 1679*. Norwich, [1906]. 21·5 cm., pp. [ii], 15, [3]. The oration translated by Edward Bensley. Reprinted from *Norfolk Archaeology* (1905–7), XVI, 132–45. With a reproduction of the painting of the Browne family.

WILLIAMSON, G. *Seventeenth Century Contexts*. Faber and Faber. London, 1960. For references see index.

—— *Milton and Others*. Faber and Faber. London, 1965 (Dryden, Marvell, Donne, Vaughan, Browne: 'The Purple of *Urn Burial*').

WILSON, F. P. *Seventeenth Century Prose, Five Lectures*. Cambridge, 1960, pp. 67–87. 'Sir Thomas Browne.'

WILSON, R. D. *N. & Q.* (1885–6), S. 6, XI, 421–2; S. 7, I, 163–4. 'Notes on some passages in Sir T.B.'s *Religio Medici*, &c.', with reference to the recent editions by Dr Greenhill.

WISE, J. N. *Dissertation Abstracts* (1965)

XXV, 7250–1. 'Some Seventeenth Century Animadversions on Sir T.B.'s *Religio Medici*.'

WOLEDGE, G. *Mod. Langu. Rev.* (1921), XVI, 65–6. 'An Allusion in Browne's *Religio Medici*' (Part I, section 30, 'The Maid of Germany').

WOOD, G. B. *Country Life* (1940), 20 Jan. 'A little known manor', Shibden Hall, Halifax, the supposed residence of Browne, with reproductions of photographs.

WOODBRIDGE, B. M. jr. *Mod. Langu. Notes* (1954), LXIX, 188–9. 'Sir T.B., Lamb and Machado de Assis.'

WOOLF, H. *N. & Q.* (1939), CXXVI, 243. 'Browne and Bede.' An example of Browne's inaccuracy (in *Misc. Tracts, Works*, 1964, III, 85–6).

WOOSTER, H. D. *Bibliophile* (1908), I, 296–8. 'A Note on Sir T.B.' as prose poet.

WRIGHT, R. *New Statesman* (1924), 9 Aug. Review of Keynes, *Bibliography of Browne*, and *Letter to a Friend*, Hazlewood reprint.

WRIGHT, W. ALDIS. *N. & Q.* (1887), S. 7, IV, 386. A note showing that Browne had read Sandys' *Travels* with reference to 'The Great Antonio' in *A Letter to a Friend*.

YOST, G. *Princeton Dissertation* (unpublished). 'Sir Thomas Browne and Aristotle.'

ZEITLIN, J. *Seventeenth Cent. News*, New York (1926).

ZIEGLER, D. K. *In Divided and Distinguished Worlds*. Religion and Rhetoric in the Writings of Sir Thomas Browne. Cambridge, Mass., Harvard University Press Office, 1943. Pp. x, 105. An attempt to dissociate Browne's religion from his science.

ADDENDA

ENDICOTT, N. J. 'Some aspects of Self-Revelation and Self-Portraiture in *Religio Medici*', in *Essays in English Literature from the Renaissance to the Victorian Age*, Presented to A. S. F. Woodhouse. University of Toronto Press, 1964, pp. 85–102.

—— *Univ. of Toronto Quart.* (1964), XXXIII, 324–8. 'Sir Thomas Browne.' Review of Bennett's *Sir Thomas Browne*, 1962, Huntley's *Sir Thomas Browne*, 1962, and *Religio Medici*, ed. Winny, 1963.

APPENDIX I

Religio Medici:
Imitators

BIBLIOGRAPHICAL PREFACE

The title of Browne's *Religio Medici* seems to have been entirely original. It was one of those happy inspirations which appear obvious by reason of their very simplicity, but no thought of such a title appears to have occurred to anyone before Browne. Wilkin (II, 16) mentioned that in the course of his researches he came upon a reference to a work entitled *Religio Patiens* (Cologne, 1566). A copy of this very rare, but entirely unimportant, book is now in my collection; it consists of a tedious Latin tragedy, which cannot be regarded as in any way a forerunner of *Religio Medici*, the title being as follows:

A. F. Leodii Religio Patiens. Tragoedia, qua nostri seculi calamitates deplorantur, & principes causæ, quibus misere nunc affligitur Christi Ecclesia, reteguntur. Ad Pium Quintum Pontificem Maximum. Coloniæ, Apud Maternum Cholinum. M. D. LXVI. A–F⁸ G⁴.

It is very unlikely that this work had ever come under Browne's eye. In fact the first relevant title seems to be the *Religio Laici* of Edward, Lord Herbert of Cherbury, first printed in 1645. Many others have followed up to the present time and the list given here contains 74 different books, several of which have run through a number of editions. Many of these books are both obscure and uncommon; some are of considerable interest and merit. They form a curious compendium of human aspirations, but none can rival in literary form or in philosophical interest their begetter, Browne's *Religio Medici*. It must be admitted that in some instances the books have little in common with Browne's work except the title. Among those with marginal claims to inclusion is, for example, Edward Ward's *The Secret History of the Calves-Head Club, Complt. Or the Republican Unmask'd. Wherein is fully shewn, The Religion of the Calves-Head Heroes, in their Anniversary Thanksgiving-Songs...London,* 1703. 8°. There is no mention of *The Religion of the Calves-Head Heroes* in the text or the head-lines, and this tract against the regicides has not been included.

In 1824 Charles Lamb facetiously suggested to the Quaker poet, Bernard Barton, the title *Religio Tremuli* or *Tremebundi* for one of his books. Barton's reply is not recorded, but Lamb himself published two years later an essay entitled 'The Religion of Actors'.

DE RELIGIONE LAICI: Edward, Lord Herbert of Cherbury   1645–56

De Veritate...Primus De Causis Errorum; alter De Religione Laici...Londini 1645 a⁴ A–Z⁴ Aa–Ii⁴ A–V⁴ X² A–B⁴ *A*⁴.

Note: Religio Laici on second R1–X2, but without heading.

Copies: BLO, BM, ULC; NU.

De Veritate...Editio Tertia [*on sub-title of* De Causis Errorum: Excud. Cura Philemonis Stephani] Londini, 1645 Formula as before.

Note: Religio Laici placed as before.

Copies: ULC; MH.

De Veritate...Editio Tertia. [n.p.] CIƆ IƆ CLVI. A–O¹² A–I¹².

Note: Religio Laici on G5–I5 without heading.

Copies: BLO, BM, EUL, K; BN, MH, Y.

RELIGIO LAICI: Edward, Lord Herbert of Cherbury   [*c.* 1645]

In The Modern Language Review. Vol. xxviii. Cambridge. 1933. Pp. 295–307. 'An Unpublished Manuscript by Lord Herbert of Cherbury entitled "Religio Laici".' By Herbert G. Wright.

Note: The text of this manuscript, which is now in the National Library of Wales (MS. 5295 E), is distinct from the printed work with the same title. It appears to have been copied from another manuscript now in the Osler Library, McGill University, Montreal. It is believed to have been copied because the Osler version has later corrections made by Herbert's own hand. This has been described by Professor S. E. Sprott in *The Library* (1956) (S. 5, XI, 120–2), and shown to have been plagiarized, much of it verbatim, by Charles Blount in his *Religio Laici* (1683), a fact already noted by Dr W. W. Francis in the *Bibliotheca Osleriana* (1929).

RELIGIO JURISCONSULTI: J Botrie   1649

Religio Jurisconsulti. London, Printed for Henry Hood, and are to be sold at his shop in St. Dunstans Church-yard. 1649. A–D⁸ E⁴.

Note: Subscribed at the end: *Sic cogitavit J. Botrie.*

Copies: BM; CH, MMO.

RELIGIO PHILOSOPHI PERIPATETICI: Christopher Davenport   1662

Religio Philosophi Peripatetici discutienda...Authore Reverendo Adm. P. F. Francisco Davenporto vulgo, a S. Clara...Duaci, Typis Baltasaris Belleri, sub Circino aureo. Anno 1662. a⁶ A–L⁸.

Note: James Crossley supplied Wilkin with a long note on Christopher Davenport (Wilkin, II, xvii). He stated that the tract was written on the occasion of a miracle performed by the Virgin Mary in 1640. It was reprinted in *Operum Omnium...F. Francisci a S. Clara.* Douai, f°, 1665.

Copies: BM, ULC.

RELIGIO PHILOSOPHI: Gideon Harvey 1663

Religio Philosophi, or Natural Theology. The First Part. The fourth Book... London, Printed by A.M. for Samuel Thomson at the Sign of the Bishops-head in St Paul's Church-yard. 1663. Aa² Bb-Rr⁴.

Note: This is the first part of Harvey's *Archelogia Philosophica Nova, or New Principles of Philosophy* (London, 1663). Harvey does not attack, or even mention Browne, but he had ridiculed him in another book, *The Conclave of Physicians* (1686). The author of the *Dialogue between Philiater and Momus* (1686) came to Browne's defence and took the opportunity of accusing Harvey of having plagiarized his title from *Religio Medici*: 'The Virtuoso, among all the rest, that you pitch upon to sneer at, forsooth, that famed Doctor of Norwich, the very man to whom you were so highly beholding for furnishing you with the notable hint of *Religio Philosophi*, taken plainly from that leading card, *Religio Medici*. But it is not fair, that because one excellent physician, a man of sense, did once write a *Religio Medici*, that therefore every Sylliton must follow the Example, and broach New Religions, or rather Irreligious Whimsies to the World's end.' See no. 292.

Copies: BLO, BM, EUL, K, RCP, ULC; LC, MH, YUL.

RELIGIO GENTILIUM: Edward, Lord Herbert of Cherbury 1663

De Religione Gentilium, errorumque apud eos causis...Amstelædami, Typis Blæviorum, M DC LXIII. ∏², A–Z⁴ Aa–Gg.⁴

Copy: BM.

De Religione Gentilium...Amstelædami, apud Joannem Wolters. MDCC. ∏² A–V⁸ X⁶.

Copy: BM.

The Ancient Religion of the Gentiles, and Causes of their Errors Considered... London: Printed for John Nutt, near Stationers-Hall, 1705. A–Z⁸ Aa–Bb⁸.

Note: Translated by William Lewis from the edition of 1663.

Copy: BM.

RELIGION OF A PHYSICIAN: Edmund Gayton 1663

The Religion of a Physician: or, Divine Meditations upon The Grand and Lesser Festivals...London: Printed by J.G. for the Author. 1663. A⁴ (a)⁴ (b)² B–N⁴ O².

Note: The author (1608–66), adopted son of Ben Jonson, describes himself on the title-page as 'Batchelor of Physic And Captain Lieutenant of Foot to James Duke of York'. On (a)4 he excuses himself for using a title already adopted by Browne. 'A poore Dwarf upon that Giant's shoulders dares not undervalue his Supporters, or stalk proudly and forget the Stilts and Props are under him.' The book should have an engraved frontispiece with a portrait of the author.

Copies: BM, K; CH, MH.

RELIGIO STOICI.

Acts, I. II.

—Ye men of Galilee, why stand ye gazing up into heaven?—

LONDON,
Printed for *George Sawbridge*, and are to be sold at his Shop, at the Sign of the Bible, on *Ludgate-hill*, 1663.

RELIGIO STOICI: Sir George Mackenzie 1663–93

Religio Stoici...Edinburgh, Printed for Robert Brown, and are to be sold at his Shop, at the Sign of the Sun, over against the Cross, 1663. A⁴ A⁸ B⁴ B–L⁸.

Note: The two leaves A3–4 with the address 'The Stoick to his Censurers' have usually been removed. In addition, E4 has been cancelled and reprinted, and F7–8 have been replaced by a single reprinted leaf. The original text had no doubt given offence to the Presbyterians. F. S. Ferguson (*Edinburgh Bibliographical Society Publications* (1936), 1, 13, 'A Bibliography of the Works of Sir George Mackenzie') records that two copies in the National Library of Scotland have the two leaves with 'The Stoick to his Censurers'. In both my copies they have been removed, the stubs being visible in one; the other leaves have been cancelled as mentioned above.

Copies: AUL, K(2), NLS(2).

Religio Stoici...London, Printed for George Sawbridge, and are to be sold at his Shop, at the Sign of the Bible, on Ludgate-hill, 1663. [formula as before.]

Note: This issue is printed from the same setting as the last, only the imprint on the title-page being changed. This must have been done while the book was in the press. The variant is known in only a single copy now in my collection. It is unusual in that the two leaves of 'The Stoick to his Censurers' are present and the leaves in sections E and F are uncancelled.

Copy: K.

Religio Stoici...Edinburgh. Printed for R. Broun. 1663. [formula as before]

Note: All copies lack the two leaves and have the cancels as above.

Copies: BLO, BM(2); MMO.

Religio Stoici. With a friendly Adresse To the Phanaticks Of all Sects and Sorts...Edinburgh: Printed for R. Broun, and are to be sold by Booksellers in London. 1665. A–K⁸ L⁴.

Note: F. S. Ferguson, *loc. cit.*, suspects that both this edition and the next were printed in London. They are from different settings of type, though one is a line-for-line reprint of the other. They do not have 'The Stoick to his Censurers', and the passages previously cancelled and reprinted are given in their original form. There is a short additional sentence at the end of chapter IX.

Copies: BLO, K, NLS, TCC; BN, CN, MH, YML.

Religio Stoici. With a Friendly Addresse To the Phanaticks Of all Sects and Sorts...Edenburgh. Printed for R. Broun, and are to be Sold by Booksellers in London, 1665. A–K⁸ L⁴.

Note: The title-page of this edition has a different type-ornament border from the other and minor changes in the type setting.

Copies: BLO, K, ULC; MMO, Y.

The Religious Stoic: Or a short Discourse on These several Subjects...By Sir G.M....Edinburgh Printed, and reprinted at London, and are to be Sold by R. Taylor near Stationers-Hall. 1685. A–M⁸.

Note: This is an exact reprint of the edition of 1665, including, as F. S. Ferguson, *loc. cit.*, notes, the error 'Theory' for 'Theology' in the heading to Chap. VI. Wing S.T.C. records a variant, *By T.B.* 1685.

Copies: K, NLS, TCC.

The Religious Stoic...The Second Edition. By Sir George Mackenzie. London, Printed by S. Briscoe over against Will's Coffee-House in Russel street, Covent-Garden, 1693.

Note: Though called 'The Second Edition', this is a re-issue of the edition of 1685 with a new title-page.

Copies: BM, GUL, K, ULC.

RELIGIO CLERICI: T.A. 1681–9

Religio Clerici. [*quotation from Epictetus*] By T.A. London: Printed for Henry Brome, at the Gun in St. Pauls Church-yard. 1681. A⁶ B–E¹².

Note: The author's identity is not known. Re-issued in the same year.

Copies: BLO, K, TCC; MH, MMO.

Religio Clerici. [*quotations from Epictetus and 1 Tim. 4. 16*] London: Printed for Henry Brome, at the Gun in St. Pauls Church-yard. 1681. A⁶ B–L¹².

Note: This issue consists of sheets B–E of the first issue, with the preliminary matter extended and reset in a smaller type-face and with additional matter at the end. E11–12 should be cancelled, but sometimes have been left, so that pp. 93–6 occur twice. The author's initials are omitted from the title-page. A frontispiece illustrating Matthew xiv. 30 and engraved by T. H. Van Hove, 1680, has been added.

Copies: BLO, K; MMO.

Religio Clerici...London, Printed and are to be sold by Randal Taylor, near Stationers-Hall. 1689. A⁶ B–L¹².

Note: A re-issue of the last edition with a new title-page.

Copies: BLO, DWL; TCD.

RELIGIO LAICI: John Dryden 1682–1710

Religio Laici or A Laymans Faith. A Poem. Written by Mr. Dryden...London, Printed for Jacob Tonson at the Judge's Head in Chancery-lane, near Fleet-street. 1682. a⁴ b² (c)² B–D⁴ E².

Note: There are three issues of this edition with small differences, the third having no date on the title-page. For details see Hugh Macdonald, *John Dryden A Bibliography*, Oxford, 1929, 16ai–iii, p. 34.

Copies: ai–ii, BLO, BM, K, NLS, TCD, ULC(3); aiii, BLO.

RELIGIO
Clerici.

Σπένδειν κὴ θύειν κͭ τὰ πά-
τεια ἑκάςοις πεοσήκει, κα-
θαρῶς κὴ μὴ ἀμελῶς.
Epictet.

By *T. A.*

LONDON:

Printed for *Henry Brome*,
at the Gun in St. *Pauls*
Church-yard. 1681.

Religio Laici...1682. a–b⁴ B–D⁴ E².

Note: Another edition of the last entry. See Macdonald, *loc. cit.* 16*b*, p. 34.

Copies: BM, TCC(2).

Religio Laici...1683. A⁴ a⁴ B–D⁴ E².

Note: The third edition. See Macdonald, *loc. cit.* 16*c*, p. 35. Reprinted in several collections of Dryden's poems.

Copies: BLO, BM, K, TCD; CH, MH, YUL.

Religio Laici...London. Printed and Sold by H. Hills, in Black-fryars near the Water-side. 1710. A⁸ B⁴.

Copies: KUL, ULC.

RELIGIO LAICI: [Charles Blount] 1683

Religio Laici. Written in a Letter to John Dryden Esq....London, Printed for R. Bentley, and S. Magnes, in Russel street, in Covent-garden. 1683. A–E¹².

Note: By Charles Blount, the deist (1654–93). The dedication to Dryden is signed C.B. This work was largely plagiarized from Lord Herbert of Cherbury's unprinted *Religio Laici*, a different work from that printed in 1645.

Copies: BM, K (Henry Gardiner's copy), TCC, ULC; MH, MMO, YUL.

RELIGIO JURISPRUDENTIS: Mark Hildesley 1685

Religio Jurisprudentis: or, the Lawyer's Advice to His Son, In Counsels, Essays, and other Miscellanies...Per Philanthropum...London, Printed for J. Harrison at Lincolns-Inn-Gate, and R. Taylor in Amen Corner. Anno Regni Regis Jacobo II. Primo, 1685. A–H¹².

Note: Sometimes contains a portrait of the author engraved by R. White. There is a reference to 'Dr. Brown' and the fear of death on p. 133.

Copies: BLO, BM, K; MH, MMO, YUL.

PRODROMUS RELIGIONIS MEDICI 1688

Jani Philadelphi consultatio desultoria de optima Christianorum secta, et Vitiis Pontificorum. Prodromus Religionis Medici. Patav. 1688.

Note: Ascribed to Sir T. Browne in Jöcher's *Allgem. Gelehrt. Lex.* (see Wilkin, I, 12). Not verified.

RELIGIO LAICI: J.R. 1688

Religio Laici, or a Laymans Faith, Touching the Supream Head and Infallible Guide of the Church. In Two Letters to a Friend in the Country. By J.R. A Convert of Mr. Bays's. Licensed June the 1st. 1688. London, Printed for John Newton, at three Pigeons over against the Inner-Temp[l]e Gate in Fleet-street. 1688. A² B–D⁴ E².

RELIGIO
LAICI.

Written in a Letter to

JOHN DRYDEN Esq.

Juvenal, Sat. 8.

*Quod modo propofui non eft
Sententia, verum
Credite me vobis folium
recitare Sibyllæ.*

LONDON,

Printed for *R. Bentley*, and
S. Magnes, in *Ruſſelſtreet*, in
Covent-garden. 1683.

Note: The author, J.R., has not been identified. Written against Dryden after his change of faith.

Copies: BLO, BM, K, NLS; CH, MH, WF.

LAYMAN'S RELIGION: [Anonymous] 1690

The Lay-Man's Religion: Humbly offered as a Help to a Modest Enquiry... London, Printed by Eliz. Holt for Walter Kettilby, at the Bishop's-Head in St. Paul's Church-Yard, in the Year 1690. A–E⁴; Second Part, A–B⁴ C².

Note: The author has not been identified.

Copies: BM, K; MH, NU.

The Lay-Man's Religion...The Second Edition...London, Printed by Eliz. Holt for Walter Kettilby, at the Bishop's Head in St. Paul's Church-Yard, in the Year 1690. A–E⁴ F²; Second Part, A–B⁴ C².

Note: A reprint of the first edition with a 'Dedication' added on A3–4.

Copies: BM, K; MH, YUL.

RELIGIO MILITIS: C.B. 1690

Religio Militis: or, The Moral Duty of a Soldier, shewing How he ought to behave himself towards God, his King and Country...London, Printed by H.C. for John Taylor, at the Ship in St. Paul's Church-Yard, 1690. A² B–E⁴.

Note: The dedication to the Duke of Schenberg is signed C.B., but the author is unidentified.

Copies: BLO, BM, K, TCD, ULC; YUL.

RELIGIO BIBLIOPOLÆ: [John Dunton] 1691–1742

Religio Bibliopolæ. In Imitation of Dr. Browns Religio Medici. With a supplement to it. By Benj. Bridgwater, Gent. London, Printed for P. Smart, and are to be sold at the Raven in the Poultry. 1691. A⁴ B–G⁸ H⁴.

Note: Partly by John Dunton (1659–1733), but much of it was written by Benjamin Bridgewater, a literary hack, of Trinity College, Cambridge. James Crossley stated (Wilkin, II, xix) that the book is largely plagiarized from other writers, including Glanvill, Howell, Norris and Boyle. It is again stated in the preface to be 'an imitation of that exquisite Piece of Dr. Brown call'd *Religio Medici*'. Wilkin, *loc. cit.*, mentions an edition of 1694, but this seems to be an error for 1691. It was reprinted twice after 1700, and in an extended form as *The New Practice of Piety* (1704), &c.

Copies: BLO, BM, K; BN, MH, MMO, YUL.

Religio Bibliopolæ. The Religion of a Bookseller After the Manner of the Religio Medici, By the Late Ingenious and Learned Sir Thomas Browne, M.D. ...London: Printed for C. Corbett, opposite St. Dunstan's Church, Fleet-Street. [Price 1s. 6d.] [?1702] A² B–L⁴ M².

Religio Bibliopolæ.

THE
Religion of a *Bookseller.*

After the Manner of the
Religio Medici,

By the Late INGENIOUS and LEARNED
Sir *THOMAS BROWNE*, M.D.

As the greatest and most universal Mischief Mankind suffers under, is the Delusion of a false and unrectified Imagination, it is the Business of this excellent Author to enable us to make a true Estimate of Things, that we may become our own Masters, and use the Faculties we are endued with, to the Ends and Purposes for which they are intended.

L O N D O N:
Printed for C. CORBETT, opposite St. *Dunstan's* Church,
Fleet-Street.   [Price .   ]

Note: The edition has a new preface omitting the reference to 'Dr. Brown'.
Copies: BM, K; MMO.

Religio Bibliopolæ: or the Religion of a Bookseller: Which is likewise Not improper to be perus'd by those of any other Calling or Profession... London: Printed, and sold by T. Warner at the Black Boy in Paternoster-row, MDCCXXVIII. Price One Shilling and Sixpence. A–P⁴ [8°].
Note: The preface of 1694 has been restored to this edition.
Copies: BM, K.

Religio Bibliopolæ oder die Religion eines Buch-Handlers...aus dem Englischen in Deutsche übersetzet. Ander und verbesserte Auflage. Frankfurt und Leipzig bei Johann Christian Martini Anno 1737
Note: The description on the title-page suggests that there had already been a previous edition in German.
Copy: BM.

Religio Bibliopolæ: or, the Religion of a Bookseller: Originally written By One of that Calling, And now Publish'd For the Benefit of All. London: Printed for W. Warren; and sold at the Three-Flower de Luces in the Old-Bailey. MDCCXLII. (Price One Shilling.) A–P⁴ [8°].
Note: This consists of the sheets of the edition of 1728 with a new title-page.
Copy: BM.

Religio Bibliopolæ. London. 1750.
Note: An edition of this date is mentioned by Wilkin, II, xix, but no copy has yet been seen.

LIBERTINE'S RELIGION: Richard Ames   1693
The Rake: or, The Libertine's Religion. A Poem...London, Printed for R. Taylor, near Stationers Hall, 1693. A² B–C⁴ D–E².
Note: The poem is in favour of sobriety and continence.
Copies: BLO, BM, K, ULC; MH, YUL.

GENTLEMAN'S RELIGION: Edward Synge   1693–1800
A Gentleman's Religion: with the Grounds and Reasons of it...By a Private Gentleman. London, Printed for A. and J. Churchill, at the Black Swan in Paternoster-Row. 1693. A–F¹².
Note: By Edward Synge, D.D., Archbishop of Tuam (1659–1741).
Copies: BLO, BM, K, TCC, ULC; MH, MMO.

A Gentleman's Religion: In Three Parts...London, Printed for A. & J. Churchill in Pater-noster-Row; and R. Sare at Grays-Inn gate in Holborn. 1698. A–F¹² A⁴ B–M¹² N² A–B⁶, with general title-page inserted before A1.

Note: A reprint of Part 1, with two parts added (dated 1697) and an Appendix (dated 1698).

Copies: BM, K, TCD.

La Religion d'un Honneste Homme Qui n'est pas Théologien de profession. Avec les fondemens & les raisons qui l'établissent...Traduit de l'Anglois. Seconde Edition augmentée d'une 2. & 3. Partie. A Amsterdam. Chez Pierre Brunel, à la Bible d'or. 1699. A–E¹² A–I¹² K⁶.

Note: With an engraved frontispiece by A. de Wint. Translated from the second edition of 1698.

Copies: K; BN, MMO (lacking the second and third parts).

A Gentleman's Religion: In Three Parts...The Second Edition. London: Printed for A. and J. Churchill...and R. Sare...1703. A–D¹² E⁶ A–K¹².

Copies: BM, CLN, K.

A Gentleman's Religion: In Three Parts...The Fourth Edition. London: Printed for A. and J. Churchill...and R. Sare...1710. A–N¹².

Copies: BM, K; MMO.

A Gentleman's Religion: in Three Parts...The Fifth Edition. London: Printed for the Executors of R. Sare, and sold by R. Williamson near Gray's-Inn-Gate in Holbourn. 1726. A–N¹².

Copies: BM, K.

A Gentleman's Religion: In Three Parts...The Sixth Edition Corrected. Dublin: Printed by S. Powell, For George Risk...George Ewing...And William Smith...M DCC XXX. A⁴ B–U⁸ X².
A Supplement to A Gentleman's Religion...Dublin: Printed by S. Powell, [&c. as before] M DCC XXX. A–M¹² A–N¹².

Note: This seems to be the only edition of the second volume containing the Supplement.

Copy: K.

A Gentleman's Religion...The Sixth Edition. London, Printed for Thomas Trye near Gray's-Inn-Gate in Holbourn. MDCCXXXVII. A–N¹².

Copy: K.

A Gentleman's Religion: with the Grounds and Reasons of it...Oxford: At the Clarendon Press. 1800. A⁴ B–S⁸ T².

Copy: K.

LADY'S RELIGION: [Anonymous]   1697–1748

A Lady's Religion. In a Letter To the Honourable My Lady Howard. By a
Divine of the Church of England. With a Prefatory Epistle to the same Lady,
By a Lay-Gentleman. London, Printed by Tho. Warren for Richard Baldwin,
at the Oxford-Arms in Warwick-lane, 1697. A–D¹².

Copies: K, GL.

A Lady's Religion...The Second Edition. To which is added, A Second Letter
to the same Lady, concerning the Import of Fear in Religion. By a Divine of
the Church of England. London: Printed for A. and J. Churchill at the
Black-Swan in Paternoster-Row. 1704. A–E¹².

Note: In a preliminary note by the Publisher to the Reader it is mentioned that the
Letter has been translated into several modern languages, and this is followed by the
'Preface to the French Translation'; the latter has not been verified.

Copy: K.

A Lady's Religion...Third Edition...Printed by Tho. Norris at the Looking-
glass on London Bridge. 1721. 12°, pp. 91.

Note: Offered in a bookseller's catalogue in 1922. Not verified.

The Religion of a Lady. Written by a Right Reverend Prelate of the Church of
England, and published by command of a Noble Lady. Proper to be read by
All, but more particularly the Ladies of Great-Britain. London: Printed for
J. Torbuck, in Clare-Court, near Drury-Lane, and sold by the Booksellers of
London and Westminster. 1736. A–D¹², with a leaf inserted before A1.

Note: Torbuck's edition of *Religio Medici*, 1736, is advertised on the leaf inserted before
the title-page (see no. 15).

Copy: CLN.

A Lady's Religion...Glasgow, Printed and sold by R. and A. Foulis. MDCCXLVIII.
A–I⁶.

Copy: Mitchell Library, Glasgow.

A Lady's Religion...The Third Edition...To which is added, A Letter to a
Lady on the Death of her Husband, By the Editor. London, Printed for
W. Owen at Homer's Head near Temple-Bar. MDCCXLVIII. Π² a–b⁶ A–H⁶ I².

Note: The Editor's preface and the letter added at the end are signed F.W. The letter
is dated August 1744. The Preface to the French Translation is printed as in the
second edition.

Copies: K; MMO.

RELIGIO POETÆ: [Anonymous]   1703

Religio Poetæ: or, A Satyr on the Poets. *Dicere verum Quid vetat?* London:
Printed in the Year 1703. A–D².

Religio Poetæ:

OR, A

SATYR

ON THE

POETS

Dicere verum
Quid vetat ?

LONDON:

Printed in the Year 1703.

[reduced]

Contents: A1 title; A2*a–b* *The Dedication to the Poets*; B1*a*–D2*b* *Religio Poetae*; *errata* at bottom of D2*b*.

Note: This anonymous satire, formerly bound with a number of other folio pieces by Pope and others, is hitherto unrecorded. It was read in 1943 by the late Sir Harold Williams, who found it of great interest, though he was unable to make any guess as to the authorship. In the dedication the author styles himself 'this poetical De Foe', but gives no other clue. It was advertised in Defoe's *Review*, 18 July 1704, and was listed in the *Term Catalogue* for Michaelmas, 1703.

Copy: K; YUL.

NEW PRACTICE OF PIETY: [John Dunton; H.N.]   1704–5

The New Practice of Piety; Writ in Imitation of Dr. Browne's Religio Medici: or The Christian Virtuoso: Discovering The Right Way to Heaven Between All Extreams. To which is Added, A Satyr On the House of Lords...London: Printed in the Year MDCCIV. A–N⁴ O² [8°].

Note: This is an extended version of Dunton's *Religio Bibliopolæ*, with a new dedication to John Locke signed H.N. It contains a reference to *Religio Medici* on B3. Dunton himself described this book as follows: 'My fifth Project has been preparing for the press for these ten years, and is entituled, "The New Practice of Piety", writ in imitation of Dr. Brown's *Religio Medici*: or, a System of uncommon Thoughts extracted from the Experience of Forty Years' (see Nichols' *Literary Anecdotes*, London, 1812, V, 73).

Copy: BLO.

The New Practice of Piety...By a Member of the New Athenian Society: The Second Edition. Dedicated to the Learned Mr. John Lock...London: Printed for S. Malthus, in London-House-Yard, at the West-End of St. Pauls. 1704. A–N⁴ O² [8°].

Note: The same book as the last with a new title-page.

Copy: BM.

The New Practice of Piety...The Third Edition...London: Printed for John Marshall at the Bible in Grace-church-street. MDCCV. A–O⁴ [8°].

Note: The two extra leaves in this edition are occupied by 'Books Printed for, and Sold by J. Marshall'.

Copy: K.

RELIGION OF A PRINCE: [William Nicholls]   1704

The Religion of a Prince; Shewing the Precepts of the Holy Scripture are the best Maxims of Government...London, Printed by W.S. for Thomas Bennet at the Half-Moon in St. Paul's Church-yard. 1704. A–O⁸ P⁴.

Note: By William Nicholls, D.D. (1664–1712), Canon of Chichester.

Copies: BM, K.

RELIGIO LIBERTINI: Richard Burridge 1712

Religio Libertini: Or, The Faith of a Converted Atheist. Occasionally set forth by Mr. Richard Burridge, Who was lately Convicted of Blasphemy...To which is prefixed A Narration of his Life...London: Printed for Sam. Briscoe, and Sold by John Graves, next White's Chocolate-House in St. James's Street, and J. Morphew, near Stationer's Hall, 1712. A–L⁴ (8°).

Note: Reprinted as pp. 4–80 of *The History Of the Rise and Growth of Schism in Europe, To the great Scandal of the Christian Religion* (London, 1714). The book was written while the author was under confinement.

Copies: BLO, K; MMO(1714).

RELIGIO REGIS: King James I 1715

Religio Regis; or the Faith and Duty of a Prince. Written by King James I. being Instructions to his Son Prince Henry. London: Printed in the Year, MDCCXV.

Note: Extracted from James I's ΒΑΣΙΛΙΚΟΝ ΔΩΡΟΝ (1603), and printed as pp. 43–80 (C10–E4) of *The Prince's Cabala: or Mysteries of State*...London: for R. Smith, &c. 1715. 12°, with sub-title as above.

Copy: K.

RELIGION OF THE WITS: [C.N.] 1716

The Religion of the Wits at Button's Refuted...In a Dialogue between a Politician, and a Divine. London: Printed for Bernard Lintott, between the Two Temple-Gates, in Fleet-street, 1716. A² B–E⁸ F².

Note: The dedication to Samuel Fuller Esq., Member of Parliament for Petersfield, is signed C.N.

Copies: K; MH.

RELIGION OF A CHURCH OF ENGLAND WOMAN: Anon. 1717

The Christian Religion As Profess'd by a Daughter of the Church of England... London: Printed by W.B. for R. Wilkin, at the King's-Head in St. Paul's-Church-Yard. 1717. A² B–Z⁸ Aa–Bb⁴ Cc².

Note: On p. 2 the author remarks, 'tho' the Press has help'd us to the Religion of a *Physician*, a *Layman*, a *Gentleman*, and a *Lady*, yet in my poor opinion, they have all of them but one Religion if they are Christians'. The headlines throughout give the title as 'The Religion of a Church of England Woman'.

Copy: K.

RELIGION EINES MEDICI [Alexandre le François] 8° 1731

Die Religion eines Medici Aus dem Frantzösischen Ins Teutsche übersetzet Und Nebst einen Vorbericht zum Druck befordert Von J.A.R. Med.D. Halberstadt | Zufinden in Christian Friedrich Schopps Buch-laden, 1731.)(^{8} χ^4 A–C^8.

Note: Dedicated to Eberhard Christian Baron von Hohlenthal. Translated by J.A. Roeper *ex Alexandro le François* (Heister, *Apologia pro medicis*, 1736, pp. 4–5). The preface contains a brief review of other writings on the religion of doctors, including Browne's *Religio Medici*.

Copy: Nationalbibliothek, Vienna; (microfilm in ULC).

RELIGION OF A SOLDIER: Major General F-d-g   1747

The New-Year's Miscellany. Containing, I. The Religion of a Soldier, by the late Major General F-d-g. [&c.] London: Printed for A. Freeman, in Fleet-Street; and sold at all the Pamphlet-Shops. 1747. [Price One Shilling.] A–H^4 [8°].

Note: 'The Religion of a Soldier' occupies pp. 1–16. The remainder is a miscellaneous collection of prose and verse.

Copy: K.

RELIGIO PHILOSOPHI: William Hay   1753

Religio Philosophi: Or, the Principles of Morality and Christianity...London: Printed for R. Dodsley in Pall-mall, 1753. A^4 B–P^8 Q^4.

Note: William Hay (1695–1755) was a barrister and Member of Parliament for Seaford. He inscribed his book to the Speaker, Arthur Onslow. It was many times reprinted (1754, 1760, 1771, &c.). In my collection is a French translation in manuscript done from the fourth edition of 1771.

Copies: BM, K, &c.

RELIGIO LAICI: [Stephen Tempest]   1764–72

Religio Laici: or, a Layman's Thoughts upon his Duty to God, his Neighbour, and Himself. London: Printed for S. Crowder, in Pater-noster Row; W. Nicoll, and W. Bristow, in St. Paul's Church-Yard; and C. Etherington, in York, 1764. [Price Two Shillings.] Π^2 a^2 A–T^4 (8°).

Note: By Stephen Tempest of Bracewell in Craven, Yorkshire (see Whittaker's *History of Craven*, p. 88). Leaves Π1 and T4 are missing in the copy quoted.

Copy: MMO.

Religio Laici...The Second Edition. London: Printed for W. Nicoll, in St. Paul's Church-Yard; and Sold by T. Wilson, C. Etherington, W. Tessey-man, J. Todd and H. Sotheran, and D. Peck, in York, 1768. [Price One Shilling.] Π^3 A–H^6 I^1.

Note: The first three leaves appear to have been imposed with the last leaf signature I.

Copy: K.

Religio Laici...The Third Edition. London: Printed for P. Shatwell, opposite the Adelphi Buildings in the Strand. MD.CC.LXXII.

Note: This consists of the sheets of the second edition with a new title-page.

Copy: K.

RELIGIO MEDICI: W. Walton   1766

Religio Medici. A Sermon preached at a Visitation, holden in The Parish Church of All-Saints in the Town of Huntingdon, April 4. 1766. By W. Walton, M.D. Rector of Upton, in Huntingdonshire...Cambridge, Printed by J. Bentham Printer to the University; For J. Paris in Cambridge...M.DCC.LXVI. (Price 1s.) Π⁴ B–D⁴ E².

Note: The half-title (missing in my copy) may have been printed as E2 and folded back (see *Bibliotheca Osleriana*, 4609).

Copies: K; MMO.

SECOND RELIGIO MEDICI: Isaac Hawkins Browne   1768

Fragmentum Isaaci Hawkins Browne, Arm. Sive Anti-Bolingbrokius. Liber Primus. Translated, for a Second *Religio Medici*. By Sir William Browne, Late Præsident, now Father of the College of Physicians: and Fellow of the Royal Society...London, MDCCLXVIII. Printed and Sold, by W. Owen near Temple-bar. Price One Shilling Six Pence. A–D² [4°].

Note: Also printed in *Poems by Isaac Hawkins Browne*, London, 1768, 8°. It was written to confute the opinions of Lord Bolingbroke 'concerning the moral attributes of the Deity, and the Doctrine of a future State'. The reference to *Religio Medici* on the title-page was inserted by the translator, who wrote the continuation recorded in the next entry. All the copies listed below are presentation copies from the translator.

Copies: BM, K, ULC; MMO.

RELIGIO MEDICI ALTERA: Sir William Browne   1769

Fragmentum Isaaci Hawkins Browne, Arm. completum. Anti-Bolingbrokius. Liber secundus. Religio Medici Altera. Adiecta versione anglica. Auctore D. Gulielmo Browne, Equ. Aur....London, MDCCLXIX. Printed and Sold, by W. Owen, near Temple-bar... A–D² [4°].

Copies: BM, K, ULC; MMO.

RELIGION OF A LAWYER: [Anonymous]   1786

The Religion of a Lawyer, A Crazy Tale, (In Four Canto's;) Analytical of the Kentish Story of Brookland Steeple. *Nugis addere pondus*.—Hor. Ep. London: Printed for J. Walker, in Paternoster-Row. M DCC LXXXVI. A² B–E⁸ E⁸.

Copies: K; MMO.

RELIGIO CLERICI: [Edward Smedley]   1818

Religio Clerici, A Churchman's Epistle.

> 'Tis too much prov'd, that with devotion's visage,
> And pious action, we do sugar o'er
> The devil himself.   *Hamlet*, Act III, Scene 1.

London: John Murray, Albemarle-Street. 1818. 22 cm., pp. [vi], 35.

Note: Edward Smedley (1788–1836) was a prebendary of Lincoln. His *Religio Clerici* in verse was reprinted in the same year and again with *A Churchman's Second Epistle* in 1821.

RELIGIO CHRISTIANI: [Anonymous]   1818

Religio Christiani, A Churchman's Answer to 'Religio Clerici'. Cambridge: Printed by James Hodson: For J. Deighton and Sons, Cambridge; Sold also by J. Hatchard, Piccadilly. 1818. 21 cm., pp. 31, [1].

RELIGION OF ACTORS: [Charles Lamb]   1826

In The New Monthly Magazine. [Vol. XVI] 1826. Part 1. London: Henry Colburn, New Burlington Street (pp. 405–7).

Note: Lamb refers in his article to a work entitled *Br—'s Religio Dramatici*, but this is probably fictitious. E. V. Lucas, Lamb's editor, suggested (*Works*, 1903, I, 504) that ' John Braham, the tenor, 1774?–1856, né Abraham, had put forth a manifesto stating that he had embraced the Christian faith'.

RELIGIO MILITIS: [Moyle Sherer]   1827

Religio Militis; or, Christianity for the Camp.

> I have so abject a conceit...that will dye at the command of a serjeant.
>   *Religio Medici*

London: Printed for Longman, Rees, Orme, Brown, and Green, Paternoster-Row. 1827. 16 cm., pp. v, [i], 151, [1].

Note: Moyle Sherer (1789–1869) was a Wykehamist, who served in the army until 1836. He lived at Claverton Farm, Bath, and wrote Sketches of India, a Life of Wellington, Romances, &c. The quotation from *Religio Medici* is from Part 1, section 38.

RELIGIO MEDICORUM: [Thomas Laycock]   1855

Religio Medicorum: A Critical Essay on Medical Ethics...Reprinted for private circulation. York. 1855. 19 cm., pp. 42, [2].

Note: The title-page was reprinted to read: *Religio Medicorum: A Critical Review of various Works on Medical Ethics...Reprinted for Private Distribution, from the British and Foreign Medico-chirurgical Review for 1848*. It was also printed for Adam and Charles Black, Edinburgh, 1855. The author was Thomas Laycock, M.D. of Edinburgh. First printed in *Brit. and Foreign Med.-Chir. Rev.* (1848), II, 1–30.

RELIGIO CHEMICI: George Wilson　　　　　　　　　　　　1862

Religio Chemici. Essays by George Wilson, F.R.S.E....London and Cambridge: Macmillan and Co. 1862. 19 cm., pp. xii, 386, [2].

RELIGIO LAICI: Thomas Hughes　　　　　　　　　　　　*c.* 1875

Tracts for Priests and People. No. 1. Religio Laici. By Thomas Hughes, author of 'Tom Brown's School Days' etc. Cambridge: Macmillan and Co. and... London. [n.d.] 17 cm., pp. 39, [1].

RELIGIO PSYCHO-MEDICI: W. A. F. Browne　　　　　　　1877

In The Journal of Psychological Medicine. Ed. L. S. Forbes Winslow. New Series vol. III London Baillière Tindall & Cox 1877

Note: Pp. 17–31. 'Religio Psycho-medici', part 1, by Wm. Alex Francis Browne. Pp. 215–31, part 2, with references to Browne's *Religio Medici*.

RELIGIO MEDICI OCCUPATI: John Watson　　　　　　　1879

Poems by John Watson M.D. London: Williams and Norgate. 1879. 18·5 cm., pp. [viii], 396.

Note: Called *Religio et Sententiæ Medici Occupati* on the half-title.

NEW RELIGIO MEDICI: Frederick Robinson　　　　　　　1887

The New Religio Medici. By Frederick Robinson M.D. London: Elliot Stock. 1887. 20·5 cm., pp. viii, 172.

RELIGIO VIATORIS: [Cardinal Manning]　　　　　　　　1887

Religio Viatoris. London: Burns & Oates, Limited. New York: Catholic Publication Society Co. 1887. 19 cm., pp. [viii], 85, [3].

RELIGIO MUSICÆ: E. Dyke　　　　　　　　　　　　　　1890

In The Sun. Paisley and London. 1890. Vol. iii, pp. 191–2. 'Religio Musicæ', by E. Dyke.

RELIGIO MEDICI: J. Todhunter　　　　　　　　　　　　1893

In Book-songs. An Anthology of poems of books and bookmen from modern authors. Edited by Gleeson White. New York. 1893.

Note: Contains 'Religio Medici', a poem of twenty lines by John Todhunter (b. 1839).

RELIGIO POETÆ: Coventry Patmore　　　　　　　　　　1893

Religio Poetæ etc. By Coventry Patmore London George Bell and Sons 1893 16 cm., pp. viii, 229, [3].

RELIGIO SCRIPTORIS: R. Le Gallienne   1893

The Religion of a Literary Man (Religio Scriptoris) by Richard Le Gallienne
London: Elkin Mathews and John Lane, Vigo Street New York: G. P.
Putnam's Sons: 1893 23 cm., pp. xi, [i], 119, [1].

RELIGIO CLERICI: A. Starkey   1895

Religio Clerici and other poems. By Alfred Starkey. London: Elliot Stock.
1895. 19 cm., pp. 147, [1].

RELIGIO ATHLETAE: A. Lynch   1895

Religio Athletae by Arthur Lynch Remington and Co., Limited, London and
Sydney. 1895 17·5 cm., pp. viii, 96, [8].

RELIGIO PICTORIS: H. B. Merriman   1899

Religio Pictoris by Helen Bigelow Merriman Boston and New York Houghton
Mifflin and Company The Riverside Press Cambridge MDCCCXCIX 20 cm.,
pp. [vi], 250, [2].

RELIGION OF A GENTLEMAN: C. Fletcher   [1900]

The Religion of a Gentleman. Boston. [1900]

Note: Recorded in *Bibliotheca Osleriana*, 4581A. The title-page is stated to be a cancel.

RELIGIO LAICI: H. C. Beeching   1902

Religio Laici A series of studies addressed to Laymen By the Rev. H. C.
Beeching, M.A. London Smith Elder & Co. 1902 19 cm., pp. [ii], viii, [ii],
270, [6].

RELIGIO MEDICI: [L. S. Beale]   1902

Religio Medici: Religio Scientiæ, Religio Vitæ. 1901. By a Student of Science
and Medicine 1849–99 Charles Good and Company Burleigh Street,
Strand 1902 18·5 cm., pp. viii, 216.

RELIGION OF AN EDUCATED MAN: F. G. Peabody   1903

The Religion of An Educated Man By Francis Greewood Peabody Plummer
Professor of Christian Morals in Harvard University New York The
Macmillan Company London Macmillan & Co. Ltd. 1903 [Harvard Library
Lectures] 19 cm., pp. [viii], 190, [2], 8.

RELIGIO CRITICI: [Anonymous]   1904

Religio Critici; or, Chapters on Great Themes. By Ἄγνωστος London: Society
for Promoting Christian Knowledge 1904 18 cm., pp. [viii], 190, [2], 8.

RELIGIO OBSTETRICI: A. R. Simpson   1905

Religio Obstetrici A Farewell Address to the Graduates of the University of
    Edinburgh on July 28th, 1905 By Professor A. R. Simpson, M.D., D.Sc.
    Reprinted from The Scottish Medical and Surgical Journal, August 1905.
    22 cm., pp. 16. Reprinted from *Scot. Med. and Surg. Journ.* (1905), XVII, 97–109.

RELIGION OF A PLAIN MAN: R. H. Benson   1906

The Religion of a Plain Man by Father Robert Hugh Benson Burns and Oates
    London 1906 18 cm., pp. ix, [iii], 164, 16.

RELIGION OF A LAYMAN: [Anonymous]   1907

The Religion of a Layman...together with a Review of The Westminster
    Confession of Faith Edinburgh Waddie and Co. Limited 1907 18·5 cm.,
    pp. [iv], 226, [2].

CONFESSIO MEDICI, RELIGIO DISCIPULI: [Stephen Paget]   1908

Confessio Medici By the Writer of 'The Young People'...Macmillan and Co.
    Limited...1908 20·5 cm., pp. ix, [iii], 158.

Note: The theme of the book links it unquestionably with the *Religio* series. In the
section (pp. 11–25) entitled 'Hospital Life' the author refers to his ideals as the
Religio Discipuli.

RELIGIO DOCTORIS: ed. G. S. Hall   1913

Religio Doctoris; meditations upon life and thought, by a retired college
    president with an introduction by G. Stanley Hall. Boston R. G. Badgar
    1913 19·5 cm., pp. viii, 183, [1].

RELIGIO MEDICI MODERENI   1915

Religio Medici Modereni Being the beliefs and opinions of an old medicine man
    by NeoKama, M.D. London John Bale, Sons & Danielsson, Ltd....1915
    18·5 cm., pp. iv, [ii], 118.

Note: With a quotation from Browne on p. 11.

RELIGIO GRAMMATICI: Gilbert Murray   1918

Religio Grammatici The Religion of a 'Man of Letters' By Gilbert Murray
    LL.D., D.Litt., F.B.A....London: George Allen & Unwin Ltd. [1918]
    16·5 cm., pp. 47, [1].

Note: Also published by Houghton Mifflin and Co., Boston and New York, 1918.

RELIGIO RELIGIOSI: Cardinal Gasquet   1918

Religio Religiosi The Object and Scope of the Religious Life By Cardinal
    Gasquet London R. & T. Washbourne...MCMXVIII 19·5 cm., pp. [viii],
    126, [2].

Note: 'The name I have given to this little book is no doubt suggested by that of the *Religio Medici* and Cardinal Manning's *Religio Viatoris*.' Printed by the Benedictine Dames of Stanbrook Abbey, Worcester.

RELIGION OF A DOCTOR: T. Bodley Scott   1919

The Religion of a Doctor. By T. Bodley Scott. London: T. Fisher Unwin Ltd. [1919] 18·5 cm., pp. 98, [2].

Note: Pp. 7–33, 'The Religion of a Doctor', and on left-hand headlines throughout.

MODERN RELIGIO MEDICI: [James W. Dawson, M.D.]   1920

The Spirit of Leisure and the Spirit of Work Some Aspects of a Modern 'Religio Medici' Printed for private circulation [n.d.] 21 cm., pp. [ii], 24.

Note: Printed for the Edinburgh Women's Medical Society. Reprinted in *The Edinburgh Medical Journal* (January 1924), and published by Oliver and Boyd, Edinburgh and London, 23 cm., pp. 23, [1].

RELIGIO MATHEMATICI: D. E. Smith   1921

In The American Mathematical Monthly, October 1921.

Note: Contains 'Religio Mathematici' by D. E. Smith. Not verified.

RELIGION OF THE WISE MEN: G. F. Wates   1923

The Religion of Wise Men By G. F. Wates London George Allen & Unwin Ltd. [1923] 18·5 cm., pp. 127, [1].

RELIGIO JOURNALISTICI: C. Morley   1924

Religio Journalistici By Christopher Morley Garden City New York Doubleday, Page & Company 1924 18·5 cm., pp. [vi], 62.

RELIGION OF A DARWINIST: Sir Arthur Keith   1925

Conway Memorial Lecture The Religion of a Darwinist Delivered at South Place Institute on March 26, 1925 by Sir Arthur Keith, F.R.S....London: Watts & Co. 17·5 cm., pp. 76, [2].

RELIGION OF AN ARTIST: John Collier   1926

The Religion of an Artist By the Hon. John Collier London 1926.

Note: Not seen. The BM copy is mislaid.

CONSECRATIO MEDICI: H. Cushing   1926

In The Journal of the American Medical Association. Vol. LXXXVII, no. 8, 21 August 1926.

Note: Pp. 539–42. 'Consecratio Medici', by Harvey Cushing M.D., Boston. Delivered as the Commencement Address at the Jefferson Medical College, Philadelphia, 5 June 1926. Reprinted in Cushing's *Consecratio Medici and Other Papers* (Boston, Little, Brown and Co., 1928) (reprinted 1928, 1929; new edition 1940, reprinted 1940). The author had Paget's *Confessio Medici* in mind when writing his address—and therefore Browne's *Religio Medici* also, though he did not name it.

RELIGIO LAICI: Sir Henry Slesser   1927

Religio Laici and other Essays and Addresses...A. R. Mowbray & Co. Ltd. London...[1927] 19 cm., pp. [viii], 135, [1].

Note: Pp. 1–8, 'Religio Laici', and on left-hand headlines throughout.

RELIGIO MILITIS: A. Hopkinson   1927

Religio Militis By Austin Hopkinson a member of parliament and formerly a private of dragoons London: Martin Hopkinson & Co. Ltd....1927 19·5 cm., pp. [viii], 195, [1].

RELIGIO MEDICI YALENSIS: Anon   1932

In The New York Times March 1932 (editorial).

RELIGIO MEDICI: P. Mairet   1935

In The Criterion. [Edited by T. S. Eliot.] Vol. xiv, no. lvi, April 1935 London: Faber & Faber.

Note: Pp. 369–73 'Religio Medici', by Philip Mairet; a note on the psychological theories of Georg Groddeck, German alienist.

MEDITATIO MEDICI: W. C. Bosanquet   1937

Meditatio Medici A Doctor's Philosophy of Life. By W. Cecil Bosanquet D.M.Oxon. Aldershot: Gale & Polden, Ltd. [1937] 22·5 cm., pp. [xii], 162, [2].

RELIGIO JUVENIS: [D. G. Evans]   1938

In Saint Bartholomew's Hospital Journal. Vol. xlv, no. 12, September 1935.

Note: Pp. 296–8. 'Religio Juvenis.' By E. [David Gordon Evans].

RELIGIO CHIRURGICI: J. R. Goodall   1947

The History of man's concept of the soul. By James Robert Goodall. Montreal, privately printed, 1947.

Note: Part of the author's unfinished *Religio Chirurgici*.

RELIGIO BIBLIOGRAPHICI: Geoffrey Keynes   1953

Religio Bibliographici by Geoffrey Keynes...London The Bibliographical Society 1953.

Note: Delivered as a Presidential Address to the Bibliographical Society, March 1953, and reprinted from *The Library*, Series 5, vol. VIII, no. 2 (June 1953), pp. 63–76. Fifty copies printed. Printed again as an introduction to the author's catalogue of his library (*Bibliotheca Bibliographici*, 1964).

RELIGIO MEDICI: D. Horton 1956

In The Harvard Medical Alumni Bulletin, October, 1956. 'Religio Medici', by Douglas Horton.

RELIGIO MEDICI: F. Marti-Ibañez 1964

In Ariel, Essays on the Arts and the History and Philosophy of Medicine M.D. Publications Inc. New York 1964.

Note: 'Religio Medici' by Felix Marti-Ibañez, M.D.

APPENDIX II

Vulgar Errors:

Forerunners and Imitators

BIBLIOGRAPHICAL PREFACE

Sir Thomas Browne in his preface to *Pseudodoxia Epidemica* mentions several authors whose works of a similar nature had anticipated his, saying: 'We hope it will not be unconsidered, that we find no open tract, or constant manuduction in this Labyrinth; but are oft-times fain to wander in the *America* and untravelled parts of Truth. For though not many years past, Dr. Primrose hath made a learned Discourse of Vulgar Errors in Physick, yet have we discussed but two or three thereof. *Scipio Mercurii* hath also left an excellent Tract in *Italian*, concerning Popular Errors; but confining himself only unto those in Physick, he hath little conduced unto the generality of our Doctrine. *Laurentius Joubertus*, by the same Title led our expectation into thoughts of great relief; whereby notwithstanding we reaped no advantage; it answering scarce at all the promise of the Inscription.[1] Nor perhaps (if it were yet extant) should we find any farther Assistance from that ancient piece of *Andreas*, pretending the same Title. And therefore we are often constrained to stand alone against the strength of Opinion, and to meet the *Goliath* and Gyant of Authority, with contemtible pibbles, and feeble Arguments, drawn from the scrip and slender stock of ourselves. Nor have we indeed scarce named any Author whose Name we do not honour; and if detraction could invite us, discretion surely would contain us from any derogatory intention, where highest Pens and friendliest Eloquence must fail in commendation.'

Of the authors named Joubert and Mercurii are well known, but Andreas is obscure. Wilkin remarked that he is 'known only from a reference in Athenaeus'. It has been conjectured[2] that Browne is more likely to have meant the writer, Johann Valentin Andreæ, or Andreas, author of a number of controversial works, such as *Peregrini in Patria Errores* (Utopiae, 1618), and *Turris Babel sive Judiciorum de Fraternitate Rosaceæ Crucis Chaos* (Argentorati, 1619). Andreas was concerned to discredit the Rosicrucian fraternity as an 'epidemic pseudodoxy', but none of the titles of his books quite bring them into the series and Browne would scarcely have described any of them as 'that ancient piece'. He would be more likely to mean the early Greek physician of that name.

It is not clear why Browne should write so slightingly of the work of Laurent Joubert (1529–82), a distinguished physician, called on the title-pages of his book: *Conselher & Medecin ordinaire du Roy, & du Roy de Navarre, premier docteur regeant stipandié, Chancelher & juge de l'université an Medecine de Montpellier*. Perhaps it was because Joubert confined himself for the most part to medical errors (as announced on his title-pages), whereas Browne ranged far more widely. Nevertheless, it may be suspected that Joubert's book had a larger part than Browne cared to admit in prompting the compilation of his own. Joubert's work is interesting and important, and it has not been generally appreciated that he

---

[1] According to the sale catalogue of his library Browne possessed the edition of 1600.
[2] By the late Col. W. E. Moss, personal communication.

appended to Part I a section on the vulgar question what language a child who had never heard human speech would speak, a question which should have caught Browne's fancy. Joubert also discussed in Part II, among the *Propos Fabuleus* several non-medical subjects, including the Viper, the Salamander, and the Bear, all treated afterwards by Browne.

Joubert dedicated the early editions of Part I to Marguerite of Navarre, but in 1579 he dropped this in favour of a dedication to M. Gui de Faur, Seigneur de Pibrac. Perhaps the free discussion of sexual matters in his book did not please the Queen. The first part achieved immediate popularity, and in an *Épistre Apologetique* by B. Cabrol, surgeon of Montpellier, defending the book against *envieux et animeux propos*, it is stated that the book was published in Bordeaux, Paris, Lyons, and Avignon in editions of not less than 1,600 copies. The editions published in Bordeaux and Paris are described here, but the others have not been seen. According to the Bibliothèque Nationale Catalogue an Avignon edition was published by P. Roux, 1586. Part I was published in Italian in 1592, and a portion of Part I was translated into Latin and printed with commentaries in 1600. A number of editions of both parts were printed in the years 1579–1608 and are briefly described here, but the list may be incomplete.

Joubert is to be regarded as Browne's principal forerunner on the continent of Europe in criticism of Vulgar Errors. His chief forerunner in England was George Hakewill, D.D. (1578–1649), Fellow of Exeter College, Oxford, and later chaplain to Prince Charles. In 1642 he was elected Rector of Exeter College and remained there until his death in 1649. He was a famous preacher and according to Boswell his writings helped to form Johnson's style.[1] His major work, *An Apologie or Declaration of the Power and Providence of God in the Government of the World* (1627), was written against Bishop Godfrey Goodman's *The Fall of Man* (1616) arguing that both man and his world were in process of decay. Although Hakewill's title-page refers only to 'the Common Error touching Natures perpetuall and universall Decay', his long and learned book deals with a great variety of Vulgar Errors in history, astronomy, natural history, &c., including even some in anatomy and medicine, such as the length of the duodenum in man and the amount of blood in the body. It is surprising that Browne did not refer to Hakewill in the preface to *Pseudodoxia*, having dealt with many of the same subjects as his predecessor.

Many other writers followed up to the present time and are recorded here. A watch has been kept for them for many years; yet more could perhaps be found, dealing with errors in special branches of knowledge, if a sufficiently exhaustive search were to be made.

---

[1] Birkbeck Hill, *Boswell's Life of Johnson*, 1934, I, 219.

BAKER, George   1574

The Composition or making of the moste excellent and pretious Oil called
Oleum Magistrale...A breef gathering togither of certain errours which the
common Chirurgions dayly use. [Imprinted at London at the long Shop
adioyning unto Saint Mildreds Church in the Pultrie, by John Alde. 1574.]
A–R⁴ S² (8°).

Note: On ff. 37–51 (O1–R2) is *A breef gathering togither of certain errors which the common
Chirurgions use.* George Baker (1540–1600) was Master of the Barber–Surgeons'
Company in 1597. According to the *DNB* he wrote and translated several works, but
the *Oleum Magistrale* is the only one credited to him in *STC*.

Copies: BM, ULC.

JOUBERT, Laurent   1578–1608

Erreurs Populaires au fait de la Medecine & Regime de santé. Corrigez par M.
Laur. Ioubert...Ceste-cy est de toutte l'œuure la premiere partie, contenant
cinq liures...A Bordeaux, Par S. Millanges, Imprimeur du Roi. 1578. Auec
Priuilege. ã⁸ ẽ⁸ ĩ⁸ õ⁴ A–Z⁸ Aa–Oo⁸. *Errata* on Pp. 7.

Copy: E. P. Goldschmidt & Co. (cat. 132, May 1965); BN.

Erreurs Populaires au fait de la Medecine & Regime de santé...A Paris, Pour
Vincent de Mehubert, iouxte la copie imprimee à Bordeaux, Par S. Millanges,
Imprimeur du Roy. 1578. Auec Priuilege. ã⁸ ẽ⁸ ĩ⁸ õ⁴ A–Z⁸ Aa–Pp⁸ Qq⁴.

Copies: K; BN.

Erreurs Populaires et Propos Vulgaires, touchant la Medecine et le Regime de
Sante. Expliquez et Refutez Par M. Laur Ioubert...Reueuë corrigée &
augmentée presque de la moitié...A Bordeaux. Par S. Millanges, imprimeur
ordinaire du Roy. Avec Privilege. 1579. *A*⁸ ẽ⁸ ĩ⁸ õ⁴ A–Z⁸ Aa–Mm⁸.

Note: This is the third, first enlarged, edition of *Erreurs Populaires*, first part. It may
have been bound with either the first or the second edition of the second part. There
is a sub-title to *Question Vulgaire. Quel langage parleroit un enfant, qui n'auroit iamais oui
parler* on Hh1.

Copies: K, ULC; BN, MH.

Segonde Partie des Erreurs Populaires, et Propos Vulgaires, touchant la
Medecine & le regime de santé, refutés ou expliqués par M. Laur. Ioubert...
Avec Deus Catalogues de plusieurs autres erreurs ou propos vulgaires, qui
n'ont eté mancionnes an la premiere & segonde edition de la premiere partie.
Item deus autres petis traites, concernans les Erreurs populaires, auec deus
Paradoxes du maime auteur. Plus l'Apologie de son Ortographie, diuisee an
quatre Dialogues. Le tout nouuellemant imprimé. A Paris, Pour Lucas Breyer,
tenant sa boutique au segond pillier de la grand'salle du Palais. M.D.LXXIX.
Avec privilege du Roy. ã⁸ ẽ⁸ ĩ⁸ a⁴ b–t⁸. *Errata* on a1*a*.

Note: This book contains the first edition of the second part of *Erreurs Populaires*. The fact is not clear from the Epistle Dedicatory to Monseigneur de Neufille, Seigneur de Villeroy, but it is confirmed by Isaac Joubert's address to his father on pp. 238-9, presenting a translation of the Paradoxes as a New Year's gift on 1 January 1579. There is a woodcut portrait of Laurent Joubert on a4*b*.

Copies: K; BN.

Erreurs Populaires et propos Vulgaires, touchant la Medecine et le Regime de Sante. Expliquez et refutez Par M. Laur. Ioubert...A Bordeaux. Par S. Millanges, imprimeur ordinaire du Roy. Avec Privilege. 1579 [-1580]. *A*⁸ *ẽ*⁸ *ĩ*⁸ *õ*⁴ A–Z⁸ Aa–Mm⁸, (seconde partie) A–X⁸.

Note: The second part is dated 1580.

Copies: ULC; BN.

Erreurs Populaires...[two parts] A Avignon par P. Roux. 1586. 8°, pp. 614.

Copy: BN.

Erreurs Populaires...[two parts] A Paris par C. Micard. 1587. 8°.

Copy: BN.

La Prima Parte de gli errori popolari dell'eccellentiss. sign. Lorenzo Gioberti Filosofo, et Medico...Tradotta di Franzese in lingua Toscana dal. Mag. M. Alberto Luchi da Colle...In Fiorenza Per Filippo Giunti, MDXCII... *ⁱ⁰ A–Q⁸ R⁴.

Copies: BM; BN.

Laurentii Jouberti Delphinatis Valentini,...De Vulgi Erroribus...Latinitate donabat...Ioannes Bourgesius Houpliniensis, Medicinae & Astrologiae candidatus. Antwerpiae, Ex Officina...Martini Nutij ad insigne duarum Ciconiarum, Anno M.DC. *⁸ A–L⁸ M⁴.

Copies: K, RSM, ULC; BN.

La Premiere et Seconde Partie des Erreurs Populaires...A Rouen, Chez Raphael du petit Val, Libraire & Imprimeur du Roy a l'Ange Raphaël. 1601 [-1600]. ã⁸ A–Q⁸, [second part] †⁸ ††⁸ a–p⁸.

Note: Printed by Nicolas l'Oyselet. The second part in this and in the next three issues is dated 1600.

Copies: K; BN.

La Premiere et Seconde Partie des Erreurs Populaires...A Rouen, Chez Thomas Daré, tenant sa boutique aux degrez du Palais. 1601. (formula as before)

Copy: K.

La Premiere et Seconde Partie des Erreurs Populaires...A Rouen, Chez Romain de Beauuais...1601. *⁸ [etc. as above]

Copy: BM.

La Premiere et Seconde Partie des Erreurs Populaires...A Rouen, Chez P. Calles...1601. 8°.

Copy: BN.

La Premiere et Seconde Partie des Erreurs Populaires...Rouen, Chez Th. Reinsart...1601.

Copy: Catalogue of J. Thiebaud, 1950.

La Premiere et Seconde Partie des Erreurs Populaires...Lyon, Chez P. Rigaud...1608. 8°, pp. 451.

Copies: BN, MH.

La Premiere et Seconde Partie des Erreurs Populaires...Lyon, Chez P. Rigaud...1608. 16°, pp. 614.

Copy: BN.

MERCURII, Girolamo   1603–45

De gli Errori Popolari d'Italia, Libri Sette...dell'Eccellentiss. Sig. Scipione Mercurii Filosofo, Medico, e Cittadino Romano...In Venetia, Appresso Gio. Battista Ciotti Senese, M.DCIII. a⁶ b⁸ c–d⁴ A⁴ B–Z⁸ Aa–Zz⁸ Aaa–Ddd⁸.

Note: Wilkin (II, 180) quotes a note to the effect that the book is 'by Girolamo Mercurii, who had assumed the name of Scipio, when travelling through Europe as a physician, after having thrown aside the religious habit of the Dominicans. This work is a verbose but amusing performance, containing much curious information relative to the opinions and customs of the period at which it was published, and usefully correcting many errors, though it inculcates others of equal magnitude.'

Copies: BM; MH.

De gli Errori Popolari d'Italia...In Padoua ad'Instanza di Francesco Bolzetta. M.DC.XLV. a–b⁴ A–Z⁸ Aa–Nn⁸ Oo¹² (4°).

Copies: BM, K; MH.

De gli Errori Popolari d'Italia...In Verona, nella Stamparia di Francesco Rossi, M DC XLV. a–b⁴ A–Z⁸ Aa–Nn⁸ Oo¹² (4°).

Note: The same sheets as the Padua edition with fresh preliminary leaves, a1–4.

Copy: BM.

BACHOT, Gaspard   1626

Erreurs Populaires touchant la Medicine et regime de Santé: Par M. Gaspard Bachot Bourbonnois, Conseiller & Medecin du Roy. Œuure nouuelle, desirée de plusieurs, & promise par feu M. Laurens Ioubert. A Lyon, Par Barthelemy Vincent, en ruë Merciere, à l'Enseigne de la Victoire. M. DC. XXVI. Avec privilege du Roy. a–h⁸ A–Z⁸ Aa–Ii⁸.

Note: A continuation of the work by Joubert.

Copies: BLO, K; BN, MH.

HAKEWILL, George   1627-35

An Apologie or Declaration of the Power and Providence of God in the
Government of the World. Or an Examination and Censure of the Common
Error touching Natures perpetuall and universal Decay, divided into Foure
Bookes...By G. H. D.D....Oxford, Printed by Iohn Lichfield and William
Turner, Printers to the famous University. Anno Dom. 1627. b⁴ c⁶ d⁴ e⁴ A–Z⁴
Aa–Zz⁴ Aaa–Ooo⁴ (f°, the last two leaves are blank).

Copies: BLO, BM, ULC; CH.

An Apologie or Declaration of the Power and Providence of God...The
second Edition revised...Oxford...1630. ∏² b⁴ c⁶ d⁶ e² A–Z⁶ Aa–Zz⁶ Aaa–
Ddd⁶.

Note: With an engraved title-page, leaf of explanation and index added.

Copies: BLO, BM, K, ULC; CH.

An Apologie or Declaration of the Power and Providence of God...The third
Edition revised...Oxford...1635. ∏² a⁴ b⁶ c⁶ d⁴ e⁴ A–Z⁶ Aa–Zz⁶ Aaa–Ddd⁶
Eee⁴ Aaaa⁴ Bbbb–Zzzz⁶ Aaaaa–Nnnnn⁶.

Note: With engraved title-page as before. The book has been greatly enlarged.

Copies: BLO, BM, ULC; CH.

CLAVE, Estienne de   1635

Paradoxes, ou Traitez Philosophiques des Pierres et Pierreries, contre l'opinion
vulgaire...Par Estienne de Clave, Docteur en Medecine. A Paris, Chez la
veufue Pierre Chavalier...M.DC.XXXV. Avec Approbation & Privilege.
ã⁴ ẽ⁸ A–Z⁸ Aa–Hh⁸. A folding diagram inserted.

Note: de Clave's book was based on the teaching of Bernard Palissy and he consequently
suffered persecution and destruction of his book.

Copies: BM, ULC; BN.

PRIMROSE, James   1638-89

Iacobi Primirosii, Doctoris Medici, De Vulgi in Medicinâ Erroribus Libri
quatuor. Lib. I. De Erroribus circa Medicos.
       Lib. II. De Erroribus circa Morbos quosdam & eorum curationem.
       Lib. III. De Erroribus circa Victus rationem sanorum, & ægrorum.
       Lib. IV. De Erroribus circa Remediorum usum.
Londini. Apud B.A. & T.F. pro H. Robinsonio, ad insigne trium Columbarum
in Cœmeterio S. Pauli. 1638. A⁸ B–T¹².

Note: James Primrose (*c.* 1598–1659), M.D. of Montpellier and Oxford, practised in Hull. He is chiefly known for his attack on Harvey's doctrine of the circulation of the blood, published in 1630. His work on Vulgar Errors in medicine is of much interest, and is in essence a continuation of the work of Joubert, whom he mentions in the preface. In Book IV are four chapters on Tobacco. The first edition is of considerable rarity.

Copies: BLO, BM, EUL, K, ULC; MH, MMO, YUL.

Iacobi Primerosii Doctoris Medici De Vulgi Erroribus in Medicina, Libri LV... Amstelodami Apud Ioannem Ianssonium. Anno M.DC.XXXIX. (†)⁶ A–I¹² K–L⁶.

Copies: BM, K.

Iacobi Primerosii...Amstelodami Apud Ioannem Ianssonium, Anno M.DC.XLIV. ()⁶ A–I¹² K–L⁶.

Note: A line-for-line reprint of the preceding edition.

Copy: K.

Popular Errours. Or the Errors of the People in Physick, First written in Latine by the learned Physitian James Primrose Doctor in Physick. Divided into foure Bookes...Profitable and necessary to be read of all. To which is added by the same Authour his verdict concerning the Antimoniall Cuppe. Translated into English by Robert Wittie Doctor in Physick. London, Printed by W. Wilson for Nicholas Bourne, at the South-entrance of the Royall Exchange. 1651. A–Z⁸ Aa–Hh⁸.

Note: With an engraved title-page by T. Cross showing a doctor at his patient's bedside, and an *Explication* opposite. Among the commendatory poems are two by Andrew Marvell, Latin and English. Wittie practised with Primrose at Hull.

Copies: BLO, BM, EUL, K, TCD; MH, MMO.

Jacobi Primerosii Doctoris Medici De Vulgi Erroribus in Medicina Libri IV. Ab Auctore recensiti & plus quam tertia parte auctis. Roterodami, Ex Officinâ Arnoldi Leers, M.DC.LVIII. *¹² A–Z¹² Aa⁶.

Note: Several chapters have been added to each book.

Copies: K; MH, MMO.

Jacobi Primerosii...Lugduni, Apud Jacobum Faeton Typograph. M.DC.LXIV. Cum Superiorum Permissu. *⁸ A–Z⁸ Aa–Ee⁸.

Copy: K.

Jacobi Primerosii...Editio postrema, prioribus emendatior. Roterodami, Ex Officinâ Arnoldi Leers. M.DC.LXIIX. *¹² A–Z¹² Aa⁶.

Popular Errours.

OR THE

Errours of the People

IN

PHYSICK,

First written in Latine by the learned Phyſitian JAMES PRIMROSE
Doctor in Phyſick.

Divided into foure Bookes.

viz. {
1. The firſt treating concerning Phyſicians.
2. The ſecond of the Errours about ſome diſeaſes,
and the knowledge of them.
3. The third of the Errours about the diet, as well
of the ſound as of the ſick.
4. The fourth of the Errours of the people about
the uſe of remedies.
}

Profitable and neceſſary to be read of all.

To which is added by the ſame Authour
his verdict concerning the Antimoniall Cuppe.

Tranſlated into Engliſh by ROBERT
WITTIE Doctor in Phyſick.

LONDON,
Printed by *W. Wilſon* for *Nicholas Bourne,*
at the South-entrance of the Royall
Exchange. 1 6 5 1.

Note: A close reprint of the edition of 1658.

Copy: K.

Traité de Primerose sur les Erreurs Vulgaires de la Medecine, avec des additions Tres-curieuses. Par M. de Rostagny Medecin de la Societé Royale, & de S.A.R. Madame de Guise. A Lyon, Chez Jean Certe...M.DC.LXXXIX. á⁸ é⁸ í⁸ A–Z⁸ Aa–Zz⁸ Aaa–Hhh⁸.

Copies: BM, K; BN, MH.

ESPAGNE, Jean d'   1639–71

Les Erreurs Populaires es Poincts Generaux...A la Haye De l'Imprimerie de Theodore Maire, M.DC.XXXIX. *⁎*⁴ A–H¹² I⁸ K².

Copy: K.

Les Erreurs Populaires es Poincts Generaux, qui concernent l'intelligence de la Religion. Rapportez a leurs causes, & compris en diuerse observations. Par Jean D'Espagne Ministre du S. Euangile. Se vendent a Charanton. Par Melchior Moudiere, demeurant a Paris, en la Court du Palais, aux deux Vipers. M.DC.XLIII. a⁴ A–V⁸.

Copy: BM.

Popular Errors, in General Poynts concerning the Knowledge of Religion: Having Relation to their causes, and reduced into divers observations. By Jean D'Espaigne, Minister of the Holy Gospell. London, Printed for Tho. Whittaker, at the signe of the Kings armes in Pauls Church-yard, 1648. A–O⁸ P².

Copies: BM, K.

Les Erreurs Populaires dans les Poincts Generaux...A Geneve, Par I. Ant. & Samuel De Tournes. M.DC.LXXI. Π² ⁎⁸ A–H¹² I⁶.

Copy: BM.

TAYLOR, Jeremy   1655

Unum Necessarium. Or, The Doctrine and Practice of Repentance...Rescued from Popular Errors. By Jer. Taylor D.D....London, Printed by James Flesher for R. Royston, at the Angel in Ivy-lane. 1655. A–Z⁸ Aa–Zz⁸ Aaa⁴.

Note: With engraved title by Lombart on A1.

Copies: BLO, BM, EUL, K; CH, MH, YUL.

THOMPSON, Ja.   1657

Helmont Disguised: or, The Vulgar Errors of Impericall and unskilfull Practisers of Physick confuted...In a Dialogue between Philiatrus, and

Pyrosophilus...By J.T. Esq. Student in Physick. London printed, by E. Alsop, for N. Brook, and W. Leybourn, and are to be sold at the signe of the Angel in Cornhill. 1657. A⁴ B–K⁸.

Note: The preface is signed Ja. Thompson.

Copy: ULC.

WALKER, Obadiah 1659

Περίαμμα ἐπιδήμιον: Or, Vulgar Errors in Practice Censured. Also The Art of Oratory, Composed for the benefit of Young Students. London, Printed for Richard Royston, at the Angel in Ivy-lane. 1659. A–H⁸ A⁴ B–I⁸.

Note: The first part is divided into seven chapters, 'A Censure of the Epidemicall practise of reproaching Red-Hair'd men', &c. In chapter II, 'A Censure of the general Scandall of some professions, especially that of the Profession of Physick', p. 25, is a reference to *Religio Medici*, though the author is not named, and on p. 28 to *Hydriotaphia*. The author of the book is stated in the BM copy to be Obadiah Walker (1616–99), Oxford Romanist. It has also been attributed to Ralph Battell, author of *Vulgar Errors in Divinity Removed* (1683). In the British Museum and other libraries is an anonymous work, *A Discourse of Artificial Beauty...With some Satyrical Censures on the Vulgar Errors of these Times* (London, R. Royston, 1662). The latter part of this book consists of a re-issue of sections B–H, first alphabet, of Περίαμμα ἐπιδήμιον. The book has been attributed to John Gauden, Bishop of Worcester.

Copies: BM, CLN, K, ULC; MH, MMO, PUL.

HELMONT, Jean Baptiste van 1662

Oriatrike or Physick Refined. The common Errors therein Refuted, and the whole Art Reformed & Rectified...Written By...John Baptista Van Helmont...And now faithfully rendred into English...By J. C[handler] Sometime of M.H. Oxon...London Printed for Lodowick Lloyd, and are to be sold at his Shop next the Castle in Cornhill. 1662. Π⁴ a² b–e⁴ f² B–Z⁴ Aa–Zz⁴ Aaa–Zzz⁴ Aaaa–Zzzz⁴ Aaaaa–Zzzzz⁴ Aaaaaa–Zzzzzz⁴ Aaaaaaa–Kkkkkkk⁴ Llllll².

Copies: BLO, BM, RCP, RCS, ULC; MH, YUL.

[VAUGHAN, Thomas] 1669

A Breif Natural History Intermixed with variety of Philosophical Discourses... With Refutations Of such Vulgar Errours As our Modern Authors have omitted. By Eugenius Philalethes. London Printed for Matthew Smelt next door to the Castle near Moor-Gate. 1669. A–H⁸ I⁴.

Note: By Thomas Vaughan (1622–66), alchemist and poet, twin brother of Henry Vaughan. Among the Vulgar Errors refuted (pp. 76–94) are several already dealt with by Browne. At the end the author refers the reader to '*Doctor Browns* Learned discourse of the Errors of the Vulgar'.

Copies: BM, K, GU; CH, MH, YUL.

SPENCER, John   1663–5

A Discourse Concerning Prodigies: wherein The Vanity of Presages by them is reprehended, and their true and proper Ends asserted and vindicated. By John Spencer, B.D. Fellow of Corpus Christi Colledge in Cambridge... Printed by John Field for Will. Graves Bookseller, and are to be sold at his Shop over against Great S. Maries Church in Cambridge. 1663. A–P⁴ Q².

Note: In the preface (A3 *b*) the author claims that his *Discourse* 'may be of use to reprehend a very Vulgar and Pernicious Error', namely the opinion of presages by prodigies. Browne is not named.

Copies: BM, ULC; CH, YUL.

A Discourse concerning Prodigies...To which is added a short Treatise concerning Vulgar Prophecies...London, Printed by J. Field &c. 1665. A⁸ a⁸ B–Z⁸ Aa–Cc⁸ Dd⁴ A–I⁸ K⁴.

Copies: BM, K, ULC; CH, MH, YUL.

THIERS, Jean-Baptiste   1679

Traité des Superstitions qui regardent les Sacrements...Paris. 1679. 12°.

Note: Leroy, *A French Bibliography of Sir Thomas Browne* (1931), p. 41, writes: 'In spite of its title this work deals at times with much of the same matter as *Pseudodoxia*. Cf. for instance Bk. v: *Des animaux superstitieux. De la corde de pendu, du trèfle à quatre feuilles et du cœur d'hirondelle*. Still the author does not seem to have known Browne's work or at least to have availed himself of it.' Second edition, 2 vols., Paris, 1697.

Copies: K(1697); BN

[BAYLE, Pierre]   1682

Lettre à M.L.A.D.C. Ou il est prouvé...que les Cometes ne sont point le presage d'aucun malheur. Avec plusieurs Reflexions...& la Refutation de quelques erreurs populaires. à Cologne, Chez Pierre Marteau, M.DC.LXXXII. *¹² **⁶ A–Z¹² Aa¹².

Copies: BM, K; BN.

BATTELL, Ralph   1683

Vulgar Errors in Divinity Removed. [quotations] London, Printed for Benj. Tooke and Joanna Brome in St. Pauls Church-Yard. MDCLXXXIII. A–I⁸ K⁴.

Note: The *Epistle Dedicatory* is signed by Ralph Battell (1649–1713), prebendary of Worcester.

Copies: BLO, BM, CLN, K (2, one on large paper); MH.

D., J.   1686

A Memorial for the Learned: or, Miscellany of choice Collections from most Eminent Authors. In History, Philosophy, Physick, and Heraldry. By J.D.

Gent...London: Printed for George Powell and William Powle, over against Lincolns-Inn Gate in Chancery-Lane, and in Holborn-Court in Grays-Inn. 1686. A^8 a^4 B–O^8 P^4.

Note: On pp. 132–204 are *Vulgar Errors, First–Seventh Book.* These are obviously all based on Browne's work, though he is not acknowledged. On p. 153 the reader is referred to Browne for further information on 'Properties of Plants'; on p. 170 it is stated that 'Here Sir Tho. Brown makes a very large and learned Discourse of Hermaphrodites, in several Creatures'.

Copies: BM; YUL.

REICHENBERG, Adam   1687

De Gemmis Errores Vulgares. Leipzig. 1687. 8°

Note: Mentioned by Wilkin, I, lxvii. Not seen.

LE BRUN, Pierre   1702

Histoire critique des Pratiques Superstitieuses, Qui ont séduit les Peuples, & embarassé les Sçavans...Par une Prêtre de l'Oratoire. A Rouen Chez Guillaume Behourt...M.DCCII. *^{10} ã^{12} â^2 ẽ^4 *^{4} **^{2} A–Z^{12} Aa–Dd^{12} Ee^{10}.

Note: The relation to Browne is somewhat superficial. He is not named by the author (see Leroy, *French Bibliography of Browne*, no. 78).

Copies: BM; BN.

BUFFIER, Claude   1704

Examen des Prejugez Vulgaires pour disposer l'esprit a juger sainement de tout, Paris, J. Mariette, 1704. 12°.

Note: Browne is not named (see Leroy, *loc. cit.* no. 80).

HUTCHINSON, Francis   1718

An Historical Essay concerning Witchcraft. With Observations upon Matters of Fact; tending to clear the Texts of the Sacred Scriptures, and confute the vulgar Errors about that Point...By Francis Hutchinson D. D....London: Printed for R. Knaplock, and D. Midwinter...MDCCXVIII. A–S^8.

Note: Chapter VIII, pp. 109–24, gives an account of the trial before Sir Matthew Hale at which Browne gave evidence (see no. 287). Second edition, 1720.

Copies: BM, K, ULC, &c.

DU LUDE, Comte   1723

Δαιμονολογια: or, a Treatise of Spirits. Wherein Several Places of Scripture are Expounded, against the Vulgar Errors concerning Withcraft, Apparitions, &c....By Comte Du Lude, a Presbyter of the Church of England. London: Printed for the Author, in the Year 1723. Π^2 [a]^4 A^2 B–Z^4.

Note: By Jacques de Daillon calling himself Comte du Lude.

Copies: BM, K, ULC.

FEYJOO Y MONTENEGRO, Gerónimo   1736

Theatro Critico Universal, O Discoursos Varios En Todo Genero de Materias.
Pasa Desengano De Errores Comunes. Escrito por el M.R.P.M. Fr. Benito
Geronymo Feyjoo. Quarta Impression. En Madrid: En la Imprenta de los
Herederos de Francisco del Hierro. Año de MDCCXXXVI. 9 vols. 4°.

Copy: ULC.

[COLMAN, George, and THORNTON, Bonnell]   1757

The Connoisseur. By Mr. Town, Critic and Censor General. Volume the
Fourth. The Second Edition. London: Printed for R. Baldwin...MDCCLVII.
Numb. cix. Thursday, February 26, 1756. On Vulgar Errors.—Specimen of a
Supplement to Sir Thomas Brown's Treatise.—Refutation of the following
Vulgar Errors—That a Maid cannot be with Child—That Gaming depends
on Chance—That Matrimony brings people together—That the Sabbath is a
Day of Rest—That there is any such thing as an Old Woman—That the Gospel
is an object of Belief.

Note: This essay does not appear in the first edition of *The Connoisseur* published in folio
parts in 1756. No. cix in this form is on quite a different subject, though it carries the
same date.

Copy: BM.

[CASTILLON, J. L.]   1765

Essai sur les Erreurs et les Superstititions. Par M.L.C....Amsterdam, Chez
Arckée & Merkus. M.DCC.LXV. A–V¹² X⁴.

Note: There is a reference in the preface to Browne's *Traité des erreurs populaires*. 'Mon
ouvrage commence où le sien finit. M. Brown prouve par de très bons raisonnements
la folie de ces erreurs, j'en démontre l'absurdité par l'histoire des maux et des progrès
qu'elles ont faits. Ces deux ouvrages, comme on voit; n'ont donc rien de commun.'
Many of the chapters deal with the legends concerning Mahomet; others with
astrology, magic, &c.

Copies: K; MH.

FOVARGUE, Stephen   1767

A New Catalogue of Vulgar Errors. By Stephen Fovargue, A.M. Fellow of
St. John's College, Cambridge...Cambridge, Printed for the Author: Sold by
Fletcher & Hodson in Cambridge...1767. (Price Half A Crown.) Π² a⁴ B–Z⁴
Aa–Bb⁴ Cc² (8°).

Note: The author in his introduction refers to Sir Thomas Browne, who, he points out,
was himself in error concerning the noise made by a bittern. The author deals with
this in Error III. His *Catalogue* of thirty-six errors covers a great variety of subjects.

Copies: BM, CLN, K, ULC; MH, MMO, NYAM.

[D'HOLBACH, P. H. T., Baron]   1771

J. Brunus Redivivus, ou Traité des Erreurs Populaires, Ouvrage Critique, Historique & Philosophique, Imité de Pomponace. Premiere Partie. MDCCLXXI. Π⁴ (a)–(g)⁸ (h)².

Note: 'J. Brunus' is Giordano Bruno, not Sir Thomas Browne.

Copy: K.

[BARRINGTON, Daines]   1766

Observations upon the Statutes...The Second Edition, With Corrections and Additions. London: Printed by W. Baker and J. Nichols, And sold by S. Baker...and W. Sandby...MDCCLXVI. a⁴ b² B–Z⁴ Aa–Zz⁴ Aaa–Lll⁴.

Note: pp. 369–70, a footnote on several vulgar errors in points of law.

Copies: BM, ULC, &c.

BIENVILLE, J. D. T.   1775

Traité des erreurs populaires sur la santé. La Haye. 1775. 8°.

Note: Browne is not named (see Leroy, *loc. cit.* no. 81).

Copy: BN.

MEDLEY, Thomas   1779

The Shandymonian: Containing A Conclamation of Original Pieces...Detections and Confutations of Vulgar Errors, And Errors not Vulgar...The Second Edition. By Thomas Medley, Esq; Vice President of Bollimong College, Doctor of Gallimafry, Utopian Professor of Oddities, and Fellow of Civil Society...London: Printed for W. Nicoll, G. Haweis, N. Collins and T. Stears. M DCC LXXIX. [Price Three Shillings] A² B–K⁸ L⁶.

Note: A miscellaneous collection of trifles, facetious and literary. The first edition has not been traced.

Copy: BM.

D'IHARCE, Jean-Luc   1783

Erreurs Populaires sur la Médecine...Par M. d'Iharce, Écuyer, Docteur en Médecine, & Médecin Breveté du Roi...A Paris, Chez l'auteur...Mequignon l'ainé...M.DCC.LXXXIII. Π² a¹² A–V¹².

Note: The author refers in his preface to the works of Joubert, Primrose, Browne and Bienville, noting that Browne has only a few articles relating to medicine.

Copies: K; BN.

[ANONYMOUS]   1784

Vulgar Errors. *Interdum vulgus rectum videt est ubi peccat.* London: Printed for J.
Debrett, opposite Burlington-House, Piccadilly. MDCCLXXXIV. A–C⁴ D².

Note: This is a political pamphlet directed against William Pitt.

Copy: K.

JONES, John   1797

Medical, Philosophical, and Vulgar Errors, of Various Kinds, Considered and
Refuted. By John Jones, M.B. *Morbis Nobis Hæc Otia dedit.* London: Printed
for T. Cadell, jun. & W. Davies…1797. [A]² B–O⁸ P⁴.

Note: This consists chiefly of 'Medical Vulgar Errors refuted'. The subject is treated in
a humorous, literary and technical spirit, with references to *Hudibras*, Wesley, &c.

Copies: BM, FLWC, ULC.

RICHERAND, A.   1810

Des Erreurs Populaires relatives a la Médecine, Par M. Richerand, Professeur
de la Faculté de Médecine de Paris, &c. &c.…De Limprimerie de Crapelet.
A Paris, Chez Caille et Ravier…1810. 20 cm., pp. vi, 234.

Note: A much enlarged edition (pp. viii, 384) was published in 1812 and again in 1814.
In the preface to these editions the author refers to the works of Joubert, Primrose
and Browne.

Copies: BM(1812), K(1810, 1812), RSM(1810); BN(1812), MH.

SALGUES, J. B.   1810

Des Erreurs et des Préjugés repandus dans la Société; par J. B. Salgues. A Paris,
Chez F. Buisson…1810. 3 vols. 20 cm.

Note: The author refers in his preface to the works of Joubert, Primrose, Bienville,
d'Iharce and Richerand, but adds that the most complete work is Browne's *Erreurs
Populaires*; though he is not free from errors himself, he is learned and deserves to be
consulted. Yet, as noted by Leroy (*loc. cit.*, no. 84), Salgues quotes extensively from
Browne, and his chapters 'Du Phénix', 'Pygmées', 'Chant du cygne', and 'Annibal',
are nothing but Browne in French disguise. The book was published again in
1811–13, 1825, and 1836.

Copies: BM(1812), K(1811); BN(1812).

[DYER, George]   1816

Vulgar Errors, Ancient and Modern…With A Critical Disquisition on every
station of Richard of Cirencester and Antoninus in Britain…Exeter: Printed
for G. Dyer, Bookseller…Longman, &c. London; and Constable and Co.
Edinburgh. 1816. 23 cm., pp. [iv], lxxvi, [iv], 230, [2], 25, [3].

[LAMB, Charles]   1826

In The New Monthly Magazine. Vols. XVI–XVII. London: Henry Colburn, New Burlington Street. 1826.

Note: Vol. XVI, pp. 25–30, 224–9, 258–65, 418–19, 519–25, 623–4; vol. XVII, pp. 245–7, 'Popular Fallacies', by Elia. 'I poke out a monthly crudity for Colburn in his magazine which I call "Popular Fallacies", and periodically crush a proverb or two, setting up my folly against the wisdom of nations' (*Works of Charles and Mary Lamb*, ed. Lucas, 1905, vol. VII, p. 699).

TIMBS, John   1841

Popular Errors explained and illustrated by John Timbs...London: Tilt and Bogue, Fleet Street. MDCCCXLI. 17 cm., pp. viii, 376.

Note: There are references to *Pseudodoxia Epidemica* on p. iv. A new edition was published in 1856, and the work was reprinted in *Things not generally known* (London, 1857).

[CORNWALLIS, C. F.]   1845–54

An Exposition of Vulgar and Common Errors Adapted to the Year of Grace MDCCCXLV. By Thomas Brown Redivivus, whilome Knt. and M.D. London: William Pickering. 1845. [Small Books on Great Subjects. Edited by a Few Well Wishers to Knowledge. No. VIII.] 17 cm., pp. [vi], 132.

Note: Edited, and probably written, by Caroline Frances Cornwallis. Printed by Charles Whittingham, Chiswick.

An Exposition of Vulgar and Common Errors...Second Edition. London: John W. Parker and Son, West Strand. 1854. 17 cm., pp. [vi], 132.

Note: A line-for-line reprint of the previous edition by Savill and Edwards, Chandos Street.

HARRISON, James Bower   1851

Popular Medical Errors by James Bower Harrison MRCSL, etc....London: Longman, Brown, Green, and Longmans. 1851. 17 cm., pp. vii, [i], 152, 4.

Note: The author refers to Browne's work in the introduction.

WADDINGTON, C.   1866

Des Erreurs et des Préjugés Populaires par Ch. Waddington, Agrégé de la Faculté des Lettres de Paris. Paris Librairie de L. Hachette et Cie. 1866. 15 cm., pp. 52.

Note: The text of a lecture given at the Asile impérial de Vincennes. The author refers to Browne on p. 22.

TRAQUAIR, R. H. 1896

On Popular Delusions in Natural History By R. H. Traquair M.D. LL.D. F.R.S. Printed by William Blackwood and Sons Edinburgh. MDCCCXCVI 22 cm., pp. 22.

Note: Reprinted from *Transactions of the Edinburgh Field Naturalists' and Microscopical Society*, vol. III (1895–6).

ACKERMANN, A. S. E. 1907

Popular Fallacies By A. S. E. Ackermann...Cassell and Company, Limited London...MCMVII 20 cm., pp. xii, 312.

Note: Second edition, enlarged, 1909; third edition, much enlarged, 1923.

HISTORICAL ASSOCIATION 1945

Common Errors in History by Members of the Historical Association... Published for The Historical Association by P. S. King & Staples Ltd.... 1945. 21 cm., pp. 24.

KEYNES, G. L., LINNELL, J. W. and PIERCY, J. 1946

In The British Medical Journal (1946), II, 449–52, 'Vulgar Errors in Thyroid Surgery'.

EVANS, B. 1947

The Natural History of Nonsense by Bergen Evans London Michael Joseph [1947] 20 cm., pp. 269, [1].

Note: The author calls his work a 'study in the palæontology of delusion'. There are many references to Browne.

PRINTERS, PUBLISHERS AND BOOKSELLERS

GENERAL INDEX

PRINTERS, PUBLISHERS
AND BOOKSELLERS 1642-1966

Only the producers of works by Sir Thomas Browne are included in this list
The numbers refer to the entries in the Bibliography

GENERAL INDEX

The numbers refer to the pages

PRINTED IN GREAT BRITAIN
AT THE UNIVERSITY PRINTING HOUSE, CAMBRIDGE
(BROOKE CRUTCHLEY, UNIVERSITY PRINTER)